D0946024

BRAINSTORMS

A Bradford Book

The MIT Press
Cambridge, Massachusetts
London, England

BRAINSTORMS

Philosophical Essays on Mind and Psychology

DANIEL C. DENNETT

Seventh printing, 1996

First MIT Press edition, 1981

Copyright © 1978 by Bradford Books, Publishers.
All rights reserved. No part of this work may be reproduced or transmitted in any form by any
means, electronic or mechanical, including photo-
copying and recording, or by any information
storage or retrieval system, except for a brief quotation (not to exceed 1,000 words) in a review or
professional work, without permission in writing
from the publisher.

Library of Congress Catalog Card Number 81-84118
ISBN 0-262-04064-6 (cloth), 0-262-54037-1 (paper)
Printed in the United States of America

Designed by Mary Mendell
Composition by Horne Associates, Inc., Hanover,
New Hampshire
Artwork by Kathy Harvey, Gloucester, Massachusetts

for Andrea and Peter

Contents

Preface

The essays collected here attempt to solve a wide variety of puzzles about the mind. Out of the solutions proposed emerges a relatively unified and comprehensive theory of the mind, a revised and extended version of the theory I presented in 1969, in *Content and Consciousness*. All the essays, with the exception of Chapter 6, "A Cure for the Common Code?", were written to be presented individually at conferences and departmental colloquia around the country, and they have been shaped and reshaped by the interplay with many different audiences.

Several virtues and vices spring from this fact. Virtue first: since they were composed to be heard, and comprehended on first hearing, they make for relatively easy reading—for philosophy. Another virtue is that the essays are self-contained, which permits the reader to sample the theory at the point of most initial interest, with the reasonable hope of being able to understand the theory well enough in that domain to know whether or not to pursue it further. A collateral vice is that these essays can be self-contained only by dint of a certain amount of repetition, but this vice has its virtuous side, for it permits central concepts in my theory—such as the concept of an intentional system—and central arguments—such as the arguments about incorrigibility or introspective authority—to be presented from more than one perspective, with more than one emphasis. This provides the skeptical reader with both a demonstration of the broad applicability I claim for these ideas, and several different angles from which to launch attacks.

Ten of the essays have appeared before in print, and drafts of all seventeen have been read and discussed by philosophers, psychologists, and their students, in some cases for years. The interest they have occasioned has encouraged me to bring them together and seek a wider audience, not only of philosophers and psychologists, but of reflective readers generally, for many of the questions posed are not the private property of professionals, but tantalizers and bafflers familiar to the speculations of even the most untheoretical imaginations. If I close my eyes and imagine a purple cow, is something somewhere really purple and cow-shaped? Could a brain scientist someday read my thoughts in my brain? Could a robot be truly conscious? Is free will an illusion? My answers were developed one at a time over the years, but once I finally noticed the rise in my temptation to indulge in the unseemly habit of citing my own work, I decided to succumb totally and admit that I think these essays are truly interrelated and should be read together.

The unified theory I claim to provide here is presented in much the same order as its ancestor was in *Content and Consciousness*, beginning, in Part I, with basic metaphysical and methodological concerns and then, in Part II, analyzing and defending the—careful—use of mentalistic or intentional formulations in psychological theories: the ascription of *content* to events and states in the mind. The fruits of that analysis are then exploited in Part III to provide answers to the most persistent quandaries about consciousness and its relation to the rest of the world. Part IV pushes tentatively, gropingly into the area I consider most important: the analysis of the relationship between our vision of ourselves as responsible, free, rational agents, and our vision of ourselves as complex parts of the physical world of science. For almost ten years I have been trying to concentrate on this last area only to be repeatedly driven back by complexities (and their attendant fascinations) in the groundwork theory of mind on which my assault on the ethical domain was to rest. Nothing I have learned has changed my mind about the importance or feasibility of that assault, to which I am now returning.

There are many people to thank. I am grateful to hosts, commentators, and audiences around the country for their stimulation and their responses. I am indebted to my students, at Tufts, and during very happy visits at Harvard and Pittsburgh, for their relentless, intelligent, good-natured skepticism. And I have been especially helped by the advice and criticism of Annette Baier, Ronald Barnette, Ned Block, Bo Dahlbom, Jerry Fodor, Michael Hooker, Hilary Putnam, Zenon Pylyshyn, Georges Rey, Amelie Rorty, Joseph Weizenbaum, and my colleagues at Tufts over the years. Finally, I thank my wife Susan for her invariably clear-headed stylistic advice, encouragement and understanding.

D.C.D.
Tufts University
February, 1978

Introduction

What is a philosophical theory of the mind?

I claim that the essays in this book taken together express a theory of the mind, so I should begin by explaining what I take a theory of the mind to be. Several very different sorts of intellectual productions are called theories: particle theory in physics, set theory in mathematics, game theory, literary theory, the theory of evolution, the identity theory in the philosophy of mind. Some things are called theories that might better be called hypotheses. The theory of evolution by natural selection is surely a theory of sorts, but its rival, creationism, is a theory only by courtesy. It lacks the parts, the predictive power, the organization of a theory; it is merely a hypothesis, the hypothesis that the theory of evolution by natural selection is false and that God created the species. I suspect we call it a theory to acknowledge that it is a genuine alternative to something that clearly *is* a theory. Creationism, after all, *might* be true and Darwinism false—which goes to show that one needn't always counter a theory with a *theory*. We won't need a theory of clairvoyance, for instance, if we can confirm the hypothesis that all apparent clairvoyants are cheats. Hoaxism is a worthy opponent of the most elaborate theory of clairvoyance, and it consists of but a single statement, supported, of course, by a good deal of sleuthing.

Philosophical theories are often hypotheses of this sort: large generalizations that do not ramify into vast organized structures of details, or predict novel effects (like theories in chemistry or physics), but are still vulnerable to disconfirmation (like hoaxism), and require detailed and systematic support. Thus "minds are just brains" is one very informal way of expressing a version of *physicalism* or the *identity theory* of mind (so-called because it *identifies* mental events with *physical* events in the brain), and "minds are not just brains; they're something non-physical" is one very informal way of expressing a version of *dualism* (so-called because it claims there are at least two fundamental sorts of events or things). Since philosophy often concerns itself with just such very general hypotheses, and the patterns of implication one lands oneself in when defending such hypotheses, philosophy often appears to the outsider to be a ludicrously overpopulated battlefield of "isms", with each imaginable variation on each general assertion pompously called a theory and given a proprietary name.

This appearance is untrustworthy, however, and the proliferation of theories is not really an embarrassment. It is surely initially reasonable to suppose that such a general hypothesis about the mind *makes sense*, and then it is also reasonable both to suppose that either it or its denial is true, and to wonder which. A sensible way to try to answer this question is to explore the evidence for, and implications of, the possible alternatives, and defend the most plausible candidate until proven wrong. That process however soon gets complicated, and it becomes imperative to distinguish one's hypothesis very precisely from closely resembling hypotheses whose hidden flaws one has uncovered. Technical terms—jargon—permit one to triangulate the possible positions in logical space and thus keep track of the implication chains one is avoiding or exploiting. Thus are born interactionism, anomolous monism, logical behaviorism, Turing machine functionalism and the other named locations in the logical space of possible general claims about the nature of the mind.

To a first approximation then a philosophical theory of the mind is supposed to be a consistent set of answers to the most general questions one can ask about minds, such as "are there any?", "are they physical?", "what happens in them?" and "how do we know anything about them?" Such a theory is not supposed to compete with or supplant neurophysiological or psychological theories, but rather both to ground such theories and to supplement them. It can ground such theories by providing the justification for the fundamental metaphysical assumptions such theories must unavoidably make. It can supplement them by providing answers to the simple, straightforward questions that those scientific theories are utterly unable to answer from their own resources. Every brain scientist knows that even in the Golden Age of neurophysiological knowledge, when the activity of every tract of fibers will be well understood, questions like "what is consciousness?" and "what is it about pains that makes them awful?" will find no answers in their textbooks—unless those textbooks include chapters of philosophy.

Many psychologists and brain scientists are embarrassed by the philosophical questions, and wish no one would ask them, but of course their students persist in asking them, because in the end these are the questions that motivate the enterprise. Synaptic junctures and response latencies have some intrinsic interest, to be sure, but if there were no hope that compounding enough facts about these would lead to discoveries about our *minds*, enthusiasm for such research would not be as keen as it is. The distaste of many empirical scientists for the philosophical questions is no doubt due to the fact that until very recently philosophers' attempts to answer them were conducted in blithe ignorance of and indifference to the discoveries, theories and problems of those sciences. That indifference was galling, I am sure—as galling as the counter-disdain of the scientists—but reasonable: until very recently there were few discoveries, theories or problems in the sciences that promised to illuminate the philosophical issues at all.

Times have changed. Psychology has become "cognitive" or "mentalistic" (in many quarters) and fascinating discoveries have been made about such familiar philosophical concerns as mental imagery, remembering and language comprehension. Even the brain scientists are beginning to tinker with models that founder on *conceptual* puzzles. There is, for instance, the problem of avoiding the "grandmother neuron". Many otherwise plausible theory sketches in brain science seem to lead ineluctably to the view that the "representation" of each particular "concept" or "idea" will be the responsibility of a particular neuron or other small part of the brain. Suppose your "grandmother" neuron died; not only could you not *say* "grandmother", you couldn't *see* her if she was standing right in front of you. You couldn't even *think* about grandmothers at all; you would have a complete cognitive blind spot. Nothing remotely like that pathology is observed, of course, and neurons malfunction or die with depressing regularity, so for these and other reasons, theories that require grandmother neurons are in trouble. The problem is to find a theory that avoids this difficulty in all its guises, and this is a problem so abstract as to be properly philosophical. Many other problems arising in these sciences—problems about concept learning, reasoning, memory, decision—also have an unmistakably philosophical cast.

Philosophy of mind has responded to these developments by becoming "naturalized"; it has become a branch of the philosophy of science concerning itself with the conceptual foundations and problems of the sciences of the mind.[1]* This has changed the shape and texture of philosophical theories of the mind by introducing into the discussions of the traditional issues many of the data and conceptual tools of the new scientific approaches, and raising new issues arising from the puzzles and pitfalls of those approaches.

Philosophy of mind is unavoidable. As soon as one asserts anything substantive about anything mental, one *ipso facto* answers at least by implication one or more of the traditional questions and thus places oneself in the camp of an *ism*. Perhaps some theorists arrive at their positions by methodically filling in the blanks on the branching checklist of possibilities, but this is not a strategy I recommend. The views already charted, named and catalogued have all been ably defended, but none has achieved consensus. One is not apt to find the magic words of support that will suddenly bring victory to an already articulated theory. A better strategy, or at least the strategy I have tried to follow, is to start not by looking hard at the possible answers to the traditional questions posed in traditional terms, but by looking hard at the empirical data, psychological theories, models of brain function and so forth, and letting the considerations and saliencies that appeared there suggest what would be important to keep distinct in a theory of the mind. The result is a theory that looks like an ungainly and inelegant hybrid, an unnameable hodge-podge of theory parts, when measured against the traditional pattern of categories. Since I think my theory carves nature at the joints, however, I am inclined to claim that it is the traditional pattern that is misshapen. For this reason I have until now refrained from giving my theory a name, and refrained from giving explicit answers to some of the most popular watershed questions, but the questions do remain to be answered, and now it is useful and perhaps even obligatory for me to give direct answers and take sides.

What is my theory?

My theory can be distinguished easily from its rivals via a brief and oversimplified history of recent brands of *physicalism*. In the beginning was *type identity theory*. It attempted to answer two questions. To the question, "What are mental events?" it answered, "Every mental event is (identical with) a physical event in the brain," and to the question, "What do two creatures have in common when they both believe that snow is white (both feel a twinge of pain, imagine an

---

*Numbered footnotes contain only bibliographical information, and are placed at the end of the book.

elephant, want a cracker)?" it answered, "In each case where creatures have something *mental* in common, it is in virtue of having something *physical* in common—e.g., their brains are in the same physical state or both exhibit the same physical feature." The answer to the first question made the view an identity theory; the answer to the second established that *types* of mental events were claimed to correspond to physically characterizable *types* of brain events. In answering these two questions, type identity theory attempted to discharge two obligations, one "metaphysical" and the other "scientific". The first answer amounts to the mere denial of dualism, the insistence that we don't need a category of non-physical things in order to account for mentality. The second takes on the responsibility of explaining commonalities—the task isolated by Socrates' incessant demands to know what is shared by things called by the same name.

Few today would quarrel with the first answer, but the second answer is hopelessly too strong. The claim it makes is that for *every* mentalistic term, every "mental" predicate "*M*", there is some predicate "*P*" *expressible in the vocabulary of the physical sciences* such that a creature is *M* if and only if it is *P*. Symbolically,

(1) (x) $(Mx \equiv Px)$

For instance, for all x, *x is thinking about baseball* if and only if *x has F-neurons in electro-chemical state G*; or, something *is in pain* if and only if it *has a brain in such and such a physical condition*. This is all utterly unlikely.[2] Consider some simpler cases to see why. Every clock and every can-opener is no doubt nothing but a physical thing, but is it remotely plausible to suppose or insist that one could compose a predicate in the restricted language of physics and chemistry that singled out all and only the can-openers or clocks? (What is the common physical feature in virtue of which this grandfather clock, this digital wristwatch, and this sundial can be ascribed the predicate "registers 10:00 A.M."?) What can-openers have peculiarly in common is a purpose or function, regardless of their physical constitution or even their design, and the same is true of clocks.

This recognition led to the second wave of physicalism: *Turing machine functionalism*. The minimal denial of dualism was maintained —every mental event was a physical event—but the requirements for answering the second question were revised: for every "mental" predicate "*M*" there is some predicate "*F*" expressible in some language that is physically *neutral*, but designed to specify abstract functions and functional relations. The obvious candidates for such a language were the systems used for describing computers or programs. The functional structure of a computer program can be described in an abstract way that is independent of any particular description of physical "hardware". The most general functional language is the system for describing computers as "Turing machines". (An elementary introduction to the concept of a Turing machine is provided in Chapter 13.) The states and activities of *any* digital computer or program can be given a mathematical description as states and activities of a unique (numbered) Turing machine, and this description is its mathematical fingerprint that will distinguish it from all *functionally* different computers or programs, but not from computers and programs that differ *only* in "physical realization". There are problems with this formulation, not germane to the issue at hand, but supposing them to be eliminable, the Turing machine functionalist proposed to say things like

(2) (x) (x believes that snow is white $\equiv x$ "realizes" some Turing machine k in logical state A)

In other words, for two things both to believe that snow is white, they need not be physically similar in any specifiable way, but they must both be in a "functional" condition or state specifiable in the most general functional language; they must share a Turing machine description according to which they are both in some particular logical state (which is roughly like two different computers having the same program and being in the same "place" in the program). The "reduction" of mental predicates to physical predicates attempted by type identity theory has been replaced in this view by a reduction of mental predicates to Turing machine predicates. While the resulting theory is only a *token* identity theory—each *individual* mental event is (identical with) some individual physical brain event or other—it is a *type* functionalism—each mental type is identifiable as a functional type in the language of Turing machine description.

But alas, this second answer is still too strong (as I argue in Chapter 2).[3] The supposition that there could be some principled way of describing all believers and pain-sufferers and dreamers as Turing machines so that they would be in the same logical state whenever they shared a mental epithet is at best a fond hope. There is really no more reason to believe you and I "have the same program" in *any* relaxed and abstract sense, considering the differences in our nature and nurture, than that our brains have identical physico-chemical descriptions. What could be done to weaken the requirements for the second answer still further?

Consider what I will call *token functionalism*, the view that while every mental event is indeed some physical event or other, and moreover some functional event or other (this is the minimal denial of epiphenomenalism—see footnote on p. 000), mental types are *not* definable as Turing machine types. How will we answer the Socratic question? What do two people have in common when they both believe that snow is white? I propose this:

> (3) (x) (x believes that snow is white $\equiv$ x can be predictively attributed the belief that snow is white).

This appears to be blatantly circular and uninformative—"A horse is any animal to which the term 'horse' truly applies." The language on the right seems simply to mimic the language on the left. What has happened to the goal of *reduction*? It was, I submit, a mistaken goal.[4]

All we need to make an informative answer of this formula is a systematic way of making the attributions alluded to on the right-hand side. Consider the parallel case of Turing machines. What do two different realizations or embodiments of a Turing machine have in common when they are in the same logical state? Just this: there is a system of description such that according to it both are described as being realizations of some particular Turing machine, and according to this description, which is predictive of the operation of both entities, both are in the same state of that Turing machine's machine table. One doesn't *reduce* Turing machine talk to some more fundamental idiom; one *legitimizes* Turing machine talk by providing it with rules of attribution and exhibiting its predictive powers. If we can similarly legitimize "mentalistic" talk, we will have no need of a reduction. That is the point of my concept of an *intentional system* (see Chapter 1). Intentional systems are supposed to play a role in the legitimization of mentalistic predicates parallel to the role played by the abstract notion of a Turing machine in setting down rules for the interpretation of artifacts as computational automata. I fear my concept is woefully informal and unsystematic compared with Turing's, but then the domain it attempts to systematize—our everyday attributions in mentalistic or intentional language—is itself something of a mess, at least compared with the clearly defined mathematical field of recursive function theory, the domain of Turing machines.

The analogy between the theoretical roles of Turing machines and intentional systems is more than superficial. Consider that warhorse in the philosophy of mind, *Brentano's Thesis* that intentionality is the mark of the mental: all mental phenomena exhibit intentionality and no physical phenomena exhibit intentionality. (The elusive concept of intentionality is introduced and explained in Chapters 1, 4 and 12.) This has been traditionally taken to be an *irreducibility* thesis: the mental, in virtue of its intentionality, cannot be reduced to the physical.[5] But given the concept of an intentional system, we can construe the first half of Brentano's Thesis—all mental phenomena are intentional—as a *reductionist* thesis of sorts, parallel to Church's Thesis in the foundations of mathematics. According to Church's Thesis, every "effective" procedure in mathematics is recursive, that is, Turing-computable. (The idea, metaphorically, is that any mathematical task for which there is a clear *recipe* composed of simple steps can be performed by a very simple computer, a universal Turing machine, the universal recipe-follower.) Church's Thesis is not provable, since it hinges on the intuitive and unformalizable notion of an effective procedure, but it is generally accepted, and it provides a very useful reduction of a fuzzy-but-useful mathematical notion to a crisply defined notion of apparently equivalent scope and greater power. Analogously, the claim that every mental phenomenon is *intentional-system-characterizable* would, if true, provide a reduction of the mental—a domain whose boundaries are *at best* fixed by mutual acknowledgment and shared intuition—to a clearly defined domain of entities, whose principles of organization are familiar, relatively formal and systematic.

   In Chapter 1 the question is posed: are there mental treasures that cannot be purchased with intentional coin? The negative answer, like Church's Thesis, cannot be proved, but only made plausible by the examination of a series of "tough" cases in which mental phenomena *are* (I claim) captured in the net of intentional systems. That is the major burden of the book, and individual essays tackle particular phenomena: invention in Chapter 5, dreams in Chapter 8, mental images and some of their kin in Chapters 9 and 10, pain in Chapter 11, and free will in Chapters 12 through 15. This is hardly a complete list of mental treasures, but reasons are given along the way, in these chapters and in others, for thinking that parallel treatments can be devised for other phenomena. Complete success in this project would vindicate physicalism of a very modest and undoctrinaire sort: all mental events are in the end just physical events, and commonalities between mental events (or between people sharing a mentalistic attribute) are explicated via a description and prediction system that is neutral with regard to physicalism, but just for that reason entirely compatible with physicalism. We know that a merely physical object can be an intentional system, even if we can't prove *either* that every intentional system is physically realizable in principle, *or* that every intuitively *mental* item in the world can be adequately accounted for as a feature of a physically realized intentional system.

If one insisted on giving a name to this theory, it could be called *type intentionalism*: every mental event is some functional, physical event or other, and the types are captured not by any reductionist language but by a regimentation of the very terms we *ordinarily* use— we explain *what beliefs are* by systematizing the notion of a believing-system, for instance. This theory has the virtues of fitting neatly into a niche left open by its rivals and being expressible in a few straight-forward general statements, but in that clean, uncomplicated form it is unacceptable to me. Sadly for the taxonomists, I cannot rest content with "type intentionalism" as it stands, for it appears to assume something I believe to be false: *viz*, that our *ordinary* way of picking out putative mental features and entities succeeds in picking out real features and entities. Type intentionalism as so far described would assume this by assuming the *integrity* of the ordinary mentalistic pred-icates used on the *left*-hand side of our definition schema (3). One might uncritically suppose that when we talk, as we ordinarily do, of peoples' thoughts, desires, beliefs, pains, sensations, dreams, exper-iences, we are referring to members in good standing of usefully distinct classes of items in the world—"natural kinds". Why else would one take on the burden of explaining how *these* "types" are reducible to any others? But most if not all of our familiar mentalistic idioms fail to perform this task of perspicuous reference, because they embody conceptual infelicities and incoherencies of various sorts. I argue for this thesis in detail with regard to the ordinary concepts of pain in Chapter 11, belief in Chapters 6 and 16, and experience in Chapters 8, 9, and 10, but the strategic point of these criticisms is more graph-ically brought out by a fanciful example.

Suppose we find a society that lacks our knowledge of human physiology, and that speaks a language just like English except for one curious family of idioms. When they are tired they talk of being beset by *fatigues*, of having mental fatigues, muscular fatigues, fatigues in the eyes and fatigues of the spirit. Their sports lore contains such maxims as "too many fatigues spoils your aim" and "five fatigues in the legs are worth ten in the arms". When we encounter them and tell them of our science, they want to know *what fatigues are*. They have been puzzling over such questions as whether numerically the same fatigue can come and go and return, whether fatigues have a definite location in matter or space and time, whether fatigues are identical with some particular physical states or processes or events in their bodies, or are made of some sort of stuff. We can see that they are off to a bad start with these questions, but what should we tell them? One thing we might tell them is that there simply are no such things as fatigues—they have a confused ontology. We can expect some of them to retort: "You don't think there are fatigues? Run around the block a few times and you'll know better! There are many things your science might teach us, but the non-existence of fatigues isn't one of them."

We ought to be unmoved by this retort, but if we wanted to acknowledge this society's "right" to go on talking about fatigues—it's their language, after all—we might try to accomodate by agreeing to call at least some of the claims they make about fatigues true and false, depending on whether the relevant individuals are drowsy, exhausted or feigning, etc. We could then give as best we could the physiological conditions for the truth and falsity of those claims, but refuse to take the apparent ontology of those claims seriously; that is, we could refuse to attempt any *identification* of fatigues. Depending on how much we choose to reform their usage before answering their questions at all, we will appear to be countenancing what is called the disappearance form of the identity theory, or eliminative materialism—for we legislate the putative items right out of existence. Fatigues are not good theoretical entities, however well entrenched the term "fatigues" is in the habits of thought of the imagined society. The same is true, I hold, of beliefs, desires, pains, mental images, experiences—as all these are *ordinarily* understood. Not only are *beliefs* and *pains* not good theoretical *things* (like electrons or neurons), but the *state-of-believing-that-p* is not a well-defined or definable theoretical *state*, and the *attribute, being-in-pain,* is not a well-behaved theoretical attribute. Some ordinary mental-entity terms (but not these) may perspicuously isolate features of people that deserve mention in a mature psychology; about such features I am a straightforward type-intentionalist or "homuncular functionalist", as Lycan calls me,[6] for reasons that will be clear from Chapters 5, 7, 9 and 11. About the theoretical entities in a mature psychology that eventually *supplant* beliefs, desires, pains, mental images, experiences . . . I am also a type-intentionalist or homuncular functionalist. About other putative mental entities I am an eliminative materialist. The details of my view must for this reason be built up piecemeal, by case studies and individual defenses that are not intended to generalize to all mental entities and all mental states. It is no easier to convince someone that there are no pains or beliefs than it would be to convince our imaginary people that there are no fatigues. If it can be done at all (supposing for the moment that one would want to, that it is true!), it can only be done by subjecting our intuitions and convictions about particular cases to skeptical scrutiny.

The foundation for that task is laid in Part I, where the concept of an intentional system is defined and subjected to a preliminary exploration in Chapter 1. Chapter 2 develops arguments against type functionalism and for type intentionalism, and in the second half provides a first look at some of the themes about consciousness explored in detailed in Part III. Chapter 3 examines the prospects of a very tempting extension of intentionalism: the brain writing hypothesis. If we can predict someone's behavior only by ascribing beliefs (and other intentions) to him, mustn't we suppose those beliefs are somehow *stored* in him and *used* by him to govern his behavior, and isn't a stored *sentence* a good model—if not our only model—for a stored belief? I argue that while it might turn out that there is some such brain writing that "encodes" our thoughts, the reasons for believing so are far from overwhelming. Further caveats about brain writing are developed in other chapters, especially Chapter 6. It is important to protect type intentionalism, as a general theory of the nature of mentalistic attributions, from the compelling but problem-ridden "engineering" hypothesis that all sophisticated intentional systems must share at least one design feature: they must have an internal system or language of mental representation. In some very weak sense, no doubt, this must be true, and in a variety of strong senses it must be false. What intermediate sense can be made of the claim is a subject of current controversy to which I add fuel in several of the chapters.

Part II explores the foundations of psychology in more detail, and attempts to describe the conceptual environment in which psychology could survive its infancy and grow to maturity. Current wisdom has it that behaviorism is dead and that "cognitive science", an alliance of cognitive psychology, linguistics and artificial intelligence, is the wave of the future. I share this optimism in part, but see some conceptual traps and false avenues worth pointing out. Chapters 4 and 5 attempt to diagnose both the weaknesses and underestimated strengths of behaviorism. They yield a vision of psychology more unified in both its methods and unsolved problems than the more impassioned spokesmen would have us believe. Chapter 6, a review of Fodor's important book, *The Language of Thought*, promotes a cautious skepticism about some of the theoretical underpinnings of the cognitive science movement, and Chapter 7 is an introductory travel guide to the field of artificial intelligence, recommending points of interest while warning of alien customs and unreliable accommodations. Since some enemies of artificial intelligence have viewed the piece as an unseemly glorification of the field and some workers in the field have regarded it as an unsympathetic attack, it probably strikes the right balance.

Part III then tackles some of the traditional questions that have puzzled philosophers of mind concerned with consciousness: what are sensations, dreams, mental images, pains? How can they be captured in the net of psychological theory? Together these chapters constitute a considerable revision of the account of consciousness given in the second half of *Content and Consciousness*, though most of the strong claims about the relation of consciousness to language survive in one form or another.

Part IV considers a variety of related questions that might be grouped under one general question: can psychology support a vision of ourselves as moral agents, free to choose what we will do and responsible for our actions? Many have thought that materialism or mechanism or determinism—all *apparent* assumptions of the reigning psychological theories—threaten this vision, but in Chapters 12 and 13 I consider the most persuasive of the arguments to this effect and reveal their flaws. Chapter 12 attempts to allay the worry that sheer mechanism—deterministic or indeterministic—would rule out free will and responsibility. By uncovering the missteps in the most compelling arguments for this thesis I claim not to refute it, but at least to strip it of its influence. Chapter 13 tackles the widespread conviction that Gödel's Theorem proves we cannot be "machines", and illustrates the fundamental confusions that give this idea whatever plausibility it has. Chapter 14 argues that persons can be defined as a particular subclass of intentional systems, "higher order" intentional systems with the capacity for natural language and (hence) consciousness in the fullest sense. In some regards then this is the unifying essay of the collection. Chapter 15 explores the relationship between free will and indeterminism, and argues that what is properly persuasive in the libertarians' insistence that our wills be undetermined can be captured in a neutral model of rational decision-making. Chapter 16 develops this model of decision-making a bit further and proposes a *reform* in our ordinary concept of belief, sharply distinguishing two phenomena I call belief and opinion. I view these chapters as developing fragments of a positive psychological theory of moral agents or persons. Chapter 17 is dessert.

BRAINSTORMS

I

Intentional Explanation and
Attributions of Mentality

1

Intentional Systems

I wish to examine the concept of a system whose behavior can be—at least sometimes—explained and predicted by relying on ascriptions to the system of beliefs and desires (and hopes, fears, intentions, hunches, . . .). I will call such systems *intentional systems*, and such explanations and predictions intentional explanations and predictions, in virtue of the intentionality of the idioms of belief and desire (and hope, fear, intention, hunch, . . .).[1]

I used to insist on capitalizing "intentional" wherever I meant to be using Brentano's notion of *intentionality*, in order to distinguish this technical term from its cousin, e.g., "an intentional shove", but the technical term is now in much greater currency, and since almost everyone else who uses the term seems content to risk this confusion, I have decided, with some trepidation, to abandon my typographical eccentricity. But let the uninitiated reader beware: "intentional" as it occurs here is *not* the familiar term of layman's English.[2] For me, as for many recent authors, intentionality is primarily a feature of linguistic entities—idioms, contexts—and for my purposes here we can be satisfied that an idiom is intentional if substitution of codesignative terms do not preserve truth or if the "objects" of the idiom are not capturable in the usual way by quantifiers. I discuss this in more detail in *Content and Consciousness.*[3]

I

The first point to make about intentional systems[4] as I have just defined them is that a particular thing is an intentional system only in relation to the strategies of someone who is trying to explain and predict its behavior. What this amounts to can best be brought out by example. Consider the case of a chess-playing computer, and the different strategies or stances one might adopt as its opponent in trying to predict its moves. There are three different stances of interest to us. First there is the *design stance*. If one knows exactly how the computer is designed (including the impermanent part of its design: its program) one can predict its designed response to any move one makes by following the computation instructions of the program. One's prediction will come true provided only that the computer performs as designed—that is, without breakdown. Different varieties of design-stance predictions can be discerned, but all of them are alike in relying on the notion of *function*, which is purpose-relative or teleological. That is, a design of a system breaks it up into larger or smaller functional parts, and design-stance predictions are generated by assuming that each functional part will function properly. For instance, the radio engineer's schematic wiring diagrams have symbols for each resistor, capacitor, transistor, etc.—*each with its task to perform*—and he can give a design-stance prediction of the behavior of a circuit by assuming that each element performs its task. Thus one can make design-stance predictions of the computer's response at several different levels of abstraction, depending on whether one's design treats as smallest functional elements strategy-generators and consequence-testers, multipliers and dividers, or transistors and switches. (It should be noted that not all diagrams or pictures are designs in this sense, for a diagram may carry no information about the functions—intended or observed—of the elements it depicts.)

We generally adopt the design stance when making predictions about the behavior of mechanical objects, e.g., "As the typewriter carriage approaches the margin, a bell will ring (provided the machine is in working order)," and more simply, "Strike the match and it will light." We also often adopt this stance in predictions involving natural objects: "Heavy pruning will stimulate denser foliage and stronger limbs." The essential feature of the design stance is that we make predictions solely from knowledge or assumptions about the system's functional design, irrespective of the physical constitution or condition of the innards of the particular object.

Second, there is what we may call the *physical stance*. From this stance our predictions are based on the actual physical state of the particular object, and are worked out by applying whatever knowledge we have of the laws of nature. It is from this stance alone that we can predict the malfunction of systems (unless, as sometimes happens these days, a system is *designed* to malfunction after a certain time, in which case malfunctioning in one sense becomes a part of its proper functioning). Instances of predictions from the physical stance are common enough: "If you turn on the switch you'll get a nasty shock," and, "When the snows come that branch will break right off." One seldom adopts the physical stance in dealing with a computer just because the number of critical variables in the physical constitution of a computer would overwhelm the most prodigious calculator. Significantly, the physical stance is generally reserved for instances of breakdown, where the condition preventing normal operation is generalized and easily locatable, e.g., "Nothing will happen when you type in your questions, because it isn't plugged in," or, "It won't work with all that flood water in it." Attempting to give a physical account or prediction of the chess-playing computer would be a pointless and herculean labor, but it would work in principle. One could predict the response it would make in a chess game by tracing out the effects of the input energies all the way through the computer until once more type was pressed against paper and a response was printed. (Because of the digital nature of computers, quantum-level indeterminacies, if such there be, will cancel out rather than accumulate, unless of course a radium "randomizer" or other amplifier of quantum effects is built into the computer).

The best chess-playing computers these days are practically inaccessible to prediction from either the design stance or the physical stance; they have become too complex for even their own designers to view from the design stance. A man's best hope of defeating such a machine in a chess match is to predict its responses by figuring out as best he can what the best or most rational move would be, given the rules and goals of chess. That is, one assumes not only (1) that the machine will function as designed, but (2) that the design is optimal as well, that the computer will "choose" the most rational move. Predictions made on these assumptions may well fail if either assumption proves unwarranted in the particular case, but still this *means* of prediction may impress us as the most fruitful one to adopt in dealing with a particular system. Put another way, when one can no longer hope to beat the machine by utilizing one's knowledge of physics or programming to anticipate its responses, one may still be able to avoid defeat by treating the machine rather like an intelligent human opponent.

We must look more closely at this strategy. A prediction relying on the assumption of the system's rationality is relative to a number of things. First, rationality here so far means nothing more than optimal design relative to a goal or optimally weighted hierarchy of goals (checkmate, winning pieces, defense, etc., in the case of chess) and a set of constraints (the rules and starting position). Prediction itself is, moreover, relative to the nature and extent of the information the system has at the time about the field of endeavor. The question one asks in framing a prediction of this sort is: What is the most rational thing for the computer to do, given goals $x,y,z, \ldots$, constraints $a,b,c,$ $\ldots$ and information (including misinformation, if any) about the present state of affairs $p,q,r, \ldots$? In predicting the computer's response to my chess move, my assessment of the computer's most rational move may depend, for instance, not only on my assumption that the computer has information about the present disposition of all the pieces, but also on whether I believe the computer has information about my inability to see four moves ahead, the relative powers of knights and bishops, and my weakness for knight-bishop exchanges. In the end I may not be able to frame a very good prediction, if I am unable to determine with any accuracy what information and goals the computer has, or if the information and goals I take to be given do not dictate any one best move, or if I simply am not so good as the computer is at generating an optimal move from this given. Such predictions then are very precarious; not only are they relative to a set of postulates about goals, constraints, and information, and not only do they hinge on determining an optimal response in situations where we may have no clear criteria for what is optimal, but also they are vulnerable to short-circuit falsifications that are in principle unpredictable from this stance. Just as design-stance predictions are vulnerable to malfunctions (by depending on the assumption of no malfunction), so these predictions are vulnerable to design weaknesses and lapses (by depending on the assumption of optimal design). It is a measure of the success of contemporary program designers that these precarious predictions turn out to be true with enough regularity to make the method useful.

The dénouement of this extended example should now be obvious: this third stance, with its assumption of rationality, is the *intentional stance*; the predictions one makes from it are intentional predictions; one is viewing the computer as an intentional system. One predicts behavior in such a case by ascribing to the system *the possession of certain information* and supposing it to be *directed by certain goals*, and then by working out the most reasonable or appropriate action on the basis of these ascriptions and suppositions. It is a small step to calling the information possessed the computer's *beliefs*, its goals and subgoals its *desires*. What I mean by saying that this is a small step, is that the notion of possession of information or misinformation is just as intentional a notion as that of belief. The "possession" at issue is hardly the bland and innocent notion of storage one might suppose; it is, and must be, "epistemic possession"—an analogue of belief. Consider: the Frenchman who possesses the *Encyclopedia Britannica* but knows no English might be said to "possess" the information in it, but if there is such a sense of possession, it is not strong enough to serve as the sort of possession the computer must be supposed to enjoy, relative to the information it *uses* in "choosing" a chess move. In a similar way, the goals of a goal-directed computer must be specified intentionally, just like desires.

Lingering doubts about whether the chess-playing computer *really* has beliefs and desires are misplaced; for the definition of intentional systems I have given does not say that intentional systems *really* have beliefs and desires, but that one can explain and predict their behavior by *ascribing* beliefs and desires to them, and whether one calls what one ascribes to the computer beliefs or belief-analogues or information complexes or intentional whatnots makes no difference to the nature of the calculation one makes on the basis of the ascriptions. One will arrive at the same predictions whether one forthrightly thinks in terms of the computer's beliefs and desires, or in terms of the computer's information-store and goal-specifications. The inescapable and interesting fact is that for the best chess-playing computers of today, intentional explanation and prediction of their behavior is not only common, but works when no other sort of prediction of their behavior is manageable. We do quite successfully treat these computers as intentional systems, and we do this independently of any considerations about what substance they are composed of, their origin, their position or lack of position in the community of moral agents, their consciousness or self-consciousness, or the determinacy or indeterminacy of their operations. The decision to adopt the strategy is pragmatic, and is not intrinsically right or wrong. One can always refuse to adopt the intentional stance toward the computer, and accept its checkmates. One can switch stances at will without involving oneself in any inconsistencies or inhumanities, adopting the intentional stance in one's role as opponent, the design stance in one's role as redesigner, and the physical stance in one's role as repairman.

This celebration of our chess-playing computer is not intended to imply that it is a completely adequate model or simulation of Mind, or intelligent human or animal activity; nor am I saying that the attitude we adopt toward this computer is precisely the same that we adopt toward a creature we deem to be conscious and rational. All that has been claimed is that on occasion, a purely physical system can be so complex, and yet so organized, that we find it convenient, explanatory, pragmatically necessary for prediction, to treat it as if it had beliefs and desires and was rational. The chess-playing computer is just that, a machine for playing chess, which no man or animal is; and hence its "rationality" is pinched and artificial.

Perhaps we could straightforwardly expand the chess-playing computer into a more faithful model of human rationality, and perhaps not. I prefer to pursue a more fundamental line of inquiry first.

When should we expect the tactic of adopting the intentional stance to pay off? Whenever we have reason to suppose the assumption of optimal design is warranted, and doubt the practicality of prediction from the design or physical stance. Suppose we travel to a distant planet and find it inhabited by things moving about its surface, multiplying, decaying, apparently reacting to events in the environment, but otherwise as unlike human beings as you please. Can we make intentional predictions and explanations of their behavior? If we have reason to suppose that a process of natural selection has been in effect, then we can be assured that the populations we observe have been selected in virtue of their design: they will respond to at least some of the more common event-types in this environment in ways that are normally appropriate—that is, conducive to propagation of the species.* Once we have tentatively identified the perils and succors of the environment (relative to the constitution of the inhabitants, not ours), we shall be able to estimate which goals and which weighting of goals will be optimal relative to the creatures' *needs* (for survival and propagation), which sorts of information about the environment will be *useful* in guiding goal-directed activity, and which activities will be appropriate given the environmental circumstances. Having doped out these conditions (which will always be subject to revision) we can proceed at once to ascribe beliefs and desires to the creatures. Their behavior will "manifest" their beliefs by being seen as the actions which, given the creatures' desires, would be appropriate to such beliefs as would be appropriate to the environmental stimulation. Desires, in turn, will be "manifested" in behavior as those appropriate desires (given the needs of the creature) to which the actions of the creature would be appropriate, given the creature's beliefs. The circularity of these interlocking specifications is no accident. Ascriptions of beliefs and desires must be interdependent, and the only points of anchorage

---

*Note that what is *directly* selected, the gene, is a diagram and not a design; it is selected, however, because it happens to ensure that its bearer has a certain (functional) design. This was pointed out to me by Woodruff.

are the demonstrable needs for survival, the regularities of behavior, and the assumption, grounded in faith in natural selection, of optimal design. Once one has ascribed beliefs and desires, however, one can at once set about predicting behavior on their basis, and if evolution has done its job—as it must over the long run—our predictions will be reliable enough to be useful.

It might at first seem that this tactic unjustifiably imposes human categories and attributes (belief, desire, and so forth) on these alien entities. It is a sort of anthropomorphizing, to be sure, but it is conceptually innocent anthropomorphizing. We do not have to suppose these creatures share with us any peculiarly human inclinations, attitudes, hopes, foibles, pleasures, or outlooks; their actions may not include running, jumping, hiding, eating, sleeping, listening, or copulating. All we transport from our world to theirs are the categories of rationality, perception (information input by some "sense" modality or modalities—perhaps radar or cosmic radiation), and action. The question of whether we can expect them to share any of our beliefs or desires is tricky, but there are a few points that can be made at this time; in virtue of their rationality they can be supposed to share our belief in logical truths,* and we cannot suppose that they normally desire their own destruction, for instance.

II

When one deals with a system—be it man, machine, or alien creature—by explaining and predicting its behavior by citing its beliefs and desires, one has what might be called a "theory of behavior" for the system. Let us see how such intentional theories of behavior relate to other putative theories of behavior.

One fact so obvious that it is easily overlooked is that our "commonsense" explanations and predictions of the behavior of both men and animals are intentional. We start by assuming rationality. We do not *expect* new acquaintances to react irrationally to particular topics or eventualities, but when they do we learn to adjust our strategies accordingly, just as, with a chess-playing computer, one sets out with a high regard for its rationality and adjusts one's estimate downward wherever performance reveals flaws. The presumption of rationality is so strongly entrenched in our inference habits that when our predic-

*Cf. Quine's argument about the necessity of "discovering" our logical connectives in any language we can translate in *Word and Object* (Cambridge, Mass.: MIT, 1960), Section 13. More will be said in defense of this below.

tions prove false, we at first cast about for adjustments in the information-possession conditions (he must not have heard, he must not know English, he must not have seen x, been aware that y, etc.) or goal weightings, before questioning the rationality of the system as a whole. In extreme cases personalities may prove to be so unpredictable from the intentional stance that we abandon it, and if we have accumulated a lot of evidence in the meanwhile about the nature of response patterns in the individual, we may find that a species of design stance can be effectively adopted. This is the fundamentally different attitude we occasionally adopt toward the insane. To watch an asylum attendant manipulate an obsessively countersuggestive patient, for instance, is to watch something radically unlike normal interpersonal relations.

Our prediction of animal behavior by "common sense" is also intentional. Whether or not sentimental folk go overboard when they talk to their dogs or fill their cats' heads with schemes and worries, even the most hardboiled among us predict animals' behavior intentionally. If we observe a mouse in a situation where it can see a cat waiting at one mousehole and cheese at another, we know which way the mouse will go, providing it is not deranged; our prediction is not based on our familiarity with maze-experiments or any assumptions about the sort of special training the mouse has been through. We suppose the mouse can see the cat and the cheese, and hence has beliefs (belief-analogues, intentional whatnots) to the effect that there is a cat to the left, cheese to the right, and we ascribe to the mouse also the desire to eat the cheese and the desire to avoid the cat (subsumed, appropriately enough, under the more general desires to eat and to avoid peril); so we predict that the mouse will do what is appropriate to such beliefs and desires, namely, go to the right in order to get the cheese and avoid the cat. Whatever academic allegiances or theoretical predilections we may have, we would be astonished if, in the general run, mice and other animals falsified such intentional predictions of their behavior. Indeed, experimental psychologists of every school would have a hard time devising experimental situations to support their various theories without the help of their intentional expectations of how the test animals will respond to circumstances.

Earlier I alleged that even creatures from another planet would share with us our beliefs in logical truths; light can be shed on this claim by asking whether mice and other animals, in virtue of being intentional systems, also believe the truths of logic. There is something bizarre in the picture of a dog or mouse cogitating a list of tautologies, but we can avoid that picture. The assumption that something is an intentional system is the assumption that it is rational; that is, one gets nowhere with the assumption that entity x has beliefs $p,q,r, \ldots$ unless one also supposes that x believes what follows from $p,q,r, \ldots$; otherwise there is no way of ruling out the prediction that x will, in the face of its beliefs $p,q,r, \ldots$ do something utterly stupid, and, if we cannot rule out *that* prediction, we will have acquired no predictive power at all. So whether or not the animal is said to *believe* the *truths* of logic, it must be supposed to *follow* the *rules* of logic. Surely our mouse follows or believes in *modus ponens*, for we ascribed to it the beliefs: (a) *there is a cat to the left*, and (b) *if there is a cat to the left, I had better not go left*, and our prediction relied on the mouse's ability to get to the conclusion. In general there is a trade-off between rules and truths; we can suppose x to have an inference rule taking A to B or we can give x the belief in the "theorem": *if A then B*. As far as our predictions are concerned, we are free to ascribe to the mouse either a few inference rules and belief in many logical propositions, or many inference rules and few if any logical beliefs.* We can even take a patently nonlogical belief like (b) and recast it as an inference rule taking (a) to the desired conclusion.

Will all logical truths appear among the beliefs of any intentional system? If the system were ideally or perfectly rational, all logical truths would appear, but any actual intentional system will be imperfect, and so not all logical truths must be ascribed as beliefs to any system. Moreover, not all the inference rules of an actual intentional system may be valid; not all its inference-licensing beliefs may be truths of logic. Experience may indicate where the shortcomings lie in any particular system. If we found an imperfectly rational creature whose allegiance to *modus ponens*, say, varied with the subject matter, we could characterize that by excluding *modus ponens* as a rule and ascribing in its stead a set of nonlogical inference rules covering the *modus ponens* step for each subject matter where the rule was followed. Not surprisingly, as we discover more and more imperfections (as we banish more and more logical truths from the creature's beliefs), our efforts at intentional prediction become more and more cumbersome and undecidable, for we can no longer count on the beliefs, desires, and actions going together that *ought* to go together. Eventually we end up, following this process, by predicting from the

*Accepting the argument of Lewis Carroll, in "What the Tortoise Said to Achilles", *Mind* (1895), reprinted in I. M. Copi and J. A. Gould, *Readings on Logic* (New York: MacMillan, 1964), we cannot allow all the rules for a system to be replaced by beliefs, for this would generate an infinite and unproductive nesting of distinct beliefs about what can be inferred from what.

design stance; we end up, that is, dropping the assumption of rationality.*

This migration from common-sense intentional explanations and predictions to more reliable design-stance explanations and predictions that is forced on us when we discover that our subjects are imperfectly rational is, independently of any such discovery, the proper direction for theory builders to take whenever possible. In the end, we want to be able to explain the intelligence of man, or beast, in terms of his design, and this in turn in terms of the natural selection of this design; so whenever we stop in our explanations at the intentional level we have left over an unexplained instance of intelligence or rationality. This comes out vividly if we look at theory building from the vantage point of economics.

Any time a theory builder proposes to call any event, state, structure, etc., in any system (say the brain of an organism) a *signal* or *message* or *command* or otherwise endows it with content, he *takes out a loan* of intelligence. He implicitly posits along with his signals, messages, or commands, something that can serve as a signal-*reader*, message-*understander*, or *commander*, else his "signals" will be for naught, will decay unreceived, uncomprehended. This loan must be repaid eventually by finding and analyzing away these readers or comprehenders; for, failing this, the theory will have among its elements unanalyzed man-analogues endowed with enough intelligence to read the signals, etc., and thus the theory will *postpone* answering the major question: what makes for intelligence? The intentionality of all such talk of signals and commands reminds us that rationality is being taken for granted, and in this way shows us where a theory is incomplete. It is this feature that, to my mind, puts a premium on the yet unfinished task of devising a rigorous definition of intentionality, for if we can lay claim to a purely formal criterion of intentional discourse, we will have what amounts to a medium of exchange for assessing theories of behavior. Intentionality *abstracts* from the inessential details of the various forms intelligence-loans can take (e.g., signal-readers, volition-emitters, librarians in the corridors of memory, egos and superegos) and serves as a reliable means of detecting exactly where a theory is *in the red* relative to the task of explaining intelligence; wherever a theory relies on a formulation bearing the logical marks of intentionality, there a little man is concealed.

*This paragraph owes much to discussion with John Vickers, whose paper "Judgment and Belief", in K. Lambert, *The Logical Way of Doing Things* (New Haven, Conn.: Yale, 1969), goes beyond the remarks here by considering the problems of the relative strength or weighting of beliefs and desires.

This insufficiency of intentional explanation from the point of view of psychology has been widely felt and as widely misconceived. The most influential misgivings, expressed in the behaviorism of Skinner and Quine, can be succinctly characterized in terms of our economic metaphor. Skinner's and Quine's adamant prohibitions of intentional idioms at all levels of theory is the analogue of rock-ribbed New England conservatism: no deficit spending when building a theory! In Quine's case, the abhorrence of loans is due mainly to his fear that they can never be repaid, whereas Skinner stresses rather that what is borrowed is worthless to begin with. Skinner's suspicion is that intentionally couched claims are empirically vacuous, in the sense that they are altogether too easy to accommodate to the data, like the *virtus dormitiva* Molière's doctor ascribes to the sleeping powder (see Chapter 4 for a more detailed discussion of these issues). Questions can be begged on a temporary basis, however, permitting a mode of prediction and explanation not totally vacuous. Consider the following intentional prediction: if I were to ask a thousand American mathematicians how much seven times five is, more than nine hundred would respond by saying that it was thirty-five. (I have allowed for a few to mis-hear my question, a few others to be obstreperous, a few to make slips of the tongue.) If you doubt the prediction, you can test it; I would bet good money on it. It seems to have empirical content because it can, in a fashion, be tested, and yet it is unsatisfactory as a prediction of an empirical theory of psychology. It works, of course, because of the contingent, empirical—but evolution-guaranteed—fact that men in general are well enough designed both to get the answer right and to want to get it right. It will hold with as few exceptions for any group of Martians with whom we are able to converse, for it is not a prediction just of *human* psychology, but of the "psychology" of intentional systems generally.

Deciding on the basis of available empirical evidence that something is a piece of copper or a lichen permits one to make predictions based on the empirical theories dealing with copper and lichens, but deciding on the basis of available evidence that something is (may be treated as) an intentional system permits predictions having a normative or logical basis rather than an empirical one, and hence the success of an intentional prediction, based as it is on no particular picture of the system's design, cannot be construed to confirm or disconfirm any particular pictures of the system's design.

Skinner's reaction to this has been to try to frame predictions purely in non-intentional language, by predicting bodily responses to physical stimuli, but to date this has not provided him with the alternative mode of prediction and explanation he has sought, as perhaps an extremely cursory review can indicate. To provide a setting for non-intentional prediction of behavior, he invented the Skinner box, in which the rewarded behavior of the occupant—say, a rat—is a highly restricted and stereotypic bodily motion—usually pressing a bar with the front paws.

The claim that is then made is that once the animal has been trained, a law-like relationship is discovered to hold between non-intentionally characterized events: controlling stimuli and bar-pressing responses. A regularity is discovered to hold, to be sure, but the fact that it is between non-intentionally defined events is due to a property of the Skinner box and not of the occupant. For let us turn our prediction about mathematicians into a Skinnerian prediction: strap a mathematician in a Skinner box so he can move only his head; display in front of him a card on which appear the marks: "How much is seven times five?"; move into the range of his head-motions two buttons, over one of which is the mark "35" and over the other "34"; place electrodes on the soles of his feet and give him a few quick shocks; the controlling stimulus is then to be the sound: "Answer now!" I predict that in a statistically significant number of cases, even *before* training trials to condition the man to press button "35" with his forehead, he will do this when given the controlling stimulus. Is this a satisfactory scientific prediction just because it eschews the intentional vocabulary? No, it is an intentional prediction disguised by so restricting the environment that only one bodily motion is available to fulfill the intentional *action* that anyone would prescribe as appropriate to the circumstances of perception, belief, desire. That it is action, not merely motion, that is predicted can also be seen in the case of subjects less intelligent than mathematicians. Suppose a mouse were trained, in a Skinner box with a food reward, to take exactly four steps forward and press a bar with its nose; if Skinner's laws truly held between stimuli and responses defined in terms of bodily motion, were we to move the bar an inch farther away, so four steps did not reach it, Skinner would have to predict that the mouse would jab its nose into the empty air rather than take a fifth step.

A variation of Skinnerian theory designed to meet this objection acknowledges that the trained response one predicts is not truly captured in a description of skeletal motion alone, but rather in a description of an environmental effect achieved: the bar going down, the "35" button being depressed. This will also not do. Suppose we could in fact train a man or animal to achieve an environmental effect, as this theory proposes. Suppose, for instance, we train a man to push a button under the longer of two displays, such as drawings or simple designs, that is, we reward him when he pushes the button under the longer of two pictures of pencils, or cigars, etc. The miraculous consequence of this theory, were it correct, would be that if, after training him on simple views, we were to present him with the Müller-Lyer arrow-head illusion, he would be immune to it, for *ex hypothesi* he has been trained to achieve an *actual* environmental effect (choosing the display that *is* longer), not a *perceived* or *believed* environmental effect (choosing the display that *seems* longer). The reliable prediction, again, is the intentional one.*

Skinner's experimental design is supposed to eliminate the intentional, but it merely masks it. Skinner's non-intentional predictions work to the extent they do, not because Skinner has truly found non-intentional behavioral laws, but because the highly reliable intentional predictions underlying his experimental situations (the rat desires food and believes it will get food by pressing the bar—something for which it has been given good evidence—so it will press the bar) are disguised by leaving virtually no room in the environment for more than one bodily motion to be the appropriate action and by leaving virtually no room in the environment for discrepancy to arise between the subject's beliefs and the reality.

Where, then, should we look for a satisfactory theory of behavior? Intentional theory is vacuous as psychology because it presupposes and does not explain rationality or intelligence. The apparent successes of Skinnerian behaviorism, however, rely on hidden intentional predictions. Skinner is right in recognizing that intentionality can be no *foundation* for psychology, and right also to look for purely mechanistic regularities in the activities of his subjects, but there is little reason to suppose they will lie on the surface in gross behavior—except, as we have seen, when we put an artificial straitjacket on an intentional regularity. Rather, we will find whatever mechanistic regularities there are in the functioning of internal systems whose design approaches the optimal (relative to some ends). In seeking knowledge of internal design our most promising tactic is to take out intelligence-loans, endow peripheral and internal events with content, and then look for mechanisms that will function appropriately with such "messages" so that we can pay back the loans. This tactic is hardly untried. Research in artificial intelligence, which has produced, among other things, the

---

*R. L. Gregory, *Eye and Brain* (London: World University Library, 1966): p. 137, reports that pigeons and fish given just this training are, not surprisingly, susceptible to visual illusions of length.

chess-playing computer, proceeds by working from an intentionally characterized problem (how to get the computer to consider the right sorts of information, make the right decisions) to a design-stance solution—an approximation of optimal design. Psychophysicists and neurophysiologists who routinely describe events in terms of the transmission of information within the nervous system are similarly borrowing intentional capital—even if they are often inclined to ignore or disavow their debts.

Finally, it should not be supposed that, just because intentional theory is vacuous as psychology, in virtue of its assumption of rationality, it is vacuous from all points of view. Game theory, for example, is inescapably intentional,[5] but as a formal normative theory and not a psychology this is nothing amiss. Game-theoretical predictions applied to human subjects achieve their accuracy in virtue of the evolutionary guarantee that man is well designed as a game player, a special case of rationality. Similarly, economics, the social science of greatest predictive power today, is not a psychological theory and presupposes what psychology must explain. Economic explanation and prediction is intentional (although some is disguised) and succeeds to the extent that it does because individual men are in general good approximations of of the optimal operator in the marketplace.

III

The concept of an intentional system is a relatively uncluttered and unmetaphysical notion, abstracted as it is from questions of the composition, constitution, consciousness, morality, or divinity of the entities falling under it. Thus, for example, it is much easier to decide whether a machine can be an intentional system than it is to decide whether a machine can *really* think, or be conscious, or morally responsible. This simplicity makes it ideal as a source of order and organization in philosophical analyses of "mental" concepts. Whatever else a person might be—embodied mind or soul, self-conscious moral agent, "emergent" form of intelligence—he is an intentional system, and whatever follows just from being an intentional system is thus true of a person. It is interesting to see just how much of what we hold to be the case about persons or their minds follows directly from their being intentional systems. To revert for a moment to the economic metaphor, the guiding or challenging question that defines work in the philosophy of mind is this: are there mental treasures that cannot be purchased with intentional coin? If not, a considerable unification of science can be foreseen in outline. Of special importance for such an examination is the subclass of intentional systems that have language, that can communicate; for these provide a framework for a theory of consciousness. In *Content and Consciousness,* part II, and in parts III and IV of this volume I have attempted to elaborate such a theory; here I would like to consider its implications for the analysis of the concept of belief. What will be true of human believers just in virtue of their being intentional systems with the capacity to communicate?

Just as not all intentional systems currently known to us can fly or swim, so not all intentional systems can talk, but those which can do this raise special problems and opportunities when we come to ascribe beliefs and desires to them. That is a massive understatement; without the talking intentional systems, of course, there would be no ascribing beliefs, no theorizing, no assuming rationality, no predicting. The capacity for language is without doubt the crowning achievement of evolution, an achievement that feeds on itself to produce ever more versatile and subtle rational systems, but still it can be looked at as an adaptation which is subject to the same conditions of environmental utility as any other behavioral talent. When it is looked at in this way several striking facts emerge. One of the most pervasive features of evolutionary histories is the interdependence of distinct organs and capacities in a species. Advanced eyes and other distance receptors are of no utility to an organism unless it develops advanced means of locomotion; the talents of a predator will not accrue to a species that does not evolve a carnivore's digestive system. The capacities of belief and communication have prerequisites of their own. We have already seen that there is no point in ascribing beliefs to a system unless the beliefs ascribed are in general appropriate to the environment, and the system responds appropriately to the beliefs. An eccentric expression of this would be: the capacity to believe would have no survival value unless it were a capacity to believe truths. What is eccentric and potentially misleading about this is that it hints at the picture of a species "trying on" a faculty giving rise to beliefs most of which were false, having its inutility demonstrated, and abandoning it. A species might "experiment" by mutation in any number of inefficacious systems, but none of these systems would deserve to be called belief systems precisely because of their defects, their nonrationality, and hence a false belief system is a conceptual impossibility. To borrow an example from a short story by MacDonald Harris, a soluble fish is an evolutionary impossibility, but a system for false beliefs cannot even be given a coherent description. The same evolutionary bias in favor of truth prunes the capacity to communicate as it develops; a capacity for false communication would not be a capacity for communication at all, but just an emission proclivity of no systematic value to the species. The faculty of communication would not gain ground in evolution unless it was by and large the faculty of transmitting true beliefs, which means only: the faculty of altering other members of the species in the direction of more optimal design.

This provides a foundation for explaining a feature of belief that philosophers have recently been at some pains to account for.[6] The concept of belief seems to have a normative cast to it that is most difficult to capture. One way of putting it might be that an avowal like "I believe that *p*" seems to imply in some fashion: "One ought to believe that *p*." This way of putting it has flaws, however, for we must then account for the fact that "I believe that *p*" seems to have normative force that "He believes that *p*", said of me, does not. Moreover, saying that one ought to believe this or that suggests that belief is voluntary, a view with notorious difficulties.[7] So long as one tries to capture the normative element by expressing it in the form of moral or pragmatic injunctions to believers, such as "one ought to believe the truth" and "one ought to act in accordance with one's beliefs", dilemmas arise. How, for instance, is one to follow the advice to believe the truth? Could one abandon one's sloppy habit of believing falsehoods? If the advice is taken to mean: believe only what you have convincing evidence for, it is the vacuous advice: believe only what you believe to be true. If alternatively it is taken to mean: believe only what is in fact the truth, it is an injunction we are powerless to obey.

The normative element of belief finds its home not in such injunctions but in the preconditions for the ascription of belief, what Phillips Griffiths calls "the general conditions for the possibility of application of the concept". For the concept of belief to find application, two conditions, we have seen, must be met: (1) In general, normally, more often than not, if *x* believes *p*, *p* is true. (2) In general, normally, more often than not, if *x* avows that *p*, he believes *p* [and, by (1), *p* is true]. Were these conditions not met, we would not have rational, communicating systems; we would not have believers or belief-avowers. The norm for belief is evidential well-foundedness (assuring truth in the long run), and the norm for avowal of belief is accuracy (which includes sincerity). These two norms determine pragmatic implications of our utterances. If I assert that *p* (or that I believe that *p*—it makes no difference), I assume the burden of defending my assertion on two fronts: I can be asked for evidence for the truth of *p*, and I can be asked for behavioral evidence that I do in fact believe *p*.[8] I do not need to examine my own behavior in order to be in a position to avow my belief that *p*, but if my sincerity or self-knowledge is challenged, this is where I must turn to defend my assertion. But again, challenges on either point must be the exception rather than the rule if belief is to have a place among our concepts.

Another way of looking at the importance of this predominance of the normal is to consider the well-known circle of implications between beliefs and desires (or intentions) that prevent non-intentional behavioral definitions of intentional terms. A man's standing under a tree is a behavioral indicator of his belief that it is raining, but only on the assumption that he desires to stay dry, and if we then look for evidence that he wants to stay dry, his standing under the tree will do, but only on the assumption that he believes the tree will shelter him; if we ask him if he believes the tree will shelter him, his positive response is confirming evidence only on the assumption that he desires to tell us the truth, and so forth *ad infinitum*. It is this apparently vicious circle that turned Quine against the intentional (and foiled Tolman's efforts at operational definition of intentional terms), but if it is true that in any particular case a man's saying that *p* is evidence of his belief only conditionally, we can be assured that in the long run and in general the circle is broken; a man's assertions are, unconditionally, indicative of his beliefs, as are his actions in general. We get around the "privacy" of beliefs and desires by recognizing that in general anyone's beliefs and desires must be those he "ought to have" given the circumstances.

These two interdependent norms of belief, one favoring the truth and rationality of belief, the other favoring accuracy of avowal, normally complement each other, but on occasion can give rise to conflict. This is the "problem of incorrigibility". If rationality is the mother of intention, we still must wean intentional systems from the criteria that give them life, and set them up on their own. Less figuratively, if we are to make use of the concept of an intentional system in particular instances, at some point we must cease *testing* the assumption of the system's rationality, adopt the intentional stance, and grant without further ado that the system is qualified for beliefs and desires. For mute animals—and chess-playing computers—this manifests itself in a tolerance for less than optimal performance. We continue to ascribe beliefs to the mouse, and explain its actions in terms of them, after we have tricked it into some stupid belief. This tolerance has its limits of course, and the less felicitous the behavior—especially the less adaptable the behavior—the more hedged are our ascriptions. For instance, we are inclined to say of the duckling that "imprints" on the first moving thing it sees upon emerging from its shell that it "believes" the thing is its mother, whom it follows around, but we emphasize the scare-quotes around "believes". For intentional systems that can communicate—persons for instance—the tolerance takes the form of the convention that a man is incorrigible or a special authority about his own beliefs. This convention is "justified" by the fact that evolution does guarantee that our second norm is followed. What better source could there be of a system's beliefs than its avowals? Conflict arises, however, whenever a person falls short of perfect rationality, and avows beliefs that either are strongly disconfirmed by the available empirical evidence or are self-contradictory or contradict other avowals he has made. If we lean on the myth that a man is perfectly rational, we must find his avowals less than authoritative: "You *can't* mean—understand—what you're saying!"; if we lean on his "right" as a speaking intentional system to have his word accepted, we grant him an irrational set of beliefs. Neither position provides a stable resting place; for, as we saw earlier, intentional explanation and prediction cannot be accommodated either to breakdown or to less than optimal design, so there is no coherent intentional description of such an impasse.*

Can any other considerations be brought to bear in such an instance to provide us with justification for one ascription of beliefs rather than another? Where should one look for such considerations? The Phenomenologist will be inclined to suppose that individual introspection will provide us a sort of data not available to the outsider adopting the intentional stance; but how would such data get used? Let the introspector amass as much inside information as you please; he must then communicate it to us, and what are we to make of his communications? We can suppose that they are incorrigible (barring corrigible verbal errors, slips of the tongue, and so forth), but we do not need Phenomenology to give us that option, for it amounts to the decision to lean on the accuracy-of-avowal norm at the expense of the rationality norm. If, alternatively, we demand certain standards of consistency and rationality of his utterances before we accept them as authoritative, what standards will we adopt? If we demand perfect rationality, we have simply flown to the other norm at the expense of the norm of accuracy of avowal. If we try to fix minimum standards at something less than perfection, what will guide our choice? Not

---

*Hintikka takes this bull by the horns. His epistemic logic is acknowledged to hold only for the ideally rational believer; were we to apply this logic to persons in the actual world in other than a normative way, thus making its implications *authoritative* about actual belief, the authority of persons would have to go by the board. Thus his rule A.CBB* (*Knowledge and Belief*, pp. 24–26), roughly that if one believes *p* one believes that one believes *p*, cannot be understood, as it is tempting to suppose, as a version of the incorrigibility thesis.

Phenomenological data, for the choice we make will determine what is to count as Phenomenological data. Not neurophysiological data either, for whether we interpret a bit of neural structure to be endowed with a particular belief content hinges on our having granted that the neural system under examination has met the standards of rationality for being an intentional system, an assumption jeopardized by the impasse we are trying to resolve. That is, one might have a theory about an individual's neurology that permitted one to "read off" or predict the propositions to which he would assent, but whether one's theory had uncovered his *beliefs*, or merely a set of assent-inducers, would depend on how consistent, reasonable, true we found the set of propositions.

John Vickers has suggested to me a way of looking at this question. Consider a set T of transformations that take beliefs into beliefs. The problem is to determine the set T_s for each intentional system S, so that if we know that S believes p, we will be able to determine other things that S believes by seeing what the transformations of p are for T_s. If S were ideally rational, every valid transformation would be in T_s; S would believe every logical consequence of every belief (and, ideally, S would have no false beliefs). Now we know that no actual intentional system will be ideally rational; so we must suppose any actual system will have a T with less in it. But we also know that, to qualify as an intentional system at all, S must have a T with some integrity; T cannot be empty. What rationale could we have, however, for fixing some set between the extremes and calling it *the* set for belief (for S, for earthlings, or for ten-year-old girls)? This is another way of asking whether we could replace Hintikka's normative theory of belief with an empirical theory of belief, and, if so, what evidence we would use. "Actually," one is tempted to say, "people do believe contradictions on occasion, as their utterances demonstrate; so any adequate logic of belief or analysis of the concept of belief must accommodate this fact." But any attempt to *legitimize* human fallibility in a theory of belief by fixing a permissible level of error would be like adding one more rule to chess: an Official Tolerance Rule to the effect that any game of chess containing no more than k moves that are illegal relative to the other rules of the game is a legal game of chess. Suppose we discovered that, in a particular large population of poor chess-players, each game on average contained three illegal moves undetected by either opponent. Would we claim that these people *actually* play a different game from ours, a game with an Official Tolerance Rule with k fixed at 3? This would be to confuse the norm they follow with what gets by in their world. We could claim in a similar vein that people *actually* believe, say, all synonymous or intentionally isomorphic consequences of their beliefs, but not all their logical consequences, but of course the occasions when a man resists assenting to a logical consequence of some avowal of his are unstable cases; he comes in for criticism and cannot appeal in his own defense to any canon absolving him from believing nonsynonymous consequences. If one wants to get away from norms and predict and and explain the "actual, empirical" behavior of the poor chess-players, one stops talking of their *chess moves* and starts talking of their proclivities to move pieces of wood or ivory about on checkered boards; if one wants to predict and explain the "actual, empirical" behavior of believers, one must similarly cease talking of belief, and descend to the design stance or physical stance for one's account.

The concept of an intentional system explicated in these pages is made to bear a heavy load. It has been used here to form a bridge connecting the intentional domain (which includes our "common-sense" world of persons and actions, game theory, and the "neural signals" of the biologist) to the non-intentional domain of the physical sciences. That is a lot to expect of one concept, but nothing less than Brentano himself expected when, in a day of less fragmented science, he proposed intentionality as the mark that sunders the universe in the most fundamental way: dividing the mental from the physical.

2

Reply to Arbib and Gunderson

In December, 1972, Michael Arbib and Keith Gunderson presented papers to an American Philosophical Association symposium on my earlier book, *Content and Consciousness*, to which this essay was a reply.[1] While one might read it as a defense of the theory in my first book, I would rather have it considered an introduction to the off-spring theory. In spite of a few references to Arbib's and Gunderson's papers and my book, this essay is designed to be comprehensible on its own, though I would not at all wish to discourage readers from exploring its antecedents. In the first section the ground rules for ascribing mental predicates to things are developed beyond the account given in Chapter 1. There I claimed that since intentional stance predictions can be made in ignorance of a thing's design—solely on an assumption of the design's excellence—verifying such predictions does not help to confirm any particular psychological theory about the actual design of the thing. This implies that what two things have in common when both are correctly attributed some mental feature need be no independently describable design feature, a result that threatens several familiar and compelling ideas about mental events and states. The second section threatens another familiar and compelling idea, *viz.*, that we mean one *special* thing when we talk of consciousness, rather than a variety of different and improperly united things.

I

Suppose two artificial intelligence teams set out to build *face-recognizers*. We will be able to judge the contraptions they come up with, for we know in advance what a face-recognizer ought to be able to do. Our expectations of face-recognizers do not spring from induction over the observed behavior of large numbers of actual face-recognizers, but from a relatively *a priori* source: what might be called our intuitive epistemic logic, more particularly, "the logic of our concept" of recognition. The logic of the concept of recognition dictates an open-ended and shifting class of appropriate further tasks, abilities, reactions and distinctions that *ideally* would manifest themselves in any face-recognizer under various conditions. Not only will we want a face-recognizer to answer questions correctly about the faces before it, but also to "use" its recognition capacities in a variety of other ways, depending on what else it does, what other tasks it performs, what other goals it has. These conditions and criteria are characterized intentionally; they are a part of what I call the theory of intentional systems, the theory of entities that are not just face-recognizers, but theorem-provers, grocery-choosers, danger-avoiders, music appreciators.

Since the Ideal Face-Recognizer, like a Platonic Form, can only be approximated by any hardware (or brainware) copy, and since the marks of successful approximation are characterized intentionally, the face-recognizers designed by the two teams may differ radically in material or design. At the physical level one might be electronic, the other hydraulic. Or one might rely on a digital computer, the other on an analogue computer. Or, at a higher level of design, one might use a system that analyzed exhibited faces via key features with indexed verbal labels—"balding", "snub-nosed", "lantern-jawed"—and then compared label-scores against master lists of label scores for previously encountered faces, while the other might use a system that reduced all face presentations to a standard size and orientation, and checked them quasi-optically against stored "templates" or "stencils". The contraptions could differ this much in design and material while being equally good—and quite good—approximations of the ideal face-recognizer. This much is implicit in the fact that the concept of recognition, unlike the concepts of, say, protein or solubility, is an intentional concept, not a physical or mechanistic concept.

But obviously there must be *some* similarity between the two face-recognizers, because they are, after all, both face-recognizers. For one thing, if they are roughly equally good approximations of the ideal, the intentional characterizations of their behaviors will have a good deal in common. They will often both be said to believe the same propositions about the faces presented to them, for instance. But what implications about further similarity can be drawn from the fact that their intentional characterizations are similar? Could they be similar only in their intentional characterizations?

Consider how we can criticize and judge the models from different points of view. From the biological point of view, one model may be applauded for utilizing elements bearing a closer resemblance in function or even chemistry to known elements in the brain. From the point of view of engineering, one model may be more efficient, fail-safe, economical and sturdy. From an "introspective" point of view, one model may appear to reflect better the actual organization of processes and routines we human beings may claim to engage in when confronted with a face. Finally, one model may simply recognize faces better than the other, and even better than human beings can. The relevance of these various grounds waxes and wanes with our purposes. If we are attempting to model "the neural bases" of recognition, sturdiness and engineering economy are beside the point—except to the extent (no doubt large) that the neural bases are sturdy and economical. If we are engaged in "artificial intelligence" research as contrasted with "computer simulation of cognitive processes",[2] we will not care if our machine's ways are not those of the man in the street, and we will not mind at all if our machine has an *inhuman* capacity for recognizing faces.

Now as "philosophers of mind", which criterion of success should we invoke? As guardians of the stock of common mentalistic concepts, we will not be concerned with rival biological theories, nor should we have any predilections about the soundness of "engineering" in our fellow face-recognizers. Nor, finally, should we grant the last word to introspective data, to the presumed phenomenology of face-recognition, for however uniform we might *discover* the phenomenological reports of human face-recognizers to be, we can easily imagine discovering that people report a wide variety of feelings, hunches, *gestalts*, strategies, intuitions while sorting out faces, and we would not want to say this variation cast any doubt on the claim of each of them to be a *bona fide* face-recognizer. Since it seems we must grant that two face-recognizers, whether natural or artificial, may accomplish this task in different ways, this suggests that even when we ascribe the same belief to two systems (e.g., the belief that one has seen face *n* more than once before), there need be no elements of design, and *a fortiori* of material, in common between them.

Let us see how this could work in more detail. The design of a face-recognizer would typically break down at the highest level into sub-systems tagged with intentional labels: "the feature *detector* sends a *report* to the *decision unit*, which *searches* the *memory* for records of similar features, and if the result is positive, the system *commands* the printer to write 'I have seen this face before'"—or something like that. These intentionally labelled subsystems themselves have parts, or elements, or states, and *some* of these may well be intentionally labelled in turn: the decision unit goes into the *conviction-that-I've-*

seen-this-face-before state, if you like. Other states or parts may not suggest any intentional characterization—e.g., the *open* state of a particular switch may not be aptly associated with any particular belief, intention, perception, directive, or decision. When we are in a position to ascribe the single belief that *p* to a system, we must, in virtue of our open-ended expectations of the ideal believer-that-*p*, be in a position to ascribe to the system an indefinite number of further beliefs, desires, etc. While no doubt *some* of these ascriptions will line up well with salient features of the system's design, other ascriptions will not, even though the system's behavior is so regulated overall as to justify those ascriptions. There need not, and cannot, be a separately specifiable state of the mechanical elements for each of the myriad intentional ascriptions, and thus it will not in many cases be possible to isolate any feature of the system at any level of abstraction and say, "*This* and *just this* is the feature in the design of this system responsible for those aspects of its behavior in virtue of which we ascribe to it the belief that *p*." And so, from the fact that both system *S* and system *T* are well characterized as believing that *p*, it does not follow that they are both in some state uniquely characterizable in any other way than just as the state of believing that *p*. (Therefore, *S* and *T*'s being in the same belief state need not amount to their being in the same logical state, if we interpret the latter motion as some Turing-machine state for some shared Turing-machine interpretation, for they need not share any relevant Turing-machine interpretation.)

This brings me to Arbib's first major criticism. I had said that in explaining the behavior of a dog, for instance, precision in the intentional story was not an important scientific goal, since from any particular intentional ascription, no precise or completely reliable inferences about other intentional ascriptions or subsequent behavior could be drawn in any case, since we cannot know or specify how close the actual dog comes to the ideal. Arbib finds this "somewhat defeatist", and urges that "there is nothing which precludes description at the intentional level from expressing causal sequences providing our intentional language is extended to allow us to provide descriptions with the flexibility of a program, rather than a statement of general tendencies". Now we can see that what Arbib suggests is right. If we put *intentional labels* on parts of a computer program, or on states the computer will pass through in executing a program, we gain access to the considerable predictive power and precision of the program.* When we put an intentional label on a program state, and want a prediction of what *precisely* will happen when the system is in that intentional state, we get our prediction by taking a close look not at the terms used in the label—we can label as casually as you like—but at the specification of the program so labelled. But if Arbib is right, I am not thereby wrong, for Arbib and I are thinking of rather different strategies. The sort of precision I was saying was impossible was a precision *prior* to labelling, a purely lexical refining which would permit the intentional calculus to operate more determinately in making its idealized predictions. Arbib, on the other hand, is talking about the access to predictive power and precision one gets when one sullies the ideal by using intentional ascriptions as more or less justifiable labels for program features that have precisely specified functional interrelations.

One might want to object: the word "label" suggests that Arbib gets his predictive power and precision out of intentional description by mere arbitrary fiat. If one assigns the intentional label "the *belief-that-p* state" to a logical state of a computer, C, and then predicts from C's program what it will do in that state, one is predicting what it will do when it believes that *p* only in virtue of that assignment, obviously. Assignments of intentional labels, however, are not arbitrary: it can become apt so to label a state when one has designed a program of power and versatility. Similarly, one's right to call a subsystem in his system the memory, or the nose-shape-detector, or the jawline analyzer hinges on the *success* of the subsystem's design rather than any other feature of it. The inescapably idealizing or normative cast to intentional discourse about an artificial system can be made honest by excellence of design, and by nothing else.

This idealizing of intentional discourse gives play to my tactic of ontological neutrality, which Gunderson finds so dubious. I wish to maintain physicalism—a motive that Gunderson finds congenial—but think identity theory is to be shunned. Here is one reason why. Our imagined face-recognizers were presumably purely physical entities, and we ascribed psychological predicates to them (albeit a very

---

*These predictions are not *directly* predictions of *causal* sequences, as he suggests, since what a system *is programmed to do* when in a certain state, and what its being in the associated physical state *causes to happen* can diverge if there is malfunction, but if our hardware is excellent we can safely predict causal sequences from the program.

restricted set of psychological predicates, as we shall see). If we then restrict ourselves for the moment to the "mental features" putatively referred to in these ascriptions, I think we should be able to see that identity theory with regard to them is simply without appeal. The usual seductions of identification are two, I think: ontological economy, or access to generalization (since *this* cloud is identical with a collection of water droplets, *that* cloud is apt to be as well). The latter motive has been all but abandoned by identity theorists in response to Putnam's objections (and others), and in this instance it is clearly unfounded; there is no reason to suppose that the physical state one identified with a particular belief in one system would have a physical twin in the other system with the same intentional characterization. So if we are to have identity, it will have to be something like Davidson's "anomolous monism".[3] But what ontic house-cleaning would be accomplished by identifying each and every intentionally characterized "state" or "event" in a system with some particular physical state or event of its parts? In the first place there is no telling how many *different* intentional states to ascribe to the system; there will be indefinitely many candidates. Is the state of believing that $100<101$ distinct from the state of believing that $100<102$, and if so, should we then expect to find distinct physical states of the system to ally with each? For *some* ascriptions of belief there will be, as we have seen, an isolable state of the program well suited to the label, but for each group of belief-states thus anchored to saliencies in our system, our intuitive epistemic logic will tell us that anyone who believed $p,q,r,\ldots$ would have to believe s, t, u, v, $\ldots$ as well, and while the behavior of the system would harmonize well with the further ascription to it of belief in s, t, $u,v,\ldots$ (this being the sort of test that establishes a thing as an intentional system), we would find nothing in particular to point to in the system as the state of belief in s, or t or u or v. $\ldots$ This should not worry us, for the intentional story we tell about an entity is not a history of actual events, processes, states, objects, but a sort of abstraction.* The desire to identify each and every part of it with some node or charge or region just because *some* parts can be so identified, is as misguided as trying to identify each line of longitude and latitude with a trail of molecules—changing,

---

*Cf. G.E.M. Anscombe, *Intention* (2nd ed. 1963), p. 80: "But if Aristotle's account [of the practical syllogism] were supposed to describe actual mental processes, it would in general be quite absurd. The interest of the account is that it describes an order which is there whenever actions are done with intentions."
See also Quine "On the Reasons for Indeterminacy of Translation", *Journal of Philosophy*, LXVII (March 26, 1970).

of course, with every wave and eddy—just because we have seen a bronze plaque at Greenwich or a row of posts along the Equator.

It is tempting to deny this, just because the intentional story we tell about each other is so apparently full of *activity* and *objects*: we are convicted of *ignoring something* in our *memory*, *jumping* to a *conclusion*, *confusing* two different *ideas*. Grammar can be misleading. In baseball, *catching a fly ball* is an exemplary physical event-type, tokens of which turn out on analysis to involve a *fly ball* (a physical object) which is *caught* (acted upon in a certain physical way). In crew, *catching a crab* is just as bruisingly physical an event-type, but there is no crab that is caught. Not only is it not the case that oarsmen catch real live (or dead) crabs with their oars; and not only is it not the case that for each token of catching a crab, a physically similar thing—each token's crab—is caught, it is not even the case that for each token there is a thing, its crab, however dissimilar from all other such crabs, that is caught. The parallel is not strong enough, however, for while there are no isolable crabs that are caught in crew races, there are isolable catchings-of-crabs, events that actually happen in the course of crew races, while in the case of many intentional ascriptions, there need be no such events at all. Suppose a programmer informs us that his face-recognizer "is designed to ignore blemishes" or "normally assumes that faces are symmetrical aside from hair styles". We should not suppose he is alluding to recurrent activities of blemish-ignoring, or assuming, that his machine engages in, but rather that he is alluding to aspects of his machine's design that determine its behavior along such lines as would be apt in one who ignored blemishes or assumed faces to be symmetrical. The pursuit of identities, in such instances, seems not only superfluous but positively harmful, since it presumes that a story that is, at least in large part, a calculator's fiction is in fact a history of actual events, which if they are not physical will have to be non-physical.

At this point Gunderson, and Thomas Nagel,[4] can be expected to comment that these observations of mine may solve the mind-body problem for certain machines—a dubious achievement if there ever was one—but have left untouched the traditional mind-body problem. To see what they are getting at, consider Gunderson's useful distinction between "program-receptive and program-resistant features of mentality".[5] Some relatively colorless mental events, such as those involved in recognition and theorem-proving, can be well-simulated by computer programs, while others, such as pains and sensations, seem utterly unapproachable by the programmer's artifices. In this instance the distinction would seem to yield the observation that so far only some program-receptive features of mentality have been spirited away unidentified, leaving such program-resistant features as pains, itches, images, yearnings, thrills of lust and other raw feels unaccounted for. Doesn't my very Rylean attempt fall down just where Ryle's own seems to: on the undeniable *episodes* of conscious experience? It is certainly clear that the intentional features so far considered have a less robust presence in our consciousness than the program-resistant variety, and as Gunderson insists, the latter are the sort to which we are supposed to have incorrigible or infallible or privileged access. The former, on the other hand, are notoriously elusive; we are often deceived about our own beliefs; we often do not know what train of "subconscious" choices or decisions or inferences led to our recognition of a face or solution to a problem. So there is some plausibility in relegating these putative events, states, achievements, processes to the role of idealized fictions in an action-predicting, action-explaining calculus, but this plausibility is notably absent when we try the same trick with pains or after-images.

That is one reason why Gunderson is unsatisfied. He sees me handling the easy cases and thinks that I think they are the hard cases. It is embarrassing to me that I have given Gunderson and others that impression, for far from thinking that intentional ascriptions such as belief, desire, and decision are the stumbling blocks of physicalism, I think they are the building blocks. I agree with Gunderson that it is a long way from ascribing belief to a system to ascribing pain to a person (especially to *myself*), but I think that describing a system that exhibits the program-receptive features is the first step in accounting for the program-resistant features. As Gunderson says, the big problem resides in the investigational asymmetries he describes, and more particularly, in the ineliminable sense of *intimacy* we feel with the program-resistant side of our mentality. To build a self, a first-person, with a privileged relation to some set of mental features, out of the third-person stuff of intentional systems is the hard part, and that is where $awareness_1$, the notion Arbib finds of dubious utility, is supposed to play its role. Content is only half the battle; consciousness is the other.

II

In *Content and Consciousness* I proposed to replace the ordinary word "aware" with a pair of technical terms, defined as follows:

(1) A is $aware_1$ that p at time t if and only if p is the content of the input state of A's "speech center" at time t.

(2) A is $aware_2$ that p at time t if and only if p is the content of an internal event in A at time t that is effective in directing current behavior.[6]

The point of my $aware_1$-$aware_2$ distinction* was to drive a wedge between two sorts of allusions found in our everyday ascriptions of awareness or consciousness: allusions to *privileged access* and to *control*. What I want to establish is that these two notions *wrongly coalesce* in our intuitive grasp of what it is to be conscious of something. Many disagree with me, and Arbib is, I think, one of them, for he offers a new definition of his own, of an "$awareness_{1.5}$", that is supposed to split the difference and capture what is important in *both* my terms, and perhaps capture some other important features of consciousness as well. But what I will argue is that Arbib has gravitated to the emphasis on control *at the expense of* the emphasis on privileged access, and that the result is that his new notion offers some refinements to my crude definition of "$aware_2$" but does not capture at all what I hoped to capture with "$aware_1$". First, to the refinements of "$aware_2$". Arbib points out that since a behavioral control system can tap sources of information or subprograms that find no actual exploitation in current behavior control but are only "potentially effective", and since from such a multiplicity of sources, or "redundancy of potential command", a higher-order choosing or decision element must pick or focus on one of these, it would be fruitful to highlight such target items as the objects of awareness for such a control system. So Arbib offers the following definition (which in its tolerance for hand-waving is a match for my definitions—he and I are playing the same game): "*A* is $aware_{1.5}$ that *p* at time *t* if and only if *p* is a projection of the content of the mental state of *A* which expresses the concentration of *A*'s attention at time *t*". I think this captures the connotations of control in our concept of awareness quite satisfactorily—better than my definition of "$aware_2$". If we want to *attract the attention* of a dog so he will be *aware* of our commands, or if we hope to *distract the attention* of a chess-playing computer from a trap we hope to spring (before it becomes *aware* of what we are doing), this definition does at least rough justice to those features of the situation we are trying to manipulate.

Let us suppose, as Arbib claims, that this notion of $awareness_{1.5}$ can be interesting and useful in the analysis of complex natural and artificial behavioral control systems. Nevertheless, no matter how fancy such a control system becomes, if this is the only sort of awareness it has, it will never succeed in acquiring a soul. As Nagel would put it,

---

*In subsequent writing about consciousness (see Part III of this volume) I have not exploited this distinction from *Content and Consciousness*, but I have not renounced it either, for the reasons given here. This half of the chapter might be read to more advantage with Part III.

there will not be something it is like to be that control system.[7] This is surprising, perhaps, for complex control systems seem in the first blush of their intentionality to exhibit all the traditional marks of consciousness. They exhibit a form of *subjectivity*, for we distinguish the objective environment of the system from how the environment *seems* or *appears* to the system. Moreover, their sensory input divides into the *objects of attention* on the one hand, and the part temporarily ignored or relegated to the background on the other. They even may be seen to exhibit signs of *self-consciousness* in having some subsystems that are the objects of scrutiny and criticism of other, overriding subsystems. Yet while they can be honored with some mental epithets, they are not yet persons or selves. Somehow these systems are all outside and no inside, or, as Gunderson says, "always at most a he or she or an it and never an I or a me to me."

The reason is, I think, that *for purposes of control*, the program-receptive features of mentality suffice: belief, desire, recognition, analysis, decision and their associates can combine to control (nonverbal) activity of any sophistication. And since even for creatures who are genuine selves, *there is nothing it is like* to believe that *p*, desire that *q*, and so forth, you can't build a self, a something it is like something to be, out of the program-receptive features by themselves.

What I am saying is that belief does not have a phenomenology. Coming to believe that *p* may be an event often or even typically accompanied by a rich phenomenology (of feelings of relief at the termination of doubt, glows of smugness, *frissons* of sheer awe) but it has no phenomenology of its own, and the same holds for the other program-receptive features of mentality. It is just this, I suspect, that makes them program-receptive.

If we are to capture the program-resistant features in an artificial system, we must somehow give the system a phenomenology, an inner life. This will require giving the system something about which it is in a privileged position, something about which it is incorrigible, for whatever else one must be to have a phenomenology, one must be the ultimate authority with regard to its contents. On that point there is widespread agreement. Now I want to claim first that this incorrigibility, properly captured, is not just a necessary but a sufficient condition for having a phenomenology, and second, that my notion of awareness$_1$ properly captures incorrigibility (see Chapter 9). This brings me to Arbib's criticisms of the notion of awareness$_1$, for they call for some clarifications and restatements on my part.

First Arbib points out, "the inadequacy of our verbal reports of our mental states to do justice to the richness that states must exhibit to play the role prescribed for them in system theory" (p. 583). At best, the utterances for which I claim a sort of infallibility express only a *partial sampling* of one's inner state at the time. The content of one's reports does not exhaust the content of one's inner states. I agree. Second, he points out that such a sample may well be unrepresentative. Again, I agree. Finally, he suggests that it is "a contingent fact that some reports are sufficiently reliable to delude some philosophers into believing that reports of mental states are infallible" (p. 584), and not only do I find a way of agreeing with this shrewd observation; I think it provides the way out of a great deal of traditional perplexity. We are confused about consciousness because of an almost irresistible urge to overestimate the extent of our incorrigibility. Our incorrigibility is real; we feel it in our bones, and being real it is, of course, undeniable, but when we come to characterize it, we generously endow ourselves with capacities for infallibility beyond anything we have, or could possibly have, and even the premonition that we could not possibly have such infallibility comforts rather than warns us, for it ensures us that we are, after all, mysterious and miraculous beings, beyond all explaining. Once we see just how little we are incorrigible about, we can accomodate the claim that this incorrigibility is the crux of our selfhood to the equally compelling claim that we are in the end just physical denizens of a physical universe.

Arbib observes that "it follows from any reasonable theory of the evolution of language that certain types of report will be highly reliable." (p. 584). Indeed, for event-types in a system to acquire the status of reports at all, they must be, in the main, reliable (see Chapter 1, page 15). The trick is not to confuse what we are, and must be, highly reliable about, with what we are incorrigible about. We are, and must be, highly reliable in our reports about what we believe, and desire, and intend, but we are not infallible. We must grant the existence of self-deception, whether it springs from some deep inner motivation, or is the result of rather mundane breakdowns in the channels between our behavior-controlling states and our verbal apparatus.* What Arbib suggests, quite plausibly, is that some philosophers have confused the (correct) intuition that we must be authoritative *in general* in our reports of all our mental states, with the (false) intuition that we are incorrigible or infallible with regard to all our reports of our mental states. Infallibility, if it exists, must be a more modest endowment.

*I did not emphasize this sufficiently in *Content and Consciousness*, though it is implicit in the discussions on p. 153 and p. 167.

Let us consider how these highly reliable, but not incorrigible, reports of our inner, controlling states might issue from the states they report. Following Arbib, we can grant that one's controlling state (one's state of awareness$_{1.5}$) at any time is immensely rich in functional capacities, and hence in content. Let us suppose that at some moment part of the content of Smith's state of awareness$_{1.5}$ is the belief, visually inculcated, that a man is approaching him. Since Smith is a well-evolved creature with verbal capacities, we can expect a further part of the content of this state of awareness$_{1.5}$ to be a conditional command to report: "I see a man approaching," or words to that effect. Using Putnam's analogy, we can say that Smith's state of awareness$_{1.5}$ is rather like a Turing Machine state consisting of very many conditional instructions, one of which is the conditional instruction to print: "I see a man approaching." Let us call Smith's *whole* state of awareness$_{1.5}$ *state A*. Suppose Smith now says, "I see a man approaching." His verbal report certainly does not do justice to state *A*, certainly represents a partial and perhaps unrepresentative sample of the content of state *A*, and moreover, can occur in situations when Smith is not in state *A*, for there will no doubt be many other states of awareness$_{1.5}$ that include the conditional instruction to say, "I see a man approaching," or, due to malfunction or faulty design, Smith's verbal apparatus may execute that instruction spuriously, when Smith's state of awareness$_{1.5}$ would not normally or properly include it. But suppose we break down state *A* into its component states, one for each instruction. Then being in state *A* will *ipso facto* involve being in state *B*, the state of being instructed to report: "I see a man approaching." Now let us rename state *B* the state of awareness$_1$ that one sees a man approaching. *Abracadabra*, we have rendered Smith "infallible", for while his report "I see a man approaching" is only a highly reliable indicator that he is in state *A* (which would ensure that he would do the other things appropriate to believing a man is approaching, for instance), it is a foolproof indicator that he is in state *B*. This does not leave Smith being infallible about very much, but then we shouldn't expect him to be—he's only human, and infallibility about great matters is a Godlike, i.e., inconceivable, power.

Smith's infallibility has been purchased, obviously, by a cheap trick: it is only by skewing the identity conditions of the state reported so that reportorial truth is guaranteed that we get reportorial infallibility. But the trick, while cheap, is not worthless, for states of awareness$_1$ so defined have a role to play in the description of systems with verbal capacities: we must be able to distinguish the *command states* of a system's verbal apparatus, what the system "means to say" in a particular instance, so that subsequent failures in execution—the merely verbal slips—can have a standard against which to be corrected.

Smith has not reported that he sees a man approaching if he makes a verbal slip, or misuses a word, even if the end result is his utterance of the words: "I see a man approaching." Smith has reported that he sees a man approaching only if he said what he meant to say: that is, only if his actual utterance as executed meets the standards set by his state of awareness$_1$. But if that is what it is for Smith to *report*, and not merely *utter sounds*, then whenever Smith reports, his reports will be guaranteed expressions of his state of awareness$_1$.

This does not mean that we can give independent characterizations of some of Smith's utterances, namely his reports, that happen to be foolproof signs that Smith is in certain independently characterized internal states, namely his states of awareness$_1$. That would be miraculous. But we wouldn't want to do that in any case, for if we could tell, by examination, which of Smith's utterances were his genuine, error-corrected reports, he would not have *privileged* access, for we could be in a *perfect* position to determine his states of awareness$_1$. The relationship between internal physical states of Smith, and their external manifestations in utterance is just garden-variety causation, and so any normal linkages between them are subject to all the possibilities of error or malfunction any physical system is subject to. It is just that the concepts of a *report* and of *awareness$_1$* are so defined that Smith has an infallible capacity to report his states of awareness$_1$. But does this amount to anything at all of interest? Well, *if* we happened to want to know what state of awareness$_1$ Smith was in, *we could do no better* than to wait on Smith's report, and if we were unsure as to whether what we heard was a genuine report of Smith's, again we could do no better than to rely on Smith's word that it was, or on the voucher implicit in his refraining from taking back or correcting what he said. But would we ever want to know what anyone's state of awareness$_1$ was? If we wanted to know whether what Smith said was what he meant to say, we would. And we might be interested in that, for if Smith said what he meant to say, we have a highly reliable, though not infallible, indicator of Smith's state of awareness$_{1.5}$. Or, if we suspected that something was awry in Smith's perceptual apparatus (because his account of what he saw did not match what was in front of his eyes), we would be interested in his states of awareness$_1$, for if Smith said what he meant to say, then our response to his aberrant perceptual reports would be not, "That *can't* be what you are aware of, since there is no man approaching," but, "*Since* you are aware of a man approaching, when there is no man approaching, there must be something wrong with your eyes or your brain."

Note that Smith's access to his states of awareness$_1$ is both privileged and non-inferential, unlike ours. When we want to know what state of awareness$_1$ Smith is in, we must ask him, and then infer on the basis of what happens what the state is. Or we might someday be able to take Smith's brain apart, and on the basis of our knowledge of its interconnections make a prediction of what Smith would say, were we to ask him, and what he would say, were we further to ask him if his report was sincere, etc., and on the basis of these predictions *infer* that he was in a particular state of awareness$_1$. But Smith doesn't have to go through any of this. When we ask him what state of awareness$_1$ he is in, he does not have to ask anyone or investigate anything in turn: he just answers. Being asked, he comes to mean to say something in answer, and whether what he means to say then is right or wrong (relative to what he *ought* to mean to say, what he would say if his brain were in order, if he were aware$_1$ of what he is aware$_{1.5}$ of), *if* he says it, he will thereby say what he is aware$_1$ of.* By being a system capable of verbal activity, Smith enters the community of communicators. He, along with the others, can ask and answer questions, make reports, utter statements that are true or false. If we consider this group of persons and ask if there is some area of concern where Smith is the privileged authority, the answer is: in his reports of awareness$_1$.** Other persons may make fallible, inferential statements about what Smith is aware$_1$ of. Smith can do better.

I have said that the extent of our infallibility, as opposed to our high reliability, is more restricted than some philosophers have supposed. Our infallible, non-inferential access consists only in our inevitable authority about what we would mean to say at a particular moment, whether we say it or not. The picture I want to guard against is of our having some special, probing, evidence-gathering faculty that has *more* access to our inner states (our states of awareness$_{1.5}$ perhaps) than it chooses to express in its reports. Our coming to mean to say something is all the access we have, and while it is infallible access to what we mean to say, it is only highly reliable access to what state is

---

*Smith is not, of course, infallible about *what he means* by what he says when he says something meaning to say it, not even *that he means* what he says.

**The *truth* of the utterance as a *report* of the occurrence of a state of awareness$_1$ is guaranteed by the *success* of expression (if the utterance *is* a successful expression), since the *content* of the state of awareness$_1$ is at the same time its individuating characteristic (what makes it the particular state of awareness$_1$ it is) and the standard against which success in utterance-execution is measured.

currently controlling the rest of our activity and attitudes. Some philosophers have supposed otherwise. Gunderson, for example says,

> Consider *any* intentional sentence of the form "I ____ that there are gophers in Minnesota" where '____' is to be filled in by an intentional verb ('believe', 'suppose', 'think', etc., and contrast our way of knowing its truth (or falsity) with any non-first-person variant thereof . . . That is, if I know that "I suppose that there are gophers in Minnesota" is true, the way in which I come to know it is radically different from the way I might come to know that "Dennett supposes that there are gophers in Minnesota" is true. (*my italics*)

The verb "suppose" has been nicely chosen; if it is taken in the sense of episodic thinking, what Gunderson at this very moment is supposing to himself, then Gunderson has special, non-inferential incorrigible access to what he supposes, but if it is taken as a synonym for "believe", then Gunderson is in only a contingently better position than I am to say whether he supposes there are gophers in Minnesota, for he is more acquainted with his own behavior than I happen to be. It would be odd to suppose (in the sense of "judge") that there are gophers in Minnesota without supposing (in the sense of "believe") that there are gophers in Minnesota, but not impossible.[8] That is, Gunderson's episode of meaning to himself that there are gophers in Minnesota is something to which his access is perfect but it is itself only a highly reliable indicator of what Gunderson believes. Lacking any remarkable emotional stake in the proposition "There are gophers in Minnesota", Gunderson can quite safely assume that his judgment is not a piece of self-deception, and that deep in his heart of hearts he really does believe that there are gophers in Minnesota, but that is to make a highly reliable inference.

There is more than one verb that straddles the line as "suppose" does. "Think" is another, and a most important one. If one supposes that it is our thinking that actually controls our behavior, then we must grant that we do our thinking subconsciously, beyond our direct access, for we have only fallible and indirect, though highly reliable, access to those states, events, processes that occur in our control systems. If one supposes on the other hand that one's thinking is one's "stream of consciousness", the episodes to which we have privileged access, then we must grant that thinking is an activity restricted to language-users, and only circumstantially related to the processes that account for their self-control. The two notions of thinking can each lay claim to being ordinary. Arbib champions one, and Gunderson the other. When Arbib says of a verbal report that "the phrase is but a projection of the thought, not the thought itself . . . Thus utterances like 'I see a man approaching' express mere aspects of the robot's total state", he seems to be identifying the total state of awareness$_{1.5}$ with the robot's thoughts, for he says "many different aspects of its current 'thoughts' could have been *elicited* by different questions" (my italics). The current thoughts, it seems, coexist not *serially* in a stream of consciousness, not as distinct episodes to which anyone, even the robot, has access in any sense, but in parallel, in the processes of control. I don't think it is *wrong* to think of thought in this way, and I also don't think it is wrong to think of thought as that contentful stream to which I have privileged, non-inferential access. I even think that in the last analysis one is not thinking about *thought* unless one is thinking of something with both these features.[9] It is only wrong, I think, to think that this dual prescription can actually be filled by any possible entities, states, or events. In just the same way someone would be mistaken who thought there was some physical thing that was all at once the voice I can strain, lose, recognize, mimic, record, and enjoy.[10]

There is, then, a sense in which I am saying there is no such thing as a thought. I am not denying that there are episodes whose content we are incorrigible about, and I am not denying that there are internal events that control our behavior and can, in that role, often be ascribed content. I am denying, however, that in providing an account or model of one of these aspects one has provided in any way for the other. And I am insisting that *thoughts* and *pains* and other program-resistant features of mentality would have to have both these aspects to satisfy their traditional roles. The pain in my toe, for instance, is surely not just a matter of my meaning to tell you about it, nor is it something I am only inferentially or indirectly aware of, that is disrupting or otherwise affecting the control of my behavior. Then, since I am denying that any entity could have the features of a pain or a thought, so much the worse for the ontological status of such things.

3

Brain Writing and Mind Reading

What are we to make of the popular notion that our brains are some-how libraries of our thoughts and beliefs? Is it *in principle* possible that brain scientists might one day know enough about the workings of our brains to be able to "crack the cerebral code" and read our minds? Phi-losophers have often rather uncritically conceded that it *is* possible in principle, usually in the context of making some point about privacy or subjectivity.[1] I read Anscombe to deny the possibility. In *Intention*[2] she seems to be arguing that the *only* information about a person that can be brought to bear in a determination of his beliefs or intentions is information about his past and future actions and experiences; a per-son's beliefs and intentions are whatever they must be to render his behavioral biography coherent, and neurological data could not pos-sibly shed light on this. This is often plausible. Suppose Jack Ruby had tried to defend himself in court by claiming he didn't know (or be-lieve) the gun was loaded. Given even the little we know about his biography, could we even make sense of a neurologist who claimed that he had scientific evidence to confirm Ruby's disclaimer? But in other cases the view is implausible. Sometimes one's biography seems com-pletely compatible with two different ascriptions of belief, so that the Anscombean test of biographical coherence yields no answer. Sam the reputable art critic extols, buys, and promotes mediocre paintings by his son. Two different hypotheses are advanced: (a) Sam does not believe the paintings are any good, but out of loyalty and love he does this to help his son, or (b) Sam's love for his son has blinded him to the faults of the paintings, and he actually believes they are good. Presum-ably if (a) were true Sam would deny it to his grave, so his future biography will look the same in either case, and his past history of big-heartedness, we can suppose, fits both hypotheses equally well. I think many of our intuitions support the view that Sam really and objectively has one belief and not the other, and it goes against the grain to accept the Anscombean position that in the absence of telltale behavioral biography there is simply nowhere else to look. Couldn't the brain scientist (in principle) work out the details of Sam's belief mechanisms, discover the *system* the brain uses to store beliefs, and then, using correlations between brain states and Sam's *manifest* beliefs as his Rosetta Stone, extrapolate to Sam's covert beliefs? Having deciphered the brain writing, he could read Sam's mind. (Of course, if we could establish this practice for Sam the art critic, we would have to reopen the case of Jack Ruby, but perhaps, just perhaps, we could then devise a scenario in which neurologists were able to confirm that Ruby was the victim of a series of unlikely but explainable beliefs—as revealed by his "cerebroscope".)

I admit to finding the brain-writing hypothesis tempting,* but suspect that it is not coherent at all. I have been so far unable to concoct a proof that it is incoherent, but will raise instead a series of difficulties that seem insuperable to me. First, though, it would be useful to ask just why the view is plausible at all. Why, for instance, is the brain-writing hypothesis more tempting than the hypothesis that on the lining of one's stomach there is a decipherable record of all the meals one has ever eaten? Gilbert Harman offers the first few steps of an answer:

> We know that people have beliefs and desires, that beliefs and desires influence action, that interaction with the environment can give rise to new beliefs, and that needs and drives can give rise to desires. Adequate psychological theories must reflect this knowledge and add to it. So adequate models must have states that correspond to beliefs, desires and thoughts such that these states function in the model as psychological states function in the person modeled, and such that they are representational in the way psychological states are representational. Where there is such representation, there is a system of representation; and that system may be identified with the inner language in which a person thinks.
>
> This reduces the claim that there is an inner language, which one thinks in, to the trivial assertion that psychological states have a representational character.[3]

*I claimed it was a distinct possibility with regard to intentions in "Features of Intentional Actions", *Philosophy and Phenomenological Research*, XXIX (1968): 232-244.

The first point, then, is that human behavior has proven to be of such a nature that the only satisfactory theories will be those in which inner *representations* play a role (though not necessarily a role that is not eliminable at another level of theory). Diehard peripheralist behaviorists may still wish to deny this, but that is of concern to historians of science, not us. It is Harman's next point that strikes me as controversial: where there is representation there is system, and this system may be *identified* with a person's inner language. Are all representations bound up in systems? Is *any* system of representations like a language? Enough like a language to make this identification more useful than misleading? Or is Harman's claim rather that whatever sorts of representations there may be, the sorts we need for human psychology must be organized in a system, and this system must be more like the system of a language than not? Assuming Harman's claim survives these questions, we still would not have an argument for the full-fledged brain-writing hypothesis. Two more steps are needed. First, we need the claim that these psychological models with their language-style representations must be realized in brainware, not ectoplasm or other ghostly stuff.* This ought to be uncontroversial; though psychologists may ignore the details of realization while elaborating and even testing their models, the model-making is ultimately bound by the restriction that any function proposed in a model must be physiologically or mechanically realizable one way or another. Second, it must be claimed that it will be possible to determine the details of such realizations from an empirical examination of the brainware and its causal role in behavior. This second point raises some interesting questions. Could the functional organization of the brain be so inscrutable from the point of view of the neurophysiologist or other physical scientist that no fixing of the representational role of any part were possible? Could the brain use a system that no outsider could detect? In such a case what would it mean to say the brain used a system? I am not sure how one would go about giving direct answers to these questions, but light can be shed on them, I think, by setting up a crude brain-writing theory and refining it as best we can to meet objections.

Again Harman gives us the first step:

In a simple model, there might be two places in which representa-

*Cf. Wilfrid Sellers, "Notes on Intentionality", *Journal of Philosophy*, LXI (1964): 663, where he discusses mental acts as tokens expressing propositions, and claims that all tokens must be *sorts* of tokens and must have a determinate factual character, and proposes identifying them with neurophysiological episodes.

tions are stored. Representations of things believed would be stored in one place; representations of things desired in the other. Interaction with the environment would produce new representations that would be stored as beliefs. Needs for food, love, etc., would produce representations to be stored as desires. Inferences could produce changes in both the set of beliefs and the set of desires. (*Ibid.*, p. 34)

No doubt we would also want to distinguish more or less permanent storage (belief and desire) from the more fleeting or occurrent *display* of representations (in perception, during problem solving, sudden thoughts, etc.). In any case we already have enough to set some conditions on the brain-writing hypothesis. Some formulations of it are forbidden us on pain of triviality. For instance, claiming that there is brain writing, but that each representation is written in a different language, is just an oblique way of asserting that there is no brain writing. I think the following six conditions will serve to distinguish genuine brain-writing hypotheses from masqueraders.

(1) The system of representations must have a generative grammar. That is, the system must be such that if you understand the system and know the finite vocabulary you can generate the representations—the sentences of brain writing—you haven't yet examined. Otherwise the language will be unlearnable.[4] Only if there were a generative grammar could the investigator get himself into a position to extrapolate from manifest beliefs and desires to covert beliefs and desires. There need not be a single generative grammar covering all representations, however. Just so long as there is a finite number of different "languages" and "multi-lingual" functional elements to serve as interpreters, the learnability condition will be met.

(2) Syntactical differences and similarities of the language must be reflected in physical differences and similarities in the brain. That is, the tokens of a syntactical type must be physically distinguishable by finite test from the tokens of other syntactical types. That does not mean that all tokens of a type must be physically similar. What physical feature is peculiar to spoken and written tokens of the word "cat"? There must simply be a finite number of physical sorts of token of each type. Tokens and "strings" of tokens may of course align themselves in physical dimensions other than those of natural language. For instance, lexical items might be individuated not by shape but by spatial location, and ordering in the strings might be accomplished not by a sequence in space or time but by degree of electric potential.

(3) Tokens must be physically salient. This is a "practical" point.

Tokens might bear physical similarities, but similarities so complex, so diffuse and multidimensional that no general *detection* mechanism could be devised: no frequency filters, stereo-locators, litmus papers, or simple combination of these could be built into a token detector. If tokens turned out not to be physically salient—and this is rather plausible in the light of current research—the brain-writing hypothesis would fail for the relatively humdrum reason that brain writing was illegible. It is worth mentioning only to distinguish it from more important obstacles to the hypothesis.

(4) The representation store must meet Anscombe's condition of biographical coherence. The sentences yielded by our neurocryptographer's radical translation must match well with the subject's manifest beliefs and desires, and with common knowledge. If too many unlikely beliefs or obvious untruths appear in the belief store, we will decide that we have hit upon something strange and marvelous—like finding the Lord's Prayer written in freckles on a man's back—but not his belief store. To give a more plausible example, we might discover that certain features of brain activity could be interpreted as a code yielding detailed and accurate information about the relative tensions of the eye muscles, the orientation of the eyeball, the convexity of the lens, etc., and this might give us great insight into the way the brain controlled the perceptual process, but since a man does not ordinarily have any beliefs about these internal matters, this would not be, except indirectly, a key to his belief store.*

(5) There must be a reader or playback mechanism. It must be demonstrated that the physical system in which the brain writing is accomplished is functionally connected in the appropriate ways to the causes of bodily action, and so forth. Of course, if we were to find the cortex written all over with sentences expressing the subject's manifest beliefs, we would be convinced this was no coincidence, but until the operation of the mechanisms that utilized the writing was discovered, we would not have a theory. (A person who discovered such a marvel would be roughly in the same evidential position as a clairvoyant who, we can imagine, might be able to predict with uncanny accuracy what

---

*Discovering such a code is not establishing that the information the code carries for the scientist is also carried for the person, or even for his brain. D. H. Perkel and T. H. Bullock, in "Neural Coding" in F. Schmitt, T. Melnechuk, et al., eds., *Neurosciences Research Symposium Summaries*, vol. 3 (Cambridge, Mass.: M.I.T. Press, 1969), discuss the discovery of a code "carrying" phasic information about wing position in the locust; it is accurately coded, but the "insect apparently makes no use of this information". (Blocking this input and substituting random input produces no loss of flying rhythm, ability, etc.)

a person would say, etc., and yet could not be supposed to have any authority—in a court of law, for instance—about a person's beliefs.)

(6) The belief store must be—in the main—consistent. If our translation manual yields sentences like "My brother is an only child" and pairs of sentences like "All dogs are vicious" and "My dog is sweet-tempered" one of several things must be wrong. If the subject declines to assert or assent to these anomalous sentences, we will discredit the translation manual (cf. Quine on radical translation); if, on the other hand, the man issues forth these sentences, we will conclude that we have discovered a pathological condition, and our brain-writing system will be viewed as a sort of assent-inducing tumor.*

A more graphic way of looking at this point is to ask whether the neurocryptographer could do a bit of tinkering and thereby *insert* a belief in his subject: if he can *read* brain writing he ought to be able to *write* brain writing. Let us suppose we are going to insert in Tom the false belief: "I have an older brother living in Cleveland." Now, can the neurocryptographer translate this into brain writing and do a bit of rewiring? Let us suppose he can do any rewiring, as much and as delicate as you wish. This rewiring will either impair Tom's basic rationality or not. Consider the two outcomes. Tom is sitting in a bar and a friend asks, "Do you have any brothers or sisters?" Tom says, "Yes, I have an older brother living in Cleveland." "What's his name?" Now what is going to happen? Tom may say, "Name? Whose name? Oh, my gosh, what was I saying? I don't have an older brother!" Or he may say, "I don't know his name," and when pressed he will deny all knowledge of this brother, and assert things like, "I am an only child and have an older brother living in Cleveland." In neither case has our neurocryptographer succeeded in wiring in a new belief. This does not show that wiring in beliefs is impossible, or that brain writing is impossible, but just that one could only wire in one belief by wiring in many (indefinitely many?) other cohering beliefs so that neither biographical nor logical coherence would be lost.** (I examine this case more fully in Chapter 12.)

---

*This condition of rationality has some slack in it. We do permit some small level of inconsistency, but large-scale illogicality must be indicative of either a defect in the subject so serious as to disqualify him as a believer at all, or a defect in our translation hypotheses. See Chapter 1.

**Joan Straumanis has pointed out to me that there is some experimental evidence that suggests that another outcome of the rewiring experiment could be that Tom spontaneously and unconsciously fabricates a web of cohering beliefs to "protect" the inserted belief and his others from each other (a sort of pearl-in-the-oyster effect).

Now suppose we have a brain-writing theory that meets all of these conditions: we have a storage facility functionally tied to behavior that is somehow administered to preserve logical and biographical coherence, and the mode of storage involves elements having physically salient syntactical parts for which we have a generative grammar. This system is going to take up some room. How much room do we need? Marvin Minsky has an optimistic answer: "One can't find a hundred things that he knows a thousand things about. . . . I therefore feel that a machine will quite critically need to acquire on the order of a hundred thousand elements of knowledge in order to behave with reasonable sensibility in ordinary situations. A million, if properly organized, should be enough for a very great intelligence."[5] If Minsky's estimate were realistic, the brain, with its ten billion neurons or trillions of molecules would be up to the task, no doubt. But surely his figure is much too low. For in addition to all the relatively *difficult* facts I have mastered, such as that New York is larger than Boston and salt is sodium chloride, there are all the easy ones we tend to overlook: New York is not on the moon, or in Venezuela; salt is not sugar, or green, or oily; salt is good on potatoes, on eggs; tweed coats are not made of salt; a grain of salt is smaller than an elephant. . . . Surely I can think of more than a thousand things I know or believe about salt, and salt is not one of a hundred, but one of thousands upon thousands of things I can do this with. Then there is my knowledge of arithmetic: two plus two is four, twenty plus twenty is forty. . . . My beliefs are apparently infinite, which means their storage, however miniaturized, will take up more room than there is in the brain. The objection, of course, seems to point to its own solution: it must be that I *potentially* believe indefinitely many things, but I *generate* all but, say, Minsky's hundred thousand by the activity of an extrapolator-deducer mechanism attached to the core library. So let us attach such a mechanism to our model and see what it looks like.

It has the capacity to extract axioms from the core when the situation demands it, and deduce further consequences. To do this, it needs to have an information store of its own, containing information about what items it would be appropriate at any time to retrieve from the core, and, for instance, the metalinguistic information it needs to analyze the contradiction in "all cats are black" and "my cat is brown". Perhaps it does this by storing the information that what is black is not brown, or maybe *that* information is in the core storage, and the metalinguistic information stored in the extrapolator-deducer mechanism is to the effect that the core element "what is black is not brown" is relevant to an analysis of the contradiction. Now how will the extrapolator-deducer mechanism store its information? In its own core library of brain-writing sentences? If it has a core library, it will also need an extrapolator-deducer mechanism to act as librarian, and what of *its* information store? Recalling Lewis Carroll's argument in "What the Tortoise Said to Achilles",[6] we can see that the extrapolator-deducer will be hamstrung by a vicious regress if it must always rely on linguistically stored beliefs which it must retrieve and analyze about what can be deduced from what. This *a priori* point has been "empirically discovered" in the field by more than one frustrated model-builder. As one team sums it up: "...a memory that merely stores *propositions* leads to technological, or organic, monstrosities and frustrates, rather than facilitates inductive operations".[7]

The conclusion is that writing—for instance, brain writing—is a *dependent* form of information storage. The brain must store at least some of its information in a manner not capturable by a brain-writing model. Could it do without brain writing altogether? I think we can get closer to an answer to this by further refining our basic model of belief.

Representations apparently play roles at many different levels in the operation of the brain. I have already mentioned the possibility of codes representing information about the tension of eye muscles and so forth, and these representations do not fall into the class of our beliefs. At another level there is the information we "use" to accomplish depth perception. Psychologists ascribe to us such activities as *analyzing depth cues* and *arriving at conclusions* about distance based on *information we have* about texture gradients, binocular interaction, and so forth. Yet it is nothing conscious that I do in order to perceive depth, and if you ask me what beliefs I have about texture gradients I draw a blank. Closer to home, a child can demonstrate his understanding of addition by reeling off sums without being able to formulate or understand propositions about the commutativity of addition. His performance indicates that he has caught on to commutativity, but should we say that among his beliefs is the belief that addition is commutative? To give one more case, while driving down a familiar road I am suddenly struck by the thought that its aspect has changed—somebody has painted his shutters or a tree has blown down, or something. Do I have a *belief* about how it used to be that grounds my current judgment that it has changed? If so, it is a belief to which I can give no expression and about which I am quite in the dark. Somehow, though, the information is there to be used.

Suppose we partition our information store into the part that is verbally retrievable and the part that is not. I would not want to claim that this separates our beliefs from everything else. Far from it. Our preanalytical notion of belief would permit young children and dumb animals to have beliefs, which must be verbally irretrievable. Perhaps, though, a strong case can be made out that at least our verbally retrievable beliefs are stored in brain writing. The picture that emerges is not, I think, implausible: there are on the one hand those representations that are available for our conscious, personal use and apprehension, and on the other hand, those that operate behind the scenes to keep us together. If any representations are stored in brain writing, the former will be, for they are in intimate relation to our natural languages. Included in this group will be the bits of factual knowledge we pick up by asking questions and reading books, especially the facts that only language-users could apprehend, such as the fact that Thanksgiving is always on Thursday. With regard to this group of representations Minsky's figure of a hundred thousand looks more realistic, provided we have an extrapolator-deducer mechanism.

If ever it seems that we are *storing sentences*, it is when we are picking up facts in this verbal manner, but are these things we pick up our beliefs? Sometimes we salt away a sentence because we like the sound of it, or because we will later be rewarded for producing it on demand, or just because it has a sort of staying power in our imagination. In Chekhov's *Three Sisters*, Tchebutykin, reading a journal, mutters: "Balzac was married in Berditchev," and then repeats it, saying he must make a note of it. Then Irina dreamily repeats it: "Balzac was married in Berditchev." Did they acquire a belief on that occasion? Whether *they* did or not, the sentence has stuck in *my* mind, and yet I wouldn't say it was one of my beliefs. I have deliberately not looked it up in the encyclopedia; probably it's true—why would Chekhov insert a distracting falsehood—for mischief? No doubt if someone offered me a thousand dollars if I could tell him where Balzac was married, I'd say Berditchev (wherever that is), but it would be wrong for him to conclude that this was a belief of mine. (This distinction is developed further in Chapter 16.)

If brain writing served only for such storage of words and sentences that we pick up for various reasons, at least we could all breathe a lot easier about the prospects of evil scientists reading our every seditious thought and turning us over to the authorities. Imagine the Loyalty Commissar asking the neurocryptographer if the man in the cerebroscope is a true patriot. "Let's see," says the scientist, "Here is the sentence we've been looking for: 'I pledge allegiance to the flag . . .'" Would finding the sentence "America's the greatest land of all" satisfy the Commissar? I think not.

The matter of verbally retrievable beliefs is in any case more complicated than the picture we've just been examining. Whereas if I am asked who won the Super Bowl in 1969, it does seem a bit as if I am searching for a ready-made sentence to utter in response, in other cases this sort of account does not ring true at all. Suppose I am watching the shell game, intent on which shell the little pea is under. At any moment it seems to be true that I have a belief about where the pea is, and can tell you if you ask, but it does not seem plausible that this is accomplished by a rapid writing and erasing of successive sentences: "Now it's left, now it's center, now right," and the flashing on and off of the negation sign in front of, "It's under the center shell." For one thing, if asked to give you my perceptual beliefs of a moment I may have to work a bit to formulate them, yet the perceptual representation was what it was before I was asked. The representationality—or intentionality—of something (e.g., a belief or perception) is compatible with its being vague or indeterminate in some respects.[8] The effort of retrieval is often an effort to formulate a sentence that is an approximation of a belief, and we are often distressed by the hard edge of determinacy our verbal output substitutes for the fuzziness of our convictions.

The answer we formulate, the judgment we find an expression for when asked for our belief, is determinate and individuated, because it consists of a specific string of words in our natural language, whether we then speak it aloud or not. *These* representations, not the beliefs to which we have verbal access, but the occurrent, datable judgments themselves, have the syntactic parts we have been looking for, and about these the brain-writing hypothesis looks much more workable. Not only are judgments determinate; they are, as Harman has pointed out, lexically and syntactically unambiguous.[9] If it occurs to me that our mothers bore us, I know for sure whether I am thinking of birth or ennui. So it is proper to view a judgment not as a sentence *simpliciter* but as a deep structure or sentence under an analysis. Judgments, unlike beliefs, occur one at a time; we have at any moment indefinitely many beliefs, but can be thinking just one thought. We saw that the brain-writing hypothesis with regard to storage of beliefs did not really effect any economies of design, because however systematic and efficient one's grammar is, one still needs infinite space to store infinitely many tokens, but with regard to representation of judgments the situation is different. A finite mechanism incorporating a generative grammar would be an efficient means of representing, one at a time, any of an infinite set of propositions.

The interesting thing about judgments is that although each of us is authoritative about the *content* of his judgments, and although each of us is authoritative about his sincerity or lack of sincerity in giving outward verbal expression of a judgment, we are not in a privileged position when it comes to the question of whether our judgments are reliable indicators of our beliefs.[10] Normally there is harmony between our judgments and our behavior, and hence between our judgments and our beliefs, but when we are afflicted by Sartre's *mauvaise foi*, our sincerest judgments can be lies about our beliefs. I may judge to myself that a man is innocent, while believing him guilty. (This point is explored further in Chapter 16).

This suggests that even if we were to discover a brain-writing system that represented our judgments, the mind reading that could be accomplished by exploiting the discovery would not uncover our beliefs. To return to the case of Sam the art critic, if our neurocryptographer were able to determine that Sam's last *judgment* on his deathbed was, "My consolation is that I fathered a great artist," we could still hold that the issue between the warring hypotheses was undecided, for this judgment may have been a self-deception. But at this point I think we are entitled to question the intuition that inspired the search for brain writing in the first place. If discovering a man's judgments still leaves the matter of belief ascription undecided, and if in fact either ascription of belief accounts for, explains, predicts Sam's behavior as well as the other, are we so sure that Sam determinately had one belief or the other? Are we sure there is a difference between his really and truly believing his son is a good artist, and his deceiving himself out of love while knowing the truth in his heart of hearts? If there were brain writing, of course, there would have to be a physical difference between these two cases, but now, what reasons do we have for supposing there is brain writing?

We are thrown back on our conviction that the brain must be an organ that *represents*, but I hope it is no longer obvious that the brain must represent in sentences. In fact we know that at least some of the representation must be accomplished in some more fundamental way. Must there be a *system* for such representation? I cannot yet see that there must. In particular, I cannot yet see that there must be a *learnable* system, in Davidson's sense, for it is not clear to me that the brain must —or can—learn (the way a child learns a language) its own ways of representing. Certainly information can be transmitted by means of unlearnable languages. Consider a string of nine light bulbs in a row; there are 512 different patterns of lit and unlit bulbs possible in this array, and so we can use the array to transmit the natural numbers from 0 to 511. There are all sorts of systems one might use to assign patterns to numbers. An obvious and efficient one would be binary notation: 000000001 is 1, 000000010 is 2, and so forth. Once a person knows the system, he can generate the numbers he has not yet observed, but suppose instead of using this or any other system, the patterns are assigned numbers randomly; a random assignment will carry the information just as well; the outsider will simply not be in a position to predict the balance of the assignments, having learned some of them. Can the brain "use" information carried by unlearnable systems? At some levels of "coding" it obviously does—where the "codes" carry very specific and limited information. In general can the brain get along without learnable representation systems? Until we can say a lot more about what it is for a system to use representations, I for one cannot see how to answer this question. If the answer is no, then there must be brain writing, but how it overcomes the difficulties I have raised here is beyond me. If the answer is yes, then the only way translation of representation can be accomplished is "sentence by sentence", assigning meaning to representations by determining their functional role in the behavior of the whole system. But where competing translations are behaviorally indistinguishable, the content of the representation will be indeterminate.

Postscript, 1978

In the seven years since this essay was written many books and articles have appeared dealing with the nature of mental representation. Compared with the models discussed today, the model described here is naive, but the conclusions I draw from it can still be drawn from today's sophisticated models, though less obviously. It has become clearer in recent years that strictly "propositional" data-structures lack the powers required to serve as models of the fundamental "mental representations", but few uncontroversial assertions can be made about the structure or function of non-propositional or quasi-propositional representations. The trade-off between storing information in "compiled" or "propositional" or "coded" form, and storing it "tacitly" in the organization of the representational system, has been fruitfully explored by people in artificial intelligence and cognitive psychology. Discussions of these developments are found in Chapters 6, 7 and 9.

II

The Nature of Theory in Psychology

4

Skinner Skinned

B. F. Skinner has recently retired, after a long and distinguished career at Harvard, and for better or for worse it appears that the school of psychology he founded, Skinnerian behaviorism, is simultaneously retiring from the academic limelight. Skinner's army of enemies would like to believe, no doubt, that his doctrines are succumbing at last to their barrage of criticism and invective, but of course science doesn't behave like that, and the reasons for the decline in influence of behaviorism are at best only indirectly tied to the many attempts at its "refutation". We could soften the blow for Skinner, perhaps, by putting the unwelcome message in terms he favors: psychologists just don't find behaviorism very *reinforcing* these days. Skinner might think this was unfair, but if he demanded *reasons*, if he asked his critics to *justify* their refusal to follow his lead, he would have to violate his own doctrines and methods. Those of us who are not Skinnerians, on the other hand, can without inconsistency plumb the inner thought processes, reasons, motives, decisions and beliefs of both Skinner and his critics, and try to extract from them an analysis of what is wrong with Skinnerian behaviorism and why.

This is not an easy task, in large measure because of a spiralling escalation of vituperation between Skinner and his critics. Skinner began as a naive and achingly philistine social thinker, so the first rounds of *humanist* criticism of his position were contemptuous, and largely conducted in ignorance of Skinner's technical work or the background of theories against which it was developed. Skinner, recognizing this, did not conceal his contempt in turn for his arrogant and ignorant humanist opponents, and so it has continued, with both sides willfully misreading and misattributing, secure in the knowledge that the other side is vastly underestimating its opponent. Somewhat surprisingly, Skinner's scientific critics have often fallen into similarly unedifying ruts.

Although counting myself among Skinner's opponents, I want to try to avoid the familiar brawl and do something diagnostic. I want to show *how* Skinner goes astray, through a series of all too common slight errors. He misapplies some perfectly good principles (principles, by the way, that his critics have often failed to recognize); he misdescribes crucial distinctions by lumping them all together; and he lets wishful thinking cloud his vision—a familiar enough failure. In particular, I want to show the falsehood of what I take to be Skinner's central philosophical claim, on which all the others rest, and which he apparently derives from his vision of psychology. The claim is that *behavioral science proves that people are not free, dignified, morally responsible agents.* It is this claim that secures what few links there are between Skinner's science and his politics. I want to show how Skinner arrives at this mistaken claim, and show how tempting in fact the path is. I would like to proceed by setting out with as much care as I can the steps of Skinner's argument for the claim, but that is impossible, since Skinner does not present arguments—at least, not wittingly. He has an ill-concealed disdain for arguments, a bias he feeds by supposing that brute facts will sweep away the most sophisticated arguments, and that the brute facts are on his side. His impatience with arguments does not, of course, prevent him from relying on arguments, it just prevents him from seeing that he is doing this—and it prevents him from seeing that his brute facts of behavior are not facts at all, but depend on an interpretation of the data which in turn depends on an an argument, which, finally, is fallacious. To get this phantom— but utterly central—argument out in the open will take a bit of reconstruction.

The first step in Skinner's argument is to characterize his enemy, "mentalism". He has a strong gut intuition that the *traditional* way of talking about and explaining human behavior—in "mentalistic" terms of a person's beliefs, desires, ideas, hopes, fears, feelings, emotions— is somehow utterly disqualified. This way of talking, he believes, is disqualified in the sense that not only is it not science as it stands; it could not be turned into science or used in science; it is inimical to science, would *have* to be in conflict with *any* genuine science of human behavior. Now the first thing one must come to understand is this antipathy of Skinner's for all things "mentalistic". Once one understands the antipathy, it is easy enough to see the boundaries of Skinner's enemy territory.

Skinner gives so many different reasons for disqualifying mentalism that we may be sure he has failed to hit the nail on the head—but he does get close to an important truth, and we can help him to get closer. Being a frugal Yankee, Skinner is reluctant to part with *any* reason, however unconvincing, for being against mentalism, but he does disassociate himself from some of the traditional arguments of behaviorists and other anti-mentalists at least to the extent of calling them relatively unimportant. For instance, perhaps the most ancient and familiar worry about mentalism is the suspicion that

(1) mental things must be made of *non-physical* stuff

thus raising the familiar and apparently fatal problems of Cartesian interactionism. Skinner presents this worry,[1] only to downplay it,[2] but when all else fails, he is happy to lean on it.[3] More explicitly, Skinner rejects the common behaviorist claim that it is

(2) the *privacy* of the mental

in contrast to the public objectivity of the data of behavior that makes the mental so abhorrent to science. "It would be foolish to deny the existence of that private world, but it is also foolish to assert that because it is private it is of a different nature from the world outside."[4] This concession to privacy is not all that it appears, however, for his concept of privacy is not the usual one encountered in the literature. Skinner does not even consider the possibility that one's mental life might be *in principle* private, *non-contingently* inaccessible. That is, he supposes without argument that the only sort of privacy envisaged is the sort that could someday be dispelled by poking around in the brain, and since "the skin is not that important as a boundary",[5] what it hides is nothing science will not be able to handle when the time comes. So Skinner suggests he will *not* object to the privacy of mental events, since their privacy would be no obstacle to science. At the same time Skinner often seeks to discredit explanations that appeal to some inner thing "we cannot see", which seems a contradiction.[6] For if we read these as objections to what we cannot *in principle* see, to what is necessarily unobservable, then he must after all be appealing tacitly to a form of the privacy objection. But perhaps we should read these disparagements of appeals to what we cannot see merely as disparagements of appeals to what we cannot *now* see, but whose existence we are *inferring*. Skinner often inveighs against appealing to

(3) events whose occurrence "can only be inferred".[7]

Chomsky takes this to be Skinner's prime objection against mentalistic psychology,[8] but Skinner elsewhere is happy to note that "Science often talks about things it cannot see or measure"[9] so it cannot be that simple. It is not that all inferred entities or events are taboo, for

Skinner himself on occasion explicitly infers the existence of such events; it must be a particular sort of inferred events. In particular,
(4) *internal* events
are decried, for they "have the effect of diverting attention from the external environment".[10] But if "the skin is not that important as a boundary", what can be wrong with internal events as such? No doubt Skinner finds *some* cause for suspicion in the mere internality of some processes; nothing else could explain his persistent ostrich-attitude towards physiological psychology.[11] But in his better moments he sees that there is nothing intrinsically wrong with inferring the existence of internal mediating events and processes—after all, he admits that some day physiology will describe the inner mechanisms that account for the relations between stimuli and responses, and he could hardly deny that in the meantime such inferences may illuminate the physiological investigations.[12] It must be only when the internal mediators are of a certain sort that they are anathema. But what sort? Why, the "occult", "prescientific", "fictional" sort, the "*mental* way station" sort,[13] but these characterizations beg the question. So the first four reasons Skinner cites are all inconclusive or contradicted by Skinner himself. If there is something wrong with mentalistic talk, it is not necessarily because mentalism is dualism, that mentalism posits nonphysical things, and it is not *just* that it involves internal, inferred, unobservable things, for he says or implies that there is nothing wrong with these features by themselves. If we are to go any further in characterizing Skinner's enemy we must read between the lines.[14]

In several places Skinner hints that what is bothering him is the *ease* with which mentalistic explanations can be concocted.[15] One *invents* whatever mental events one needs to "explain" the behavior in question. One falls back on the "miracle-working mind", which, just because it *is* miraculous, "explains nothing at all".[16] Now this is an ancient and honorable objection vividly characterized by Molière as the *virtus dormitiva*. The learned "doctor" in *Le Malade Imaginaire*, on being asked to explain what it was in the opium that put people to sleep, cites its *virtus dormitiva* or sleep-producing power. Leibniz similarly lampooned those who forged

> expressly occult qualities or faculties which they imagined to be like little demons or goblins capable of producing unceremoniously that which is demanded, just as if watches marked the hours by a certain horodeictic faculty without having need of wheels, or as if mills crushed grains by a fractive faculty without needing any thing resembling millstones.[17]

By seeming to offer an explanation, Skinner says, inventions of this sort "bring curiosity to an end". Now there can be no doubt that convicting a theory of relying on a *virtus dormitiva* is fatal to that theory, but getting the conviction is not always a simple matter—it often has been, though, in Twentieth Century psychology, and this may make Skinner complacent. Theories abounded in the early days of behaviorism which posited curiosity drives, the reduction of which explained why rats in mazes were curious; untapped reservoirs of aggressiveness to explain why animals were aggressive; and invisible, internal punishments and rewards that were postulated solely to account for the fact that unpunished, unrewarded animals sometimes refrained from or persisted in forms of behavior. But mentalistic explanations do not *seem* to cite a *virtus dormitiva*. For instance, explaining Tom's presence on the uptown bus by citing his desire to go to Macy's and his belief that Macy's is uptown does not look like citing a *virtus dormitiva*: it is not as empty and question-begging as citing a special uptown-bus-affinity in him would be. Yet I think it is clear that Skinner does think that all mentalistic explanation is infected with the *virtus dormitiva*.[18] This is interesting, for it means that *mentalistic* explanations are on a par for Skinner with a lot of bad *behavioristic* theorizing, but since he offers no discernible defense of this claim, and since I think the claim is ultimately indefensible (as I hope to make clear shortly), I think we must look elsewhere for Skinner's best reason for being against mentalism.

There is a special case of the *virtus dormitiva*, in fact alluded to in the Leibniz passage I quoted, which is the key to Skinner's objection: sometimes the thing the desperate theoretician postulates takes the form of a little man in the machine, a *homunculus*, a demon or goblin as Leibniz says. Skinner often alludes to this fellow. "The function of the inner man is to provide an explanation which will not be explained in turn."[19] In fact, Skinner identifies this little man with the notion of an autonomous, free and dignified moral agent: he says we must abolish "the autonomous man—the inner man, the homunculus, the possessing demon, the man defended by the literature of freedom and dignity".[20] This is a typical case of Skinner's exasperating habit of running together into a single undifferentiated lump a number of distinct factors that are related. Here the concept of a moral agent is identified with the concept of a little man in the brain, which in turn is identified with the demons of yore. Skinner, then, sees superstition and demonology every time a claim is made on behalf of moral responsibility, and every time a theory seems to be utilizing a homunculus. It all looks the same to him: bad. Moreover, he lumps *this* pernicious bit of superstition (the moral-autonomous-homunculus-goblin) with all the lesser suspicions we have been examining; it turns out that "mental" means "internal" means "inferred" means "unobservable" means "private" means "*virtus dormitiva*" means "demons" means "superstition". Psychologists who study physiology (and hence look at *internal* things), or talk of *inferred* drives, or use mentalistic terms like "belief" are all a sorry lot for Skinner, scarcely distinguishable from folk who believe in witches, or, perish the thought, in the freedom and dignity of man. Skinner brands them all with what we might call guilt by free association. For instance, in *Beyond Freedom and Dignity*, after all Skinner's claims to disassociate himself from the lesser objections to mentalism, on p. 200 he lets all the sheep back into the fold:

> Science does not dehumanize man; it de-homunculizes him . . . Only by *dispossessing* him can we turn to the *real* causes of human behavior. Only then can we turn from the *inferred* to the observed, from the miraculous to the natural, from the *inaccessible* to the manipulable. (*my italics*)[21]

But I was saying that hidden in this pile of dubious and inconsequential objections to mentalism is something important and true. What is it? It is that Skinner sees—or almost sees—that there is a special way that questions can be begged in psychology, and this way is *akin to* introducing a homunculus. Since psychology's task is to account for the intelligence or rationality of men and animals, it cannot fulfill its task if anywhere along the line it *presupposes* intelligence or rationality. Now introducing a homunculus does just that, as Skinner recognizes explicitly in "Behaviorism at Fifty":

> . . . the little man . . . was recently the hero of a television program called "Gateways to the Mind" . . . The viewer learned, from animated cartoons, that when a man's finger is pricked, electrical impulses resembling flashes of lightning run up the afferent nerves and appear on a television screen in the brain. The little man wakes up, sees the flashing screen, reaches out, and pulls the lever . . . More flashes of lightning go down the nerves to the muscles, which then contract, as the finger is pulled away from the threatening stimulus. *The behavior of the homunculus was, of course, not explained.* An explanation would presumably require another film. And it, in turn, another. (*my italics*)[22]

This "explanation" of our ability to respond to pin-pricks depends on the intelligence or rationality of the little man looking at the TV screen in the brain—and what does *his* intelligence depend on? Skinner sees clearly that introducing an unanalyzed homunculus is a dead end for psychology, and what he sees dimly is that a homunculus is hidden in effect in your explanation *whenever you use a certain vocabulary*, just because the use of that vocabulary, like the explicit introduction of a homunculus, presupposes intelligence or rationality. For instance, if I say that Tom is taking the uptown bus because he *wants* to go to Macy's and *believes* Macy's is uptown, my explanation of Tom's action *presupposes* Tom's intelligence, because if Tom weren't intelligent enough to put two and two together, as we say, he might fail to see that taking the uptown bus was a way of getting to Macy's. My explanation has a suppressed further premise: expanded it should read: Tom believes Macy's is uptown, and Tom wants to go to Macy's, so *since Tom is rational* Tom wants to go uptown, etc. Since I am relying on Tom's rationality to give me an explanation, it can hardly be an explanation of what makes Tom rational, even in part.

Whenever an explanation invokes the terms "want", "believe", "perceive", "think", "fear"—in short the "mentalistic" terms Skinner abhors—it must presuppose in some measure and fashion the rationality or intelligence of the entity being described.[23] My favorite example of this is the chess-playing computer. There are now computer programs that can play a respectable game of chess. If you want to predict or explain the moves the computer makes you can do it mechanistically (either by talking about the opening and closing of logic gates, etc., or at a more fundamental physical level by talking about the effects of the electrical energy moving through the computer) or you can say, "If the computer *wants* to capture my bishop and *believes* I wouldn't trade my queen for his knight, then the computer will move his pawn forward one space," or something like that. We need not take seriously the claim that the computer *really* has beliefs and desires in order to use this way of reasoning. Such reasoning about the computer's "reasoning" may in fact enable you to predict the computer's behavior quite well (if the computer is well-programmed), and in a sense such reasoning can even explain the computer's behavior—we might say: "Oh, now I understand why the computer didn't move its rook."—but in another sense it doesn't explain the computer's behavior at all. What is awesome and baffling about a chess-playing computer is how a mere mechanical thing could be made to be so "smart". Suppose you were to ask the designer, "How did the computer 'figure out' that it should move its knight?" and he replied: "Simple; it recognized that its opponent couldn't counterattack without losing a rook." This would be highly unsatisfactory to us, for the question is, how was he able to make a computer that *recognized* anything in the first place? So long as our explanation still has "mentalistic" words like "recognize" and "figure out" and "want" and "believe" in it, it will presuppose the very set of capacities—whatever the capacities are that go to make up intelligence—it ought to be accounting for. And notice: this defect in the explanation need have nothing to do with postulating any non-physical, inner, private, inferred, unobservable events or processes, because it need not postulate any processes or events at all. The computer designer may know exactly what events are or are not going on inside the computer, or for that matter on its highly visible output device: in choosing to answer by talking of the computer's *reasons* for making the move it did, he is not asserting that there are any extra, strange, hidden processes going on; he is simply explaining the *rationale* of the program without telling us how it's done. Skinner comes very close to seeing this. He says:

> Nor can we escape. . . . by breaking the little man into pieces and dealing with his wishes, cognitions, motives, and so on, bit by bit. The objection is not that those things are mental but that they offer no real explanation and stand in the way of a more effective analysis. [24]

The upshot of this long and winding path through Skinner's various objections to mentalism is this: if we ignore the inconsistencies, clear away the red herrings, focus some of Skinner's vaguer comments, and put a few words in his mouth, he comes up identifying the enemy as a certain class of terms—the "mentalistic" terms in his jargon—which when used in psychological theories "offer no real explanation" because using them is something like supposing there is a little man in the brain. Skinner never says the use of these terms presupposes rationality, but it does. Skinner also never gives us an exhaustive list of the mentalistic terms, or a definition of the class, but once again we can help him out. These terms, the use of which presupposes the rationality of the entity under investigation, are what philosophers call the *intentional idioms.* [25] They can be distinguished from other terms by several peculiarities of their logic, which is a more manageable way of distinguishing them than Skinner's. [26] Thus, spruced up, Skinner's position becomes the following: *don't use intentional idioms in psychology.*

Spruced-up Skinner is not alone in being opposed to intentional idioms in psychology. His Harvard colleague, Quine, has been most explicit on the topic. [27] One might suppose their congruence on this issue came out of discussion or collaboration, but Skinner is so apparently oblivious of Quine's arguments against intentional psychology, and so diffuse in his own objections to "mentalism" that this is most unlikely. For Quine's objections to intentional idioms have never had anything to do with their presupposing rationality or offering no explanation; rather he has argued that intentional idioms are to be foresworn because, as Chisholm argues, we cannot translate sentences containing intentional idioms into sentences lacking them.[28] Sentences containing intentional idioms refuse to "reduce" to the sentences of the physical sciences, so we must learn to do without them; Skinner on the other hand is blithely confident that such translations are possible,[29] and indeed *Beyond Freedom and Dignity* consists in large measure of samples of Skinner's translations.[30]

If Skinner never avails himself of the Chisholm-Quine untranslatability argument, and never makes explicit the presupposition of rationality argument, he does nevertheless muddy the water with a few other inconclusive objections. Intentional explanations tend to be "unfinished", he says, in that an action is explained, for instance, by reference to an opinion, without the existence of the opinion being explained in turn. But explaining an explosion by citing a spark is similarly incomplete, and since Skinner admits that both the former and the latter explanation could be completed, this is hardly a telling objection.[31] He also suggests that intentional explanations are not predictive, which is manifestly false. (See Chapters 1 and 15 of this volume.) Knowing that Tom wants to go to Macy's and believes the uptown bus will take him there, my prediction that he will take the uptown bus is, while not foolproof, highly reliable. Skinner sometimes hints that intentional explanations are only *vaguely* predictive, but this does not distinguish them from his own explanations until we are given some parameters by which to measure vagueness, which for human behavior are not forthcoming.

So let us put words in Skinner's mouth, and follow the phantom argument to its conclusion. We can, then, "agree" with Skinner when we read him between the lines to be asserting that no satisfactory psychological theory can *rest* on any use of intentional idioms, for their use presupposes rationality, which is the very thing psychology is supposed to explain. So if there is progress in psychology, it will inevitably be, as Skinner suggests, in the direction of eliminating ultimate appeals to beliefs, desires, and other intentional items from our explanations. So far so good. But now Skinner appears to make an important misstep, for he seems to draw the further conclusion that *intentional idioms therefore have no legitimate place in any psychological theory.* But this has not been shown at all. There is no reason why

intentional terms cannot be used provisionally in the effort to map out
the functions of the behavior control system of men and animals, just
so long as a way is found eventually to "cash them out" by designing a
mechanism to function as specified (see Chapters 1, 5 and 7). For
example, we may not now be able to describe mechanically how to
build a "belief store" for a man or animal, but if we specify how such
a belief store must function, we can use the notion in a perfectly
scientific way pending completion of its mechanical or physiological
analysis. Mendelian genetics, for instance, thrived as a science for years
with nothing more to feed on than the concept of a gene, a whatever-
it-turns-out-to-be that functions as a transmitter of a heritable trait.
All that is required by sound canons of scientific practice is that we
not suppose or claim that we have reached an end to explanation in
citing such a thing. Skinner, or rather phantom-Skinner, is wrong, then,
to think it follows from the fact that psychology cannot make any
final appeal to intentional items, that there can be no place for intentional idioms in psychology.

It is this misstep that leads Skinner into his most pervasive confusion.
We have already seen that Skinner, unlike Quine, thinks that translation
of intentional into non-intentional terms is possible. But if so, why
can't intentional explanations, in virtue of these bonds of translation,
find a place in psychology? Skinner vacillates between saying they can
and they can't, often within the space of a few pages.

> Beliefs, preferences, perceptions, needs, purposes, and opinions
> are possessions of autonomous man which are *said to* change
> when we change minds. What *is* changed in each case is a prob-
> ability of action. (*my italics*) [32]

How are we to interpret this? As meaning that we change probabilities,
not beliefs, or as meaning that changing beliefs *is just* changing probabilities of action? Skinner's very next sentence strongly suggests the latter:

> A person's belief that the floor will hold him as he walks across it
> depends upon his past experience.

but a few sentences later he hedges this by putting "belief" in scare-
quotes:

> We build "belief" when we increase the probability of action by
> reinforcing behavior.

Does this passage mean that it is *all right* to talk of building belief, so
long as we understand it as increasing action probabilities, or that it is

wrong to talk that way since *all* we are doing is increasing action probabilities?[33] On the next page he takes the hard line:

> We change the relative strengths of responses by differential rein-
> forcement of alternative courses of action; we do *not* change
> something called a preference. We change the probability of an
> act by changing a condition of deprivation or aversive stimula-
> tion; we do *not* change a need. We reinforce behavior in particular
> ways; we do *not* give a person a purpose or an intention. (*my
> italics*)

This vacillation is typical of Skinner. The exclusivity expressed in
the last quotation is rampant in *Beyond Freedom and Dignity*: "Our
age is not suffering from anxiety but from the accidents, crimes, . . ."
(p. 14) Young people refuse to get jobs "not because they feel alienated
but because of defective social environments . . ." (p. 15) A man
"makes a distinction not through some mental act of perception but
because of prior contingencies". (p. 187) (See also, pp. 26, 30, 157,
101, 189, 190, 204) Yet the contrary claim that these intentional
terms can all be translated, and hence, presumably, can be used to
make true statements in psychology, is just about as widespread. We
have just seen what may be Skinner's definition of "believe"; "want"
is defined on p. 37, and "intend" on p. 72, and p. 108. Intentional
idioms occur by the dozens in crucial roles in all of Skinner's books,
and Skinner explicitly justifies or excuses this practice in several places.
For instance, in *Beyond Freedom and Dignity* (p. 24), he says, "No
doubt many of the mentalistic expressions imbedded in the English
language cannot be as rigorously translated as 'sunrise', but acceptable
translations are not out of reach." In *About Behaviorism* (p. 17) he
says, "Many of these expressions I 'translate into behavior'. I do so
while acknowledging that *traduttori traditori*—translators are traitors—
and that there are perhaps no exact behavioral equivalents . . ." But
the context shows that Skinner thinks he only loses the flavor—the
connotations—not the predictive or inferential power or referential
accuracy of the terms.

It is unfathomable how Skinner can be so sloppy on this score, for
reflection should reveal to him, as it will to us, that this vacillation is
over an absolutely central point in his argument.[34] For surely Skinner
is right in seeing that the validity of our conceptual scheme of moral
agents having dignity, freedom and responsibility stands or falls on the
question: can men ever be *truly* said to have beliefs, desires, intentions?
If they can, there is at least some hope of retaining a notion of the

dignity of man; if they cannot, if men never can be said truly to want or believe, then surely they never can be said truly to act responsibly, or to have a conception of justice, or know the difference between right and wrong. So Skinner's whole case comes down to the question: can intentional explanations (citing beliefs, desires, etc.) on the one hand, and proper, ultimate, scientific explanations on the other hand, *co-exist*? Can they ever *both* be true, or would the truth of a scientific explanation always *exclude* the other?

In spite of his vacillation in print, it is clear that Skinner must come down in favor of the exclusive view, if his argument is to work. Certainly the majority of his remarks favor this view, and in fact it becomes quite explicit on p. 101 of *Beyond Freedom and Dignity* where Skinner distinguishes the "pre-scientific" (i.e., intentional) view of a person's behavior from the scientific view, and goes on to say, "Neither view can be proved, but it is in the nature of scientific inquiry that the evidence should shift in favor of the second." Here we see Skinner going beyond the correct intuition that it is in the nature of scientific inquiry that ultimate appeals to intentional idioms must disappear as progress is made, to the bolder view that as this occurs intentional explanations will be rendered false, not reduced or translated into other terms.

I argue at length in Chapter 12 that intentional and mechanistic or scientific explanations *can* co-exist, and have given here an example supposed to confirm this: we know that there is a purely mechanistic explanation of the chess playing computer, and yet it is *not false* to say that the computer *figures out* or *recognizes* the best move, or that it *concludes* that its opponent cannot make a certain move, any more than it is false to say that a computer *adds* or *multiplies*. There has often been confusion on this score. It used to be popular to say, "A computer can't really think, or course; all it can do is add, subtract, multiply and divide." That leaves the way open to saying, "A computer can't really multiply, of course; all it can do is add numbers together very, very fast," and that must lead to the admission: "A computer cannot really add numbers, of course; all it can do is control the opening and closing of hundreds of tiny switches," which leads to: "A computer can't really control its switches, of course; it's simply at the mercy of the electrical currents pulsing through it." What this chain of claims adds up to "prove", obviously, is that computers are really pretty dull lumps of stuff—they can't do anything interesting at all. They can't really guide rockets to the moon, or make out paychecks, or beat human beings at chess, but of course they can do all that and more. What the computer programmer can do if we give him the chance is not *explain away* the illusion that the computer is doing these things, but *explain how* the computer truly is doing these things.

Skinner fails to see the distinction between explaining and explaining away. In this regard he is succumbing to the same confusion as those who suppose that since color can be explained in terms of the properties of atoms which are not colored, nothing is colored. Imagine the Skinner-style exclusion claim: "The American flag is *not* red, white and blue, but rather a collection of colorless atoms." Since Skinner fails to make this distinction, he is led to the exclusive view, the view that true scientific explanations will exclude true intentional explanations, and typically, though he asserts this, he offers no arguments for it. Once again, however, with a little extrapolation we can see what perfectly good insights led Skinner to this error.

There are times when a mechanistic explanation obviously does exclude an intentional explanation. Wooldridge gives us a vivid example:

When the time comes for egg laying the wasp *Sphex* builds a burrow for the purpose and seeks out a cricket which she stings in such a way as to paralyze but not kill it. She drags the cricket into her burrow, lays her eggs alongside, closes the burrow, then flies away, never to return. In due course, the eggs hatch and the wasp grubs feed off the paralyzed cricket, which has not decayed, having been kept in the wasp equivalent of deep freeze. To the human mind, such an elaborately organized and seemingly purposeful routine conveys a convincing flavor of logic and thoughtfulness—until more details are examined. For example, the wasp's routine is to bring the paralyzed cricket to the burrow, leave it on the threshold, go inside to see that all is well, emerge, and then drag the cricket in. If, while the wasp is inside making her preliminary inspection the cricket is moved a few inches away, the wasp, on emerging from the burrow, will bring the cricket back to the threshold, but not inside, and will then repeat the preparatory procedure of entering the burrow to see that everything is all right. If again the cricket is removed a few inches while the wasp is inside, once again the wasp will move the cricket up to the threshold and re-enter the burrow for a final check. The wasp never thinks of pulling the cricket straight in. On one occasion, this procedure was repeated forty times, always with the same result.[35]

In this case what we took at first to be a bit of intelligent behavior is unmasked. When we see how simple, rigid and mechanical it is, we realize that we were attributing too much to the wasp. Now Skinner's experimental life has been devoted to unmasking, over and over again, the behavior of pigeons and other lower animals. In "Behaviorism at Fifty" he gives an example almost as graphic as our wasp. Students watch a pigeon being conditioned to turn in a clockwise circle, and Skinner asks them to describe what they have observed. They all talk of the pigeon *expecting, hoping* for food, *feeling* this, *observing* that, and Skinner points out with glee that they have observed nothing of the kind; he has a simpler, more mechanical explanation of what has happened, and it *falsifies* the students' unfounded *inferences.* Since in this case explanation is unmasking or explaining away, it always is.[36] Today pigeons, tomorrow the world. What Skinner fails to see is that it is not the fact that he has an explanation[37] that unmasks the pretender after intelligence, but rather that his explanation is so simple (see Chapter 12 of this volume). If Skinner had said to his students, "Aha! You think the pigeon is so smart, but here's how it learned to do its trick," and proceeded to inundate them with hundreds of pages of detailed explanation of highly complex inner mechanisms, their response would no doubt be that yes, the pigeon did seem, on his explanation, to be pretty smart.

The fact that it is the simplicity of explanations that can render elaborate intentional explanations false is completely lost to Skinner for a very good reason: the only *well-formulated, testable* explanations Skinner and his colleagues have so far come up with have been, per-force, relatively simple, and deal with the relatively simple behavior controls of relatively simple animals. Since all the explanations he has so far come up with have been of the unmasking variety (pigeons, it turns out, do not have either freedom or dignity), Skinner might be forgiven for supposing that all explanations in psychology, including all explanations of human behavior, must be similarly unmasking.

It might, of course, turn out to be the case that all human behavior could be unmasked, that all signs of human cleverness are as illusory as the wasp's performance, but in spite of all Skinner's claims of triumph in explaining human behavior, his own testimony reveals this to be wishful thinking. Even if we were to leave unchallenged all the claims of operant conditioning of human beings in experimental situations,[38] there remain areas of human behavior that prove completely intractable to Skinner's mode of analysis. Not surprisingly, these are the areas of deliberate, intentional action. The persistently recalcitrant features of human behavior for the Skinnerians can be grouped under the headings of novelty and generality. The Skinnerian must explain all behavior by citing the subject's past history of similar stimuli and responses, so when someone behaves in a novel manner, there is a problem. Pigeons do not exhibit very interesting novel behavior, but human beings do. Suppose, to borrow one of Skinner's examples, I am held up and asked for my wallet.[39] This has never happened to me before, so the correct response cannot have been "reinforced" for me, yet I do the smart thing: I hand over my wallet. Why? The Skinnerian must claim that this is not truly novel behavior at all, but an instance of a *general sort* of behavior which has been previously conditioned. But what sort is it? Not only have I not been trained to hand over my wallet to men with guns, I have not been trained to empty my pockets for women with bombs, nor to turn over my possessions to armed entities. None of these things has ever happened to me before. I may never have been threatened before at all. Or more plausibly, it may well be that most often when I have been threatened in the past, the "reinforced" response was to *apologize* to the threatener for something I'd said. Obviously, though, when told, "Your money or your life!" I don't respond by saying, "I'm sorry. I take it all back." It is perfectly clear that what experience has taught me is that if I *want* to save my skin, and *believe* I am being threatened, I should do what I *believe* my threatener *wants* me to do. But of course Skinner cannot permit this intentional formulation at all, for in ascribing wants and beliefs it would presuppose my rationality. He must insist that the "threat stimuli" I now encounter (and these are not defined) are similar in some crucial but undescribed respect to some stimuli encountered in my past which were followed by responses of some sort similar to the one I now make, where the past responses were reinforced somehow by their consequences. But see what Skinner is doing here. He is positing an external *virtus dormitiva*. He has no record of any earlier experiences of this sort, but *infers* their existence, and moreover *endows* them with an automatically theory-satisfying quality: these postulated earlier experiences are claimed to resemble-in-whatever-is-the-crucial-respect the situation they must resemble for the Skinnerian explanation to work. Why do I hand over my wallet? Because I must have had in the past some experiences that reinforced wallet-handing-over behavior in circumstances like this.

When Skinner predicts pigeon behavior he makes use of his knowledge of their reinforcement history, but when he predicts human behavior, he does not. This can be vividly seen if we consider once again the chess-playing computer. Suppose we set up a contest between Skinner and an intentionalist to see who could make the best predictions of the computer's moves. Skinner would proceed by keeping a careful cumulative record of every move the computer ever made, keeping track of each move's consequences, to see which moves were "reinforced" by their consequences. Would he have a chance of making good predictions? Mathematically, it can be shown that there is no guarantee that he would get anywhere with this method unless he knew the *internal* starting state of the computer; the computer's past biography of moves is not enough.[40] But for the sake of argument we can suppose that the importance of the initial state would recede as the computer made more and more moves (not a universally plausible supposition), so that Skinner could get closer and closer to good predictions in spite of his ignorance of this crucial variable. Skinner's predictions would take this form: there is a high probability that the computer will move queen to king's bishop-4 because when stimulated by similar (not necessarily identical) board positions in the past, the computer has been reinforced for making similar (not necessarily identical) moves. There is obviously much that is problematical about such formulations—e.g., what are the shared features of the similar board positions and similar moves?—but let us suppose Skinner succeeds, after years of cumulative recording, in arriving at good predictions. This would not be as flashy and easy a method as the intentionalist's, who would simply ask himself at each point in the game: "Now if I were the computer, knowing what I know and wanting what I want, which move would I believe to have the best consequences?" but Skinner could comfort himself by recalling Russell's phrase, and claiming that his opponent's method had all the advantages of theft over honest toil.

But suppose we complicate the picture. Suppose we wrote some chess-playing programs that could "learn" as they played, and improve as a result of "experience"—by the relatively simple expedient of adjusting weightings in their evaluation formulae for positions as a function of their "track record". Now suppose we set two different chess-playing computers to playing a series of games against each other, but do not provide for the recording of the games. We turn them on at night, and in the morning discover two very much improved chess-playing computers (one of them, probably, would have established its mastery over the other—something we couldn't discover until we watched a few games). It must be possible to determine mathematically what these evolved programs are now (if we know exactly what program each had to begin with, and that there is no randomizing element in either program, and that no uncorrected malfunctions occurred during the night, and if we know exactly how many games were played in the time available)—or we could, in principle, take the computers apart, figuring out what their programs were in that way. But for practical purposes both of these methods are ruled out. Can we still make predictions of their behavior? Of course. The intentionalist can predict their behavior just as well (no better) than he can predict the behavior of a novel human opponent, a stranger in town. He would assume his opponent had some intelligence, and hence would expect him to make the most intelligent moves available. But Skinner would have to claim ignorance; the fact that the biography of the computers would be lost would mean that Skinner would not be able to use his method. He would say that too much conditioning of which he had no record had intervened overnight. But he *could* do this: he could make the same predictions (roughly, depending on his ability at chess) as the intentionalist, and *on the same grounds*, namely that it was the best move he could see, and then "deduce" the fact that the computer during the night *must have* been "reinforced" for making moves "similar in some respect" to the one he is now predicting. Here it would be crystal clear that Skinner would have no grounds for such a hypothesis except that his theory required it, and no way of being specific about the "similarity" of the overnight experiences.[41]

I am suggesting that once Skinner turns from pigeons to people, his proffered "explanations" of human behavior are no better than this. If Skinner complains that mentalistic explanations are too easy, since we always know exactly what mental events to postulate to "explain" the behavior, the same can be said of all the explanation sketches of complex human behavior in Skinner's books. They offer not a shred of confirmation that Skinner's basic mode of explanation—in terms of reinforcement of operants—will prove fruitful in accounting for human behavior. It is hard to be sure, but Skinner even seems to realize this. He says at one point, "The instances of behavior cited in what follows are not offered as 'proof' of the interpretation", but he goes right on to say, "The proof is to be found in the basic analysis." But insofar as the "basic analysis" proves anything, it proves that people are not like pigeons, that Skinner's unmasking explanations will not be forthcoming. Certainly if we discovered that people only handed over their wallets to robbers after being conditioned to do this, and, moreover, continued to hand over their wallets after the robber had shown his gun was empty, or when the robber was flanked by policemen, we would have to admit that Skinner had unmasked the pretenders; human beings would be little better than pigeons or wasps, and we would have to agree that we had no freedom and dignity.

Skinner's increasing reliance, however, on a *virtus dormitiva* to "explain" complex human behavior is a measure of the difference between pigeons and persons, and hence is a measure of the distance between Skinner's premises and his conclusions. When Skinner speculates about the past history of reinforcement in a person in order to explain some current behavior, he is saying, in effect, "I don't know which of many possible equivalent series of events occurred, but one of them did, and that explains the occurrence of this behavior now." But what is the equivalence class Skinner is pointing to in every case? What do the wide variety of possible stimulus histories have in common? Skinner can't tell us in his vocabulary, but it is easy enough to say: the stimulus histories that belong to the equivalence class have in common the fact that they *had the effect of teaching the person that p*, of storing certain information. In the end Skinner is playing the same game with his speculations as the cognitivist who speculates about internal representations of information. Skinner is simply relying on a more cumbersome vocabulary.

Skinner has failed to show that psychology without mentalism is either possible or—in his own work—actual, and so he has failed to explode the myths of freedom and dignity. Since that explosion was to have been his first shot in a proposed social revolution, its misfiring saves us the work of taking seriously his alternately dreary and terrifying proposals for improving the world.

5

Why the Law of Effect Will Not Go Away

The poet Paul Valéry said: "It takes two to invent anything." He was not referring to collaborative partnerships between people but to a bifurcation in the individual inventor. "The one", he says, "makes up combinations; the other one chooses, recognizes what he wishes and what is important to him in the mass of the things which the former has imparted to him. What we call genius is much less the work of the first one than the readiness of the second one to grasp the value of what has been laid before him and to choose it."[1] This is a plausible claim. Why? Is it true? If it is, what kind of truth is it? An empirical generalization for which there is wide scale confirmation? Or a "conceptual truth" derivable from our concept of invention? Or something else?

Herbert Simon, in *The Sciences of the Artificial*, makes a related claim: "human problem solving, from the most blundering to the most insightful, involves nothing more than varying mixtures of trial and error and selectivity."[2] This claim is also plausible, I think, but less so. Simon presents it as if it were the conclusion of an inductive investigation, but *that*, I think, is not plausible at all. An extensive survey of human problem solving may have driven home this thesis to Simon, but its claim to our assent comes from a different quarter.

I want to show that these claims owe their plausibility to the fact that they are implications of an abstract principle whose "necessity" (such as it is) consists in this: we can know independently of empirical research in psychology that any adequate and complete psychological theory must exploit some version or other of the principle. The most familiar version of the principle I have in mind is the derided darling of the behaviorists: the Law of Effect. "The rough idea", Broadbent observes,[3] "that actions followed by reward are repeated, is one which is likely to occur to most intelligent people who think about possible explanations of behavior." This rough idea, refined, is the Law of Effect, and my claim is that it is not just part of *a* possible explanation of behavior, but of *any* possible adequate explanation of behavior.

In order to establish this condition of adequacy for psychological theories, we must first be clear about the burden of psychology. Consider the way the rest of the social sciences depend on the more basic science of psychology. Economics, or at any rate classical economics, assumes at the outset an ontology of rational, self-interested agents, and then proposes to discover generalizations about how such agents, the "atoms" of economics, will behave in the market-place. This assumption of intelligence and self-interest in agents is not idle; it is needed to ground and explain the generalizations. Consider the law of supply and demand. There is no mystery about why the law holds as reliably as it does: *people are not fools*; they want as much as they can get, they know what they want and how much they want it, and they know enough to charge what the market will bear and buy as cheap as they can. If that didn't explain why the law of supply and demand works, we would be utterly baffled or incredulous on learning that it did. Political science, sociology, anthropology and social psychology are similarly content to *assume* capacities of discrimination, perception, reason and action based on reason, and then seek interesting generalizations about the exploitation of these capacities in particular circumstances. One way of alluding to this shared feature of these social sciences is to note that they are all *intentional*: they utilize the intentional or "mentalistic" or "cognitive" vocabulary—they speak of belief, desire, expectation, recognition, action, etc.—and they permit explanations to come to an end, at least on occasion, with the citation of a stretch of practical reasoning (usually drastically enthymematic): the voters elected the Democrat *because* they were working men and believed the Republican candidate to be anti-labor; the stock market dropped *because* investors believed other havens for their money were safer. These sciences leave to psychology the task of explaining *how there come to be* entities—organisms, human beings—that can be so usefully assumed to be self-interested, knowledgeable and rational. A fundamental task of psychology then is to explain intelligence. For the super-abstemious behaviorist who will not permit himself to speak even of intelligence (that being too "mentalistic" for him) we can say, with Hull, that a primary task of psychology "is to understand . . . why . . . behavior . . . is so generally adaptive, i.e., successful in the sense of reducing needs and facilitating survival . . .".[4] The account of intelligence required of psychology must not of course be question-begging. It must not explain intelligence in terms of intelligence, for instance by assigning responsibility for the existence of intelligence in creatures to the munificence of an intelligent Creator, or by putting clever homunculi at the control panels of the nervous system (see Chapter 4).[5] If that were the best psychology could do, then psychology could not do the job assigned it.

We already have a model of a theory that admirably discharges just this *sort* of burden in the Darwinian theory of evolution by natural selection, and as many commentators have pointed out, the Law of Effect is closely analogous to the principle of natural selection. The Law of Effect presumes there to be a "population" of stimulus-response pairs, more or less randomly or in any case arbitrarily mated, and from this large and varied pool, reinforcers *select* the well-designed, the adaptive, the fortuitously appropriate pairs in an entirely mechanical way: their recurrence is made more probable, while their maladaptive or merely neutral brethren suffer "extinction", not by being *killed* (all particular stimulus-response pairs come to swift ends), but by *failing to reproduce*. The analogy is very strong, very satisfying, and very familiar.

But there has been some misinterpretation of the nature of its appeal. Broadbent observes:

> The attraction both of natural selection and of the Law of Effect, to certain types of mind, is that they do not call on explanatory principles of a quite separate order from those used in the physical sciences. It is not surprising therefore that the Law of Effect had been seized on, not merely as a generalization which is true of animals under certain conditions, but also as a fundamental principle which would explain all adaptive behaviour.[6]

It is certainly true that these analogous principles appeal to physicalists or materialists because they are mechanistically explicable, but there is a more fundamental reason for favoring them: they both can provide clearly non-question-begging accounts of *explicanda* for which it is very hard to devise non-question-begging accounts. Darwin explains a world of final causes and teleological laws with a principle that is, to be sure, mechanistic but—more fundamentally—utterly independent of "meaning" or "purpose". It assumes a world that is *absurd* in the existentialist's sense of the term: not ludicrous but pointless, and this assumption is a necessary condition of any non-question-begging account of *purpose*. Whether we can imagine a *non*-mechanistic but also non-question-begging principle for explaining design in the biological world is doubtful; it is tempting to see the commitment to non-question-begging accounts here as tantamount to a commitment to mechanistic materialism, but the priority of these commitments is clear. It is not that one's prior prejudice in favour of materialism gives one reason to accept Darwin's principle because it is materialistic, but rather that one's prior acknowledgment of the constraint against begging the question gives one *reason to adopt materialism*, once one sees that Darwin's non-question-begging account of design or purpose in nature is materialistic. One argues: Darwin's materialistic theory may not be the only non-question-begging theory of these matters, but it is one such theory, and the only one we have found, which is quite a good reason for espousing materialism.

A precisely parallel argument might occur to the psychologist trying to decide whether to throw in with the behaviorists: theories based on the Law of Effect may not be the only psychological theories that do not beg the question of intelligence, but they *are* clearly non-question-begging in this regard, and their rivals are not, which is quite a good reason for joining the austere and demanding brotherhood of behaviorists. But all is not well in that camp, and has not been for some time. Contrary to the claims of the more optimistic apologists, the Law of Effect has not been knit into any theory with anything remotely like the proven power of the theory of natural selection. The Law of Effect has appeared in several guises since Thorndike introduced it as a principle of learning; most influentially, it assumed centrality in Hull's behaviorism as the "law of primary reinforcement" and in Skinner's as the "principle of operant conditioning",* but the history of these attempts is the history of ever more sophisticated failures to get the Law of Effect to *do enough work.* It may account for a *lot* of learning, but it can't seem to account for it all. Why, then, not look for another fundamental principle of more power to explain the balance? It is not just mulishness or proprietary pride that has kept behaviorists from following this suggestion, but rather something like the conviction that the Law of Effect is not just *a* good idea, but the only possible good idea for this job. There is something right in this conviction, I want to maintain, but what is wrong in it has had an ironic result: allegiance to the Law of Effect in its behavioristic or peripheralistic versions has forced psychologists to beg small questions left and right in order to keep from begging the big question. One "saves" the Law of Effect from persistent counter-instances by the *ad hoc* postulation of reinforcers and stimulus histories for which one has not the slightest

---

*Skinner explicitly identifies his principle with the Law of Effect in *Science and Human Behavior* (1953), p. 87.

grounds except the demands of the theory. For instance one postulates curiosity drives, the reduction of which is reinforcing, in order to explain "latent" learning, or presumes that when one exhibits an apparently novel bit of intelligent behavior, there *must have been* some "relevantly similar" responses in one's past for which one was reinforced. These strategies are not altogether bad; they parallel the evolutionist's speculative hypothetical ancestries of species, which are similarly made up out of whole cloth to begin with, but which differ usually in being clearly confirmable or disconfirmable. These criticisms of behaviorism are not new,[7] and not universally fair in application either. I am convinced, nevertheless, that no behaviorism, however sophisticated, can elude all versions of these familiar objections, but that is not a claim to be supported in short compass. It will be more constructive to turn to what I claim is right about the Law of Effect, and to suggest another way a version of it can be introduced to take up where behaviorism leaves off.

The first thing to note is that the Law of Effect and the principle of natural selection are not just analogues; they are designed to work together. There is a kind of intelligence, or pseudo-intelligence, for which the principle of natural selection itself provides the complete explanation, and that is the "intelligence" manifest in tropistic, "instinctual" behavior control. The environmental appropriateness, the biological and strategic wisdom, evident in bird's-nest-building, spider-web-making and less intricate "innate" behavioral dispositions is to be explained by the same principle that explains the well-designedness of the bird's wings or the spider's eyes. We are to understand that creatures so "wired" as to exhibit useful tropistic behavior in their environmental niches will have a survival advantage over creatures not so wired, and hence will gradually be selected by the vicissitudes of nature. Tropistic behavior is not plastic in the individual, however, and it is evident that solely tropistically controlled creatures would not be evolution's final solution to the needs-versus-environment problem. *If* creatures with some plasticity in their input-output relations were to appear, *some* of them might have an advantage over even the most sophisticated of their tropistic cousins. Which ones? Those that were able to distinguish good results of plasticity from bad, and preserve the good. The problem of selection reappears and points to its own solution: let some class of events in the organisms be genetically endowed with the capacity to increase the likelihood of the recurrence of behavior-controlling events upon which they act. Call them reinforcers. Some mutations, we can then speculate, appear with inappropriate reinforcers, others with neutral reinforcers, and a lucky few with appropriate reinforcers. Those lucky few survive, of course, and their progeny are endowed genetically with a capacity to *learn*, where learning is understood to be nothing more than a change (in the environmentally appropriate direction) in stimulus-response probability relations. The obviously adaptive positive reinforcers will be events normally caused by the presence of food or water, by sexual contact, and by bodily well-being, while the normal effects of injury and deprivation will be the obvious negative reinforcers, though there could be many more than these.*

The picture so far is of creatures well endowed by natural selection with tropistic *hard-wiring*, including the hard-wiring of some reinforcers. These reinforcers, in turn, permit the further selection and establishment of adaptive soft-wiring, such selection to be drawn from a pool of essentially arbitrary, *undesigned* temporary interconnections. Whenever a creature is fortunate enough to have one of its interconnections be followed by an environmental effect that in turn produces a reinforcer as "feedback", that interconnection will be favored. Skinner is quite explicit about all this. In *Science and Human Behavior* he notes that "The process of conditioning has survival value", but of course what he means is that the *capacity* to be conditioned has survival value. "Where inherited behavior leaves off, the inherited modifiability of the process of conditioning takes over."[8] So let us use the term "Skinnerian creatures" for all creatures that are susceptible to operant conditioning, all creatures whose learning can be explained by the Law of Effect. Skinnerian creatures clearly have it over merely tropistic creatures, but it seems that there are other creatures, e.g., at least ourselves and many other mammals, that have it over merely Skinnerian creatures.

The trouble, intuitively, with Skinnerian creatures is that they can learn only by actual behavioral trial and error in the environment. A useful bit of soft-wiring cannot get selected until it has had an opportunity to provoke some reinforcing feedback from the environment, and the problem seems to be that merely *potential*, as yet *unutilized* behavioral controls can *ex hypothesi* have no environmental effects which could lead to their being reinforced. And yet experience seems

---

*Cf. Skinner, *Science and Human Behavior*, p. 83. Skinner speaks of food and water *themselves* being the reinforcers, but commenting on this difference would entail entering the familiar and arid 'more peripheral than thou' controversy. A point of Skinner's that is always worth reiterating, though, is that negative reinforcers are not *punishments*; they are events the cessation of which is positively reinforcing, that is, their cessation *increases* the probability of recurrence of the behaviour followed by cessation.

to show that we, and even monkeys, often think out and select an adaptive course of action without benefit of prior external feedback and reinforcement. Faced with this dilemma, we might indulge in a little wishful thinking: if only the Law of Effect could provide for the reinforcement of merely potential, unutilized bits of behavior control wiring! If only such unutilized controls could have some subtle effect on the environment (i.e., if only merely "thinking about the solution" could have some environmental effect) and if only the environment were benign enough to bounce back the appropriate feedback in response! But that, it seems, would be miraculous.

Not so. We can have all that and more by simply positing that creatures have *two* environments, the outer environment in which they live, and an "inner" environment they carry around with them. The inner environment is just to be conceived as an input-output box for providing feedback for events in the brain.* Now we can run just the same speculative argument on Skinnerian creatures that we earlier ran on tropistic creatures. Suppose there appear among the Skinnerian creatures of the world mutations that have inner environments of the sort just mentioned. Some, we can assume, will have maladaptive inner environments (the environments will make environmentally inappropriate behavior more likely); others will have neutral inner environments; but a lucky few will have inner environments that happen to reinforce, by and large, only adaptive *potential* behavioral controls. In a way we are turning the principle of natural selection on its head: we are talking of the evolution of (inner) environments to suit the organism, of environments that would have survival value in an organism. Mutations equipped with such benign inner environments would have a distinct survival advantage over merely Skinnerian creatures in any exiguous environment, since they could learn faster and *more safely* (for trial and error learning is not only tedious; it can be dangerous). The advantage provided by such a benign inner environment has been elegantly expressed in a phrase of Karl Popper's: it "permits our hypotheses to die in our stead".

The behaviorist, faced with the shortcomings of the Law of Effect, insisted that all we needed was more of the same (that only more of same could explain what had to be explained), and that is what we have given him. He was just construing "the same" too narrowly. The *peripheralism* of behaviorist versions of the Law of Effect turns out to

*This is not Simon's distinction between inner and outer environment in *The Sciences of the Artificial*, but a more restrictive notion. It also has *nothing whatever* to do with any distinction between the 'subjective' or 'phenomenal' world and the objective, public world.

be not so essential as they had thought. For instance, our talk of an inner *environment* is merely vestigial peripheralism; the inner environment is just an inner something that selects. Ultimately of course it is environmental effects that are the measure of adaptivity and the mainspring of learning, but the environment can delegate its selective function to something in the organism (just as death had earlier delegated its selective function to pain), and if this occurs, a more intelligent, flexible, organism is the result.

It might be asked if behaviorists haven't already, in fact long ago, taken this step to inner reinforcement or selection. I think the fairest answer is that some have and some have not, and even those that have have not been clear about what they are doing. On the one hand there are the neo-Skinnerians who have no qualms about talking about the operant conditioning that results in the subject who *imagines* courses of action followed by reinforcing results, and on the other hand you have the neo-Skinnerians that still rail against the use of such mentalistic terms as "imagine". Skinner himself falls into both camps, often within the compass of a single page.* "The skin", says Skinner, "is not that important as a boundary",[9] but it is hard to believe he sees the implications of this observation. In any event it will be clearer here to suppose that behaviorists are "classical" peripheralists who do not envisage such a reapplication of the Law of Effect via an inner environment.

At this point it is important to ask whether this proposed principle of selection by inner environment hasn't smuggled in some incoherency or impossibility, for if it has not, we can argue that since our hypothesized mutations would clearly have the edge over merely Skinnerian creatures, there is no reason to believe that operant conditioning was evolution's final solution to the learning or intelligence problem, and we could then safely "predict" the appearance and establishment of such mutations. Here we are, we could add. We could then go on to ask how powerful our new principle was, and whether there was learning or intelligence *it* couldn't explain. And we could afford to be more open-minded about this question than the behaviorist was, since if we thought there *was* learning it couldn't handle, we would know where to look for yet a stronger principle: yet a *fourth* incarnation of our basic principle of natural selection (or, otherwise viewed, yet a *third* incarnation of our basic psychological principle of the Law of Effect). In fact we can already see just what it will be. Nothing requires the inner environment to be entirely genetically hard-wired. A more versatile capacity would be one in which the inner environment *itself* could

*See Chapter 4 for detailed confirmation of this and similar vacillation in Skinner.

evolve in the individual as a result of—for starters—operant conditioning. We not only learn; we learn better how to learn, and learn better how to learn better how to learn.*

So is there anything incoherent about the supposition of inner environments that can select adaptive features of *potential* behavior control systems (and favor their incorporation into *actual* behavior controls—for that is what reinforcement amounts to in this application)? Is anything miraculous or question-begging being assumed here? The notion of an inner environment was *introduced* in explicitly non-intentional language: the inner environment is simply any internal region that can affect and be affected by features of potential behavioral control systems. The benign and hence selected inner environments are simply those in which the result of these causal interactions is the increased conditional probability of the actualization of those potential controls that would be adaptive under the conditions in which they are probable. The way the notion is introduced is thus uncontaminated by covert appeal to intelligence, but it is still not obvious that an inner environment could "work".

What conditions must we put on features of bits of brain design to ensure that their selection by an optimally designed selector-mechanism will yield a better than chance improvement in ultimate performance? Since selection by inner environment is ultimately a mechanical sorting, which can key only on physical features of what is sorted, at the very least there would have to be a *normal* or *systematic* correlation between the physical event types selected and what we may call a *functional role* in some control program. A physically characterized type of wiring could not consist in the main of reliably adaptive tokens unless those tokens normally played a particular function.** This is the same condition, raised one level, that we find on operant conditioning: if physically characterized *response* classes do not produce a normally uniform environmental effect, reinforcement cannot be adaptive. So if and when this principle works, it works to establish high probabilities that particular appropriate functional roles will be filled at the appropriate times in control programs. Functional roles will be *discriminated*, and thereby control programs will become well designed.

*At a glance it seems that ultimately we want one-shot learning to change the inner environment. In ordinary perspective, we want to account for the fact that if I am trying to solve a problem, *someone can tell me*, once, what won't work and I can take this lesson to heart immediately.

**See Simon, *op. cit.*, p. 73, also pp. 90–2. He argues that *efficient* evolution of design also requires a hierarchical organization of design elements. My treatment of these issues is heavily indebted to Simon's illuminating and lucid account.

It is hard to keep track of these purported functions and effects while speaking in the sterilized vocabulary of the behaviorist, but there is an easier way of talking: we can say that physical event tokens of a selected type have—in virtue of their normally playing a certain role in a well-designed functional organization—a *meaning* or *content*. We have many familiar examples of *adaptive potential behavior control elements*: accurate *maps* are adaptive potential behavior control elements, and so are true *beliefs*, warranted *expectations*, clear *concepts*, well-ordered *preferences*, sound *plans of action*, in short all the favorite tools of the cognitive psychologist. As Popper says, it is *hypotheses*—events or states endowed with an intentional characterization—that die in our stead. Is *cognitive* psychology then bound ultimately to versions of the Law of Effect? That it is, I hope to show by looking at artificial intelligence (AI) research.

AI program designers work backwards on the same task behaviorists work forwards on. We have just traced the behaviorists' cautious and self-denying efforts to build from mechanistic principles towards the levels of complexity at which it becomes apt and illuminating to speak in intentional terms about what they claim is going on. The AI researcher *starts* with an intentionally characterized problem (e.g., how can I get a computer to *understand* questions of English?), breaks it down into sub-problems that are also intentionally characterized (e.g., how do I get the computer to *recognize* questions, *distinguish* subjects from predicates, *ignore* irrelevant parsings?) and then breaks these problems down still further until finally he reaches problem or task descriptions that are obviously mechanistic. Here is a way of looking at the process. The AI programmer begins with an intentionally characterized problem, and thus frankly views the computer anthropomorphically: if he *solves* the problem he will say he has designed a computer that can understand questions in English. His first and highest level of design breaks the computer down into subsystems, each of which is given intentionally characterized tasks; he composes a flow chart of evaluators, rememberers, discriminators, overseers and the like. These are *homunculi* with a vengeance; the highest level design breaks the computer down into a committee or army of intelligent homunculi with purposes, information and strategies. Each homunculus in turn is analysed into *smaller* homunculi, but, more important, into *less clever* homunculi. When the level is reached where the homunculi are no more than adders and subtractors, by the time they need only the intelligence to pick the larger of two numbers when directed to, they have been reduced to functionaries "who can be replaced by a machine". The aid to comprehension of anthropomorphiz-ing the elements just about lapses at this point, and a mechanistic view of the proceedings becomes workable and comprehensible. The AI pro-grammer uses intentional language fearlessly because he *knows* that if he succeeds in getting his program to run, any questions he has been begging provisionally will have been paid back. The computer is more unforgiving than any human critic; if the program works then we can be certain that all homunculi have been discharged from the theory.*

Working backwards in this way has proved to be a remarkably fruit-ful research strategy, for powerful principles of design have been developed and tested, so it is interesting to note that the overall shape of AI models is strikingly similar to the organization proposed for our post-Skinnerian mutations, and the problems encountered echo the problems faced by the behaviorist. A ubiquitous strategy in AI pro-gramming is known as *generate-and-test*, and our opening quotation of Paul Valéry perfectly describes it. The problem solver (or inventor) is broken down at some point or points into a generator and a tester. The generator spews up candidates for solutions or elements of solutions to the problems, and the tester accepts or rejects them on the basis of stored criteria. Simon points out the analogy, once again, to natural selection (*op. cit.* pp. 95–98).

The tester of a generate-and-test subroutine is none other than a part of the inner environment of our post-Skinnerian mutations, so if we want to know how well the principle of selection by inner environ-ment can work, the answer is that it can work as well as generate-and-test methods can work in AI programs, which is hearteningly well.** Simon, as we saw at the outset, was prepared to go so far as to con-clude that *all* "human problem solving, from the most blundering to the most insightful" can be captured in the net of generate-and-test programming: "varying mixtures of trial and error and selectivity." This claim is exactly analogous to the behaviorists' creed that the Law of Effect could explain all learning, and again we may ask whether this

---

*Cf. Chapters 1 and 11. In *Content and Consciousness* I scorned theories that replaced the little man in the brain with a committee. This was a big mistake, for this is just how one gets to "pay back" the "intelligence loans" of intentionalist theories. Several levels of homuncular discharge are pictured in the flow charts from Colby's *Artificial Paranoia* reproduced on pp. 119–121.

**Hubert Dreyfus would disagree—see *What Computers Can't Do: A Critique of Artificial Reason* (Harper & Row, 1973)—but Dreyfus has not succeeded in demon-strating any *a priori* limits to generate-and-test systems hierarchically organized, so his contribution to date is salutary scepticism, not refutation.

is short-sighted allegiance to an idea that is good, but not the only good idea. Generate-and-test programs can simulate, and hence account for (in one important sense)* a lot of problem-solving and invention; what grounds have we for supposing it is powerful enough to handle it all? The behaviorist was in no position to defend his creed, but the AI researcher is in better shape.

Some AI researchers have taken their task to be the *simulation* of particular cognitive capacities "found in nature"—even the capacities and styles of particular human individuals[10] —and such research is known as CS or "cognitive simulation" research, but others take their task to be, not simulation, but the construction of intelligent programs *by any means whatever*. The only constraint on design principles in AI thus viewed is that they should *work*, and hence any boundaries the AI programmer keeps running into are arguably boundaries that restrict *all possible* modes of intelligence and learning. Thus, if AI is truly the study of all possible modes of intelligence, and if generate-and-test is truly a necessary feature of AI learning programs, then generate-and-test is a necessary feature of all modes of learning, and hence a necessary principle in any adequate psychological theory.

Both premises in that argument need further support. The first premise was proposed on the grounds that AI's guiding principle is that *anything is permitted that works*, but isn't AI really more restrictive than that principle suggests? Isn't it really that AI is the investigation of all possible *mechanistically realizable* modes of intelligence? Doesn't AI's claim to cover all possible modes beg the question against the vitalist or dualist who is looking for a non-question-begging but also non-mechanistic psychology? The AI researcher is a mechanist, to be sure, but a mechanist-*malgré-lui*. He typically does not know or care what the hardware realizations of his designs will be, and often even relinquishes control and authorship of his programs at a point where they are still replete with intentionalistic constructions, still several levels away from machine language. He can do this because it is merely a clerical problem for compiler programs and the technicians that feed them to accomplish the ultimate "reduction" to a mechanistic level. The constraints of mechanism do not loom large for the AI researcher,

---

*There is a tradition of overstating the import of successful AI or CS (cognitive simulation) programs (e.g., "programs are theories and successful programs are confirmed theories"). For the moment all we need accept is the minimal claim that a successful program proves a particular sort of capacity to be in principle mechanistically realizable and hence mechanically explicable. Obviously much more can be inferred from successful programs, but it takes some detailed work to say what, where and why.

for he is confident that any design he can state *clearly* can be mechanized. The operative constraint for him, then, is something like clarity, and in practice clarity is ensured for anything expressible in a programming language of some level. Anything thus expressible is clear; what about the converse? Is anything clear thus expressible? The AI programmer believes it, but it is not something subject to proof; it is, or boils down to, some version of Church's Thesis (e.g., anything computable is Turing-machine computable). But now we can see that the supposition that there might be a non-question-begging non-mechanistic psychology gets you nothing, unless accompanied by the supposition that Church's Thesis is false. For a non-question-begging psychology will be a psychology that makes no ultimate appeals to unexplained intelligence, and that condition can be reformulated as the condition that whatever functional parts a psychology breaks its subjects into, the smallest, or most fundamental, or least sophisticated parts must not be supposed to perform tasks or follow procedures requiring intelligence. That condition in turn is surely strong enough to ensure that any procedure admissible as an "ultimate" procedure in a psychological theory falls well within the intuitive boundaries of the "computable" or "effective" as these terms are presumed to be used in Church's Thesis. The intuitively computable functions mentioned in Church's Thesis are those that "any fool can do", while the admissible atomic functions of a psychological theory are those that "presuppose *no* intelligence". If Church's Thesis is correct, then the constraints of mechanism are no more severe than the constraint against begging the question in psychology, for any psychology that stipulated atomic tasks that were "too difficult" to fall under Church's Thesis would be a theory with undischarged homunculi.* So our first premise, that AI is the study of all possible modes of intelligence, is supported as much as it could be, which is *not quite* total support, in two regards. The first premise depends on two unprovable but very reasonable assumptions: that Church's Thesis is true, and that *there can be*, in principle, an adequate and complete psychology.

That leaves the second premise to defend: what reason is there to believe that generate-and-test is a necessary and not merely handy and ubiquitous feature of AI learning programs? First, it must be granted

---

*Note that this does *not* commit the AI researcher to the view that "men are Turing machines". The whole point of generate-and-test strategies in program design is to *permit* computers to *hit on* solutions to problems they cannot be *guaranteed* to solve either because we can prove there is no algorithm for getting the solution or because if there is an algorithm we don't know it or couldn't use it. Hence the utility of generate-and-test and heuristics in programming (see also Chapter 13).

that many computer programs of great sophistication do not invoke any variety of generate-and-test. In these cases the correct or best steps to be taken by the computer are not selected but *given*; the program's procedures are completely designed and inflexible. These programs are the analogues of our merely tropistic creatures; their design is *fixed* by a prior design process. Sometimes there is a sequence of such programs, with the programmer making a series of changes in the program to improve its performance. Such genealogical developments do not so much represent problems solved as problems deferred, however, for the trick is to get the program to become self-designing, "to get the teacher out of the learner". As long as the programmer must, in effect, reach in and rewire the control system, the system is not *learning*. Learning can be viewed as *self-design*, and Simon suggests we "think of the design process as involving first the generation of alternatives and then the testing of these alternatives against a whole array of requirements and constraints" (*op. cit.*, p. 74). Of course he would suggest this, and we can follow his suggestion, but are there any alternatives? Is there any way of thinking (coherently) about the design process that is incompatible with (and more powerful than) thinking of it as an evolution wrought by generate-and-test? It seems not, and here is an argument supposed to show why. I suspect this argument could be made to appear more rigorous (while also, perhaps, being revealed to be entirely unoriginal) by recasting it into the technical vocabulary of some version of "information theory" or "theory of self-organizing systems". I would be interested to learn that this was so, but am content to let the argument, which is as intuitive as it is sketchy, rest on its own merits in the meantime.

We are viewing learning as ultimately a *process* of self-design. That process is for the purposes of this argument defined only by its *product*, and the product is a *new* design. That is, as a result of the process something comes to have a design it previously did not have. This new design "must come from somewhere". That is, it takes *information* to distinguish the new design from all other designs, and that information must come from somewhere—either all from outside the system, or all from inside, or a bit of both. If all from outside, then the system does not redesign itself; this is the case we just looked at, where the all-knowing programmer, who *has* the information, *imposes* the new design on the system from without. So the information must all come from inside, or from both inside and outside. Suppose it all comes from inside. Then either the information already exists inside or it is created inside. What I mean is this: either the new design *exists ready made* in the old design in the sense that its implementation at this time is already guaranteed by its old design, or the old design does not determine in this way what the new design will be. In the former case, the system has not really redesigned itself; it was designed all along to go into this phase at this time, and we must look to a prior design process to explain this. In the latter case, the new design is *underdetermined* by the old design. This is a feature shared with the one remaining possibility: that the information comes from both inside and outside. In both of these cases the new design is underdetermined by the old design by itself, and only in these cases is there "genuine" learning (as opposed to the merely "apparent" learning of the merely tropistic creature). In any such case of underdetermination, the new design is either underdetermined period—there is a truly random contribution here; nothing takes up all the slack left by the underdetermination of the old design—or the new design is determined by the combination of the old design and contributions (from either inside or outside or both) that are themselves *arbitrary*, that is, *undesigned* or *fortuitous*. But if the contribution of arbitrary elements is to yield a better than chance probability of the new design being an improvement over the old design, the old design must have the capacity to *reject* arbitrary contributions on the basis of design features— information—already present. In other words, there must be a *selection* from the fortuitous contributions, based on the old design. If the arbitrary or undesigned contribution comes from within, what we have is a non-deterministic automaton.* A non-deterministic automaton is one such that at some point or points its further operations must wait on the result of a procedure that is undetermined by its program and input. In other words, some tester must wait on some generator to produce a candidate for its inspection. If the undesigned contribution comes from the outside, the situation is much the same; the distinction between *input* and *random contribution* is just differently drawn. The automaton is now deterministic in that its next step is a determinate function of its program and its input, but what input it gets is a fortuitous matter. In either case the system can *protect itself* against merely fortuitous response to this merely fortuitous input only by *selecting* as a function of its old design from the fortuitous "stimulation" presented. Learning must tread the fine line between the idiocy of pre-programmed tropism on the one hand and the idiocy of an over-plastic domination by fortuitous impingements on the other. In short, every process of genuine learning (or invention, which is just

---

*Gilbert Harman points out in *Thought* (New Jersey: Princeton, 1973), that non-deterministic automata can be physically deterministic (if what is random relative to the program is determined in the machine).

a special sort of learning) must invoke, at at least one but probably many levels, the principle of generate-and-test.

The moral of this story is that cognitivist theoreticians of all stamps may proceed merrily and *fruitfully* with temporarily question-begging theoretical formulations, but if they expect AI to *pay their debts* some day (and if anything can, AI can), they must acknowledge that the *processes* invoked will inevitably bear the analogy to natural selection exemplified by the Law of Effect. The moral is *not*, of course, that behaviorism is the road to truth in psychology; even our hypothesized first-generation mutations of Skinnerian creatures were too intelligent for behaviorism to account for, and we have every reason to believe actual higher organisms are much more complicated than that. The only solace for the behaviorist in this account is that his theoretical paralysis has been suffered in a Good Cause; he has not begged the question, and if the high-flying cognitivists ever achieve his probity, it will only be by relying on principles fundamentally analogous to his.

This leaves open where these inevitable principles of selection will be invoked, and how often. Nothing requires generate-and-test formats to be simple and obviously mechanistic in any of their interesting realizations. On the contrary, *introspective* evidence, of a sort I will presently illustrate, seems to bear out the general claim that generate-and-test is a common and recognizable feature of human problem solving, at the same time that it establishes that the generators and testers with which we are *introspectively* familiar are themselves highly sophisticated—highly intelligent homunculi. As Simon points out, generate-and-test is not an efficient or powerful process unless the *generator* is endowed with a high degree of selectivity (so that it generates only the most likely or most plausible candidates in a circumstance), and since, as he says, "selectivity can always be equated with some kind of feedback of information from the environment" (p. 97), we must ask, of each sort and degree of selectivity in the generator, where *it* came from—is it learned or innate—and at the end of any successful answer to that question will be a generate-and-test process, either of natural selection if the selectivity is innate, or of some variety of learning, if it is not. A consequence of this is that we cannot tell by any simple inspection or introspection whether a particular stroke of genius we encounter is a bit of "genuine" invention at all—that is, whether the invention occurred just *now*, or is the result of much earlier processes of invention that are now playing out their effects. Did Einstein's genetic endowment guarantee his creativity, or did his genetic endowment together with his nurture, his stimulus history, guarantee his creativity or did he genuinely create (during his own thought processes), his great insights? I hope it is clear how little hinges on knowing the answer to this question.

At this point I am prepared to say that the first part of Valéry's claim stands vindicated: it takes two to invent anything: the one makes up combinations; the other one chooses. What of the second part of this claim: "What we call genius is much less the work of the first one than the readiness of the second one to grasp the value of what has been laid before him and to choose it"? We have seen a way in which this must be true, in the strained sense that the *ultimate* generators must contain an element of randomness or arbitrariness. "The original solution to a problem must lie in the category of luck."* But it does not seem that Valéry's second claim is true on any ordinary interpretation. For instance, it does not seem to be true of all *inter-personal* collaborations that the choosers are more the geniuses than their "idea-men" are. Some producers seldom offer poor suggestions; their choosers are virtual yes-men. Other producers are highly erratic in what they will propose, and require the censorship of severe and intelligent editors. There appears to be a trade-off here between, roughly, spontaneity or fertility of imagination on the one hand, and a critical eye on the other. A task of invention seems to require both, and it looks like a straightforwardly empirical question subject to continuous variation how much of each gets done by each collaborator.

Valéry seems to slight the contribution of the first, but perhaps that is just because he has in mind a collaboration at one end of the spectrum, where a relatively undiscriminating producer of combinations makes a lot of work for his editor. Of course, as said at the outset, Valéry is not talking about actual interpersonal collaboration, but of a bifurcation in the soul. He is perhaps thinking of his own case, which suggests that he is one of those who are *aware* of considering and rejecting many bad ideas. He does not credit *his* producer-homunculus with much genius, and is happy to identify with the *responsible* partner, the chooser. Mozart, it seems, was of the same type: "When I feel well and in a good humor, or when I am taking a drive or walking after a good meal, or in the night when I cannot sleep, thoughts crowd into my mind as easily as you would wish. Whence and how do they come? I do not know and *I have nothing to do with it.* Those which please me I keep in my head and hum them; at least others have told me that I

*Arthur Koestler, in *The Act of Creation* (1964):p. 559, quotes the behaviorist E. R. Guthrie to this effect, but it is a misquotation, sad to say, for had Guthrie said what Koestler says he said, he would have said something true and important. Perhaps he did say it, but not on the page, or in the book, where Koestler says he said it.

do so."[11] In such cases the producer-chooser bifurcation lines up with the unconscious and conscious selves bifurcation. One is conscious only of the *products* of the producer, which one then consciously tests and chooses.

Poincaré, in a famous lecture of 1908, offers an "introspective" account of some mathematical inventing of his own that is more problematic: "One evening, contrary to my custom, I drank black coffee and could not sleep. Ideas rose in crowds; I felt them collide until pairs interlocked, so to speak, making a stable combination."[12] In this instance the chooser seems to have disappeared, but Poincaré has another, better interpretation of the incident. In this introspective experience he has been given a rare opportunity to glimpse the *processes* in the generator; what is normally accomplished out of sight of consciousness is witnessed on this occasion, and the ideas that form stable combinations are those few that would normally be presented to the conscious chooser for further evaluation. Poincaré supposes he has watched the selectivity within the generator at work. I am not a little sceptical about Poincaré's claimed *introspection* here (I think all introspection involves elements of rational reconstruction, and I smell a good deal of that in Poincaré's protocol), but I like his categories. In particular, Poincaré gives us, in his discussion of this experience, the key to another puzzling question.

For I have really had two burdens in this paper. The first, which I take to have discharged, is to explain why the Law of Effect is so popular in its various guises. The other is to explain why it is so *unpopular* in all its guises. There is no denying that the Law of Effect seems to be an affront to our self-esteem, and a lot of the resistance—even hatred— encountered by behaviorists is surely due to this. Poincaré puts his finger on it. He was, if anyone ever has been, a creative and original thinker, and yet his own analysis of how he accomplished his inventions seemed to deny him *responsibility* for them. He saw only two alternatives, both disheartening. One was that his unconscious self, the generator with whom he does not or cannot *identify* "is capable of discernment; it has tact, delicacy; it knows how to choose, to divine. What do I say? It knows better how to divine than the conscious self since it succeeds where that has failed. In a word, is not the subliminal self superior to the conscious self? I confess that, for my part, I should hate to accept this."[13] The other is that the generator is an automaton, an ultimately absurd, blind trier of all possibilities. That is of course no better a homunculus with whom to identify oneself. One does not want to be the generator, then. As Mozart says of his musical ideas: "Whence and how do they come? I do not know and I have nothing to do with it.''* Nor does one want to be just the tester, for then one's chances of being creative depend on the luck one has with one's collaborator, the generator. The fundamental passivity of the testing role leaves no room for the "creative self."** But we could not have hoped for any other outcome. If we are to have any adequate *analysis* of creativity, invention, intelligence, it must be one in which intelligence is analysed into something none of whose parts is intelligence, and at that level of analysis, of course, no "self" worth identifying with can survive.

The mistake in this pessimism lies in confusing explaining with explaining away. Giving a non-question-begging account of *how* creatures are intelligent can hardly prove that they aren't intelligent. If we want to catch a glimpse of a creative self, we should look, for instance, at M. Poincaré, for *he* (and not any of his proper parts) was certainly a genius.

Finally, I cannot resist passing on a wonderful bit of incidental intelligence reported by Hadamard: the Latin verb *cogito* is derived, as St. Augustine tell us, from Latin words meaning *to shake together*, while the verb *intelligo* means *to select among*. The Romans, it seems, knew what they were talking about.

*Peter Kivy has drawn my attention to the fact that Mozart scholars agree that the famous letter quoted above is spurious. Mozart, then, may not have been the Valéry type, but the author of the letter did in any case accurately describe one sort of creative process.

**This passivity is curiously evoked by Koestler in his account of "underground games" in *The Act of Creation*. It is a tell-tale sign of the inescapability of the principle of selectivity discussed here that Koestler, the arch-enemy of behaviorism, can do no better, when he sets himself the task of composing a rival account of creativity, than to accept the generate-and-test format and then endow the generator with frankly mysterious effects of uncoincidental coincidence.

6

A Cure for the Common Code?

We and other creatures exhibit intelligent behavior, and since the regular production of such behavior requires thought, and since thought requires representation, and since nothing can represent except within a system, we must be endowed with and utilize a system of internal representation having its own "grammar" and "vocabulary", which we might call the language of thought.

This argument has seldom been brought into the open and examined, but behind the scenes it has motivated and flavored large bodies of philosophical doctrine, and strongly influenced research strategies and theories in psychology, linguistics, computer science and neurophysiology. It is worth asking why such an influential move has been so comfortably ignored until recently. It is not plausibly one of those drifts of thought that seem too obvious to need spelling out; perhaps it has been avoided because once one attempts to put the argument in proper and explicit shape, incoherencies, paradoxes, infinite regresses and other alarming implications seem to arise at every turning. Now Jerry Fodor, in *The Language of Thought*, Crowell, 1975, has done us the fine service of propounding and defending a vigorous, unblinking, and ingenious version of the argument. Many of his conclusions seem outrageous, and the threats of incoherency are now close to the surface, but Fodor argues with great persuasiveness that these are in fact parts of the foundation of deservedly esteemed schools of thought in philosophy, cognitive psychology and linguistics. If he has produced an unintended *reductio ad absurdum* (a possibility he cheerfully admits), some of our favorite edifices will topple with him. He may be wrong, of course, but the challenge is well presented, and since recently thinkers in all the jeopardized fields have been converging on just the perplexities Fodor discusses, the challenge will not be ignored. The main issue treated in Fodor's book is fast becoming a major topic of interdisciplinary interest, and philosophers of mind who have squeezed the last drops of enlightenment out of the debate over the identity theory or the individuation of actions should be pleased to find here some important and fascinating problems to engage their talents. What is needed is nothing less than a completely general theory of representation, with which we can explain how words, thoughts, thinkers, pictures, computers, animals, sentences, mechanisms, states, functions, nerve impulses, and formal models (*inter alia*) can be said to represent one thing or another. It will not do to divide and conquer here—by saying that these various things do not represent in the same sense. Of course that is true, but what is important is that there is something that binds them all together, and we need a theory that can unify the variety. Producing such a theory is surely a philosophical endeavor, but philosophers must recognize that some of the most useful and suggestive work currently being done on the problems is being done by psychologists, linguists, and workers in artificial intelligence.

For what it is worth, Fodor probably holds uniquely strong professional credentials for the task of consolidating the insights from these fields, for he holds a joint appointment in psychology and philosophy (at M.I.T., a major centre for work in linguistics and artificial intelligence) and has made important contributions to experimental psycholinguistics and linguistics in addition to his work in philosophy. Fodor is not beset by the philosophical naiveté of many of his colleagues in psychology and he has as powerful a grasp of current thinking in linguistics and psychology as anyone in philosophy. Indeed, the overall savvy of his book is one of its most striking characteristics, mainly for good but also for ill. There cannot be many readers well equipped or disposed to appreciate all his knowing nudges; the uninitiated will perhaps be the unpersuaded (and unamused) as well. I fear that Fodor's unfailing high spirits and jocosity may hurt his cause by irritating as many readers as they amuse. I find the book genuinely witty, however, and can only urge those who resent being tickled while engaged in such serious business to make an extra effort to distinguish the medium from the message.

Fodor's message has three parts. First he describes and promotes a brand of theorizing he calls cognitive psychology, but clearly he means to cast his net wider, and in places narrower, than that term would suggest. The distinguishing mark of this theorizing is the unapologetic utilization of intentional characterizations of processes and "intellectualist" analyse of perception and other "cognitive processes" in terms of information-flow, hypothesis-testing, inference and decision-making. Within its boundaries fall much current psychology, linguistics, artificial intelligence, and some strains of thought in current philosophy. Let us call it neocognitivism, for it is not markedly continuous with earlier schools of cognitive psychology, nor is it all clearly psychology. It has developed largely in recognition of the impotence of (psychological and logical) behaviorism, and its inspiration is drawn largely from linguistics, computer science and (come to think of it) the last three hundred years of epistemology. Fodor attempts to establish the credentials of neocognitivism by showing how it avoids the doldrums of Rylean logical behaviorism, steers between the Scylla of dualism and the Charybdis of reductionism to emerge as the only straw floating—as Jerome Lettvin once put it. In this first part Fodor has a strong and persuasive case on almost all counts.

Fodor's second task is to show that this best hope for a confirmed, powerful psychological theory inescapably requires the postulation of internal representational systems. These systems, though designed for computation rather than communication, have structures—and other features—so like those of natural languages that we may—and should—speak of the language of thought: the medium in which the computational transactions are performed that ultimately govern our behavior and the behavior of other intelligent creatures as well. This is the philosophic heart of Fodor's book, and will receive detailed attention below.

Third, Fodor completes his book with two lengthy chapters purporting to show how evidence from linguistics and psychology establishes answers to an impressive variety of questions about 'the structure of the internal code'. Having proved the existence of Planet X, he proceeds to detail its climate and geography for us, using data that had been available but hitherto mute. These chapters are undeniably compelling, for every now and then one gets glimmers of the sort of fruitful falling-into-place so seldom encountered in psychology or philosophy of mind. Whereas, for instance, behaviorism has always worn the guise of a properly endorsed method (a "methodology") in dogged search of results, here we seem to see an abundance of results and tempting hypotheses to test for which we must somehow concoct methodological permission.

For example, linguists have devised a variety of competing formal systems for more or less algorithmically generating or analysing sentences, and a question the psycholinguist asks is which if any proposed formalism has "psychological reality", or in other words describes or mirrors real psychological processes occurring in the production or comprehension of sentences. This empirical question is to be settled independently of the elegance or power of the formal systems. (One way of dividing 67 by 12 is to subtract 12 from 67, then subtract 12 from 55, and so forth, while counting the subtractions; another is long division; which if either has "psychological reality" for an individual human calculator is surely an empirical question, and *asking the calculator* is not the only, or always the best, way of answering the question.) Subtle studies of reaction times, relative difficulty of comprehension, patterns of errors, and so forth often provide satisfyingly clearcut verdicts on these questions, but often only if we make just the sorts of assumptions about representational machinery Fodor is attempting to vindicate. Whether these investigations will continue to ramify nicely is far from assured, however, and there is an abundance of danger signals for skeptics to make of what they can.

The conclusion Fodor wishes to draw from this examination is bracingly unqualified: " . . . having a propositional attitude is being in some *computational* relation to an internal representation". "Attitudes to propositions are . . . 'reduced' to attitudes to formulae, though the formulae are couched in a proprietary inner code" (p. 198). The inner code is innate, and one's innate vocabulary of predicates must be sufficient to represent, by logical construction, any predicate of any natural language one can learn. Once one learns such a predicate one may augment one's inner code with a synonym, as it were, of the natural language predicate and henceforward use this non-native inner word as an abbreviation for the cumbersome truth-functional molecule of native mentalese (p. 152). We are not born with an inner code word for "airplane" but if we couldn't form at the outset a predicate of inner mentalese at least coextensive with "airplane" we could never learn what "airplane" meant, could never add an "airplane"-synonym to our basic stock. So there is a sense in which one cannot "acquire new concepts" by learning a language, even one's mother tongue.

All this (and there is more) is hard to swallow, but what are the alternatives? Thinkers as diverse as B. F. Skinner, Norman Malcolm and Hubert Dreyfus have insisted that the very concept of neural systems of representation is a monstrous error. Let us call that the extreme right wing view. On the extreme left, then, would be researchers such as McConnell and Ungar, who take brain-writing so literally that they suppose one might physically extract token sentences of the inner code from one creature and teach another by injection or ingestion. (Ungar reports he has trained cats to fear the dark and then isolated a substance in them, "scotophobin", which injected into untrained cats causes them to fear the dark!) Middle-of-the-road positions have yet to be formulated in satisfactory detail, but it is safe to say that Fodor has laid claim to a position far to the left of center and is insisting that no less extreme position can provide the foundations for the promising theories of neocognitivism.

Let us return to the beginning and examine Fodor's case in some detail. Fodor takes his first task to be protecting neo-cognitivism from two philosophic threats: Ryle's attack on intellectualist theorizing, and the physicalist demand that all theoretical terms be reducible somehow to the terms of physics. Fodor sees these as in different ways suggesting the charge that neo-cognitivism is dualistic (a verdict Fodor would view as at least discouraging and probably fatal). The charge is familiar: the characteristic predicates of cognitive psychology are intentional or "mentalistic" idioms, and since mentalism is dualism, cognitive psychology is dualistic. Certainly in the past this has been an influential train of thought; Brentano did after all reintroduce the concept of intentionality precisely as the distinguishing mark of the non-physical, and (though probably not influenced by Brentano) Skinner has for years seen the spectre of dualism in every variety of "mentalistic" theorizing. The claim has not however figured influentially in recent philosophic work in the area. On the contrary, the coexistence of physicalistic doctrine with intentional or mentalistic vocabulary, while perhaps not having received the justification it ought to have, is a typically undefended and unattacked feature of current discussions.

It is a bit curious then that a rebuttal of the dualism charge should find pride of place in Fodor. Perhaps he is addressing the many psychologists who haven't heard and are still swayed by Skinner's suspicions. More curious still is Fodor's choice of Ryle as the initial target of his rebuttal. In *Psychological Explanation* (1968) Fodor went to great lengths to refute his version of Ryle's "logical behaviorism" and in 1975 he has still not been able to remove his hands from this tar-baby. Now it is clearer why Ryle should exercise him so, for he has clarified his interpretation with a cute example: "Why are Wheaties (as the ads say) the breakfast of champions?" "Because," says the dietician, "they contain vitamins, etc." "Because," says the Rylean, "they are eaten for breakfast by a non-negligible number of champions." The former is a "causal" explanation, the latter a "conceptual" explanation and, according to Fodor, Ryle's view is that the latter explanation is in competition with the former. When a question should have a conceptual answer, it cannot have a causal answer as well. Questions like "What makes the clown's clowning clever?" have conceptual answers and, according to Fodor's Ryle, therefore cannot have causal answers —"Alas for the psychology of clever clowning."

Fodor's demolition of this notion should be, and is, obvious, and as an interpretation of Ryle it is almost right: the Wheaties example does most effectively illuminate a central Rylean distinction, and there are many passages in *The Concept of Mind* that could be cited to support the claim that Ryle deserves to be so interpreted. But Ryle does not, as Fodor thinks, offer *The Concept of Mind* as a psychological theory or as a substitute for psychology or as a proof that psychology can't be done. Fodor seems to be pointing out that questions like "What makes the clowning clever?" are ambiguous, but he does not see, or accept, the implication that in such cases there are two questions one can be asking. If there are two questions, it can be true that one cannot answer a question requiring a conceptual answer with a causal answer, which is Ryle's point, without it being true that psychology and philosophy of mind are in competition. Fodor has construed Ryle's attack on intellectualist theorizing (involving the postulation of inner cognitive processes) as an attack on intellectualist solutions to problems in psychology, while Ryle intended it primarily as an attack on intellectualist solutions to the conceptual problems of philosophy. In fairness to Fodor's interpretation, Ryle does strongly suggest that cognitivistic or "para-mechanical" hypotheses and the like are bankrupt as psychology as well (see especially the last chapter of *The Concept of Mind*) and against that excessive strain in Ryle's thought Fodor's arguments—and indeed the whole book—are a welcome antidote. But in the process of magnifying and rebutting the worst in Ryle, Fodor misconstrues Ryle in another fashion that leads him to overlook a more penetrating Rylean objection to his enterprise. "Ryle assumes", Fodor tells us, ". . . that a mentalist must be a dualist; in particular, that mentalism and materialism are mutually exclusive." Hence the "tendency to see the options of dualism and behaviorism as exhaustive in the philosophy of mind" (p. 4). Were we to replace "Ryle" with "Skinner" and "philosophy of mind" with "psychology" in this passage there would be no quarrel, but in the sense of the term in which behaviorism is the chief rival empirical theory to Fodor's mentalism, Ryle is no behaviorist but a sort of mentalist himself. Ryle does not attempt, as Skinner does, to explicate mentalistic predicates "(just) in terms of stimulus and response variables" (p. 8). On the contrary, his explications are typically replete with intentional idioms. Ryle's familiar account of vanity, for instance (whatever its problems) is not that vanity is a disposition to perform certain locomotions, utter certain sounds, respond to certain stimuli, but that it is a disposition to try to make oneself prominent, to ignore criticism, talk about oneself, avoid recalling past failures, "indulge in roseate daydreams about his own successes" (*The Concept of Mind*, p. 86). What kind of behaviorism is that? Not any kind to be found in psychology. Ryle's disagreements with Fodor are fundamental, but they are not to be discovered by allying Ryle with Skinner.

Perhaps Ryle's view can again be illuminated by a fanciful example. Suppose someone were benighted enough to think the monthly bank statement he received was a historical description of actual transfers of currency among thousands of labelled boxes in bank vaults. He is informed of an overdraft and puts forward a theory of anti-dollars, vacuums and vortices to explain it. The Rylean explains that *nothing like that* is what makes it the case that the account is overdrawn and gives a "conceptual" account of the situation. The "logical behaviorist" account of overdrafts is the one we are usually interested in. Of course there is a mechanical story about what happens at the bank that can be told as well, and perhaps knowing it will help us understand the conceptual account, but the two are distinct.

Fodor does not seem to see this point in application to psychology, for he wishes to maintain with regard to the clever clown "that it is the fact that the behavior was caused by such [inner cognitive] events that makes it the kind of behavior it is; that intelligent behavior *is* intelligent because it has the kind of etiology it has" (p. 3—but see also n. 2 of p. 29, where Fodor qualifies this). This claim burkes Ryle's distinction and leads Fodor, I hope to show later, to a mistaken account of of what makes it the case that something represents something.

Setting aside this difficulty, Fodor has shown, *contra* Ryle, that there is some real work that the mentalistic terms of cognitive psychology might do, but could they do this work while being faithful to the spirit of materialism? Fodor argues that the reasonable belief in the generality of physics, and the reasonable desire that the various sciences be somehow unified, have engendered unreasonably strong demands that the theoretical predicates of the "special" sciences, and psychology in particular, be "reducible" to the predicates of physics. Fodor's critique of reductionism and concomitant defence of functionalism is consonant with other recent accounts, especially Putnam's, but makes important additions of detail to this emerging orthodoxy. The unreasonableness of reductionism is nicely illustrated by a discussion of its application to Gresham's Law; a very clear account is given of type and token physicalism and natural kinds, and there is an especially useful development of the claim that it is a mistake to try to make the laws of the unreduced sciences exceptionless. We should look for the laws of physics to be exceptionless, but these laws should not, as the reductionist requires, guarantee that the laws of the reduced sciences have no exceptions, but rather provide an explanation of the exceptions encountered. To reconstrue the laws of the special sciences so that their predicates were locked with the predicates of physics would be to abandon the very utility of the predicates that gave birth to the special sciences in the first place.

Fodor offers a specific positive account of the logical relations that may hold between the terms of a special science (say psychology) and a reducing science (either physiology or physics) which goes far toward establishing the proper independence of the former. I think it could go farther. Fodor shows how a special science can be neutral with regard to variation in physical realization, and can tolerate variety in the physical tokenings of its types even within the individual, but I think he unnecessarily rules out the possibility that there could be a law of a special science, even an exceptionless law, where there were no *laws* of the reducing sciences relating all the tokenings (because the regularities in token sequences could only be described by conditionals with highly disjunctive antecedents and consequents). It seems essential that he allow for and explain this possibility, for it is fundamental to the capacity of well designed systems to "absorb" random or merely fortuitous noise, malfunction, interference. The account Fodor gives does not permit the brain to tolerate typographical errors in the inner code, so far as I can see.

Fodor supposes his arguments obtain methodological permission to use mentalistic predicates in theory construction. Why should we want them? Because it is "self-evident that organisms often believe the behavior they produce to be of a certain kind and that it is often part of the explanation of the way that an organism behaves to advert to the beliefs it has about the kind of behavior it produces" (p. 28). In other words, Fodor does not believe another reasoned obituary of behaviorism would be worth space in his book. Very well, but what, exactly, is "self-evident"? Fodor believes that the everyday, lay explanations of behavior (of both people and beasts) in terms of beliefs and desires are of a piece with the sophisticated information-flow explanations of the neo-cognitivists, so that the self-evident acceptability of "the dog bit me because he thought I was someone else" ensures the inevitable theoretical soundness of something like "the dog's executive routine initiated the attack subroutine because in the course of perceptual analysis it generated and misconfirmed a false hypothesis about the identity of an object in its environment". Fodor recognizes that it is a fairly large step from everyday, personal-level intentional explanations to theory-bound sub-personal level intentional explanations but impatiently dismisses the worry that anything important to his enterprise might hinge on how he took the step: "There is, obviously, a horribly difficult problem about what determines what a person (as distinct from his body, or parts of his body) did. Many philosophers care terrifically about drawing this distinction . . . but . . . there is no particular reason to suppose that it is relevant to the purposes of cognitive psychology" (p. 52). We shall see.

Fodor's next task is to show how neo-cognitivist theory is unavoidably committed to a language of thought. He begins by offering three different but related demonstrations, and similar problems attend each. First, Fodor presents a schema for neo-cognitivist theories of "considered action". Any such theory will suppose the

agent finds himself in a certain situation (S) . . . believes that a certain set of behavioral options . . . are available to him . . ., computes a set of hypotheticals roughly of the form if B_1 is performed in S, then, with a certain probability, C_1 . . . . A preference ordering is assigned to the consequences. . . . The organism's choice of behavior is determined as a function of the preferences and the probabilities assigned (p. 28-29).

In other words, a normative decision theory is to be adapted as a natural history of cognitive processes in the organism, and for such a history to be true, agents must "have means for representing their behavior to themselves". "For, according to the model, deciding is a computational process; the act the agent performs is the consequence of computations defined over representations of possible actions. No representations, no computations. No computations, no model" (p. 31). Moreover, "an infinity of distinct representations must belong to the system" for "there is no upper bound to the complexity of the representation that may be required to specify the behavioral options available to the agent" (p. 31).

Note that this argument assumes there is a clear line between computational processes and other processes, and another between considered action and mere reactivity. Fodor does not intend his argument to apply only to the psychology of human beings, but how plausible is it that a mole or a chicken or a fish is capable of representing behavioral options of unbounded complexity? The famous four F's (fighting, fleeing, feeding and sexual intercourse) would seem to be a plausible initial tally of options, and even if we allow, say, a dozen variations on each theme, we hardly need a productive representation system to provide internal vehicles for them all, and the process that led to the appropriate "choice" in such a case would not often appear to be computational, unless all processes are. Presumably a diving bell does not compute its equilibrium depth in the water, though it arrives at it by a process of diminishing "corrections". Does a fish compute its proper depth of operations? Is there an important qualitative difference between the processes in the fish and the diving bell?

Fodor's way of dealing with these problems is best understood by contrast with the paths not taken. Fodor could have claimed that only the behavior of human beings (and other smart creatures of his choosing) is governed by truly computational processes, or he could have gone to the other extreme and granted the diving bell its computational processes. Or he could have defended an intermediate position along these lines: all creatures of noticeable intelligence make decisions (I who "care terrifically" would insist that at best something decision-like occurs within them) and as we ascend the phylogenetic scale the decision-processes are more and more aptly characterized as computational; all creatures of noticeable intelligence have at least rudimentary representational systems, but only in higher creatures are these systems language-like in being productive or generative. Instead, he adopts the line that there is a radical discontinuity between computational and non-computational processes: "What distinguishes what organisms do . . . is that a *representation of the rules they follow constitutes one of the causal determinants of their behavior*" (p. 74, n. 15). If Fodor is to distinguish this claim from the other options he must mean that these rules are *explicitly* represented (not implicitly represented in virtue of functional organization, that is), and this is the radical heart of Fodor's position. I will discuss some problems with it later.

Fodor's second demonstration concerns what he calls concept learning: roughly, coming to distinguish and attach importance to some particular class of things or stimuli in one's environment (e.g., learning about green apples, or learning not to press the bar until the buzzer sounds, or learning to put the red circles in one pile and everything else in another). Fodor claims that "there is only one kind of theory that has ever been proposed for concept learning—indeed, there would seem to be only one kind of theory that is conceivable—and this theory [that concept learning proceeds by hypothesis formation and confirmation] is incoherent unless there is a language of thought" (p. 36). Why? Because the hypotheses formed must be "couched" in representations. A striking point Fodor makes about this is that experiments can distinguish between *logically equivalent* but "notationally" different formulations of hypotheses in concept learning. The idea is that taking the spades out of a deck of cards is easier, oddly enough, than leaving all the cards that are not spades in the deck. When presented with the latter task if one does not think "in other words . . ." one's performance will suffer. Does this consideration, and similar ones, not establish beyond a shadow of a doubt the "psychological reality" of the representations? As in the first case, it all depends on how far Fodor is prepared to descend with his talk of representations. What is somewhat plausible in the case of human beings is not at all plausible in the case of lower animals, and it seems that even insects can achieve *some* concept learning. Either some very primitive concept learning does not require hypothesis formation and confirmation, or if it all does, some hypotheses are formed but not "couched", or just about any feature on the inside of a creature can be considered a representation. Certainly the psychological reality of something functioning in some ways rather like a representation is established by the results Fodor cites, but Fodor has prepared a buttered slide for us and anyone who does not want to get on it might well dig in the heels at this point and ask for more details.

Fodor's third demonstration concerns perception. Here his point is that, as empiricists have insisted (for all the wrong reasons) "the sensory data which confirm a given perceptual hypothesis are typically internally represented in a vocabulary that is impoverished compared to the vocabulary in which the hypotheses themselves are couched" (p. 44). For instance, the empiricists would say that my hypothesis is that there is an apple out there, and my data are that I seem to see this red round patch. Fodor likes the idea of perception proceeding by a series of computational processes taking descriptions in one vocabulary and using them to confirm hypothesized descriptions in another vocabulary, and the main thing he sees wrong with empiricist versions of this is their penchant for couching the given in the "theory-free language of qualia" rather than the "theory-laden language of values of physical parameters" (p. 48). What is given is the excitation of a sensory mechanism sensitive to a physical property. "Hence, there is no reason to believe that the organism cannot be mistaken about what sensory descriptions apply in any given case" (p. 48). But here Fodor seems to me to have lost track of the important distinction between the content of a signal to the system it informs, and the content we on the outside can assign it when we describe the signal and the system of which it is a part. For instance, one badly misconceives the problem of perception if one views the retinal receptors as "telling" the first level of hypotheses testers "red wavelength light at location L again", for that level does not utilize or understand (in *any* impoverished sense) information of that sort. What it gets in the way of data are at best reports with uninterpreted dummy predicates ("it is intensely F at location L again") and out of these it must confirm its own dummy hypotheses.* In fact is either way of talking appropriate? The *vocabulary* of the signals is not something that is to be settled by an examination of tokens, at least at this level, and when we turn to indirect evidence of "psychological reality" any evidence we turn up will perforce be neutral between interpreted and uninterpreted predicates.

What content is to be assigned to events in the nervous system subserving perception? That, I take it, is a rather important question for cognitive psychology to answer. It cannot be answered, I submit, until one gets quite careful about who (or what, if anything) has access to the candidate representation—for whom or for what the thing in question is a representation. As Michael Arbib has suggested, what the frog's eye tells the frog's brain is not what the frog's eye tells the frog.

Fodor rather nonchalantly dismisses such distinctions. Why are they important? Suppose we make the following extension of his main argument. The only psychology that could possibly succeed is neo-cognitivist, which requires the postulation of an internal system of representations. However, nothing is intrinsically a representation of anything; something is a representation only *for* or *to* someone; any representation or system of representations requires at least one *user* of the system who is external to the system. Call such a user an *exempt agent.* Hence, in addition to a system of internal representations, neo-cognitivism requires the postulation of an inner exempt agent or agents—in short, undischarged homunculi. Any psychology with undischarged homunculi is doomed to circularity or infinite regress, hence psychology is impossible (see Chapters 5 and 7 of this volume, where these claims are expanded and examined at length).

The problem is an old one. Hume wisely shunned the notion of an inner self that would intelligently manipulate the ideas and impressions, but this left him with the necessity of getting the ideas to "think for themselves". His associationistic couplings of ideas and impressions, his pseudo-chemical bonding of each idea to its predecessor and successor, is a notorious non-solution to the problem. Fodor's analogous problem is to get the internal representations to "understand themselves", and one is initially inclined to view Hume's failure as the harbinger of doom

---

*Cf. J. J. C. Smart, *Philosophy and Scientific Realism* (London: Routledge & Kegan Paul, 1963), on "topic-neutral reports". The epistemic status of reports with uninterpreted predicates and reports with qualia-predicates would seem to be the same.

for all remotely analogous enterprises. But perhaps the *prima facie* absurd notion of self-understanding representations is an idea whose time has come, for what are the "data structures" of computer science if not just that: representations that understand themselves? In a computer, a command to dig goes straight to the shovel, as it were, eliminating the comprehending and obeying middleman. Not *straight* to the shovel, of course, for a lot of sophisticated switching is required to get the right command going to the right tools, and for some purposes it is illuminating to treat parts of this switching machinery as analogous to the displaced shovellers, subcontractors and contractors. The beauty of it all, and its importance for psychology, is precisely that it promises to solve Hume's problem by giving us a model of vehicles of representation that function without exempt agents for whom they are ploys. Alternatively, one could insist that the very lack of exempt agents in computers to be the users of the putative representations shows that computers do not contain representations—real representations—at all, but unless one views this as a rather modest bit of lexicographical purism, one is in danger of discarding one of the most promising conceptual advances ever to fall into philosophers' hands.

Fodor almost parenthetically makes these points (in a footnote on p. 74, where he roundly rebuts an ill-considered version of the homunculus argument of mine). He is justly unafraid of homunculi, for they are at most just picturesquely described parts of the switching machinery that ensures the functional roles of the inner messages, but fails to recognize that they still play the theoretical role of fixing the "topic" and "vocabulary" of the messages they communicate. If viewing messages of the inner code as self-understanding representations in this fashion can save Fodor's enterprise from incoherence—and in principle I think it can—it does so by adding constraints to the notion of an internal representation system that emphasize rather than eliminate the distinction between personal level attributions of beliefs and desires and sub-personal level attributions of content to intrasystemic transactions. If there is any future for internal systems of representation it will not be for languages of thought that "represent our beliefs to us", except in the most strained sense. Fodor notices the the strain (p. 52) but decides to tolerate it. The result, for all its vividness, is at least misleading in a way that has an analogy in the history of science. The problem of genetic inheritance used to look all but insoluble. Did the sperm cell contain a tiny man, and if so did the tiny man have sperm cells containing tiny men and so forth *ad infinitum*? Or did the sperm cell contain a picture or description of a human being, and if so, what looked at the picture or read the description? The truth turns out to be scarcely less marvellous than the "absurd" speculations, what with self-reading, self-duplicating codes and their supporting machinery, but anyone who had insisted all along that somehow the mother finds out from the sperm what sort of baby the father wants would not have been pointing in just the right direction. (This sidelong glance at DNA serves the additional purpose of reminding the skeptics who view the contraptions of artificial intelligence as hopelessly inefficient and 'inorganic' that nature has proved not to be stingy when it comes to micro-engineering solutions to hard problems.)

Earlier I claimed that Fodor's view of computational processes commits him to a radical view of representation. The problems with this hard line on the psychological reality of explicit representations are apparent—indeed, are deliberately made apparent, to Fodor's credit— in his discussion of language learning. His argument is that the process of learning the meaning of a word, even the initial words of one's native tongue, is and must be a process of hypothesis formation and confirmation, and in particular,

> among the generalizations about a language that the learner must hypothesize and confirm are some which determine the extensions of the predicates of that language. A generalization that effects such a determination is, by stipulation, a *truth rule*. (p. 59)

For instance, the truth rule for "is a chair" is "⌜y is a chair⌝ is true iff* Gx" where "G" is a predicate of one's internal code. Fodor seems to think that the only hypotheses which could *determine* the extension of a natural language predicate would have to be confirmed hypotheses explicitly about that predicate and having the explicit form of a truth rule. But to play Fodor's own game for a moment, couldn't a child learn *something that determined* the extension of "is a chair" by *disconfirming* the following hypotheses (and others):

⌜x is a chair⌝ is true iff x is red
⌜x is a chair⌝ is true iff x is in the living room
⌜x is a chair⌝ is true iff x has a cushion

and, perhaps, confirming—even *mis*confirming—others, e.g., "⌜x is a chair⌝ is true if x is this object here or that object there", and "⌜x is a chair⌝ is true only if x would support Daddy's weight", without ever *explicitly* representing a confirmed truth rule for "is a chair"? I suspect that Fodor's reply would be that to learn something determining the

*The term "iff" is logicians' shorthand for "if and only if".

extension of "is a chair" the child must explicitly conjoin all the confirmed hypotheses and the negations of the disconfirmed hypotheses and that somehow this amounts to the confirmation of the explicit truth rule for "is a chair", but aside from the implausibility of this as a story of real computational processes (but remember DNA) one wants to know what could conceivably count against the presumably empirical claim that whatever could determine the extension of a predicate has the explicit form of a truth rule, if this example did not.

Perhaps Fodor has gratuitously overstated his own best case, for it seems as if he is committed to the impossible view that only explicit representation is representation, and (roughly) nothing can be believed, thought about or learned without being explicitly represented.

That is, one might think of cognitive theories as filling in explanation schema[ta] of, roughly, the form: *having the attitude R to proposition P is contingently identical to being in computational relation C to the formula (or sequence of formulae) F.* A cognitive theory, insofar as it was both true and general, would presumably explain the productivity of propositional attitudes by entailing infinitely many substitution instances of this schema: one for each of the propositional attitudes that the organism can entertain (p. 77).

Perhaps we "entertain" propositional attitudes either seriatim or at least in manageably small numbers at any one time, but the propositional attitudes we *have* far outstrip those we (in some sense) actively entertain. For instance, it should come as no news to any of you that zebras in the wild do not wear overcoats, but I hazard the guess that it *hadn't occurred* to any of you before just now. We all have believed it for some time but were not born believing it, so we must have come to believe it between birth and, say, age fifteen, but it is not at all plausible that this is a hypothesis any of us has explicitly formed or confirmed in our childhood, even unconsciously. It is not even plausible that having formed and confirmed other hypotheses entailing this fact about zebras, we (in our spare time?) explicitly *computed* this implication.

Fodor does seem to be committed to some such view as this, however. He backs into this corner by underestimating the viability of what he takes to be the only alternative, which he characterizes as a dispositional behavioral analysis of propositional attitudes. "A number of philosophers who ought to know better do, apparently, accept such views" Fodor says, never doubting that he has seen clearly to the very heart of such silliness. His version of dispositional analysis is so simplistic, however, that he thinks the notion is adequately buried by a quip:

"Pay me enough and I will stand on my head iff you say chair. But I know what 'is a chair' means all the same" (p. 63). It is of course true that the arduous piecemeal composition of dispositional definitions of propositional attitudes would be a bootless methodology for psychology (Ryle knew better than to attempt to say, precisely, just what his "multi-track" dispositions were), but if, as Fodor supposes, the representation-talk of cognitive psychology ultimately gets vindicated by such ploys as computer modelling of cognitive systems and processes, he must be committed in spite of himself to a version of Rylism. For a computer program is just a very complicated specification of a multi-track disposition (a disposition to be disposed under conditions A, B, C to be disposed under conditions X, Y, Z to be disposed . . . to give output O . . . etc.). Notationally distinct but equivalent programs are equivalent precisely in that they determine the same multi-track disposition.

Suppose research reveals all the psychologically real computational processes in Mary, and artificial intelligencers program a robot, Ruth, whose internal processes "model" Mary's as perfectly as you like. Suppose that Mary believes that *p*. So then does Ruth. But suppose the artificial intelligencers then give another robot, Sally, a program equivalent to Ruth's, but notationally and computationally different. Sally may not be a good psychological model of Mary, but Sally, like Ruth and Mary, believes that *p*.* That is, the ascription of all Mary's beliefs and desires (etc.) to Sally will be just as predictive as their ascription to Ruth so far as prediction of action goes. Sally's response delays, errors, and the like may not match Mary's, but this it not what belief ascription is supposed to predict or explain (cf. Fodor, p. 123). If one agrees with Fodor that it is the job of cognitive psychology to map the psychologically real processes in people, then since the ascription of belief and desire is only indirectly tied to such processes, one might well say that beliefs and desires are not the proper objects of study of cognitive psychology. Put otherwise, cognitivist theories are or should be theories of the subpersonal level, where beliefs and desires disappear, to be replaced with representations of other sorts on other topics.

But unless I am misreading Fodor, he will have none of this. His position simply is that since believing that snow is white could not be having a disposition to behave, it must be having a token of the mentalese translation of "snow is white" installed in some wonderful

*Perfect equivalence of programs is a very strong condition. I would hold it is a sufficient but not necessary condition for sharing intentional characterizations.

way in one's head. Perhaps I am misreading him by interpreting "being in a computational relation to a formula of the inner code" as implying the existence of a real token of that formula in some functionally characterized relation to the rest of the machinery, but the weaker alternative, *viz.*, that one is in a computational relation to a formula if one *can or would produce or use* a token of that formula in some way under some circumstance, invokes dispositionalism of just the sort Fodor has presumably forsworn.

None of this is to say that neural representations, even tokens of brain-writing, are impossible. It is not even to deny that the existence of such representations is a necessary condition for cognition. It may well turn out to be. But Fodor, by making explicit coding *criterial* for representation or contentfulness, has committed the very sin he imputes to Ryle: he has confused a conceptual answer with a causal answer. Like neo-cognitivists generally, Fodor wants to be able to assign content to events or other features of systems, to treat them as information-bearers or messages. What makes it the case ultimately that something in this sense represents something within a system is that it has a function within the system, in principle globally specifiable.* To say that it has the function of bearing a certain message or transmitting certain information is to talk in circles, but often in useful circles for the time being. Content is a function of function, then, but not every structure can realize every function, can reliably guarantee the normal relationships required. So function is a function of structure. There are, then, strong indirect structural constraints on things that can be endowed with content. If our brains were as homogeneous as jelly we could not think. Fodor, however, makes a direct leap from content to structure and seems moreover to make structure in the end criterial for content.

On his view a prescriptive theory (e.g., natural deduction or decision theory) can be predictive of behavior only if it is descriptive of inner processes. When we predict and explain the behavior of a system at the intentional level *our* calculations have a certain syntactic structure: to oversimplify, they are formal proofs or derivations, e.g., of descriptions of best actions to take given certain beliefs and preferences. We predict that the physical states or events to which we assign the premises as formulae will *cause* those states or events whose formulae are the later lines of our calculations (see, e.g., p. 73). Fodor seems to suppose that the only structures that could guarantee and explain the

---

*Ignoring for the moment the normative element in all intentional attributions (see Chapter 1 of this volume).

predictive power of our intentionalistic calculations (and permit us to assign formulae to states or events in a principled way) *must* mirror the syntax of those calculations. This is either trivially true (because the "syntactic" structure of events or states is defined simply by their function) or an empirical claim that is very interesting, not entirely implausible, and as yet not demonstrated or even argued for, so far as I can tell. For instance, suppose hamsters are interpretable as good Bayesians when it comes to the decisions they make. Must we in principle be able to find some saliencies in the hamsters' controls that are interpretable as tokens of formulae in some Bayesian calculus? If that is Fodor's conclusion, I don't see that he has given it the support it needs, and I confess to disbelieving it utterly.

In a recent conversation with the designer of a chess-playing program I heard the following criticism of a rival program: "It thinks it should get its queen out early." This ascribes a propositional attitude to the program in a very useful and predictive way, for as the designer went on to say, one can usually count on chasing that queen around the board. But for all the many levels of explicit representation to be found in that program, nowhere is anything roughly synonymous with "I should get my queen out early" explicitly tokened. The level of analysis to which the designer's remark belongs describes features of the program that are, in an entirely innocent way, emergent properties of the computational processes that have "engineering reality". I see no reason to believe that the relation between belief-talk and psychological-process talk will be any more direct.

Are all these doubts about Fodor's radical view swept away by the material in the second half of this book, where evidence is adduced about the structure, vocabulary and utilization of the inner code? The challenge of these chapters to the skeptic is to find a way of recasting what cannot be denied in them in terms less radical than Fodor's. I do not see that this cannot be done, but saying it is not doing it, and doing it would require a monograph. Fodor's account of the inner code in action is packed with detail and bold speculation, and is supported by a variety of elegant experiments and ingenious arguments. Fodor puts together a more or less Gricean theory of communication and a more or less Chomskyan view of the relation between surface features of utterances and deeper levels, but comes out forcefully against semantic primitives (at least in their familiar role in the production and comprehension of sentences). He defends images as inner representational vehicles in addition to his code formulae, and claims to show that the inner code can represent its own representations and has a vocabulary about as rich as that of English—to mention a few highlights. There are a few dubious links in the argumentation (e.g., Fodor's cat and mouse example on p. 142 seems obviously mis-analysed, but it may not matter), but time and again Fodor succeeds, in my estimation, in parrying the "obvious" philosophical objections. One exception is in his account of communication. Unless I am reading him too literally, he seems committed to the view that for A to communicate verbally with B, A and B must not only share a natural language but have the same version of mentalese as well. Once again this is a claim that might be trivial or might be almost certainly false, and we can't tell until Fodor is more explicit.

Faulting Fodor for not being sufficiently explicit in this instance is a bit ungenerous, for Fodor has offered a detailed theory in an area hitherto bereft of detailed theories, and has been more explicit than anybody else about many of the murky issues. The book is exceptionally clear, with excellent summaries of arguments and conclusions at just the right places. The view Fodor has put forward is a remarkably full view; seldom have stands on so many different issues been so staunchly taken in this area, and even where I think he is wrong, it is usually the crispness of his expression that suggests for the first time just exactly what is wrong. Fodor challenges us to find a better theory, and I fully expect that challenge to be met, but when better theories emerge they will owe a good deal to Fodor's reconnaissance.

7

Artificial Intelligence as Philosophy and as Psychology

Philosophers of mind have been interested in computers since their arrival a generation ago, but for the most part they have been interested only in the most abstract questions of principle, and have kept actual machines at arm's length and actual programs in soft focus. Had they chosen to take a closer look at the details I do not think they would have found much of philosophic interest until fairly recently, but recent work in Artificial Intelligence, or AI, promises to have a much more variegated impact on philosophy, and so, quite appropriately, philosophers have begun responding with interest to the bold manifestos of the Artificial Intelligentsia.[1] My goal in this chapter is to provide a sort of travel guide to philosophers pursuing this interest. It is well known that amateur travelers in strange lands often ludicrously miscomprehend what they see, and enthusiastically report wonders and monstrosities that later investigations prove never to have existed, while overlooking genuine novelties of the greatest importance. Having myself fallen prey to a variety of misconceptions about AI, and wasted a good deal of time and energy pursuing chimaeras, I would like to alert other philosophers to some of these pitfalls of interpretation. Since I am still acutely conscious of my own amateur status as an observer of AI, I must acknowledge at the outset that my vision of what is going on in AI, what is important and why, is almost certainly still somewhat untrustworthy. There is much in AI that I have not read, and much that I have read but not understood. So traveler, beware; take along any other maps you can find, and listen critically to the natives.

The interest of philosophers of mind in Artificial Intelligence comes as no surprise to many tough-minded experimental psychologists, for from their point of view the two fields look very much alike: there are the same broad generalizations and bold extrapolations, the same blithe indifference to the hard-won data of the experimentalist, the same appeal to the deliverances of casual introspection and conceptual analysis, the aprioristic reasonings about what is impossible in principle or what must be the case in psychology. The only apparent difference between the two fields, such a psychologist might say, is that the AI worker pulls his armchair up to a console. I will argue that this observation is largely justified, but should not in most regards be viewed as a criticism. There is much work for the armchair psychologist to do, and a computer console has proven a useful tool in this work.

Psychology turns out to be very difficult. The task of psychology is to explain human perception, learning, cognition, and so forth in terms that will ultimately unite psychological theory to physiology in one way or another, and there are two broad strategies one could adopt: a *bottom-up* strategy that starts with some basic and well-defined unit or theoretical atom for psychology, and builds these atoms into molecules and larger aggregates that can account for the complex phenomena we all observe, or a *top-down* strategy that begins with a more abstract decomposition of the highest levels of psychological organization, and hopes to analyze these into more and more detailed smaller systems or processes until finally one arrives at elements familiar to the biologists. It is a commonplace that both endeavors could and should proceed simultaneously, but there is now abundant evidence that the bottom-up strategy in psychology is unlikely to prove very fruitful. The two best developed attempts at bottom-up psychology are stimulus-response behaviorism and what we might call "neuron signal physiological psychology", and both are now widely regarded as stymied, the former because stimuli and responses prove not to be perspicuously chosen atoms, the latter because even if synapses and impulse trains are perfectly good atoms, there are just too many of them, and their interactions are too complex to study once one abandons the afferent and efferent peripheries and tries to make sense of the crucial center (see Chapters 4 and 5).[2] Bottom-up strategies have not proved notably fruitful in the early development of other sciences, in chemistry and biology for instance, and so psychologists are only following the lead of "mature" sciences if they turn to the top-down approach. Within that broad strategy there are a variety of starting points that can be ordered in an array. Faced with the practical impossibility of answering the empirical questions of psychology by brute inspection (how *in fact* does the nervous system accomplish X or Y or Z?), psychologists ask themselves an easier preliminary question:

How could any system (with features $A, B, C, \ldots$) possibly accomplish X?*
This sort of question is easier because it is "less empirical"; it is an *engineering* question, a quest for a solution (*any* solution) rather than a discovery. Seeking an answer to such a question can sometimes lead to the discovery of general constraints on all solutions (including of course nature's as yet unknown solution), and therein lies the value of this style of aprioristic theorizing. Once one decides to do psychology this way, one can choose a degree of empirical difficulty for one's question by filling in the blanks in the question schema above.[3] The more empirical constraints one puts on the description of the system, or on the description of the requisite behavior, the greater the claim to "psychological reality" one's answer must make. For instance, one can ask how any neuronal network with such-and-such physical features could *possibly* accomplish human color discriminations, or we can ask how any finite system could *possibly* subserve the acquisition of a natural language, or one can ask how human memory could *possibly* be so organized so as to make it so relatively easy for us to answer questions like "Have you ever ridden an antelope?", and so relatively hard to answer "What did you have for breakfast last Tuesday?". Or, one can ask, with Kant, how anything at all could *possibly* experience or know anything at all. Pure epistemology thus viewed, for instance, is simply the limiting case of the psychologists' quest, and is *prima facie* no less valuable *to psychology* for being so neutral with regard to empirical details. Some such questions are of course better designed to yield good answers than others, but *properly carried out*, any such investigation can yield constraints that bind all more data-enriched investigations.

AI workers can pitch their investigations at any level of empirical difficulty they wish; at Carnegie Mellon University, for instance, much is made of paying careful attention to experimental data on human performance, and attempting to model human performance closely. Other workers in AI are less concerned with that degree of psychological reality and have engaged in a more abstract version of AI. There is much that is of value and interest to psychology at the empirical end

*George Smith and Barbara Klein have pointed out to me that this question can be viewed as several ways ambiguous, and hence a variety of quite different responses might be held to answer such a question. Much of what I say below about different tactics for answering a question of this form can be construed to be about tactics for answering different (but related) questions. Philosophers who intend a question of this sort rhetorically can occasionally be embarrassed to receive in reply a detailed answer of one variety of another.

of the spectrum, but I want to claim that AI is better viewed as sharing with traditional epistemology the status of being a most general, most abstract asking of the top-down question: how is knowledge possible?* It has seemed to some philosophers that AI cannot be plausibly so construed because it takes on an additional burden: it restricts itself to *mechanistic* solutions, and hence its domain is not the Kantian domain of all possible modes of intelligence, but just all possible mechanistically realizable modes of intelligence. This, it is claimed, would beg the question against vitalists, dualists and other anti-mechanists. But as I have argued elsewhere, the mechanism requirement of AI is not an additional constraint of any moment, for if psychology is possible at all, and if Church's thesis is true, the constraint of mechanism is no more severe than the constraint against begging the question in psychology, and who would wish to evade that? (See Chapter 5).[4]

So I am claiming that AI shares with philosophy (in particular, with epistemology and philosophy of mind) the status of most abstract investigation of the principles of psychology. But it shares with psychology *in distinction from philosophy* a typical tactic in *answering* its questions. In AI or cognitive psychology the typical attempt to answer a *general* top-down question consists in designing a *particular* system that does, or appears to do, the relevant job, and then considering which of its features are necessary not just to one's particular system but to any such system. Philosophers have generally shunned such elaborate system-designing in favor of more doggedly general inquiry. This is perhaps the major difference between AI and "pure" philosophical approaches to the same questions, and it is one of my purposes here to exhibit some of the relative strengths and weaknesses of the two approaches.

The system-design approach that is common to AI and other styles of top-down psychology is beset by a variety of dangers of which these four are perhaps the chief:

(1) designing a system with component subsystems whose stipulated capacities are *miraculous* given the constraints one is accepting. (E.g., positing more information-processing in a component than the relevant time and matter will allow, or, at a more abstract level of engineering incoherence, positing a subsystem whose duties would require it to be more "intelligent" or "knowledgeable" than the supersystem of which it is to be a part.

(2) mistaking *conditional* necessities of one's particular solution for

---

*This question (and attempts to answer it) constitutes one main branch of epistemology; the other main branch has dealt with the problem of skepticism, and its constitutive question might be: "Is knowledge possible?"

completely general constraints (a trivial example would be proclaiming that brains use LISP; less trivial examples require careful elucidation).

(3) restricting oneself artificially to the design of a subsystem (e.g., a depth perceiver or sentence parser) and concocting a solution that is systematically incapable of being grafted onto the other subsystems of a whole cognitive creature.

(4) restricting the performance of one's system to an artificially small part of the "natural" domain of that system and providing no efficient or plausible way for the system to be enlarged.

These dangers are altogether familiar to AI, but are just as common, *if harder to diagnose conclusively*, in other approaches to psychology. Consider danger (1): both Freud's ego subsystem and J.J. Gibson's invariance-sensitive perceptual "tuning forks" have been *charged* with miraculous capacities. Danger (2): behaviorists have been *charged* with illicitly extrapolating from pigeon-necessities to people-necessities, and it is often claimed that what the frog's eye tells the frog's brain is not at all what the person's eye tells the person's brain. Danger (3): it is notoriously hard to see how Chomsky's early *syntax*-driven system could interact with semantical components to produce or comprehend purposeful speech. Danger (4): it is hard to see how some models of nonsense-syllable rote memorization could be enlarged to handle similar but more sophisticated memory tasks. It is one of the great strengths of AI that when one of its products succumbs to any of these dangers this can usually be quite conclusively demonstrated.

I now have triangulated AI with respect to both philosophy and psychology (as my title suggested I would): AI can be (and should often be taken to be) as abstract and "unempirical" as philosophy in t e questions it attempts to answer, but at the same time, it should be as explicit and particularistic in its models as psychology at its best. Thus one might learn as much of value to psychology or epistemology from a *particular* but highly *un*realistic AI model as one could learn from a detailed psychology of, say, Martians. A good psychology of Martians, however unlike us they might be, would certainly yield general principles of psychology or epistemology applicable to human beings. Now before turning to the all important question: "What, so conceived, has AI accomplished?", I want to consider briefly some misinterpretations of AI that my sketch of it so far does not protect us from.

Since we are viewing AI as a species of top-down cognitive psychology, it is tempting to suppose that the decomposition of function in a computer is intended by AI to be somehow isomorphic to the decomposition of function in a brain. One learns of vast programs made up of literally billions of basic computer events and somehow so organized as to produce a simulacrum of human intelligence, and it is altogether natural to suppose that since the brain is known to be composed of billions of tiny functioning parts, and since there is a *gap of ignorance* between our understanding of intelligent human behavior and our understanding of those tiny parts, the ultimate, millenial goal of AI must be to provide a hierarchical breakdown of parts in the computer that will mirror or be isomorphic to some hard-to-discover hierarchical breakdown of brain-event parts. The familiar theme of "organs made of tissues made of cells made of molecules made of atoms" is to be matched, one might suppose, in electronic hardware terms. In the thrall of this picture one might be discouraged to learn that some functional parts of the nervous system do not seem to function in the digital way the atomic functioning parts in computers do. The standard response to this worry would be that one had looked too deep in the computer (this is sometimes called the "grain problem"). The computer is a digital device at bottom, but a digital device can simulate an "analogue" device to any degree of continuity you desire, and at a higher level of aggregation in the computer one may find the analogue elements that are mappable onto the non-digital brain parts. As many writers have observed,[5] we cannot gauge the psychological reality of a model until we are given the commentary on the model that tells us which features of the model are intended to mirror real saliencies in nature, and which are either backstage expediters of the modeling or sheer inadvertent detail. (In the Eighteenth Century, scientists built beautiful brass clockwork models of the solar system called orreries. The *gears* of an orrery are not intended to represent anything real in the firmament, nor are the reflections of one brass globe in another.) When one looks at AI programs in detail one sees mountains of digital calculation or "number crunching"; if this looks terribly unbiological, this is to be excused since that part of the model's structure is to be viewed as backstage, not part of the model we are supposed to compare with nature.

This story is fine in principle, I think, and the day may come when this imagined isomorphism down to the neuronal level (but not backstage) is proclaimed, but in fact we see nothing remotely like this in current AI work. We see instead models that diverge from nature *very* early on the downward path. AI programs typically model relatively high-level cognitive features, such as concept learning or revision of goals or beliefs, and it does indeed often take millions of basic computer events to simulate just a handful of these *intended model features* —but no one really knows or cares what these basic events are, for no one supposes that *any* of the saliencies in the mass of activity that subserves the intended features are to be taken seriously as psychology or physiology. The psychological reality of an AI program is thus usually intended to be only skin deep; only the highest levels of program description and commentary are to be counted as the model.

The *thin*ness of the psychological reality of AI models is obscured for the uninitiated by a particularly misleading feature of most of the AI programs that get into the limelight. What especially attracts audiences and evokes wonder is the marvelous verisimilitude of some of the programs. Consider this excerpt of conversation (minus the programmer's excellent commentary) between Terry Winograd's SHRDLU and its interlocutor. SHRDLU is a program that lives in an imaginary "block world" where it can manipulate colored blocks on a table in response to commands and answer questions about its life in this world. Computer responses are capitalized.

Had you touched any pyramid before you put the green one on the little cube?

YES, THE GREEN ONE.

When did you pick it up?

WHILE I WAS STACKING UP THE RED CUBE, A LARGE RED BLOCK AND A LARGE GREEN CUBE.

Why?

TO GET RID OF IT.

Why did you do that?

TO CLEAR OFF THE RED CUBE.

Why did you clear off that cube?

TO PUT IT ON A LARGE GREEN CUBE.

Why did you do that?

BECAUSE YOU ASKED ME TO.[6]

When SHRDLU replies to the last question with "Because you asked me to", one can hardly help being struck by the apparent *humanity* of the response—"SHRDLU is *one of us!*" it is tempting to exclaim. If one is naive, one will be awestruck; if one is not, one will still be titillated by the illusion, for that is largely what it is. SHRDLU's response, though perfectly appropriate to the occasion (and not by coincidence!) is "canned". Winograd has simply given SHRDLU this whole sentence to print at times like these. If a child gave SHRDLU's response we would naturally expect its behavior to manifest a general capacity which might also reveal itself by producing the response: "Because you told me to," or, "Because that's what I was asked to do," or on another occasion: "Because I felt like it," or "Because your assistant told me to," but these are dimensions of subtlety beyond SHRDLU.[7] Its behavior is remarkably versatile, but it does not reveal a rich knowledge of interpersonal relations, of the difference between requests and orders, of being cooperative with other people under appropriate circumstances. (It should be added that Winograd's paper makes it very explicit where and to what extent he is canning SHRDLU's responses, so anyone who feels cheated by SHRDLU has simply not read Winograd. Other natural language programs do not rely on canned responses, or rely on them to a minimal extent.)

The fact remains, however, that much of the antagonism to AI is due to resentment and distrust engendered by such legerdemain. Why do AI people use these tricks? For many reasons. First, they need to get some tell-tale response back from the program and it is as easy to can a mnemonically vivid and "natural" response as something more sober, technical and understated (perhaps: "REASON: PRIOR COMMAND TO DO THAT"). Second, in Winograd's case he was attempting to reveal the *minimal* conditions for correct analysis of certain linguistic forms (note all the "problems" of pronominal antecedents in the sentences displayed), so "natural" language *output* to reveal correct analysis of natural langauge *input* was entirely appropriate. Third, AI people put canned responses in their programs because it is fun. It is fun to amuse one's colleagues, who are not fooled of course, and it is especially fun to bamboozle the outsiders. As an outsider, one must learn to be properly unimpressed by AI verisimilitude, as one is by the chemist's dazzling forest of glass tubing, or the angry mouths full of teeth painted on World War II fighter planes. (Joseph Weizenbaum's famous ELIZA program,[8] the computer "psychotherapist" who apparently listens so wisely and sympathetically to one's problems, is intended in part as an antidote to the enthusiasm generated by AI verisimilitude. It is almost all clever canning, and is not a psychologically realistic model of anything, but rather a demonstration of how easily one can be gulled into attributing too much to a program. It exploits syntactic landmarks in one's input with nothing approaching genuine understanding, but it makes a good show of comprehension nevertheless. One might say it was a plausible model of a Wernicke's aphasic, who can babble on with well-formed and even semantically appropriate responses to his interlocutor, sometimes sustaining the illusion of comprehension for quite a while.)

The AI community pays a price for this misleading if fascinating fun, not only by contributing to the image of AI people as tricksters and hackers, but by fueling more serious misconceptions of the point of AI research. For instance, Winograd's real contribution in SHRDLU is *not* that he has produced an English speaker and understander that is psychologically realistic at many different levels of analysis (though that is what the verisimilitude strongly suggests, and what a lot of the fanfare—for which Winograd is not responsible—has assumed), but that he has explored some of the deepest demands on any system that can take direction (in a natural language), plan, change the world and keep track of the changes wrought or contemplated, and in the course of this exploration he has clarified the problems and proposed ingenious and plausible *partial* solutions to them. The real contribution in Winograd's work stands quite unimpeached by the perfectly true but irrelevant charge that SHRDLU doesn't have a *rich* or human understanding of most of the words in its very restricted vocabulary, or is terribly slow.

In fact, paying so much attention to the performance of SHRDLU (and similar systems) reveals a failure to recognize that AI programs are not *empirical* experiments but *thought*-experiments prosthetically regulated by computers. Some AI people have recently become fond of describing their discipline as "experimental epistemology". This unfortunate term should make a philosopher's blood boil, but if AI called itself thought-experimental epistemology (or even better: *Gedanken*-experimental epistemology) philosophers ought to be reassured. The questions asked and answered by the thought-experiments of AI are about whether or not one can obtain certain sorts of information processing—recognition, inference, control of various sorts, for instance—from certain sorts of designs. Often the answer is no. The process of elimination looms large in AI. Relatively plausible schemes are explored far enough to make it clear that they are utterly incapable of delivering the requisite behavior, and learning this is important progress, even if it doesn't result in a mind-boggling robot.

The hardware realizations of AI are almost gratuitous. Like dropping the cannonballs off the Leaning Tower of Pisa, they are demonstrations that are superfluous to those who have understood the argument, however persuasive they are to the rest. Are computers then irrelevant to AI? "In principle" they are irrelevant (in the same sense of "in principle", diagrams on the blackboard are in principle unnecessary to teaching geometry), but in practice they are not. I earlier described them as "prosthetic regulators" of thought-experiments. What I meant was this: it is notoriously difficult to keep wishful thinking out of one's thought-experiments; computer simulation *forces* one to recognize all the costs of one's imagined design. As Pylyshyn observes, "What is needed is . . . a technical language with which to discipline one's imagination."[9] The discipline provided by computers is undeniable (and especially palpable to the beginning programmer). It is both a good thing—for the reasons just stated—and a bad thing. Perhaps you have known a person so steeped in, say, playing bridge, that his entire life becomes in his eyes a series of finesses, end plays and cross-ruffs. Every morning he draws life's trumps and whenever he can see the end of a project he views it as a lay-down. Computer languages seem to have a similar effect on people who become fluent in them. Although I won't try to prove it by citing examples, I think it is quite obvious that the "technical language" Pylyshyn speaks of can cripple an imagination in the process of disciplining it.[10]

It has been said so often that computers have huge effects on their users' imaginations that one can easily lose sight of one of the most obvious but still underrated ways in which computers achieve this effect, and that is the sheer speed of computers. Before computers came along the theoretician was strongly constrained to ignore the possibility of truly massive and complex processes in psychology because it was hard to see how such processes could fail to *appear* at worst mechanical and cumbersome, at best vegetatively slow, and of course a hallmark of mentality is its swiftness. One might say that the speed of thought defines the upper bound of subjective "fast", the way the speed of light defines the upper bound of objective "fast". Now suppose there had never been any computers but that somehow (by magic, presumably) Kenneth Colby had managed to dream up these flow charts as a proposed model of a part of human organization in paranoia. (The flow charts are from his book, *Artificial Paranoia*, Pergamon, 1975; figure 7.1 represents the main program; figures 7.2 and 7.3 are blow-ups of details of the main program.) It is obvious to everyone, even Colby I think, that this is a vastly oversimplified model of paranoia, but had there not been computers to show us how all this processing and much much more can occur in a twinkling, we would be inclined to dismiss the proposal immediately as altogether too clanking and inorganic, a Rube Goldberg machine. Most programs look like that in slow motion (hand simulation) but speeded up they often reveal a dexterity and grace that appears natural, and this grace is entirely undetectable via a slow analysis of the program (cf. time lapse photography of plants growing and buds opening). The grace in operation of AI programs may be mere illusion. Perhaps nature is graceful *all the way down*, but for better or for worse, computer speed has liberated the imagination of theoreticians by opening up the possibility and plausibility of very complex interactive information processes playing a role in the production of cognitive events so swift as to be atomic to introspection.

At last I turn to the important question. Suppose that AI is viewed as I recommend, as a most abstract inquiry into the possibility of intelligence or knowledge. Has it solved any very general problems or discovered any very important constraints or principles? I think the answer is a qualified yes. In particular, I think AI has broken the back of an argument that has bedeviled philosophers and psychologists for over two hundred years. Here is a skeletal version of it: *First,* the only psychology that could possibly succeed in explaining the complexities of human activity must posit internal representations. This premise has been deemed obvious by just about everyone except the radical behaviorists (both in psychology and philosophy—both Watson and Skinner, and Ryle and Malcolm). Descartes doubted almost everything

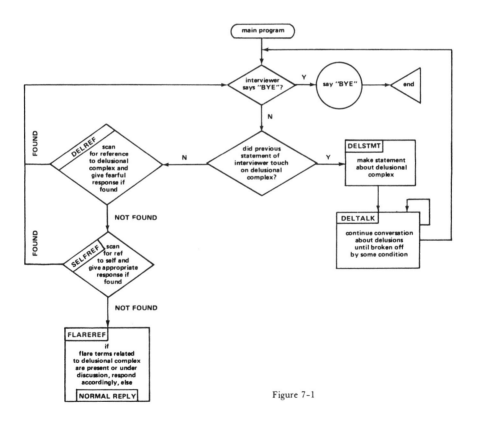

Figure 7-1

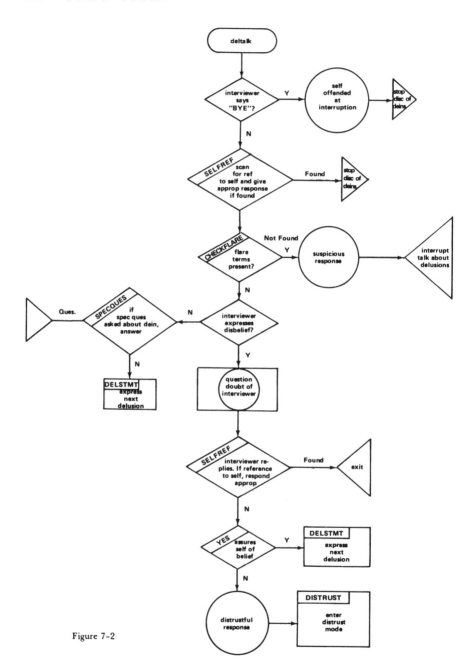

Figure 7-2

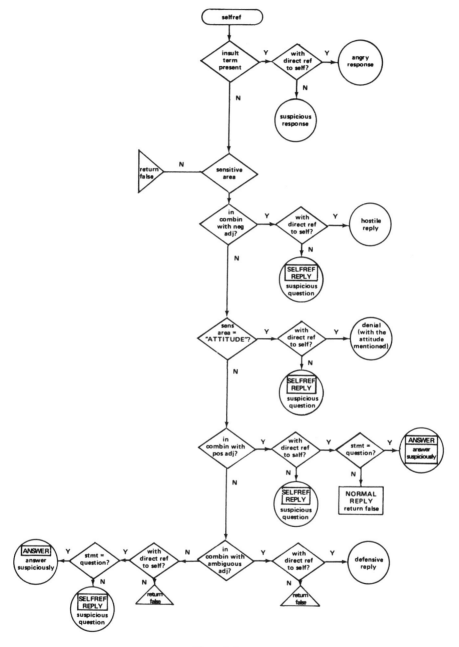

Figure 7-3

but this. For the British Empiricists, the internal representations were called ideas, sensations, impressions; more recently psychologists have talked of hypotheses, maps, schemas, images, propositions, engrams, neural signals, even holograms and whole innate theories. So the first premise is quite invulnerable, or at any rate it has an impressive mandate (see Chapter 6). But, *second*, nothing is intrinsically a representation of anything; something is a representation only *for* or *to* someone; any representation or system of representations thus requires at least one *user* or *interpreter* of the representation who is external to it. Any such interpreter must have a variety of psychological or intentional traits (see Chapter 1): it must be capable of a variety of *comprehension*, and must have beliefs and goals (so it can *use* the representation to *inform* itself and thus assist it in achieving its goals). Such an interpreter is then a sort of homunculus.

Therefore, psychology *without* homunculi is impossible. But psychology *with* homunculi is doomed to circularity or infinite regress, so psychology is impossible.

The argument given is a relatively abstract version of a familiar group of problems. For instance, it seems (to many) that we cannot account for perception unless we suppose it provides us with an internal image (or model or map) of the external world, and yet what good would that image do us unless we have an inner eye to perceive it, and how are we to explain *its* capacity for perception? It also seems (to many) that understanding a heard sentence must be somehow *translating* it into some internal message, but how will this message in turn be understood: by translating it into something else? The problem is an old one, and let's call it *Hume's Problem*, for while he did not state it explicitly, he appreciated its force and strove mightily to escape its clutches. Hume's internal representations were impressions and ideas, and he wisely shunned the notion of an inner *self* that would intelligently *manipulate* these items, but this left him with the necessity of getting the ideas and impressions to "think for themselves". The result was his theory of the self as a "bundle" of (nothing but) impressions and ideas. He attempted to set these impressions and ideas into dynamic interaction by positing various associationistic links, so that each succeeding idea in the stream of consciousness dragged its successor onto the stage according to one or another principle, all without benefit of intelligent *supervision*. It didn't work, of course. It couldn't conceivably work, and Hume's failure is plausibly viewed as the harbinger of doom for any remotely analogous enterprise. On the one hand, how could *any* theory of psychology make sense of representations that *understand themselves*, and on the other, how could *any* theory of psychology avoid regress or circularity if it posits at least one representation-understander in addition to the representations?

Now no doubt some philosophers and psychologists who have appealed to internal representations over the years have believed in their hearts that somehow the force of this argument could be blunted, that Hume's problem could be solved, but I am sure no one had the slightest idea *how to do this* until AI and the notion of data-structures came along. Data-structures may or may not be biologically or psychologically realistic representations, but they are, if not living, breathing examples, at least clanking, functioning examples of representations that can be said in the requisite sense to understand themselves.*

How this is accomplished can be metaphorically described (and any talk about internal representations is bound to have a large element of metaphor in it) by elaborating our description (see Chapter 5) of AI as a top-down theoretical inquiry. One starts, in AI, with a specification of a whole person or cognitive organism—what I call, more neutrally, an intentional system (see Chapter 1)—or some artificial segment of that person's abilities (e.g., chess-playing, answering questions about baseball) and then breaks that largest intentional system into an organization of subsystems, each of which could itself be viewed as an intentional system (with its own specialized beliefs and desires) and hence as formally a homunculus. In fact, homunculus talk is ubiquitous in AI, and almost always illuminating. AI homunculi talk to each other, wrest control from each other, volunteer, sub-contract, supervise, and even kill. There seems no better way of describing what is going on.[11] Homunculi are *bogeymen* only if they duplicate *entire* the talents they are rung in to explain (a special case of danger (1)). If one can get a team or committee of *relatively* ignorant, narrow-minded, blind homunculi to produce the intelligent behavior of the whole, this is progress. A flow chart is typically the organizational chart of a committee of homunculi (investigators, librarians, accountants, executives); each box specifies a homunculus by prescribing a function *without*

---

*Joseph Weizenbaum has pointed out to me that Turing saw from the very beginning that computers could in principle break the threatened regress of Hume's Problem, and George Smith has drawn my attention to similar early wisdom in Von Neumann. It has taken a generation of development for their profound insights to be confirmed, after a fashion, by detailed models. It is one thing—far from negligible—to proclaim a possibility in principle, and another to reveal how the possibility might be made actual in detail. Before the relatively recent inventions of AI, the belief that Hume's Problem could be dissolved somehow by the conceptual advances of computer science provided encouragement but scant guidance to psychologists and philosophers.

saying how it is to be accomplished (one says, in effect: put a little man in there to do the job). If we then look closer at the individual boxes we see that the function of each is accomplished by subdividing it via another flow chart into still smaller, more stupid homunculi. Eventually this nesting of boxes within boxes lands you with homunculi so stupid (all they have to do is remember whether to say yes or no when asked) that they can be, as one says, "replaced by a machine". One *discharges* fancy homunculi from one's scheme by organizing armies of such idiots to do the work.

When homunculi at a level interact, they do so by sending *messages*, and each homunculus has representations that it uses to execute its functions. Thus typical AI discussions *do* draw a distinction between representation and representation-user[12] : they take the *first step* of the threatened infinite regress, but as many writers in AI have observed,[13] it has gradually emerged from the tinkerings of AI that there is a trade-off between sophistication in the representation and sophistication in the user. The more raw and uninterpreted the representation—e.g., the mosaic of retinal stimulation at an instant—the more sophisticated the interpreter or user of the representation. The more interpreted a representation—the more *procedural* information is *embodied in it*, for instance—the less fancy the interpreter need be. It is this fact that permits one to get away with *lesser* homunculi at high levels, by getting their earlier or lower brethren to do some of the work. One never quite gets *completely* self-understanding representations (unless one stands back and views all representation in the system from a global vantage point), but all homunculi are ultimately discharged. One gets the advantage of the trade-off only by sacrificing versatility and universality in one's subsystems and their representations,[14] so one's homunculi cannot be too versatile nor can the messages they send and receive have the full flavor of normal human linguistic interaction. We have seen an example of how homuncular communications may fall short in SHRDLU's remark, "Because you asked me to." The context of production and the function of the utterance makes clear that this is a sophisticated communication and the product of a sophisticated representation, but it is not a full-fledged Gricean speech act. If it were, it would require too fancy a homunculus to use it.

There are two ways a philosopher might view AI data structures. One could grant that they are indeed self-understanding representations or one could cite the various disanalogies between them and prototypical or *real* representations (human statements, paintings, maps) and conclude that data-structures are not really internal representations at all. But if one takes the latter line, the modest successes of AI simply serve to undercut our first premise: it is no longer obvious that psychology needs internal representations; internal pseudo-representations may do just as well.

It is certainly tempting to argue that since AI has provided us with the only known way of solving Hume's Problem, albeit for very restrictive systems, it must be on the right track, and its categories must be psychologically real, but one might well be falling into Danger (2) if one did. We can all be relieved and encouraged to learn that there is *a* way of solving Hume's Problem, but it has yet to be shown that AI's way is the only way it can be done.

AI has made a major contribution to philosophy and psychology by revealing a particular way in which simple cases of Hume's Problem can be solved. What else has it accomplished of interest to philosophers? I will close by just drawing attention to the two main areas where I think the AI approach is of particular relevance to philosophy.

For many years philosophers and psychologists have debated (with scant interdisciplinary communication) about the existence and nature of mental images. These discussions have been relatively fruitless, largely, I think, because neither side had any idea of how to come to grips with Hume's Problem. Recent work in AI, however, has recast the issues in a clearly more perspicuous and powerful framework, and anyone hoping to resolve this ancient issue will find help in the AI discussions.[15]

The second main area of philosophical interest, in my view, is the so-called "frame problem."[16] The frame problem is an abstract *epistemological* problem that was in effect discovered by AI thought-experimentation. When a cognitive creature, an entity with many beliefs about the world, performs an act, the world changes and many of the creature's beliefs must be revised or updated. How? It cannot be that we perceive and notice *all* the changes (for one thing, many of the changes we *know* to occur do not occur in our perceptual fields), and hence it cannot be that we rely entirely on perceptual input to revise our beliefs. So we must have internal ways of up-dating our beliefs that will fill in the gaps and keep our internal model, the totality of our beliefs, roughly faithful to the world.

If one supposes, as philosophers traditionally have, that one's beliefs are a set of propositions, and reasoning is inference or deduction from members of the set, one is in for trouble, for it is quite clear (though still controversial) that systems relying only on such processes get swamped by combinatorial explosions in the updating effort. It seems that our entire conception of belief and reasoning must be radically revised if we are to explain the undeniable capacity of human beings to keep their beliefs roughly consonant with the reality they live in.

I think one can find an *appreciation* of the frame problem in Kant (we *might* call the frame problem Kant's Problem) but unless one disciplines one's thought-experiments in the AI manner, philosophical proposals of solutions to the problem, including Kant's of course, can be viewed as at best suggestive, at worst mere wishful thinking.

I do not want to suggest that philosophers abandon traditional philosophical methods and retrain themselves as AI workers. There is plenty of work to do by thought-experimentation and argumentation, disciplined by the canons of philosophical method and informed by the philosophical tradition. Some of the most influential recent work in AI (e.g., Minsky's papers on "Frames") is loaded with recognizably philosophical speculations of a relatively unsophisticated nature. Philosophers, I have said, should study AI. Should AI workers study philosophy? Yes, unless they are content to reinvent the wheel every few days. When AI reinvents a wheel, it is typically square, or at best hexagonal, and can only make a few hundred revolutions before it stops. Philosopher's wheels, on the other hand, are perfect circles, require *in principle* no lubrication, and can go in at least two directions at once. Clearly a meeting of minds is in order.*

*I am indebted to Margaret Boden for valuable advice on an early draft of this paper. Her *Artificial Intelligence and Natural Man* (Harvester, 1977), provides an excellent introduction to the field of AI for philosophers.

III

Objects of Consciousness and the Nature of Experience

8

Are Dreams Experiences?

The "received view" of dreams is that they are *experiences that occur during sleep*, experiences which we can often recall upon waking. Enlarged, the received view is that dreams consist of sensations, thoughts, impressions, and so forth, usually composed into coherent narratives or adventures, occurring somehow in awareness or consciousness, though in some other sense or way the dreamer is *un*conscious during the episode.* *Received* it certainly is; as Norman Malcolm pointed out in his book, *Dreaming*, not only has it been virtually unchallenged, it has been explicitly endorsed by Aristotle, Descartes, Kant, Russell, Moore, and Freud.[1] That was in 1959, and I think it is fair to say that in spite of Malcolm's arguments against the received view, it is still the received view. I want to reopen the case, and though my aims and presuppositions are quite antagonistic to Malcolm's, those familiar with his attack will see many points at which my discussion agrees with and gains insight and direction from his. I will not, though, go into a detailed extraction and defense of what I find valuable in Malcolm's book. My immediate purpose in what follows is to undermine the authority of the received view of dreams. My larger purpose is to introduce a view about the relationship between experience and memory that I plan to incorporate into a physicalistic theory of consciousness, a theory considerably different from the theory I have hitherto defended.[2]

The most scandalous conclusion that Malcolm attempted to draw

*Cf. Hilary Putnam's version of "a natural lexical definition": "a series of impressions (visual, etc.) occurring during sleep; usually appearing to the subject to be of people, objects, etc.; frequently remembered upon awakening" ("Dreaming and 'Depth Grammar'" in R. J. Butler, ed., *Analytical Philosophy* (Oxford, 1962):224.

from his analysis of the concept of dreaming was to the effect that contemporary dream research by psychologists and other scientists was conceptually confused, misguided, ultimately simply *irrelevant* to dreaming.[3] This conclusion strikes many as bizarre and impertinent. If scientists can study waking experience, waking sensation, thought, imagination, consciousness, they can surely study the varieties of these phenomena that occur during sleep, in dreaming. This riposte is not, of course, a consideration that would impress Malcolm, for it is simply an announcement of faith in the received view, the view that dreams do consist of sensations, thoughts, and so forth occurring during sleep, and Malcolm already knows that the view he is attacking inspires such faith. In any event, as everyone expected, Malcolm's words have had little or no discouraging effect on dream researchers. Their work continues apace to this day, apparently with a degree of fruition that makes a mockery of Malcolm's view. So let us suppose, *contra* Malcolm, that the researchers are neither the perpetrators nor the victims of a conceptual crime, and see where it leads us. Let us suppose that the dream researcher's concept of dreaming is not only received, but the true and unconfused concept of dreaming. What are the prospects, then, for the scientific elaboration of the received view?

It is well known that periods of rapid eye movements (REMs) occur during sleep, and correlate well with subsequent reports of having dreamed. There are also characteristic EEG patterns usually concurrent with the REM episodes, and other physiological correlates that go to suggest that dreams do indeed occur during sleep, and can now be timed, confirmed to occur, and measured in all manner of ways. One tantalizing finding has been the apparent occasional content-relativity of the REMs. A person whose REMs are predominantly horizontal is awakened and reports a dream in which he watched two people throwing tomatoes at each other. A predominantly vertical pattern in REMs is correlated with a dream report of picking basketballs off the floor and throwing them up at the basket.[4] A neurophysiological model* of dreaming would plausibly construe these REMs as relatively gross and peripheral effects of a more determinate content-relative process deeper in the brain, which we might hope some day to *translate*, in this sense: we might be able to *predict* from certain physiological events observed during sleep that the subsequent dream report would

---

*Putnam (*op. cit.*) points out that a crucial lacuna in Malcolm's verificationist arguments against REMs as evidence confirming the received view is his failure to consider the confirmation relations arising from the use of developed theories and models (p. 226). At a number of points this paper attempts to fill that gap.

allude to, for example, fear, falling from a height, eating something cold, even (in the Golden Age of neurocryptography) buying a train ticket to New Haven for $12.65 and then forgetting which pocket it was in. The prospect of a *generalized* capacity to predict dream narratives in such detail would be vanishingly small in the absence of a highly systematic and well-entrenched theory of representation in the brain, but let us suppose for the nonce that such a theory is not only in principle possible, but the natural culmination of the research strategies that are already achieving modest success in "translating" relatively gross and peripheral nervous-system activity.*

Now some people claim never to dream, and many people waken to report that they have dreamed but cannot recall any details. The latter usually have a strong conviction that the dream *did* have details, though they cannot recall them, and even when we can recall our dreams, the memories fade very fast, and the mere act of expressing them seems to interfere, to speed up the memory loss. Here the impression of details *there then* but *now lost* is very strong indeed. REM researchers now confidently state that their research shows that *everybody* has dreams (and every night); some of us just seldom—or never—recall them. It must be unsettling to be assured that one has dreamed when one is positive one has not; Malcolm could be expected to diagnose one's reaction to such an assurance as the shudder of conceptual violation,[5] but that would be an overstatement. The data of common experience strongly suggest a gradation in people's capacities to recall (both dreams and other items), and it should be nothing worse than an odd but obvious implication of the received view that one could *dream* without recalling, just as one can promise without recalling, or be raucously drunk without recalling.

Guided by common experience and the received view, then, we can imagine our scientists of the future isolating the memory mechanisms responsible for dream recall, and finding ways of chemically facilitating or inhibiting them. This is surely plausible; research into the chemistry of memory already suggests which chemicals might have these powers. We would expect that the scientists' claims to a theory of the dream-recall mechanism would be buttressed by systematic ties to a theory of memory mechanisms in general and by results, such as, perhaps, their ability to cure the dream-amnesiac.

---

*I have in mind such work as Hubel and Wiesel's "translation" of optic nerve signals in the cat. I argue against optimism regarding the prospects for a generalized neural theory of representation in "Brain Writing and Mind Reading" (Chapter 3 of this volume).

So we imagine future dream theory to posit two largely separable processes: first, there are neural events during sleep (more specifically during REM periods having certain characteristic EEG correlates) that systematically represent (are systematically correlatable with) the "events occurring in the dream", and during this process there is a second, memory-loading process so that these events can be recalled on waking (when the memory process works). Dreams are *presented*, and simultaneously *recorded* in memory, and we might be able to interfere with or prevent the recording without disturbing the presentation.

This posited process of memory-loading and playback must be saved from simplistic interpretation if we are to maintain any vestige of realism for our fantasy. It is rarely if ever the case that a dreamer awakens and proceeds to recite with vacant stare a fixed narrative. Dream recall is like recall generally. We interpret, extrapolate, revise; it sometimes seems that we "relive" the incidents and *draw conclusions* from this reliving—conclusions that are then expressed in what we actually *compose* then and there as our recollections. It is not easy to analyze what must be going on when this happens. What is the *raw material*, the evidence, the basis for these reconstructions we call recollections?

Consider a fictional example. John Dean, a recently acclaimed virtuoso of recollection, is asked about a certain meeting in the Oval Office. Was Haldeman present? Consider some possible replies.

(1) "No."
(2) "I can't (or don't) recall his being there."
(3) "I distinctly recall that he was not there."
(4) "I remember noticing (remarking) at the time that he was not there."

If Dean says (1) we will suspect that he is saying less than he *can* say, even if what he says is sincere and even true. At the other extreme, (4) seems to be a nearly *complete* report of the relevant part of Dean's memory. Answer (2), unlike all the others, reports an inability, a blank. Under the right circumstances, though, it carries about as strong a pragmatic implication of Haldeman's absence as any of the others (we ask: could Dean conceivably fail to recall Haldeman's presence if Haldeman had been there?). The stronger these pragmatic implications, the more disingenuous an answer like (2) will seem. Consider: "Was Dan Rather at that meeting in the Oval Office?" "I can't *recall* his being there." The answer is seen to be disingenuous because we know Dean knows, and we know, the additional supporting premises which, in conjunction with (2), imply something like (1), and we expect Dean to be reasonable and draw this conclusion for—and with—us. Then what should Dean say, if asked the question about Dan Rather? Certainly not (4), unless the paranoia in the White House in those days knew no bounds, but (3) can be heard to carry a similar, if weaker, implication. We would not expect Dean to say this because it suggests (presumably misleadingly) that his answer is closer to being *given* in his recollection, less a conclusion quickly drawn. (1) is clearly the best answer on the list under these circumstances. It *looks* like a conclusion he reaches on the basis of things he remembers. He remembers Nixon and Ehrlichman talking with him, forming a sort of triangle in the room, and on the basis of *this* he concludes that Haldeman, and Rather, were absent, though he took no notice of the fact at the time, or if he did he has forgotten it. Now suppose Dean says (1). Perhaps when he does this he recalls in his mind this triangle, but does not bother to tell us that—he does not close his eyes on the witness stand and do a little phenomenology for us; he simply offers up his conclusion as a dictate of memory. But he need not have gone through this conscious process of reliving and reasoning at all. He may say, directly, "No," and if he is pressed to be more forthcoming, any reasoning he offers based on other things he recalls will not be expressing any reasoning he knows he went through before his initial negative reply. He may not even be able to explain why or how his memory dictates this answer to the question, and yet be sure, and deservedly sure, that his reply is a sincere and reliable dictate of memory.

To summarize: sometimes we can sincerely answer a question of recollection with an answer like (4), but often we cannot, and sometimes we draw a blank, but in *all* these cases there are conclusions we can draw based on what in some sense we directly remember in conjunction with common and proprietary knowledge, and these conclusions need not be drawn in a process of *conscious* reasoning. Whatever it is that is directly remembered can play its evidentiary role in prompting an answer of recollection without coming into consciousness. This suggests that when we remember some event, there is some limited amount of information that is *there*, not necessarily in consciousness but available in one way or another for utilization in composing our recollections and answering questions we or others raise. Perhaps what occupies this functional position is an immensely detailed recording of our experience to which our later access in normally imperfect and partial (although under hypnosis it may improve). Perhaps there is enough information in this position to reconstitute completely our past experience and present us, under special circumstances, with a vivid hallucination of reliving the event.* However much is in this position in Dean, however, it is not possible that Dan Rather's absence is there except by implication, for his absence was not experienced by Dean at the time, any more than up to this moment you have been experiencing Rather's absence from this room. What the posited memory-loading process records, then, is whatever occupies this functional position at a later time. The "playback" of dream recollections, like other recollections, is presumably seldom if ever complete or uninterpreted, and often bits of information are utilized in making memory claims without being played back in consciousness at all.

In dreaming there is also a third process that is distinguished both in the layman's version of the received view and in fancier theories, and that is the *composition* of what is presented and recorded. In various ways this process exhibits intelligence: dream stories are usually coherent and realistic (even surrealism has a realistic background), and are often gripping, complex, and of course loaded with symbolism. Dream composition utilizes the dreamer's general and particular knowledge, her recent and distant experience, and is guided in familiar ways by her fears and desires, covert and overt.

Studying these three processes will require tampering with them, and we can imagine that the researchers will acquire the technological virtuosity to be able to influence, direct, or alter the composition process, to stop, restart, or even transpose the presentation process as it occurs, to prevent or distort the recording process. We can even imagine that they will be able to obliterate the "veridical" dream memory and substitute for it an undreamed narrative. This eventuality would produce a strange result indeed. Our dreamer would wake up and report her dream, only to be assured by the researcher that she never dreamed *that* dream, but rather another, which they proceed to relate to her. Malcolm sees that the scientific elaboration of the received view countenances such a possibility-in-principle and for him this amounts to a *reductio ad absurdum* of the received view,[6] but again, this is an overreaction to an admittedly strange circumstance. Given the state of the art of dream research today, were someone to contradict my clear recollection of what I had just dreamed, my utter skepticism would be warranted, but the science-fictional situation envisaged would be quite different. Not only would the researchers have proved their powers by correctly predicting dream recollections on numerous occasions, but they would have a theory that explained their successes.

*Cf. Wilder Penfield's descriptions of electrode-induced memory hallucinations, in *The Excitable Cortex in Conscious Man*, (Springfield, Illinois, 1958).

And we need not suppose the dream they related to the dreamer would be entirely *alien* to her ears, even though she had no recollection of it (and in fact a competing recollection). Suppose it recounted an adventure with some secretly loved acquaintance of hers, a person unknown to the researchers. The stone wall of skepticism would begin to crumble.

The story told so far does not, I take it, exhibit the conceptual chaos Malcolm imagines; strange as it is, I do not think it would evoke in the layman, our custodian of ordinary concepts, the nausea of incomprehension. As a premise for a science-fiction novel it would be almost pedestrian in its lack of conceptual horizon-bending.

But perhaps this is not at all the way the theory of dreaming will develop. Malcolm notes in passing that it has been suggested by some researchers that dreams may occur during the moments of waking, not during the prior REM periods. Why would anyone conjecture this? Perhaps you have had a dream leading logically and coherently up to a climax in which you are shot, whereupon you wake up and are told that a truck has just backfired outside your open window. Or you are fleeing someone in a building, you climb out a window, walk along the ledge, then fall—and wake up on the floor having fallen out of bed. In a recent dream of mine I searched long and far for a neighbor's goat; when at last I found her she bleated *baa-a-a*—and I awoke to find her bleat merging perfectly with the buzz of an electric alarm clock I had not used or heard for months. Many people, I find, have anecdotes like this to relate, but the scientific literature disparages them, and I can find only one remotely well-documented case from an experiment: different stimuli were being used to waken dreamers, and one subject was wakened by dripping cold water on his back. He related a dream in which he was singing in an opera. Suddenly he *heard and saw* that the soprano had been struck by debris falling from above; he ran to her and as he bent over her, felt water dripping on his back. [7]

What are we to make of these reports? The elaboration of the received view we have just sketched can deal with them, but at a high cost: precognition. If the terminal events in these dreams are strongly *prepared for* by the narrative, if they do not consist of radically juxtaposed turns in the narrative (for example, the goat turns into a telephone and starts ringing), then the composition process must have been directed by something having "knowledge" of the future. That is too high a price for most of us to pay, no doubt. Perhaps all these anecdotes succumb to a mixture of reasonable skepticism, statistics (coincidences do happen, and are to be "expected" once in a blue moon), the discovery of subtle influences from the environment, and various other deflating redescriptions. But if all else failed we could devise any number of variant dream theories that accommodated these "miracles" in less than miraculous ways. Perhaps, to echo the earlier conjecture, dreams are composed and presented *very fast* in the interval between bang, bump, or buzz and full consciousness, with some short delay system postponing the full "perception" of the noise in the dream until the presentation of the narrative is ready for it. Or perhaps in that short interval dreams are composed, presented, and recorded *backwards*, and then remembered front to back. Or perhaps there is a "library" in the brain of undreamed dreams with various indexed endings, and the bang or bump or buzz has the effect of retrieving an appropriate dream and inserting it, cassette-like, in the memory mechanism.

None of these theories can be viewed as a mere variation or rival elaboration of the received view. If one of them is true, then the received view is false. And since these rival theories, including the theory inspired by the received view, are all empirical, subject to confirmation and refutation, and since the rival theories even have some (admittedly anecdotal) evidence in their favor, we are constrained to admit that the received view might simply turn out to be false: dreams, it might turn out, are not what we took them to be—or perhaps we would say that it turns out that there are no dreams after all, only dream "recollections" produced in the manner described in our confirmed theory, whichever it is. Malcolm sees that all this is implied by the received view, and takes it to be yet another *reductio ad absurdum* of it: any view that could permit the discovery that "we are always only under the *illusion* of having had a dream" is "senseless".[8] But again, Malcolm's response to this implication is too drastic. The claim that we had been fooled for millennia into believing in dreams would be hard to swallow, but then we would not have to swallow it unless it had the backing of a strongly confirmed scientific theory, and then this claim would put no greater strain on our credulity than we have already endured from the claims of Copernicus, Einstein, and others. It would be rather like learning that dream-recall was like *déjà vu*—it only *seemed* that you had experienced it before—and once you believed *that*, it would no longer even seem (as strongly) that you were recalling. The experience of "dream recall" would change for us.*

My attack on the received view is not, however, a straightforward

---

*Cf. Putnam, *op. cit.*, p. 227. The naïve subject of *déjà vu* says, "I vaguely remember experiencing all this before"; the sophisticated subject is not even tempted to say this, but says, perhaps, "Hm, I'm having a *déjà vu* experience right now." The experience has changed.

empirical attack. I do not wish to aver that anecdotal evidence about dream anticipation disproves the received view, but I do want to consider in more detail what the issues would be were a rival to the received view to gain support. I hope to show that the received view is more vulnerable to empirical disconfirmation than its status as the received view would lead us to expect. Of the rival theories, the cassette-library theory runs most strongly against our pretheoretical convictions, for on the other two there still is some vestige of the presumed presentation process: it is just much faster than we had expected, or happens backwards. On the cassette view, our "precognitive" dreams are never dreamed at all, but just spuriously "recalled" on waking. If our memory mechanisms were empty until the moment of waking, and then received a whole precomposed dream narrative in one lump, the idea that precognitive dreams are *experienced episodes* during sleep would have to go by the board.

Suppose we generalize the cassette theory to cover all dreams: all dream narratives are composed directly into memory banks; which, if any, of these is available to waking recollection depends on various factors—precedence of composition, topicality of waking stimulus, degree of "repression", and so forth. On this view, the process of presentation has vanished, and although the dream cassettes would have to be filled at some time by a composition process, that process might well occur during our waking hours, and spread over months (it takes a long time to write a good story). The composition might even have occurred aeons before our birth; we might have an *innate* library of undreamed dream cassettes ready for appropriate insertion in the playback mechanism. Stranger things have been claimed. Even on the received view, the composition process is an unconscious or subconscious process of which we normally have no more *experience* than of the processes regulating our metabolism; otherwise dreams could not be suspenseful. (I say "normally" for there does seem to be the phenomenon of self-conscious dreaming, where we tinker with a dream, run it by several times, attempt to resume it where it left off. Here the theatrical metaphor that enlivens the received view seems particularly apt. After tinkering like the playwright, we must sit back, get ourselves back into the audience mood, suspend disbelief, and re-enter the play. Some researchers call these occasions *lucid dreams.* But usually we are not privy to the composition process at all, and so have no inkling about when it might occur.) Research might give us good grounds for believing- that dream narratives that were composed onto cassettes in the morning decayed faster than cassettes composed in the afternoon, or during meals.

A more likely finding of the cassette-theorist would be that the composition process occurs during sleep, and more particularly, during periods of rapid eye movements, with characteristic EEG patterns. One might even be able to "translate" the composition process—that is, predict dream recollections from data about the composition process. This theory looks suspiciously like the elaboration of the received theory, except that it lacks the presentation process. Cassette narratives, we are told, are composed in narrative order, and long narratives take longer to compose, and the decay time for cassettes in storage is usually quite short; normally the dream one "recalls" on waking was composed just minutes earlier, a fact attested to by the occasional cases of content-relativity in one of the by-products of cassette composition: rapid eye movements. On this theory dream memories are produced just the way the received theory says they are, except for one crucial thing: the process of dream-memory production is entirely unconscious, involves no awareness or experiencing at all. Even "lucid dreams" can be accommodated easily on this hypothesis, as follows: although the composition and recording processes are entirely unconscious, on occasion the composition process inserts traces of itself into the recording via the literary conceit of a dream within a dream.*

Now we have a challenge to the received view worth reckoning with. It apparently accounts for all the data of the REM researchers as well as the received view does, so there is no reason for sober investigators not to adopt the cassette theory forthwith if it has any advantages over the received view. And it seems that it does: it has a simple explanation of precognitive dreams (if there are any) and it posits one less process by eliminating a presentation process whose point begins to be lost.

But what greater point could a process have? In its presence we have experience; in its absence we have none. As Thomas Nagel would put it, the central issue between these two theories appears to be whether or not it is like anything to dream.[9] On the cassette theory it is not like anything to dream, although it is like something *to have dreamed.* On the cassette theory, dreams are not experiences we have during sleep; where we had thought there were dreams, there is only an unconscious composition process and an equally unconscious memory-loading process.

A few years ago there was a flurry of experimentation in learning-while-you-sleep. Tape recordings of textbooks were played in the

*For more on lucid dreams and their accommodation by the cassette theory, see Kathleen Emmett, "Oneiric Experiences" and my "The Onus Re Experiences: a Reply to Emmett", both forthcoming in *Philosophical Studies.*

sleeper's room, and tests were run to see if there were any subsequent signs of learning. As I recall, the results were negative, but some people thought the results were positive. If you had asked one of them *what it was like* to learn in one's sleep, the reply would presumably have been: "It was not like anything at all—I was sound asleep at the time. I went to sleep not knowing any geography and woke up knowing quite a bit, but don't ask me what it was like. It wasn't like anything." If the cassette theory of dreams is true, dream-recollection production is a similarly unexperienced process. If asked what it is like to dream one *ought* to say (because it would be the truth): "It is not like anything. I go to sleep and when I wake up I find I have a tale to tell, a 'recollection' as it were." It is Malcolm's view that this is what we ought to say, but Malcolm is not an explicit champion of the cassette theory or any other empirical theory of dreaming. His reasons, as we shall see, are derived from "conceptual analysis". But whatever the reasons are, the conclusion seems outrageous. *We all know better*, we think. But do we? We are faced with two strikingly different positions about what happens when we dream, and one of these, the received view, we are not just loath to give up; we find it virtually unintelligible that we could be wrong about it. And yet the point of difference between it (as elaborated into a theory by scientists) and its rival, the cassette theory, is apparently a technical, theoretical matter about which the layman's biases, his everyday experience, and even his personal recollections of dreams are without authority or even weight. What should we do? Sit back and wait for the experts to tell us, hoping against hope that dreams will turn out to be, after all, experiences? That seems ridiculous.

If that seems ridiculous, perhaps it *is* ridiculous. Can some way be found to protect the received view from the possibility of losing this contest? If we do not for a minute believe it could lose, we must suppose there is some principled explanation of this. One might set out in a verificationist manner.* What could possibly settle the issue between the received view and the cassette theory if subjects' recollections were deemed neutral? The conclusion of one view is that dreams are experiences, and of the other, thát they are not; but if subjects' recollections were not held to be *criterial*, nothing else could count as evidence for or against the rival theories, at least with regard to this disputed conclusion. Therefore the claimed difference between the two theories is illusory, or perhaps we should say they are both pseudo-theories. This

*This argument is inspired by the verificationist arguments of Malcolm, and its rebuttal is inspired by Putnam's objections, but Malcolm does not commit himself to this argument.

will not do. We can easily imagine the two theories to share a concept of experience, and even to agree on which data would go to show that dreams were, in this shared technical sense, experiences. Nor would this technical concept of experience have to look all that unordinary. We have many common ways of distinguishing which among the events that impinge on us are experienced and which are not, and we can imagine these theories to build from these ordinary distinctions a powerful shared set of well-confirmed empirically necessary and sufficient conditions for events to be experienced. If, for instance, some part of the brain is invariably active in some characteristic way when some event in waking life is, as we ordinarily say, experienced, and if moreover we have a theory that says why this should be so, the absence of such brain activity during REM periods would look bad for the received view and good for the cassette view.

But if that is what we should look for, the received view is in trouble, for one routinely recognized condition for having an experience is that one be conscious, or awake, and dreamers are not. A well-confirmed physiological condition for this is that one's reticular activating system be "on", which it is not during sleep. The fact that one is in a sound sleep goes a long way to confirming that one is *not* having experiences, as *ordinarily* understood. Malcolm would make this criterial, but that is one more overstatement. Lack of reticular system activity strongly suggests that nothing is being experienced during REMs, but the defender of the received view can plausibly reply that reticular activation is only a condition of *normal* experience, and can point to the frequent occurrence during REM periods of the normal physiological accompaniments of fear, anxiety, delight, and arousal as considerations in favor of an extended concept of experience. How could one exhibit an emotional reaction to something not even experienced? The debate would not stop there, but we need not follow it further now. The fact remains that the physiological data would be clearly relevant evidence in the dispute between the theories, and not all the evidence is on the side of the received view.

Still, one might say, the very relevance of physiological evidence shows the dispute not to involve our ordinary concept of experience at all, but only a technical substitute. For suppose we were told without further elaboration that the theory inspired by the received view had won the debate, had proved to be the better theory. We would not know what, if anything, had been confirmed by this finding. Which of our hunches and biases would be thereby vindicated, and are any of them truly in jeopardy?

This plausible rhetorical question suggests that none of our precious preconceptions about dreaming *could* be in jeopardy, a conclusion that "conceptual analysis" might discover for us. How might this be done? Let us return to the comparison between the cassette view of dreams and the speculation that one might learn in one's sleep. I suggested that subjects in either circumstance should, on waking, deny that it was like anything to have undergone the phenomenon. But there would be a crucial difference in their waking states, presumably. For the dreamer, unlike the sleep-learner, would probably want to add to his disclaimer: "Of course it *seems to me* to have been like something!" The sleep learner has new knowledge, or new beliefs, but not new *memories*. This is surely an important difference, but just what difference does it make? Is it that the claim:

(5) It was not like anything, but it seems to me to have been like something,

is a covert contradiction? Can one sustain the following principle?

(6) If it seems to have been like something, it was like something.

The present tense version of the principle is unassailable:

(7) If it seems to me to be like something to be *x*, then it is like something to me to be *x*.

That is what we mean when we talk of what it is like: how it seems to us.* When we try to make the principle extend through memory to the past, however, we run into difficulties. There is no good reason to deny that memories can be spurious, and there is plenty of confirmation that they can. This is somewhat obscured by some looseness in our understanding of the verb "remember". Sometimes we draw a distinction between remembering and seeming to remember such that remembering, like knowing, is veridical. On this reading it follows that if you remember something to have been *x*, it was *x*. If it was not *x*, you only seem to remember that it was. But when I say, about a restaurant we are dining in, "This isn't the way I remember it," my claim is equivocal. I may not be claiming the restaurant has changed— it may be that my memory is at fault. On this reading of "remember" there is still a distinction between remembering and seeming to remember, but it is not a distinction with veridicality on one side: for example one tells a tale of one's childhood that is shown to be false and one wonders whether one has mistaken fantasizing or confabulating for (mis)remembering. On *either* reading, however, there is no claim that can be made of the form:

---

*Cf. Nagel, "What Is It Like to Be a Bat?":440n. "[T]he analogical form of the English expression 'what is it *like*' is misleading. It does not mean 'what (in our experience) it resembles', but rather 'how it is for the subject himself'."

(8) Since I remember it to have been like something, it was like something.

On the first reading of "remember", the claim, while logically impeccable, does no work unless one claims a capacity to tell one's memories from one's seeming memories that one simply does not have. On the second reading, even if we could always tell fantasy from memory the consequent would not follow. So (5) represents a possible state of affairs. We had in fact already countenanced this state of affairs as an abnormality in supposing that the dream researchers could, by tampering, insert a spurious dream recollection. Now we are countenancing it as a possible and not even improbable account of the normal case.

Malcolm sees that nothing like (6) or (8) can be exploited in this context; we can seem to have had an experience when we have not, and for just this reason he denies that dreams are experiences! His argument is that *since* one can be under the impression that one has had an experience and yet not have had it, and since if one is under the impression that one has had a dream, one *has* had a dream,* having had a dream cannot be having had an experience; hence, dreams are not experiences.

This "criteriological" move has a curious consequence: it "saves" the authority of the wakened dream-recaller, and this *looks like* a rescue of subjectivity from the clutches of objective science, but it "saves" dreaming only at the expense of experience. What Malcolm sees is that if we permit a distinction between "remembering" and "seeming to remember" to apply to dream recollections, the concept of dreaming is cast adrift from any criterial anchoring to first-person reports, and becomes (or is revealed to be) a theoretical concept. Once we grant that subjective, introspective or retrospective evidence does not have the authority to settle questions about the nature of dreams—for instance, whether dreams are experiences—we have to turn to the other data, the behavior and physiology of dreamers, and to the relative strengths of the theories of these, if we are to settle the question, a question which the subject is not in a privileged position to answer.

---

*"That he really had a dream and that he is under the impression that he had a dream: these are the same thing" ("Dreaming and Skepticism",:32). This is the central premise of Malcolm's work on dreaming, and one he gets from Wittgenstein: "The question whether the dreamer's memory deceives him when he reports the dream after waking cannot arise unless indeed we introduce a completely new criterion for the report's 'agreeing' with the dream, a criterion which gives us a concept of 'truth' as distinguished from 'truthfulness' here" (*Philosophical Investigations*:222-223). It is Malcolm's unswerving loyalty to this remark that forces his account into such notorious claims.

Malcolm avoids this by denying that dreams are experiences, but this only concedes that one does *not* have a privileged opinion about one's own past experiences.* This concession is unavoidable, I think, and Malcolm's is not the only philosophic position caused embarrassment by it. A defender of the subjective realm such as Nagel must grant that in general, whether or not it was like something to be *x*, whether or not the subject *experienced* being *x*—questions that *define* the subjective realm—are questions about which the subject's subsequent subjective opinion is not authoritative. But if the subject's own convictions do not settle the matter, and if, as Nagel holds, no objective considerations are conclusive either, the subjective realm floats out of ken altogether, except perhaps for the subject's convictions about the specious present. Dreams are particularly vulnerable in this regard only because, as Malcolm observes, sleepers do not and cannot *express* current convictions about the specious present (if they have any) while they are dreaming. Since our only expressible access to dreams is retrospective, dreams are particularly vulnerable, but they are not alone. The argument we have been considering is more general; the dispute between the rival theories of memory-loading can be extended beyond dreaming to all experience. For instance, just now, while you were reading my remarks about Nagel, were you experiencing the peripheral sights and sounds available in your environment? Of course you were, you say, and you can prove it to your own complete satisfaction by closing your eyes and recalling a variety of events or conditions that co-occurred with your reading those remarks. While not *central* in your consciousness at the time, they were certainly *there*, being *experienced*, as your recollections show. But the cassette theorist, emboldened by the success with dreams, puts forward the *subliminal peripheral recollection-production* theory, the view that the variety of peripheral details in such cases are not consciously experienced, but merely unconsciously recorded for subsequent recall. Events outside our immediate attention are not experienced at all, our theorist says, but they do have subliminal effects on short-term memory. Our capacity to recall them for a short period does not establish that they were experienced, any more than our capacity to "recall" dreams shows that they were experienced. But this is nonsense, you say: *recording those peripheral items for subsequent recollection just is experiencing them.*

If only this bold claim were true! Look what it would do for us. The

---

*Sometimes Malcolm seems to want to "save" all "private states" in this way, thus either having to deny that experiences are private states, or having to adopt after all some principle like (8). See *Dreaming*, p. 55.

difference between the received view of dreams and the cassette theory would collapse; the presumably unconscious memory-loading process of the cassette theory would turn out to be the very presentation process dear to the received view. A "conceptual relationship" could be established between experience and memory that avoided the difficulties heretofore encountered in such claims, as follows: The conceptual relationship is *not* between experiencing and subsequent subjective convictions of memory (the latter are *not* criterial), but between experiencing and something perfectly objective: the laying down thereupon of a memory trace—for however short a time and regardless of subsequent success or failure at recollection.* The conceptual relationship would be identity. *Experire est recordare.*

Much can be said in support of this principle, but at this time I will restrict myself to a few brief persuasions. First, is remembering a *necessary* condition for experiencing? Arguably, yes, if you grant that memories may not last long. The idea of a subject, an "I", experiencing each successive state in a stream of consciousness with *no* recollection of its predecessors, is a hopelessly impoverished model of experience and experiencers. The *familiarity* and *continuity* in the world of current experiences is a necessary background for recognition and discrimination, and only short-term memory can provide this. Items that come and go so fast, or so inconspicuously, as to leave no reverberations behind in memory at all, are plausibly viewed as simply not experienced. So if remembering is a necessary condition, is it also a *sufficient* condition for experiencing? Yost and Kalish say so, without supporting argument: "Dreaming is a real experience. And since dreams can be remembered they must be conscious experiences."[10] Martin and Deutscher, in their article "Remembering", concur:

> So long as we hold some sort of 'storage' or 'trace' account of memory, it follows that we can remember only what we have experienced, for it is in our experience of events that they "enter" the storehouse.[11]

So remembering, in the sense of storing away in the memory for some time, is arguably a necessary and sufficient condition for experiencing. These are, I think, philosophically respectable arguments for the claimed identity, and to them can be added an ulterior

---

*Not completely regardless of subsequent success or failure at recollection, for identifying some process as the laying down of a memory trace is identifying some process by its function, and nothing that did not have as its normal effect enabling the subject to report truly about the past could be picked out functionally as the memory-loading process.

consideration which will appeal to physicalists if not to others. The proposed identity of experiencing and recording promises a striking simplification for physicalist theories of mind. The problematic (largely because utterly vague) presentation process vanishes as an extra phenomenon to be accounted for, and with it goes the even more mysterious *audience* or *recipient* of those presentations. In its place is just a relatively prosaic short-term memory capacity, the sort of thing for which rudimentary but suggestive physical models already abound.

The principle as it stands, however, is too strong, on two counts. Consider again Martin and Deutscher's commentary on the "storehouse" model of memory: "It is in our experience of events that they 'enter' the storehouse." What, though, of forcible or illegal entry? We need an account of something like *normal* entry into memory so that we can rule out, as experiences, such abnormally entered items as the undreamed dream surgically inserted by the dream researchers. We want to rule out such cases, not by declaring them impossible, for they are not, but by denying that they are experiences for the subject. As we shall see in a moment, the best way of doing this may have a surprising consequence. The second failing of our principle is simply that it lacks the status we have claimed for it. It is not self-evident; its denial is not a contradiction. We must not make the mistake of asserting that this is a discovered conceptual truth about experience and memory. We must understand it as a proposal, a theoretically promising adjustment in our ordinary concepts for which we may have to sacrifice some popular preconceptions. For instance, whether animals can be held to dream, or to experience anything, is rendered an uncertainty depending on what we mean by *recall*. Can animals *recall* events? If not, they cannot have experiences. More radically, subjective authority about experience goes by the board entirely. Still, we get a lot in return, not the least of which is a way of diagnosing and dismissing the Pickwickian hypothesis of subliminal peripheral recollection-production.

We are still not out of the woods on dreaming, though, for we must define normal memory-entry in such a way as to admit ordinary experience and exclude tampering and other odd cases.

When the memory gets loaded by accident or interference we will not want this to count as experience, and yet we want to grant that there is such a thing as nonveridical experience. The memory-loading that occurs during a hallucination occurs during abnormal circumstances, but not so abnormal as to lead us to deny that hallucinations are experiences. But look at a slightly different case (I do not know if this ever occurs, but it might). Suppose at noon Jones, who is wide awake, suffers some event in her brain that has a delayed effect: at

12:15 she will "recall" having seen a ghost at noon. Suppose her recollection is as vivid as you like, but suppose her actual behavior at noon (and up until recollection at 12:15) showed no trace of horror, surprise, or cognizance of anything untoward. Had she shown any signs at noon of being under the impression that something bizarre was happening, we would be strongly inclined to say she had had a hallucination then, was experiencing it then, even if she could not recount it to us until fifteen minutes later. But since she did not *react* in any such telling way at noon, but proceeded about her business, we are strongly inclined to say the hallucination occurred later, at 12:15, and was a *hallucination of recollection* of something she had never experienced, even though the cause of the hallucination occurred at noon. Since the events responsible for her later capacity to recall did not contribute to her behavior-controlling state at the time, they did not enter her experience then, whatever their later repercussions. But then when we apply this distinguishing principle to dreams, we find that it is quite likely that most dreams are not experiences. Whereas nightmares accompanied by moans, cries, cowering, and sweaty palms *would* be experiences, bad dreams dreamed in repose (though remembered in agony) would not be, unless, contrary to surface appearances, their entry into memory is accomplished by engagements of the whole behavior-controlling system sufficiently normal to distinguish these cases sharply from our imaginary delayed hallucination.*

If it turns out that sleep, or at least that portion of sleep during which dreaming occurs, is a state of more or less peripheral paralysis or inactivity; if it turns out that most of the functional areas that are critical to the governance of our wide awake acitvity are in operation, then there will be good reason for drawing the lines around experience so that dreams are included. If not, there will be good reason to deny that dreams are experiences.

Some of the relevant data are already familiar. The occurrence of REMs suggests that more then a little of the visual processing system is active during dream periods, and it should be a fairly straightforward task—perhaps already accomplished—to determine just how much is. Even strongly positive results would not be overwhelming grounds for deciding that dreams are experiences, however, for in various sorts of hysteric or psychosomatic blindness there is substantial apparently normal activity in the visual processing system, and in so-called

---

*Malcolm too sees an important distinction between "violent nightmares" and normal dreams dreamed in repose, a distinction that forces him to claim we have several different concepts of sleep. Only thus can he save as a *conceptual* truth the claim that we have no experiences while we sleep.

subliminal perception the same is true, and in neither case are we inclined to suppose that visual experience occurs. More compelling, in many ways, is the evidence that dreams serve a purpose: they seem to be used to redress emotional imbalances caused by frustrating experiences in waking life, to rationalize cognitive dissonances, allay anxieties, and so forth. When this task is too difficult, it seems, the dream mechanisms often go into a looping cycle; troubled people often report recurring obsessive dreams that haunt them night after night. It is implausible that such recurrent dreams must be recomposed each night,* so if a recurrent physiological process can be correlated with these dreams, it will appear to be a presentation process, and the presentation process will have a point: namely, to provide the emotional and cognitive-processing functional parts with the raw material for new syntheses, new accommodations, perhaps permitting a more stable or satisfying self-image for the dreamer. But even this function could easily be seen to be accomplished entirely *unconsciously*. The self-presentation tactics and perceptual interpretation ploys posited by theorists as diverse as Freud and Erving Goffman are no less plausible for being presumed to be entirely unconscious, and they serve a similar self-protective maintenance function. As Malcolm points out, dreamers' narratives can be used by Freudians and others as a valuable source of information about the internal processes that shape us, without our having to suppose that these are recollections of experiences.**

It is an *open*, and *theoretical* question whether dreams fall inside or outside the boundary of experience.*** A plausible theory of experience will be one that does justice to *three* distinguishable families of intuitions we have about experience and consciousness: those dealing

*I am indebted to Robert Nozick for raising this consideration.
***Dreaming*, p. 122. Malcolm quotes with approval this methodological suggestion of Freud's from *A General Introduction to Psychoanalysis* (Garden City:Norton, 1943), p. 76.

> Any disadvantage resulting from the uncertain recollection of dreams may be remedied by deciding that exactly what the dreamer tells is to count as the dream, and by ignoring all that he may have forgotten or altered in the process of recollection.

***Foulkes, *The Psychology of Sleep* (New York: Scribners, 1966) cites a number of telling, if inconclusive, further observations: in one study no association was found between "the excitement value of dream content and heart or respiration rate" (p. 50), a datum to be balanced by the curious fact that there are usually action-potentials discoverable in the motor-neurons in the biceps of one who is asked to *imagine* bending one's arm; similar action-potentials are found in the arms of deaf mute dreamers—people who talk with their hands. There are also high levels of activity in the sensory cortex during dreaming sleep.

with the role of experience in guiding current behavior, those dealing with our *current* proclivities and capacities to *say* what we are experiencing, and those dealing with the *retrospective* or *recollective* capacity to say. In earlier work I have sharply distinguished the first and second of these, but underestimated the distinctness and importance of this third source of demands on a theory of consciousness. A theory that does justice to these distinct and often inharmonious demands must also do justice to a fourth: the functional saliencies that emerge from empirical investigation. In the end, the concept of experience may not prove to differentiate any one thing of sufficient theoretical interest to warrant time spent in determining its boundaries. Were this to occur, the received view of dreams, like the lay view of experience in general, would not be so much disproved as rendered obsolete. It may seem inconceivable that this could happen, but armchair conceptual analysis is powerless to establish this.

9

Toward a Cognitive Theory of Consciousness

I

Philosophers of mind and epistemologists have much to learn from recent work in cognitive psychology, but one of philosophy's favorite facets of mentality has received scant attention from cognitive psychologists, and that is consciousness itself: full-blown, introspective, inner-world, phenomenological consciousness. In fact if one looks in the obvious places (the more ambitious attempts at whole theories, overviews of recent research, and more specialized work in such areas as attention and "mental imagery") one finds not so much a lack of interest as a deliberate and adroit avoidance of the issue. I think I know why. Consciousness appears to be the last bastion of occult properties, epiphenomena, immeasurable subjective states—in short, the one area of mind best left to the philosophers, who are welcome to it. Let them make fools of themselves trying to corral the quicksilver of "phenomenology" into a respectable theory.

This would permit an acceptable division of labor were it not for the fact that cognitive psychologists have skirted the domain of consciousness by so wide a margin that they offer almost no suggestions about what the "interface" between the models of cognitive psychology and a theory of consciousness should be. I propose to fill this gap and sketch a theory of consciousness that can be continuous with and help to unify current cognitivist theories of perception, problem-solving, and language use. I fear that to the extent that the view I put forward is seen to meet these desiderata, it will *seem* not to do justice to the phenomena, so it would help if first I said just what I am trying to do justice to. Nagel has epitomized the problem of consciousness with the question: "What is it like to be something?"[1] It is certainly not like anything to be a brick or a hamburger; it certainly is like something to be you or me; and it seems to be like something to be a bat or a dog or a dolphin, if only we could figure out what. The question, "Is it like something to be an X?" may in the end be the wrong question to ask, but it excellently captures the intuitions that constitute the challenge to a theory of consciousness. Until one's psychological or physiological or cybernetic theory explains how it can be like something to be something (or explains *in detail* what is wrong with this demand), one's theory will be *seriously* incomplete. It is open to the theorist, of course, to reject the challenge out of hand. One can emulate those behaviorists who (it has been charged) "feign anesthesia" and categorically deny that anyone *has* an inner life. This course has little or nothing to recommend it. Some behaviorists may find this comfortable ground to defend, but it would be awkward at the very least for the cognitivist, who has to explain what is going on when, for example, one asks one's experimental subjects to form a mental image, or to give an introspective account of problem-solving, or to attend to the sentences in the left earphone rather than the sentences in the right earphone. The cognitivist must take consciousness seriously, but there are relatively noncommittal ways of doing this. One can somewhat paradoxically treat consciousness itself as something of a "black box" from which introspective and retrospective statements issue (with their associated reaction times, and so forth), but how is this black box fastened to the other boxes in one's model? I shall propose an answer to this question, one that will also be a partial account of what is going on inside the black box.

II

There is much that happens to me and in me of which I am *not* conscious, which I do not experience, and there is much that happens in and to me of which I *am* conscious. That of which I am conscious is that to which I have *access*, or (to put the emphasis where it belongs), that to which *I* have access. Let us call this sort of access the access of personal consciousness, thereby stressing that the *subject* of that access (whatever it is) which exhausts consciousness is the *person*, and not any of the person's parts. The first step in characterizing this access is to distinguish it from two other sorts of access that play important roles in cognitive theories. The first of these can be called *computational access*. When a computer program is composed of subroutines (typically governed by an "executive" routine) one can speak of one routine having access to the output of another. This means simply that there is an information link between them: the results of computation of one subroutine are available for further computation by another subroutine. A variety of interesting issues can be couched in terms of computational access. For instance, Marvin Minsky faults the design of current chess-playing programs by pointing out that the executive programs typically do not have enough *access* (of the right sort) to the routines that evaluate the various lines of play considered. Typically, the evaluator "has to summarize the results of all the search . . . and compress them into a single numerical quantity to represent the value of being at node A . . . [but] we want S [the output of the evaluator] to tell the Move Generator which kinds of moves to consider. But if S is a mere number, this is unsuitable for much reasoning or analysis."[2] It would be better if the higher executive had more access to the details of the line of play evaluated, and not just a summary judgment.

In a very different context, Julesz' perception experiments using randomly generated dot displays show that at least some perceptual information about depth, for instance, is computed by a process that has *access* to highly uninterpreted information about the pattern of light stimulating the retinas.[3] Lines of computational access are currently being studied in cognitive psychology and related fields, and there are useful characterizations of direct and indirect access, variable access, gated access, and so forth. Computational access has nothing *directly* to do with the access of personal consciousness, for *we* do not have access to many things that various parts of our nervous systems are shown to have access to. For instance, some levels of the visual processing system must have computational access to information about inner ear state changes and saccadic eye movements, but *we* do not, and *we* have virtually no access to the information our autonomic nervous systems must have access to in order to maintain the complex homeostases of health.

The second sort of access to distinguish from both computational access and the access of personal consciousness might be called *public access*. Often it is useful to a programmer to have access to what the computer is doing, so that the computer's progress on the program can be monitored; and to this end a "trace" is provided for in the program so that the computer can print out information about the intermediate steps in its own operations. One provides for public access of this sort by designing a print-out subroutine and giving it *computational* access to whatever one wants public access to. This is a nontrivial additional provision in a program, for there is a difference between, say, the access the executive routine has to its subroutines, and the access the print-out routine has to the access the executive routine has. The domain of computational access for a system and the domain of public access for the system user are as distinct as the functions and offices of Secretary of State Henry Kissinger and Press Secretary Ron Nessen. Kissinger has computational access to much information that we the public have no access to, because Nessen, our avenue of access, has no computational access to the information. What is used for control is one thing, and what is available to the public is another, and there is at best a contingently large overlap between these domains, both in computer systems and in the White House.

The notion of public access seems to bring us closer to the personal access of consciousness, for we are speaking creatures (we have a sort of print-out faculty), and—at least to a first approximation—that of which we are conscious is that of which we can tell, introspectively or retrospectively. There is a problem, however. So far, the *subject* of public access has not been identified. On the one hand we can speak of the *public's* access via print-out or other publication to what is going on in a system, and on the other we can speak of the *print-out faculty's* computational access to the information it publishes; but surely neither of these subjects is the "I" who has access to my contents of consciousness, nor does any more suitable subject appear likely to be found in this neighborhood.

There are other worries as well, of course. Nonhuman, nonverbal creatures have no print-out faculties, or at best very rudimentary and unexpressive print-out faculties, yet some philosophers—notably Nagel —insist that full-blown, phenomenological consciousness is as much their blessing as ours. I think one can be skeptical of this claim without thereby becoming the Village Verificationist, but the issue deserves an unhurried treatment of its own.

The picture of a human being as analogous to a large organization, with intercommunicating departments, executives, and a public relations unit to "speak for the organization" is very attractive and useful. The basic idea is as old as Plato's *Republic*, but it seems to have a fatal flaw: it is not like anything to be such an organization. What is it like to be the Ford Administration? Nothing, obviously, even if it is like something to be a certain part of that administration. The whole is a very clever assemblage of coordinated *parts* that at its best acts with a unity not unlike the unity of a single person,[4] but still, it has no soul of its own, even if some of its parts do.

This apparently decisive shortcoming threatens a wide spectrum of theory-building enterprises currently receiving favorable attention in philosophy and psychology. Any philosopher of mind who (like myself) favors a "functionalist" theory of mind must face the fact that the very feature that has been seen to recommend functionalism over cruder brands of materialism—its abstractness and hence neutrality with regard to what could "realize" the functions deemed essential to sentient or intentional systems—permits a functionalist theory, however realistically biological or humanoid in flavor, to be instantiated not only by robots (an acceptable or even desirable consequence in the eyes of some), but by suprahuman organizations that would seem to have minds of their own only in the flimsiest metaphorical sense.

Davis has raised a graphic version of this objection with regard to functionalist theories of pain.[5] Let a functionalist theory of pain (whatever its details) be instantiated by a system the subassemblies of which are not such things as C-fibers and reticular systems but telephone lines and offices staffed by people. Perhaps it is a giant robot controlled by an army of human beings that inhabit it. When the theory's functionally characterized conditions for pain are now met we must say, if the theory is true, that the robot is in pain. That is, real pain, as real as our own, would exist in virtue of the perhaps disinterested and businesslike activities of these bureaucratic teams, executing their proper functions. It does *seem* that there must be more to pain than that.[6]

Psychologists cannot escape this embarrassment merely by declining to embrace philosophers' versions of functionalism, for their own theories are vulnerable to a version of the same objection. Functionalist theories are theories of what I have called the sub-personal level. Subpersonal theories proceed by analyzing a person into an organization of subsystems (organs, routines, nerves, faculties, components—even atoms) and attempting to explain the behavior of the whole person as the outcome of the interaction of these subsystems. Thus in the present instance the shortcoming emerged because the two access notions introduced, computational access *simpliciter* and the computational access of a print-out faculty, were defined at the sub-personal level; if introduced into a psychological theory they would characterize relations not between a person and a body, or a person and a state of affairs or a person and anything at all, but rather, at best, relations between *parts* of persons (or their bodies) and other things. So far as I can see, however, every cognitivist theory currently defended or envisaged, functionalist or not, is a theory of the sub-personal level. It is not at all clear to me, indeed, how a psychological theory—as distinct from a philosophical theory—could fail to be a sub-personal theory.* So the functionalists' problem of capturing the person as subject of experience must arise as well for these cognitivist theories. At best a sub-personal theory will seem to give us *no grounds* for believing its instantiations would be subjects of experience, and at worst (as we have seen) a sub-personal theory will seem to permit instantiations that *obviously are not* subjects of experience Take your favorite inchoate cognitivist theory and imagine it completed and improved along the lines of its infancy; is it not always easy to imagine the completed theory instantiated or "realized" by an entity—an engineer's contraption, for instance, or some kind of zombie—to which we have no inclination to grant an inner, conscious life?

Intuition then, proclaims that any sub-personal theory must leave out something vital, something unobtainable moreover with subpersonal resources. Intuitions can sometimes be appeased or made to go away, however, and that is the task I set myself here. I propose to construct a full-fledged "I" out of sub-personal parts by exploiting the sub-personal notions of access already introduced.

This unpromising enterprise is forced on me, as students, colleagues, and other critics have insisted over the last few years, if I am to salvage the sort of functionalist theory of the mind I have heretofore defended. Since I have no other theory of the mind to fall back on, since in fact I see no remotely plausible alternatives to tempt me, I accept this problem as mine. It is not mine alone, though, as I hope I have made clear. This is fortunate, for the problem begs for a cooperative solution; my attempt trespasses deep in psychologists' territory, and I would hope to stimulate assistance, not a boundary dispute, from that quarter.

The first step is to sketch a sub-personal flow chart, a cognitivistic model that by being sub-personal "evades" the question of personal consciousness but, unlike cognitivistic psychologies with which I am familiar, prepares attachment points for subsequent explicit claims about consciousness. The flow chart will be a philosopher's amateur production, oversimplified in several dimensions, but I think it will be fairly clear how one could go about adding complications.

*Ryle and Wittgenstein are the preeminent modern theorists of the personal level. In fact, in their different ways they invent the enterprise, by showing that there is work to be done, that there are questions that arise purely at the personal level, and that one misconceives the questions if one offers sub-personal hypotheses or theories as answers. Typically readers who do not understand, or accept, these difficult claims see them as evading or missing the point, and complain that neither Ryle nor Wittgenstein has any positive psychological theory to offer at all. That is true: the personal level "theory" of persons is not a psychological theory.

Figure 9-1

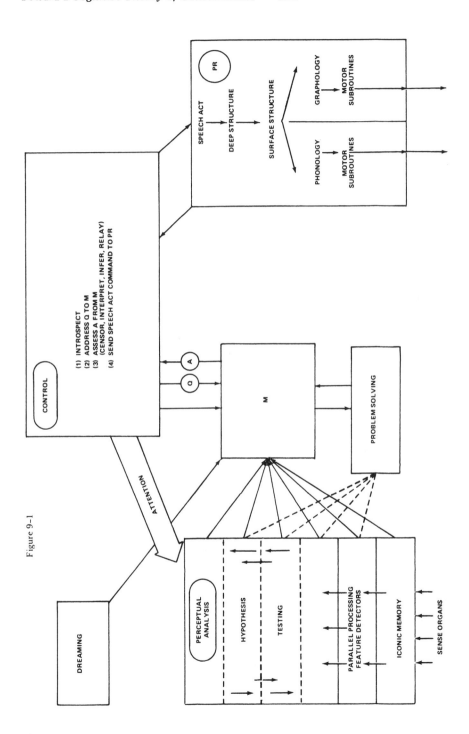

III

For clarity I restrict attention to six of the functional areas to which a theory of consciousness must do justice (see Figure 9.1). At the output end we have the print-out component, and since this is our own Ron Nessen analogue I shall call it *PR*. *PR* takes as input *orders to perform speech acts*, or *semantic intentions*, and executes these orders. The details of the organization of the *PR* component are hotly contested by psycholinguists and others, and I do not wish to adjudicate the debates. Roughly, I suppose the breakdown to be as follows: the speech act command gets turned into an *oratio obliqua* command (to say that *p*), and this gets turned into a "deep structure" specification—in "semantic markerese" perhaps—which in turn yields a surface structure or *oratio recta* specification. We can imagine this to branch into either a phonological or graphological specification, depending on whether the initial command was to speak or write. These specifications, finally, drive motor subroutines that drive the vocal or writing apparatus to yield an ultimate execution of the input intention. There is a good deal of interaction between the levels: if one has difficulty pronouncing a certain word, this may count against its inclusion in the surface structure if one intends to speak, but not if one is writing.

PR gets all its directions from a higher executive or *Control* component, but the pool of information to which *PR* has access is a special short-term memory store or buffer memory, which I shall simply call *M*. The lines of communication between Control, *M*, and *PR* are roughly as follows: suppose Control "decides" for various reasons to "introspect":

(1) it goes into its introspection subroutine, in which
(2) it directs a question to *M*;
(3) when an answer comes back (and none may) it assesses the answer: it may
  (a) censor the answer
  (b) "interpret" the answer in the light of other information
  (c) "draw inferences" from the answer, or
  (d) relay the answer as retrieved direct to *PR*
(4) The outcome of any of (a–d) can be a speech command to *PR*.

The point of the buffer memory *M* is that getting some item of information into *M* is a necessary but not sufficient condition for getting it accessed by *PR* in the form of the *content* of some speech act command.

Now what gets into *M* and how? First let us look at perception. I assume a tier of perceptual analysis levels beginning with sense-organ stimulation and arriving ultimately at highly interpreted information about the perceived world, drawing often on more than one sense modality and utilizing large amounts of stored information. The entire process is variably goal-dependent. Again, the details of this stack of processes are controversial, but I shall venture a few relatively safe points. At the lowest levels we have what Neisser calls "iconic memory",[7] a very short storage of the stimuli virtually uninterpreted. "Parallel processing" by "feature detectors" takes us up several levels and yields crude but local-specific information about edges, corners, shapes, patches of color and so forth. From there a process of "hypothesis generation and confirmation" takes over, a *sequential*, not parallel, process that utilizes both stored "world knowledge" (in the "expectation-driven mode") and the results of the parallel feature detectors (in the "data-driven mode") to determine the generation of hypotheses and their confirmation and disconfirmation. Perhaps the "data structures" at the highest levels of this process are Minsky's "frames", and perhaps they are not. All the processes of perceptual analysis, but especially the higher, sequential levels, are governed by complicated instruction from Control. As Neisser argues convincingly, with limited cognitive resources with which to perform this sophisticated task of perceptual analysis, Control must budget wisely, allocating the available cognitive resources to the sensory modality or topic of most current importance. This allocation of cognitive resources is the essence of *attention*, Neisser argues, and I partially concur. There is a notion of attention that is very definitely a matter of allocation of cognitive resources.* This notion of attention, important as it is, is only very indirectly connected with consciousness, as can be seen at a glance if one considers the fact that any problem-solving or game-playing computer pays attention, in this sense, first to one candidate course of action and then to another, and presumably it would not on this ground be deemed conscious. Or consider the fact that a somnambulist must no doubt allocate considerable cognitive resources to the job of navigating successfully and maintaining balance while being, in some important sense, unconscious (and unconscious *of* all this calculation) at the time. In this sense of attention, *unconscious attention* is no contradiction in terms, and in fact no hints at all have been given to suggest what *conscious* attention might be.

Now the perceptual analysis component sends information to *M from many levels*. Why? Because when one sees a complex scene and analyzes it as, say, a chair and a table in the middle of the room, one

*See p. 31ff above.

sees more than just that there are that chair and table there. One sees the shapes, colors, local details, and periphery too. I do not want to *identify* what one experiences with what one *can say*, but at least *if* one can say something about some current feature of the perceivable world, one has experienced it. This is vividly brought out by tachistoscopic experiments[8]. If one sees a string of four alphabetic letters flashed for a few milliseconds on a screen, one cannot usually identify them. Although the stimulus pattern persists in iconic storage after the actual external flash has ceased, this storage decays before the higher-level processors can complete their work; and once the data are lost, analysis must terminate. But one sees *something*; one can say that one has seen a flash, or a flash with some dark objects, or even four letters or symbols. Something is experienced, even though perceptual analysis is not completed. In such a case, I am supposing, the results of however much analysis gets accomplished normally go to *M*. These results will go to other places of great importance as well, no doubt, but for our purposes all that matters is what gets into *M*.**

Perception, then, sends a variety of inputs to *M*. Perceptual experience is not the only conscious experience we have, though, so what else must we suppose gets into *M*? We are normally conscious of our thinking when we set out to solve problems, so let us very artificially isolate a *problem-solving component* that sends its results to *M*. (At least for some sorts of problem-solving—"imagistic" problem-solving—it is tempting to suppose the processes utilize a lot of the machinery of perceptual analysis; hence the dotted lines in Figure 9.1.) We shall return later to this component and its interactions with *M*. Another unit that sends information to *M* is Control itself. A partial record of its goals, plans, intentions, beliefs gets installed in *M* for occasional publication when the situation demands it.

These are the essential units of the system for my purposes here, but just to illustrate how the model could be extended, I add the dream-production unit. It loads *M* as well, and, as I have argued in the preceding chapter, the question whether dreams are experiences is to be answered by assessing the nature of this memory-loading process (the "route taken" by the access arrow).

**M is a special hypothesized memory location, defined functionally by its access relations to *PR*, and it should not be confused with any already familiar functionally or anatomically defined variety of buffer memory, short-term memory, or echoic memory posited by cognitive theories to date. It may, for all I know, *coincide* nicely with some variety of memory already proposed and studied, but eclectic as my model is, I do not intend here to be appropriating any existing notion from psychology.

Before turning to the question of how such a sub-personal model could possibly say anything about consciousness, let me illustrate briefly how it is supposed to handle various phenomena. Fodor discusses an experiment by Lackner and Garrett.[9] In dichotic listening tests, subjects listen through earphones to two different channels and are instructed to *attend* to just one channel. They can typically report with great accuracy what they have heard through the attended channel, but not surprisingly they can typically say little about what was going on concomitantly in the unattended channel. Thus, if the unattended channel carries a spoken sentence, the subjects can typically report they heard a voice, or even a male or female voice. Perhaps they even have a conviction about whether the voice was speaking in their native tongue, but they cannot report *what was said*. One hypothesis, based on Broadbent's filtering theory,[10] is that a control decision is made to allocate virtually all the cognitive resources to the analysis of the attended channel, with only low-level ("preattentive") processing being done on the input from the unattended channel. Processing of the unattended channel at the level of semantic analysis, for instance, is on this hypothesis *just not done*. Lackner and Garrett's experiments disconfirm the Broadbent model in this instance, however. In the *attended* channel subjects heard ambiguous sentences, such as, "He put out the lantern to signal the attack." In the unattended channel one group of subjects received disambiguating input (e.g., "He extinguished the lantern"), while another group had neutral or irrelevant input. The former group *could not report* what they heard through the unattended channel, but they favored the suggested reading of the ambiguous sentences more than the control group. The influence of the unattended channel on the interpretation of the attended signal can be explained only on the hypothesis that the unattended input is processed all the way to a semantic level, even though the subjects have no awareness of this—that is, cannot report it. On my model, this suggests that although higher-level processing of the unattended channel goes on, only low-level results are sent to *M*. This nicely illustrates the independence of computational access for *control* (in this case, influencing perceptual set in the attended channel) from computational access for *publication*, and gives an instance of, and an interpretation of, the well-known unreliability of introspective evidence. The *absence* of introspective evidence that a certain analysis has been performed is never reliable evidence that no such analysis has been performed. The analysis in question may simply be one of the many processes that contribute in other ways to control, perception, and action, without loading

M with its results. I shall discuss more subtle cases of the relationship between such processing and introspective access later.

To pave the way for this, I want to say a bit more about the interaction proposed between *PR*, Control, and *M*. I will settle for relatively crude suggestions, but the possibilities of such interactions can be—and to some extent have been—studied systematically. Relative retrieval times, lexical biases, the reliability of "tip-of-the-tongue" judgments, similarity spaces, and the like can provide an abundance of clues to guide the model builder. Consider James' introspective account of having a forgotten name on the tip of one's tongue:

> There is a gap therein, but no mere gap. It is a gap that is intensely active. A sort of wraith of the name is in it, beckoning us in a given direction, making us at moments tingle with the sense of our closeness, and then letting us sink back without the longed for term. If wrong names are proposed to us, this singularly definite gap acts immediately so as to negate them. They do not fit into the mold. . . . The rhythm of a lost word may be there without a sound to clothe it.[11]

This passage, for all its phenomenological glories, is strikingly suggestive of purely functional interrelationships that might realistically be postulated to hold between the components of the model—or the components of a better model of course. Suppose a functionalistic model inspired by this passage were developed and supported in the usual ways: it would be part of the burden of this essay to mitigate resistance to the claim that an instantiation of such a model could *assert* (*knowing* what it meant and *meaning* what it said) just what James asserts in this passage.

Returning to the proposed interactions between *PR*, Control and *M*, suppose *PR* gets a speech act command that for one reason or another it cannot execute. Words fail it. I propose that a failure discovery like this feeds back to Control, which will deal with the situation in a number of ways. It can alter its directions to Perceptual Analysis, producing a new perceptual set. This *may* result in a reinterpretation of the incoming stimulation, producing a *changed* input (at any level) to *M*, and then a changed speech act command to *PR*. Being unable at first to describe one's perceptual experience could lead in this way to a *change* in one's perceptual experience. This would help explain, for instance, the heightened capacity to discriminate—and experience— wines that comes from learning to use the exotic vocabulary of the wine-taster. (What I am proposing is, of course, a very Kantian bit of machinery, designed in effect to knit intuitions and concepts together.

Any psychological theory must address this problem; in some models the Kantian perspective is more readily seen.) But if perceptual revision did not occur, Control could send to *PR* a direction to say that one finds the experience ineffable or indescribable and this might be followed by a series of commands to say various things about what the experience was more or less like, about just how one's words are betraying one's true semantic intentions and so forth. What I am granting is that there is no guarantee that information loaded into *M* has a publication in the native tongue that is acceptable to the system.

What kind of *information* might fail to find expression in one's native tongue? Although *M* has been characterized as an information store, nothing has been said about the *form* the information must take. What sort of "data structures" are involved? Is the information encoded "propositionally" or "imagistically" or "analogically"? These important questions deserve answers, but not here. It is important here, however, to explain why I refrain from answering them, and that will require a digression.

The current debate in cognitive psychology between the propositionalists and the lovers of images (see Chapter 10) is multifariously instructive to philosophers, not only because it contains echoes of philosophic controversies, but also because it clearly illustrates the close and systematic relationship between "pure" philosophy—especially epistemology—and empirical psychology. Psychologists, faced with the practical impossibility of answering the empirical questions of psychology by brute inspection (how does the human nervous system accomplish perception or cognition?) very reasonably ask themselves an easier preliminary question: how could *any* (physical or mechanical or biological) system accomplish perception or cognition? This question is easier because it is "less empirical"; it is an *engineering* question, a quest for a solution (any solution) rather than a discovery, but it is still dominated by a mountain of empirical facts—in particular, facts about the powers, limits, and idiosyncrasies of actual human perceivers under a wide range of conditions.

The psychological question becomes: how could any system *do all that*? It is a question one is ill-equipped to answer if one does not know what *all that* is—for instance, if one is a philosopher largely unacquainted with the psychologists' data. Yet there is a strong aprioristic element in the psychologists' investigations, because it turns out to be very difficult to compose any model at all that could conceivably *do all that*. What is wrong with most models is that they fail to satisfy some quite general constraint or constraints on all solutions. The charge often leveled against such models is not just that they fail to account for some body of data, but that they *could not conceivably* account for human perception or cognition (for instance), since they violate some proclaimed necessary condition on all solutions. This aprioristic thinking is not peculiar to psychology. Engineers can enumerate necessary conditions for being an amplifier or a motor, and biologists can set down constraints on all possible solutions to the problem of the mechanics of genetic inheritance, to give just two examples. Once one decides to do psychology this way at all, one can address oneself to the problems raised by the most particular constraints, by middling constraints, or by the most general constraints. One can ask how any neuronal network of such-and-such features can possibly accomplish human color discriminations, or one can ask how any finite organic system can possibly subserve the acquisition of a natural language, or one can ask, with Kant, how anything at all could possibly experience or know anything. Pure epistemology thus viewed is simply the limiting case of the psychologists' quest, and any constraints the philosopher finds in that most general and abstract investigation bind all psychological theories as inexorably as constraints encountered in more parochial and fact-enriched environments.

Notice, too, that the philosophers' most abstract question is not asked in a factual vacuum; when we ask aprioristically how experience is possible, or what knowledge is, or how anything can be a symbol or have meaning, we appeal to, and are thus constrained by, an enormous body of commonplace facts: the facts that anchor what we mean by "experience", "symbol", and so forth. All the philosopher need know in the way of facts is what can be learned at mother's knee, but that is not nothing. The psychologist says: "The experimental results bear me out, don't they?" The philosopher says: "That's what it is to understand an utterance, isn't it?" If recently many philosophers of mind, knowledge, and language have found it useful or imperative to descend in the direction of more data, the reason is that the issues at the less general levels are proving to be fascinating, manipulable, and apparently useful in illuminating the more abstract level.

This is particularly apparent in the current controversy over propositions and images as vehicles of information in cognitive systems, a controversy of protean guise, sometimes appearing to be pure philosophy (and hence no business of psychologists!), sometimes an abstract engineering question for cyberneticists and the like, and sometimes a question of hard psychological, biological, or phenomenological fact. It has grown popular to the point of becoming second nature to talk of *information*-processing and transmission in the nervous system, but there is uncertainty and disagreement about the *a priori* constraints on any such talk of information. There is often the illusion that no problems attend the psychologists' talk of information, since information theory has presumably provided a rigorous foundation for such talk, but it is not often that psychologists have in mind any hard-edged information-theoretic sense of the term; usually what is being alluded to is the information or content an event within the system has *for the system as a (biological) whole* (what the frog's eye tells the frog's brain, or better, as Arbib has suggested—in conversation—what the frog's eye tells the frog). The *content* (in this sense) of a particular vehicle of information, a particular information-bearing event or state, is and must be a function of its function in the system. This is the sense of "information" utilized in our model (and in psychological models generally); so when I assert that, for instance, there is a transfer of information from some perceptual analysis area to M, I endow that transfer event with content, and the content it has is to be understood as a function of the function within the whole system of that event. So far, that event's function has been only circularly characterized: it has the function of conveying information about the results of analysis at that level to a functional area that is accessible to another functional area whose function is to express in a natural language just that information obtained by that level of perceptual analysis. Such a characterization is circular, but not necessarily viciously circular. The circle is a high-level holding pattern, which permits us to consider the constraints on any theory without descending to the next, more empirical level.

We can say, though, just what that next level down is. The content of a psychological state or event is a function of its function, and its function is—in the end, must be—a function of the *structure* of the state or event and the systems of which it is a part. Not just any structures can realize the functions that we determine must be realized, but the step from functional constraint to structural constraint is treacherous[12] and takes a philosopher quite far from home. When the question of "form of information" takes on this (quite proper) guise as a question of engineering, I leave it—reluctantly—to the engineers. I shall address myself shortly to the question in its "purely philosophical" or "phenomenological" guises. So, to end the digression, it would be best, for the time being, to stay in our circle and talk only of the *content* of states and events, and not the structure of the vehicles of content.

Stopping at a level of description above the stern demands of structural realizations is thus engaging in an extended exercise in more or less well-motivated handwaving,* but this handwaving may well be saved by ultimate realizations of these information-processing components, and if it is, it will have been not only not in vain, but an essential propaedeutic to such theorizing.

One can never be sure, however. For instance, the Control component in my model is awfully fancy. It has a superb capacity to address just the right stored information in its long-term memory, a talent for asking M just the right questions, and an ability to organize its long-and short-term goals and plans in a very versatile way. This is no homunculus that any AI researcher has the faintest idea how to realize at this time. The ever-present worry is that as we devise components—lesser homunculi—to execute various relatively menial tasks near the periphery, we shall be "making progress" only by driving into the center of our system an all-powerful executive homunculus whose duties require an almost Godlike omniscience. I can make no firm claims for the soundness of my components in this model. The most I shall venture for them is that they seem to me not to reproduce the problems at deeper levels, thus merely postponing solution.

IV

With those qualifications and excuses behind me, I turn to the decisive question. Suppose an entity were all wired up in some fashion so as to realize the flow chart in Figure 9.1. What would it be like (if anything) to be such an entity? At first glance the answer seems to be: not like anything. The whole system has been designed to operate in the dark, as it were, with the various components accomplishing their tasks unperceived and unperceiving. In particular, we have not supposed any inner introspecting eye to be watching the perceptual analysis processes, the control decisions, the efforts of PR to execute its orders. And yet to us on the outside, watching such an entity, engaging it in conversation, listening to its efforts to describe the effects on it of various perceptual environments, there will be at least the illusion that it is like

*It only appears to be more specific handwaving when one talks not simply of contentful states and events but of cognitive *maps*, say, as opposed to stored *propositions*. People who like images say they are talking about images but not (of course!) about *pictures in the brain*; people who like propositions say they are talking about propositions—which are not *at all* like images—but also, of course, not *sentences in the brain*. There is plenty of doctrine about what images and propositions are *not*, but very little about what they are.

something to be the entity. In fact it will tell us (or at least seem to be telling us) just what it is like. But inside it is all darkness, a hoax. Or so it seems. Inside your skull it is also all darkness, and whatever processes occur in your grey matter occur unperceived and unperceiving. Can it be said that just as there is some other point of view that *you* have, there is some other point of view that *it* has?

It is hard to know how to answer that question. But the following may help. Suppose I put forward the bold hypothesis that you are a realization of this flow chart, and that it is in virtue of this fact that it seems—to us and to you—that there is something it is like to be you. Can you give good grounds for denying the hypothesis, and if so, what are they? What personal access do you have, and to what? Here I must abruptly shift the perspective of this paper and wax phenomenological for a while. I want to draw your attention to a class of phenomena. If you have ever had a sudden *presentiment* that someone was looking over your shoulder, or a *premonition* that something dire was about to happen, you are acquainted with the phenomena. These events are propositional episodes, thinkings that *p*; there is normally some inclination to express them (although the inclination is easily suppressed or cancelled), and we may not even express them to ourselves in "inner speech". When they occur in us, we have not the faintest idea what their etiology is (unless we have some theory about the causes of premonitions; my point is that "to introspection" they arrive from we know not where). There are other more familiar examples of coming to want to say something without knowing how or why. Witticisms "occur to us", but we do not know how we produce them (the example is Ryle's). Lashley long ago pointed out that if asked to think a thought in dactylic hexameter we (many of us) can oblige, but we have no awareness of how we do it: the *result* arrives, and that is the extent of our direct access to the whole business. Lashley's provocative comment on his example was that "no activity of the mind is ever conscious", and the interpretation of this I am supporting is that we have access—conscious access—to the *results* of mental processes, but not to the processes themselves.

My contention is that far from being rare and anomalous occurrences, propositional episodes, these thinkings that *p*, are our normal and continuous avenue to self-knowledge, that they exhaust our immediate awareness, and that the odd varieties, such as the presentiment that someone is looking over one's shoulder, are striking only because of their isolation from the preceding and following presentiments, only because of our inability to follow them up with related propositional episodes about the same topic.* Right now it occurs to me that there are pages in front of me, a presentiment whose etiology is not known directly by me, but which is, of course, perfectly obvious. It is my visual system that gives me this presentiment, along with a host of others. I *can say* all sorts of things to elaborate on and supplement my initial report. But if I am put in an abnormal perceptual environment—for instance, in a tachistoscopic experiment—I may be less sure *why* I want to say what I do. I sort of have a hunch that is was an English word you flashed on the screen, but did I really *see* it? I cannot say what word it was, or describe it in any detail.

Instead of cajoling you with further phenomenological persuasions, I shall enlarge upon my view by drawing an analogy to Hume. Hume's revolutionary step in the analysis of causation was to suggest that we had it all backwards. Earlier attempts at an account of our belief in causation supposed that when we saw a cause and then an effect we *saw* the necessary connection between them, and *thereupon and therefore* inferred or expected the effect when we saw the cause. Hume examined the cause ("turned it on all sides") and could *find* no such necessary connection to be observed, so he suggested that it was the other way around: having been conditioned, in effect, to infer or expect the effect when seeing the cause, we *found ourselves* drawing the inference, and this gave rise to an illusion of sorts that we were *seeing* a necessary connection that explained and grounded the inference we were compelled to make. The inference itself, Hume says, is psychologically and epistemically prior, and it gives rise to the belief in a "perceived" necessary connection. I am proposing a parallel account of "introspection": we find ourselves *wanting to say* all these things about what is going on in us; this gives rise to *theories* we hold about how we come to be able to do this—for instance, the notorious but

---

*Cf. Ryle's illuminating account of "unstudied utterances" in *The Concept of Mind* (London: Hutcheson, 1949) and Sellars' treatments of "thinkings out loud" and "proximate propensities" to think out loud in *Science, Perception and Reality* (London: Routledge & Kegan Paul, 1963). Ryle claims that our unstudied utterances "constitute our primary evidence for making self-comments (p. 183), and I am claiming that it is our proximate propensities to make unstudied utterances that constitute this primary evidence. Ryle probably would not deny this, for he says (p. 194): "One of the things often signified by 'self-consciousness' is the notice we take of our own unstudied utterances, including our explicit avowals, whether these are spoken aloud, muttered or said in our heads. We eavesdrop on our own voiced utterances and our own silent monologues." Ryle offers no account, however, of just what one is doing when one eavesdrops on one's silent monologues, nor could he give such an account without descending to the subpersonal level he wishes to avoid; *we* do not do anything in order so to eavesdrop; we *just are* aware of our own thinkings.

homespun theory that we "perceive" these goings on with our "inner eye", and that this *perception* grounds and explains the semantic intentions we have.

Hume might almost have arrived at this extension of his view. He claims (*Treatise*, I.iv.2) that there is a difference between our "internal impressions" and our sensations. The latter require the positing of continuously existing external bodies in order to preserve the coherence and constancy of our discontinuous impressions of sensation. (Hume's example is the fire in his study fireplace that gradually burns down, turning slowly to embers in the periods between the interrupted and different sensations he receives from the fire.) But, says Hume, "internal impressions" do not require this postulating; "on no occasion is it necessary to suppose that they have existed and operated, when they were not perceived, in order to preserve the same dependance and connexion, of which we have had experience". This claim is virtually unavoidable for Hume—given his allegiance to a Lockean doctrine of the "transparency" of the mind to itself—but it is a fundamental error. Not only must we come to accept all manner of covert influences, unconscious problem-solving processes, and the like (recall Lashley's dictum), but *mental images themselves* are the creatures of a "posit", an inference or extrapolation exactly analogous to Hume's "posit" about external bodies. This is graphically illustrated by Shepard's experiments with "rotating mental images". The subjects in these experiments are shown pairs of line drawings like those in Figure 9.2, and asked whether or not the pair are different views of the same shape. In this

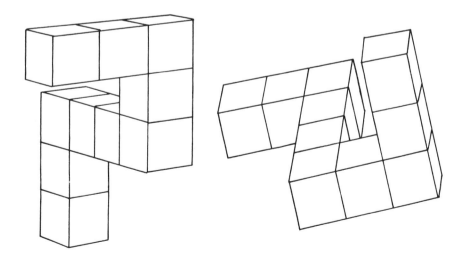

Figure 9-2

case, as you can quickly determine, the answer is yes. How did you do it? A typical answer is, "I rotated the image in my mind's eye." Amazingly, Shepard set out to see if he could determine the normal angular velocity of rotation of such images! How could he do this? The subjects were given buttons to press to give their answers. After tentative standard latency times were subtracted from both ends of the duration between display and answer, Shepard was left with durations that should, on his hypothesis, vary linearly (ignoring acceleration and deceleration) with the degrees of rotation required to bring the figures into superimposition. It should take roughly twice as long to rotate an image through 100 degrees as through 50 degrees. Shepard claims to have obtained significant positive results: he himself can rotate such mental images at an angular velocity of 62.6 degrees per second.

Now how can my view possibly accommodate such phenomena? Aren't we directly aware of an image rotating in phenomenal space in this instance? No. And that much, I think, you can quickly ascertain to your own satisfaction. For isn't it the case that if you attend to your experience more closely when you say you rotate the image you find it moves in discrete jumps—it flicks through a series of orientations. You cannot gradually speed up or slow down the rotation, can you? But now "look" again. Isn't it really just that these discrete steps are discrete propositional episodes? Now it looks like *this*, but if I imagine it turned *that* much, it would look like *that* . . . ah yes, it would eventually look just like the other one. But the flicking, you may insist, is clearly part of a motion observed—the axis of rotation is, perhaps, vertical, not horizontal. But your reason for saying this is just that your intermediate judgments define the rotation. They are judgments that fall in an order that would be the proper order of perceptual judgments in the case of watching a real image rotate around a vertical axis. If you are inclined to argue that only an internal system that actually did proceed by some rotation in space of a representation or image could explain the sequence of judgments and their temporal relations in such cases, you might be right, but your grounds are hardly overwhelming. In fact, these discrete series of judgments bear a striking resemblance to the discrete series of small flashing lights that create the illusions of perceived motion, which have received so much attention from psychologists.[14]

We know that in these situations we all "perceive" motion—even elaborate orbital motions in three dimensions—when there is no motion. When we are confronted by a small group of these sequentially flashing lights we experience an illusion; we are led irresistibly to a nonveridical perceptual judgment that there is a single light moving in a particular way. What I am suggesting is that as the discrete series of flashes is to that nonveridical judgment, so our series of judgments in the image rotation case is to the judgment that something is really rotated in our minds (or in our brains, or anywhere). There *may* be motion of something "behind" our judgments in the image rotation case, but if there is, it is something quite outside our present ken, and its very existence is suggested only by the most tenuous inference, however psychologically irresistible it may be.

My account of the Shepard phenomenon is that *however* the problem-solving process is accomplished, it yields *results*, both final and intermediate, that are available in M to be accessed by PR. These results, by the time they reach PR, are unproblematically propositional in nature: they are intentions to say that p. They are one product of perception or problem-solving. Another product is ducking when you see a flying object coming at you, but this is neither propositional nor imagistic so far as I can see. These products are perhaps only *indirect* products of perceptual processes; the *direct* or *immediate* product, one might wish to say, is experience itself, and the question is whether experience is propositional or imagistic or something else. My answer, counterintuitive as it may seem at first, is that if that question has any admissible interpretation at all, introspection cannot answer it. We have no direct personal access to the *structure* of *content*ful events within us.

V

Having given some suggestion about how the model I propose operates with a variety of phenomena, I now want to make some proposals about how the traditional categories of consciousness are to be superimposed on the model. These proposals are not supposed to be *a priori* truths about consciousness, or the dictates of conceptual analysis of our ordinary concepts, but rather suggestions about the best fit we can achieve between our pretheoretical intuitions (which are not entirely consistent) and a cognitive theory of the sort I have been sketching.

(1) One perceives more than one experiences. Perceptual analysis provides information about the world that is utilized in the control of behavior but is not accessible to introspection or consciousness, on any familiar understanding of these terms. In other words, there is nothing repugnant to theory in the notion of unconscious or subliminal perception or "subception", and any intuitions to the contrary should be discarded.

(2) The content of one's experience includes whatever enters (by normal routes) the buffer memory M. What one experiences may decay before it is in fact accessed by PR, or it may be garbled in transition to

PR, or it may be relatively inaccessible to *PR*.* In virtue of this possibility of error or malfunction between *M* and *PR*, *what one wants to say* is not an infallible or incorrigible determinant of what one has experienced or is currently experiencing. So the content of one's experience is given an *objective* characterization, and any intuition we have to the contrary that we are the sole and perfect arbiters of what we experience should be discarded.

(3) One experiences more at any time than one wants to say then. What fills the "periphery", adds detail to one's "percepts", inhabits "fringe consciousness", is, as phenomenologists have insisted, *there*. Where? In *M*. No more mysterious process of presentation or apprehension of inhabitants of phenomenal space is needed.

(4) One experiences more than one attends to—in either of two senses of attention. One experiences more than what results from higher-level allocations of cognitive resources, and one experiences, as (3) asserts, more than one is currently thinking. These are entirely different ways in which there are unattended contents of consciousness, even though there is a strong contingent link between them. Usually Control fixes things so that what one is attending to in the former sense is what one is attending to in the latter. Put otherwise, our conscious access to what we are attending to is normally excellent.

(5) One's access to one's experience is accomplished via the access relations between *M* and *PR*. As Anscombe would put it, we simply *can say* what it is we are experiencing, what it is we are up to. This is

*Ryle says: "There is, however, a proper sense in which I can be said generally to know what has just been engaging my notice or half-notice, namely that I generally could give a memory report of it, if there was occasion to do so. This does not exclude the possibility that I might sometimes give a misreport, for even short-term reminiscence is not exempt from carelessness or bias." (*The Concept of Mind*, p. 160) Ryle permits himself to call this capacity "log-keeping", and my *M* is apparently just Ryle's log-keeping system "paramechanized". But surely Ryle's own remarks on log-keeping, if taken seriously, constitute just the sort of paramechanical hypothesis he typically condemns. Why is Ryle led to such an uncharacteristic account? Not because he is *aware* of keeping logs, and not because he finds himself or observes himself keeping logs. (A Rylean would be quick to ask him embarrassing questions about how many entries he writes in his log before breakfast, and how he writes them.) Ryle is led to this (happy) lapse, I suppose, because *what must be explained*, *viz.*, our ability to report on so many different things that were just now happening, demands an explanation somehow in terms of an information—or memory—model. Another precursor of *M* that may have occurred to the reader is Freud's *preconscious*: "The question, 'How does a thing become conscious?' would be more advantageously stated: 'How does a thing become preconscious?', and the answer would be: 'Through becoming connected with the word-presentations corresponding to it.'" (*The Ego and the Id*, New York: Norton, 1962, p. 10).

accomplished without any inner eye or introspective faculty beyond the machinery invoked in the model.

(6) Our feelings of special authority in offering introspective reports —the basis for all the misbegotten theses of introspective incorrigibility and infallibility—arise from the fact that our semantic intentions, which determine what we want to say, are the standards against which we measure our own verbal productions; hence if we say what we mean to say, if we have committed no errors or infelicities of expression, then our actual utterances cannot fail to be expressions of the content of our semantic intentions, cannot fail to do justice to the access we have to our own inner lives.

(I claimed in *Content and Consciousness* that this fact explained how we were, in a very limited and strained sense, incorrigible with regard to the contents of our awareness or consciousness. Now, thanks to the relentless persuasions of John Bender, William Talbott, Thomas Blackburn, Annette Baier and others, I wish to claim that this fact explains not how we are in fact incorrigible, but rather why people—especially philosophers—so often think we are. The fact does provide for what Gunderson calls the investigational asymmetry of some first-person claims, but the asymmetry is not profitably to be viewed, as I used to claim, as any sort of even limited incorrigibility.)

VI

Having an inner life—being something it is like something to be—is on this account a matter of having a certain sort of functional organization, but the only natural entities that could be expected to have such functional organizations would be highly evolved and *socialized* creatures. The prospect of a robot artificially constructed to replicate such a functional structure is not ruled out, but when one reflects on the activities such an entity would have to engage in to be more than an instantaneous version of such a system, the claim that it would be conscious loses—at least for me—its implausibility. We might not have the imagination to engage such a thing in interpersonal relations; it might not *seem*, in its metallic skin, to have an inner life or any prospect of an inner life. Such appearances are unreliable, however, for consider the possibility of there being a truly conscious entity (whatever one supposes this involves) that was just like us except that it operated on a time scale ten thousand times slower than ours. We would have a very hard time recognizing any of its day-long emissions as speech acts, let alone witty, cheery, doleful, heartfelt speech acts, and its ponderous responses to cuts and bruises would not easily enliven our sympathies; but if so, we would *ex hypothesi* be ignoring a genuine, conscious person among us.

When we wonder if something or someone is conscious, it is tempting to view this as wondering whether or not a special light is turned on inside. This is an error, however, as we can see by asking questions about our own cases: was I conscious (or conscious of X) at time t? When we see that what settles the issues in our own case is a consideration of facts about our current capacities and past activities, and the best theory that can account for these, we are less reluctant to let the same considerations settle the issues in the case of others.

There is no *proving* that something that seems to have an inner life does in fact have one—if by "proving" we understand, as we often do, the evincing of evidence that can be seen to establish by principles already agreed upon that something is the case. In this paper I set myself the task of constructing an "I", a something it was like something to be, out of sub-personal parts of the sort encountered in cognitivistic theories. I do not now wish to claim that I have *demonstrably* succeeded in this. Suppose we consider the two questions:

(1) Would an entity instantiating this theory sketch *seem* (to "others", to "us") to have an inner conscious life?

(2) Would such an entity *in fact* have an inner conscious life?

Question (1) is an agreeably straightforward question of engineering. Perhaps the thing whose design I have sketched would impress the keenest skeptic, and perhaps it would be lamentably (or comically) unrealistic or mute or self-defeating. Whatever flaws the design has might have philosophical or psychological significance, or might be rather trivial blunders on my part. (Is my model akin to the blueprint for a perpetual motion machine, or have I merely forgotten to provide a way out for the exhaust gases?) Most if not all objections to *details* in my model can be cast—even if not so intended—as grounds for denying (1), thus:

(3) Such an entity would not even *seem* to have an inner conscious life because

. . . it lacks any provision for such human phenomena as . . .,

. . . it ignores . . .,

. . . it would respond in situation - - - by doing . . .

I must take such objections seriously because part of my goal in this paper is to reveal, by imagined counterinstance, the implausibility of the charge that no entity describable solely by the resources of cognitivistic theory could *possibly* seem to have an inner conscious life. If that charge is nevertheless true (I cannot imagine how that could be *shown*—but perhaps I shall live and learn), then cognitivism is forlorn, and this would be a fact of great importance to philosophy and psychology.

Suppose, however, that some cognitivistic model of consciousness (not mine, no doubt, but its kin, I like to think) encouraged a positive answer to question (1). Suppose some model passed all the appearance tests we could devise. How on earth should one then address question (2)? Is there a better course than mere doctrinaire verificationism on the one hand, or shoulder-shrugging agnosticism on the other? This is of course just "the problem of other minds", and I propose that progress can be made on it by reexamining *what one knows about one's own case* in the light of the most promising theories of psychology. What convinces *me* that a cognitivistic theory could capture all the dear features I discover in my inner life is not any "argument", and not just the programmatic appeal of thereby preserving something like "the unity of science", but rather a detailed attempt to describe to myself exactly those features of my life *and the nature of my acquaintance with them* that I would cite as my "grounds" for claiming that I *am*—and do not merely *seem to be*—conscious. What *I* discover are facts quite congenial to cognitivistic theorizing, and my tactic here has been to try, by persuasive redescription, to elicit the same discoveries in others. Skeptics can view the form of the argument, such as it is, as a challenge—to produce a rival description of some feature of conscious experience that is both acceptable to many (better, it should evoke enthusiastic agreement, it should ring a bell) and unassimilable by cognitivistic theorizing. I am aware of the irony of recommending something so reminiscent of the battle of descriptions that embarrassed the early introspectionists to death, but how else could anyone plausibly support the claim that one's theory was a theory of *consciousness*?

10

Two Approaches to Mental Images

"You don't believe in me," observed the Ghost.
"I don't," said Scrooge.
"What evidence would you have of my reality, beyond that of your senses?"
"I don't know," said Scrooge.
"Why do you doubt your senses?"
"Because," said Scrooge, "a little thing affects them. A slight disorder of the stomach makes them cheats. You may be an undigested bit of beef, a blot of mustard, a crumb of cheese, a fragment of an underdone potato. There's more of gravy than of grave about you, whatever you are!"

Scrooge was not much in the habit of cracking jokes, nor did he feel, in his heart, by any means waggish then. The truth is, that he tried to be smart, as a means of distracting his own attention, and keeping down his terror; for the spectre's voice disturbed the very marrow in his bones.

—*Dickens,* A Christmas Carol

Of all the controversies currently raging in philosophy and psychology, none is being conducted with more vigor—if not rigor—than the debate over the nature of, and even the very existence of, mental images. Although the issues are various and complex, and although the arguments exhibit at least some of the variety and complexity the issues demand, one can describe the situation with negligible sociological distortion by saying that there is a *single* war being fought on many fronts (or at least there seems to be in the minds of the participants), a war between the believers and the skeptics, the lovers of mental images—

let us call them *iconophiles*—and those who decry or deny them—the *iconophobes*. Both sides have apparently decided to pretend to know what *mental representations* are, and the issue is whether there are mental representations with properties peculiar to images.[1] Whatever *mental* representations are, they must be understood by analogy to *non*-mental representations, such as words, sentences, maps, graphs, pictures, charts, statues, telegrams, etc. The question is whether any of one's mental representations are more like *pictures* or *maps* than like *sentences*, to take the favored alternative.

A curious feature of the debate is the passion it evokes, which is unlike the normal passion of scientific controversy in being as accessible to the layman and spectator as to the proprietors of the various theories. People often take a lively interest in a controversy in physics or biology or astronomy without feeling the need to take sides, and indeed without deeming themselves equipped to have an opinion worth promoting, but everyone, it seems, has a fiercely confident opinion about the nature and existence of mental images. This manifests itself in remarkable ways: in unhesitating predictions of the results of novel psychological experiments, in flat disbelief in the integrity of recalcitrant experiments, in gleeful citation of "supporting" experimental evidence, coupled with bland imperviousness to contrary evidence. Since this relatively uninformed or pretheoretical partisanship comes in both varieties—iconophile and iconophobe—one breathtakingly simple explanation of the phenomenon, and one that is often proposed, is that in fact some people do have mental images and others don't. Each side naively extrapolates from its own experience. There are a variety of data that independently support this hypothesis. It is very likely that there are quite radical differences in people's "imagistic" powers. That cannot, however, be the whole explanation of this confident partisanship. I wish to show that a subtle misconception of the issue underlies this curious phenomenon, a misconception that is as apt to beguile the theorist as the innocent bystander.

I will try to bring out the misconception by first setting out a picture of the issue from the point of view of the iconophile. This picture is familiar, but *out of focus, untuned.* I will then show how the issue is transformed by attention to a few distinctions. Here, then, is the *untuned* version of the iconophile's case.

The iconophile asserts that *there are* mental images, and moreover is prepared to back up this ontological claim by saying just *where* in the scheme of things the mental images are. First, they are the typical *effects* of certain sorts of causes. Mental images are, let us say, the typical effects of veridical visual perception, the ingestion of hallucinogens, the desire to solve geometry problems in one's head, and so forth. There are all manner of mental images, but let us take a particular case for discussion. On being asked whether it is possible to touch one's right elbow to one's left knee while touching one's left elbow to one's right knee, Lucy refrains from contortions and instead *forms a mental image* of herself attempting this feat. Call the image itself, the target item in this debate, α. Here we have a certain train of events including, *inter alia*, Lucy's (A) hearing the question, (B) coming to understand it, (C) coming to desire to answer it, (D) deciding not to contort herself, and finally (E) attempting to frame an image. These are all plausibly held to be events in the causal ancestry of α. No one of them itself is, or contains, or need be held to be or contain, a mental image, but as a sequence they form a particular natural prelude to a particular mental image, namely, α.

Moreover, says our iconophile, mental images are the typical *causes* of certain sorts of effects. That is to say, the occurrence of a mental image such as α *makes a difference*: had it not occurred, later things that transpired would not have transpired, or would have transpired differently. In making this claim, our iconophile rejects epiphenomenalism, wisely, since no version of that bizarre doctrine merits attention.* Of all the effects typically produced by the occurrence of a mental image, one is singled out by its immediacy and the consequent dependence of other effects on it; let us call it the *apprehension* of the mental image, being as neutral as possible about what apprehension might be. Perhaps there could be unapprehended mental images. If so, the people visited by them *do not believe* they are visited by them, do not *make use* of them (e.g., to solve problems, to answer questions, simply to perceive), do not remember them. That is what we shall

---

*I find there are different senses of the term "epiphenomenal" in currency today. The epiphenomenalism I have just rudely dismissed is the view that there are epiphenomena that are more or less accompanying shadows of events in the brain, but that these epiphenomena *have no physical effects at all*. One might say this is one half of Cartesian interactionism: bodily events cause (or occasion) mental events (epiphenomena), but these are themselves causally inert. Some people, notably psychologists, often use "epiphenomenal" to mean, roughly, "nonfunctional". Thus if I engrave curlicues and filagrees on the connecting rods of an engine they are merely epiphenomenal in this sense—they don't contribute or detract from the normal functioning of the engine, but of course they do have have effects in the world by which their presence may be determined: they reflect and absorb light, for instance. That there are non-functional physical properties of brain events (or non-functional brain events) we already know; we will need an impressive argument to show there are non-functional (but physically efficacious) non-physical events or properties.

mean by apprehension. A mental image that fails to be apprehended is like a stimulus that fails to stimulate; one can rule either out by definition if one wishes. Note that we have left it open whether one can *mis*apprehend a mental image or *unconsciously* apprehend a mental image. As I said, we are being as neutral as possible about what apprehension might be.

But whether or not there might be unconsciously apprehended mental images, there certainly are mental images that are consciously apprehended, supposing for the moment that all we mean by "consciously apprehended" is "believed by the subject to have occurred in virtue of having been apprehended at occurrence". Thus, one of the effects of α is Lucy's subsequent belief that α has occurred. Now we could say that this belief (partially) *constituted* Lucy's apprehension of α,

$A \to B \to C \to D \to E \to \alpha \to$ Apprehension of α (=belief that α occurred &. . .),

or we could say that this belief was *caused by* an intervening apprehension of α.

$A \to B \to C \to D \to E \to \alpha \to$ Apprehension of $\alpha \to$ belief that α occurred.

In either case, we will acknowledge that such a belief is at least a typical consequence of the occurrence of a mental image such as α. It is a familiar fact that beliefs spawn beliefs with great fecundity, and no sooner would Lucy believe that α had occurred than she would also believe a host of other things about α. Let us both arbitrarily and vaguely distinguish the manifold of beliefs *quite* immediately produced by and "focussed on" or "about" α, and call this assemblage of beliefs β.

$A \to B \to C \to D \to E \to \alpha \to \beta$ (=a manifold of beliefs about α).

Up to now, "α" has been the proper name of a particular mental image of Lucy's, and "β" the proper name of one of its effects. Now generalize this bit of nomenclature. Let α be any mental image and β be its relatively direct effect in the realm of belief. There can be debate and disagreement among iconophiles over the scope and population of particular β-manifolds, but surely the conscious apprehension of an α will produce *some* beliefs about α. Put the uncontroversial beliefs in that α's β-manifold and ignore the rest, since nothing will hinge on them. The outer boundary of a β-manifold will not be important to us, but the joint between an α and its β-manifold will.

To some theorists, beliefs are themselves images or at least *like* images. Armstrong, for instance, likens beliefs to maps[2] and contrasts them to sentences. Since I want the β-manifolds to be agreed by all to be purely *non*-imagistic (whatever that means) believers in the imagistic nature of belief, if there are any, are asked to direct their attention to a slightly different item among the causal descendants of any α, namely to the causally-first entirely non-imagistic typical psychological effect of that α, and call *it* the β-manifold of that α. It might, for instance, be a manifold of *dispositions to say and do various things* in virtue of one's (imagistic) beliefs about α.

This concept of a β-manifold is unavoidably lax, but perhaps its flavor can be conveyed by another example. Suppose I am inspired by my current mental image of a unicorn to draw a picture of a unicorn, indeed to *render* my current mental image on the page. There are then *two* images: my mental image, and its good or bad copy, the drawn image. Something intervenes between them. Of all that intervenes there are myriad descriptions possible, no doubt, most of them quite unknown to us. A plausible sketch of one such description would include in roughly this sequence: first, the mental image of the unicorn; then apprehension of that image, followed by (or constituting) belief that one is having just such an image; then delight in it; a subsequent desire to produce it for others; then an intention to draw, leading to an intention to grasp the pencil *just so*—and so forth. Of all of this, I want to focus on the earliest and most immediate non-imagistic products of (or constituents of) apprehension, the manifold of beliefs about the mental image that one might suppose would remain relatively constant over changes in artistic desire, delight, boredom, and incidental knowledge, provided only that the image remained constant (supposing that notion to make sense—remember, this is the iconophile's story). One cannot get entirely precise about this. For instance, the *desire to draw* arrives hand in hand with the *belief* that the image is, shall we say, artworthy, and does *this* belief belong in the β-manifold or not? I don't think it makes any difference to my case one way or another.

Now I have tried to define β-manifolds in such a way that any iconophile will be happy to acknowledge the existence of β-manifolds as the first cognitive but non-imagistic difference the having of a mental image typically makes in us. By characterizing the β-manifold as itself non-imagistic, I mean to obtain a similar acquiescence from the iconophobe, for iconophobes do not for a moment wish to deny the existence of those manifolds of belief called by the iconophile β-manifolds. To deny that would be to deny the one truly obvious fact about mental imagery: people generally do think they have mental images and are disposed to say so. Iconophobes differ from iconophiles in denying that the normal or typical proximate causes of those manifolds are things or events having the earmarks of, and hence deserving to be called, *images*. The debate is entirely over the nature of the occupants of the α role, *the nature of the normal causes of* β-manifolds.

So far neither category is all that well characterized—not by me, and not by the participants in the psychological and philosophical debates, so it is not surprising that disagreement between iconophile and iconophobe should persist, should lack agreed-upon methods of resolution, should look like a *philosophical* dispute. It is not. It is merely *embryonic-scientific*. What is remarkable is that so many people find it so difficult to let this issue be what it ought to be: a scientific, empirical question, amenable to experimental probing. Why should anyone feel differently? Most of us laymen are quite content to be not only ignorant but opinionless about the normal causes of dandruff, inflation, earthquake and schizophrenia. We will let science tell us if only it will. But, one is mightily tempted to say, the normal cause of my β-manifold to the effect that I am having a mental image of sort x is (of course!) a mental image of sort x, and I already know more about that mental image of mine, simply in virtue of having it, than science could ever tell me. This temptation is at the heart of the misconception I hope to uncover and dispell. I hope to dispell it by pointing out and clarifying two approaches to mental images that are very different, but not at war. The *first* approach has just in fact been sketched, if fuzzily. It can be called, without intending thereby to do it special honor or dishonor, the *scientific approach*. It proceeds by defining mental images as the *normal causes* of β-manifolds. (The existence of β-manifolds is uncontroversial, however murky and ill-defined the concept is.) This approach treats the hints, avowals and protestations of image-havers as issuing in the normal way from their β-manifolds. Having various beliefs about what is going on in them, people come to say various things, and these utterances are useful *data* about the nature of mental images. The subjects have no more special authority about the nature of their own mental images, on this approach, than about the nature of their genes or germs. This approach calmly ignores the claim of the image-haver to be *authoritative* about the nature of his or her mental images.

By defining mental images as the normal causes of β-manifolds, the scientific approach virtually guarantees the *existence* of mental images— since it is highly probably that β-manifolds have some normal pattern of causation—and conducts an investigation to see whether mental images are well named. Are mental images *images* of any sort? Similarly, atoms came to be defined as the smallest units of a chemical element, and then it remained a question of whether atoms were well named. They weren't, as it turned out, and the scientific approach to mental images is just as prepared to discover non-imagistic mental images as physicists were to discover splittable atoms.

The stance of the scientific approach to the avowals of image-havers will benefit from further characterization. The scientist confronted by an organism that "talks" is free to treat the vocal emissions of the specimen as mere sounds, the causes of which are to be investigated. This is the way we treat human snores, for instance. If one makes this choice, one is not then confronted with questions concerning the semantic interpretation of the sounds, their meaning, truth or falsity. For snores this proves to be no hardship, but all attempts to treat those sounds we call human utterances in this non-semantic way have failed to produce credible accounts of their etiology, to put it mildly. Once one makes the decision to treat these sounds as utterances with a semantic interpretation on the other hand, one is committed to an intentionalistic interpretation of their etiology, for one has decided to view the sounds as the products of communicative intentions, as the expressions of beliefs, or as lies, as requests, questions, commands and so forth. Under the scientific approach to mental images, the image-haver is *not* subjected to the indignity of having her avowals and commentaries treated as mere noise: they are granted the status of expressions of belief, assertations made with both reason and sincerity. The scientific approach simply refrains from granting at the outset that the beliefs being expressed are *true* or even well grounded. In this the scientific approach deviates slightly from the normal mode of interpersonal communication. If in the course of conversation I assert that *p* and you set to wondering out loud what might *cause* me to believe that *p*, you bid fair to insult me, for your wondering leaves open the gaping possibility that my belief that *p* might lack the proper epistemic credentials, might be *merely* caused (might be caused in some way other than that mysteriously *right* sort of causal way alluded to in the various causal theories of perception, reference, memory, inference, etc.). It is this possibility that the scientific approach to mental images leaves explicitly open, just in order to investigate it. What normally causes people to believe that the sun is shining is the sun's shining, but what normally causes people to believe that everything they are now experiencing they have experienced once before is not their having experienced it all once before. The scientific approach to mental images leaves open the possibility that mental image beliefs, β-manifolds, might have an explanation more akin to the explanation of *déjà vu* than to that of normal visual perception.

The *other* approach to mental images, which I will name in due course, is initially more congenial in *not challenging* or questioning the epistemic credentials of image-havers' beliefs. Indeed, the β-manifold of a person can be endowed with a certain authority: the authority to *create a world*, the world that is the logical construct of the manifold of beliefs. Any set of beliefs determines a world; if the beliefs are all true, the world thus determined coincides with a portion of the real world. If any are false, the set determines a world that is at least partly fictional (e.g., the world of Dickens' London). If the set of beliefs is inconsistent, the world determined will contain objects with contradictory properties, but that is all right, since the objects are not real objects but merely *intentional objects*. [3]

The second approach to mental images defines them not as the *normal causes* of β-manifolds, but as the *intentional objects* of β-manifolds.

        : intentional object
        : (the path of logical construction)
A→B→C→D→E—→α——→β · · ·

By defining mental images as the intentional objects of β-manifolds, the second approach guarantees the *existence* of mental images *as logical constructs*. That is, it guarantees them the odd but surprisingly robust existence of intentional objects generally, what Brentano called "intentional inexistence". On this approach, mental images are at least as real as Santa Claus. Just as one might set out to learn all there is to be learned about Santa Claus, the intentional object, so one might set out to learn all there is to be learned about those intentional objects, people's mental images.

Note that there are truths and falsehoods about Santa Claus. It is true that Santa Claus has a white beard and drives a flying sleigh, false that he is tall and thin. Focussing on intentional objects like this does not require a presumption of fiction or falsehood. Consider the difference between setting out to learn all there is to know about Queen Elizabeth II, and setting out to learn all there is to know about Queen Elizabeth II, the intentional object constructable from the beliefs of British school children under the age of ten. The latter investigation might prove both more interesting and more useful than the former.

But to return to our second approach to mental images, why would one be interested in the logical construction route in this instance? The scientific approach was seen to be blandly *uncommitted* to the truth of β-manifolds; *its* mental images, the normal causes, exist with the features they do whether or not people's beliefs about them are true. This second approach seems blithely *unconcerned* with the truth of β-manifolds; *its* mental images, the logical constructs, or intentional objects, exist (as logical constructs) with precisely the features they are believed to have—whether or not the beliefs are true (true *of* anything real). Could one claim that this second approach would be a serious pursuit?

An extended analogy may convince us that it could be, by exhibiting in more detail the program of such a study. Suppose anthropologists were to discover a tribe that believed in a hitherto unheard of god of the forest, called *Feenoman*. Upon learning of Feenoman, the anthropologists are faced with a fundamental choice (not a deliberate, intentional choice, but a choice-point, an opportunity): they may convert to the native religion and believe wholeheartedly in the real existence and good works of Feenoman, or they can *study the cult* with an agnostic attitude. Consider the agnostic path. While not believing in Feenoman, the anthropologists nevertheless decide to study and systematize as best they can the religion of these people. They set down descriptions of Feenoman given by native informants; they look for agreement, seek to explain and eliminate disagreements (some say Feenoman is blue-eyed, others say he—or she—is brown-eyed). Gradually a logical construction emerges: Feenoman, the forest god, complete with a list of traits and habits, and a biography. These infidel scientists, or Feenomanologists as they call themselves, have described, ordered, catalogued, inventoried, the relevant belief-manifolds of the natives, and arrived at the *definitive* description of Feenoman. Note that the beliefs of the natives are authoritative (he's *their* god, after all), but only because Feenoman is being treated as *merely* an intentional object, a mere fiction as we disbelievers insist, and hence entirely a *creature* of the beliefs of the natives, a logical construct. Since those beliefs may contradict each other, Feenoman, as logical construct, may have contradictory properties attributed to him. The Feenomanologists try to present the best logical construct they can, but they have no overriding obligation to resolve all contradictions—they are prepared to discover unresolved and undismissible disagreements among the devout.

The believers, of course, don't see it that way—by definition, for they are the believers, to whom Feenoman is no *mere* intentional object, but someone as real as you or I. Their attitude toward their own authority about the traits of Feenoman is—or ought to be—a bit more complicated. On the one hand they do believe they *know* all about Feenoman—they are Feenomanists, after all, and who should know better than they? Yet unless they hold themselves severally to have some sort of papal infallibility, they allow as how they could *in principle* be wrong in some details. They could just possibly be instructed about the true nature of Feenoman. For instance, Feenoman himself might set them straight about a few details. Thus, a native Feenomanist who fell in with the visiting Feenomanologists and adopted their stance would have to adopt an attitude of distance or neutrality toward his own convictions (or shouldn't we have to say his own *prior* convictions?), and would in the process suffer some sort of crisis of faith, and pass from the ranks of the truly devout. (Cf. the old joke about Santayana's curious brand of Roman Catholicism: Santayana's creed, it was said, is that there is no God and Mary is His Mother.)

We can imagine another group of anthropologists who study the Feenomanists and their religion, who are also disbelievers or agnostics, like the Feenomanologists, but who set out to plot the normal causes of Feenomanist belief-manifolds. Their first step would be to learn what the Feenomanologists had charted out of those belief manifolds. This might provide valuable clues about the normal causes of the manifolds. This would be especially true if Feenomanism turns out to be true religion; we leave it open, that is, for the scientific cause-seekers to discover Feenoman and confirm the native religion. The whole investigation might, however, prove fruitless; perhaps there are no normal or projectible or salient patterns in the events that lead Feenomanists to their creed. (Cf. the conditioning of "superstitious" behavior in pigeons via random reinforcement schedules by Herrnstein *et al.*) What if these cause-seekers ask the Feenomanists, the believers, about the normal causes of their beliefs? The Feenomanists will insist, naturally, that the normal causes of their Feenomanist belief manifolds are the words and deeds of Feenoman. The anthropologists might discover otherwise. They might discover that the normal cause of the bulk of Feenomanist belief manifolds was the trickery of Sam the Shaman. This would be a particularly interesting case for us, for no matter how directly and reliably Sam the Shaman's activities determined the content of Feenomanist beliefs about Feenoman, we would not on that account alone be entitled or inclined to *identify* Feenoman as Sam the Shaman. Identification depends on the truth of the beliefs caused. If an impressive number of the most important traits of Feenoman are traits of Sam the Shaman, we will be tempted to identify the two. So, for that matter, will the Feenomanists themselves—a telling test. But probably two overridingly important traits of Feenoman are his immortality and his supernatural power, and no doubt the lack of these in Sam the Shaman would count decisively, both in our eyes and the Feenomanists', against identifying the intentional object of their creed with its normal cause. It seems, however, to be a matter almost of taste: we will learn which traits of Feenoman are *essential*, and for whom, when we see which Feenomanists (if any) accept the proposed identity.

It is time to start drawing morals from this extended analogy. I expect the morals I wish to draw are obvious, but since there are so many of them, and since I mean to draw them all, I must try your patience by making them all explicit. The second approach to mental images I shall *call* the *phenomenological approach*, but with the following warning: I mean to be *prescribing* an approach rather than *describing* an existing discipline. When I speak of the phenomenological approach I shall mean the approach I am here outlining *whether or not* any people who call themselves phenomenologists would accept it as an accurate description of their enterprise. My position, to put it bluntly, is that if what I call the phenomenological approach does not describe the program of Husserl, Sartre and their followers, so much the worse for their program. I intend to *defend* the phenomenological program as I describe it, and I call it the phenomenological program because it seems to me—no Husserl scholar, but an amateur of long standing—to do justice to what is best in Husserl.[4] I am even less of a Sartre scholar, but my reading of Sartre also encourages me to use this name for the approach described.[5] I would be happy to learn that my description finds favor among self-styled phenomenologists; if it does not, I shall change the name of the approach, not its description.

The phenomenological approach, then, sets out to rationalize the β-manifolds of people by describing the intentional objects that are their logical constructs. It proceeds independently of any search for the causes of those β-manifolds, and can *afford* to ignore experimental data about reaction times, interference effects and the like (I don't recommend that it turn its back on these data, but it may).[6] Its master, like the master of the New Critics, is the *text*, in this case the protocols, the introspective declarations, avowals, revisions, confessions of *subjects* or image-havers (see Chapter 9).[7] It treats these declarations, once care has been taken to allow for editorial revision, as authoritative, as *constituting* the features of the intentional objects being studied. In so viewing these declarations, the phenomenologists adopt an attitude fundamentally if subtly different from the attitude of the subjects themselves, for the phenomenologists must view the mental images that are the focus of *their* investigation as possibly only *mere* intentional objects, while by the subjects the mental images are *believed to be real*—"by definition", provided the subjects are sincere. Phenomenologists will be interested to discover inconsistencies between the accounts of different subjects, and even within the accounts of a single subject on a single occasion, and will make more or less standard efforts to remove these by queries and challenges designed to provoke thoughtful expression, retraction of misspoken claims, and so forth. But if inconsistencies remain after such purification of the text has gone as far as it can go, then the phenomenologists will be under no obligation to force consistency onto the β-manifolds they are cataloguing. Of course, the probing and challenging may well *effect a revision* in their subjects' β-manifolds, just as the anthropologists' sophisticated questions might well provoke doctrinal revision, invention, or clarification in the Feenomanists' creed. Under such probing some subjects might even come, rightly or wrongly, so to alter their β-manifolds that they no longer could be said to believe in mental images—and so *in the sense of the phenomenological approach* they would *cease to have* mental images. (Under intense anthropological scrutiny from Feenomanologists, Feenoman might cease to exist. That seems to have happened to Satan, for instance.)

Like the Feenomanists, subjects ought to have a complicated attitude toward their own authority about their mental images. On the one hand, believing as they do, they take their introspective descriptions to be truths, but if so, then they ought to grant that the real objects they are attempting to describe might turn out to have properties unrecognized by them, might turn out to be not as they believe them to be, *might* even turn out not to exist.[8] There is thus a tension between their attitude as subjects and the attitude of the phenomenologists studying them, and just as the Feenomanist turned Feenomanologist could not both cling unproblematically to his faith and study it, the *auto*phenomenologist studying his own mental images must find a built-in frustration in his efforts at "bracketing" or *epoché*, in divorcing himself from the implications of those of his beliefs he is studying at the very moment he is drawing out those implications. If he succeeds in suspending belief in them, then to that extent he succeeds in altering the β-manifold he is attempting to study. Autophenomenology is so difficult that even experts typically fail, and end up studying some artifact of their own enterprise.*

*For example, imagine the plight of the autophenomenologist who set out to study the intentional objects that accompanied his engagement in wildly abandoned sex; he would end up studying the intentional objects of someone engaged in sex while simultaneously performing *epoché*—hardly the same experience at all. According to Schacht, "Phenomenology proper is characterized by Husserl as 'the critique of transcendental experience' (*I[deas]* 29); 'transcendental experience' is said to be 'a new kind of experience' (I, 27), distinct from ordinary experience; and the 'phenomenological reduction' is held to be the operation through the performance of which this 'new kind of experience' becomes accessible to us." (*op. cit.*, p. 298.)

The tension between the attitude that takes mental images to be constituted "authoritatively" by β-manifolds and the attitude that takes mental images to be the real, normal causes of those β-manifolds, helps to create a spurious *third* approach to mental images, an approach that tries to treat mental images as both incorrigibly known and causally efficacious. Such marvelous entities would have to inhabit a medium more transparent to cognition than ordinary physical space, yet more actual and concrete than the mere logical space in which logical constructs, possible worlds, and the like reside. Call it, as many have, *phenomenal space*. It is as if our Feenomanist turned Feenomanologist were to grasp in his confusion at the desperate strategem of inventing a god-space, or heaven, for his beloved Feenoman to reside in, a space *real* enough to satisfy the believer in him, but remote and mysterious enough to hide Feenoman from the skeptic in him. Phenomenal space is Mental Image Heaven, but if mental images turn out to be *real*, they can reside quite comfortably in the physical space in our brains, and if they turn out not to be real, they can reside, with Santa Claus, in the logical space of fiction.*

This point is so central to my purpose, and people are often so resistant to it, that I wish to take a bit of time to explore its implications. I have been speaking as if β-manifolds were uniform from subject to subject, but of course they are not. Not only do people differ in the kinds of imagery they report, but they hold all manner of different *theories* about what they call their mental images, and hence their β-manifolds vary widely in content. Some people think their mental images are epiphenomena; some people think their mental images are something-or-others that happen in their brains; some may think their mental images are *merely* intentional objects, fictitious things they are mightily tempted to believe in, and hence, when they let their guard down, do believe in. (Cf. Scrooge.) Now, if anyone believes his mental images are information-carrying structures in his brain that deserve to be called images because they have certain structural and functional properties, and if science eventually confirms that the normal causes of that person's β-manifolds are just such structures, then he can happily *identify* intentional object with cause. It will

---

*Nothing I have said here *requires* materialism to be true. If the followers of the scientific approach wish to be dualists, they can set out to study dualistic causation of α, of β by α, and of behavior, etc., by β. My objections to dualism are of the familiar sort, and are recounted in other writings, but no appeal is being made to them here. Even for the dualist, I am insisting, there is no way to *merge* the two approaches. The dualist must either be investigating, or talking about, the occupants of the α-role, or intentional objects. A non-physical cause would have to bear the same relation to an intentional object as a physical cause.

turn out for him that imaging is, and has been, like normal veridical perception: just as pigs cause one to see pigs and cows cause one to see cows, images have caused him to believe he is having images. That is the scientific iconophile's prediction. If, on the other hand, that person's beliefs turn out to be false, if they turn out to be caused by things in the brain lacking the peculiar features of images, then the scientific iconophobe will turn out to be right, and we will have to say that that person's β-manifolds are composed of (largely) false beliefs, what one might call systematically illusory beliefs. We ought to be able, in such a case, to convince the person of this. Success in this attempt would eliminate those beliefs, but not necessarily the temptation or disposition to lapse back into them. (Some illusions are "stronger" than others.) Complete success would "cure" the delusions, and, from the phenomenological point of view, eradicate the mental images.

What if someone holds that his mental images are not physical events or structures in his brain at all, but rather either epiphenomena or items in phenomenal space, having automatically cognizable features, obeying a different logic from that of images in physical space, etc.? It is *not*, I am saying, an empirical question whether *he* is right: he is wrong, and it doesn't take science to prove it; it takes philosophy to prove it. Philosophy's job in this entire issue is to clear away hopeless doctrines like these, and leave the issue between scientific iconophile and scientific iconophobe as the only issue with *ontological* significance. *In principle* there could be a parallel question to dispute within the purely phenomenological approach. The debate between iconophile and iconophobe phenomenologists could only concern the correct or best extrapolation of intentional objects from β-manifolds. Such questions can be discussed with serious intent and rigor, but if scientific iconophobia turned out to be the truth, they would be of rather rarefied and diminished significance. They would be parallel to such questions as "Does Santa Claus have eight or nine reindeer? (Is Rudolph *established*?)" and "Was Apollo a murderer?" If scientific iconophilia turns out to be true, there could be a rich and interesting interaction between the scientists and the phenomenologists. It would not follow from the truth of scientific iconophilia that the images of phenomenology could be identified with the newly discovered or confirmed images in the α-position, for the latter might be, while undeniably *images*, very unlike the intentional objects they produced. Of course for any particular mental image creed that turns out to be *true religion*, the scientific approach will answer all the questions the phenomenological approach leaves indeterminate. There is always more to learn about *real* things about which we have (some) true beliefs.

A third approach of sorts to mental images can be obtained by noting the possibility of an equivocation in the notion of a *logical construct*. Suppose someone says, as I guess many philosophers are tempted to say: "*Whatever* science discovers, it can't discover that I don't have mental images when I think I do, and not merely as intentional objects of my beliefs." This is a powerful intuition, I grant, but one best combatted. If one wants, however, one can grant the point by a simple logical maneuver: define mental images as logical constructs out of β-manifolds in a different sense of logical construct: make having the β-manifold *criterial* for having a mental image; make it tantamount to having a mental image. One could then say, "What it *means* to say I am having a mental image is that I am having a certain β-manifold." This view might be called logical internal behaviorism. It is an approach of sorts, but an approach that has already reached its goal. It leaves nothing more (of interest) to be said about mental images. It is like the phenomenological approach in not being at war with the scientific approach, though people who hold such doctrines often cast their claims in terms that strongly suggest otherwise. (Cf. Norman Malcolm, *Dreaming*, 1959). Note too that on this view we already know what mental images are, and one thing is clear: they are *not* images of any sort, or anything *like* images. They are no more like images than home runs are like baseballs or fences.

Is my position then best described as iconophile or iconophobe? With regard to the legitimate scientific disagreement about the nature of mental representations, this paper is so far entirely neutral. It has so far merely attempted to clarify that issue by distinguishing it sharply from spurious—if traditional—debates about entirely mythical species of mental images: the various non-physical, phenomenal or epiphenomenal, self-intimating, transparent to cognition, unmisapprehensible, pseudo-extended, quasi-imagistic phantasms that have often been presented as mental images in the past. About these I am a devout iconophobe. What do I put in their place? What is left to be going on in one once these pretenders have been dismissed? In their place there are only the α's—the causes, and the β-manifolds—the effects, and about these I have been neutral, for the question whether either of these is properly imagistic is not a pure philosophical question, but a question of psychological theory or meta-theory. At the outset I required a definition of β-manifolds that had them non-imagistic, but now we can see that that was a temporary bit of scaffolding; at the time there seemed to be just *one* question about mental images, and that proviso was needed to isolate that one question. Now we can see that in fact there are two—indeed many more than two—roles in cognitive theories that *might* be filled by information-bearing structures that deserved to be called images. Armstrong, you recall, likens beliefs themselves to maps, and perhaps he is right: perhaps when psychological theory develops—if it ever does—to the point where there are well behaved and well attested theoretical entities playing roughly the α and β roles, it might prove appropriate to conceive of the β items as images of some sort. That is of course an issue that is far removed from any introspector's authority to settle. The considerations that count concern the power and versatility of different kinds of information-bearing structures, or data-structures as they are called in computer science. There is much that can already be said by iconophiles and iconophobes in support of their positions, but this is not the time to review that debate.* The goal of this essay has just been to clear the decks so that debate can proceed unhindered by misconceptions about what we might call the metaphysical status of mental images.

*In *Content and Consciousness*, in spite of my efforts to distinguish what I distinguish here in terms of the two approaches (there I spoke of the personal and sub-personal levels of explanation), I mixed metaphysical iconophobia, the view I have just espoused, and scientific iconophobia, a view I still favor, though cautiously. That is, many of the iconophobic arguments and claims of *Content and Consciousness* are properly viewed as contributions (good or bad) to psychology, not philosophy.

11

Why You Can't Make a Computer that Feels Pain

I

It has seemed important to many people to claim that computers cannot *in principle* duplicate various human feats, activities, happenings. Such aprioristic claims, we have learned, have an embarrassing history of subsequent falsification. Contrary to recently held opinion, for instance, computers can play superb checkers and good chess, can produce novel and unexpected proofs of nontrivial theorems, can conduct sophisticated conversations in ordinary if tightly circumscribed English. The materialist or computerphile who grounds an uncomplicated optimism in this ungraceful retreat of the skeptics, however, is in danger of installing conceptual confusion in the worst place, in the foundations of his own ascendant view of the mind. The triumphs of artificial intelligence have been balanced by failures and false starts. Some have asked if there is a pattern to be discerned here. Keith Gunderson has pointed out that the successes have been with task-oriented, *sapient* features of mentality, the failures and false starts with *sentient* features of mentality, and has developed a distinction between program-receptive and program-resistant features of mentality.[1] Gunderson's point is not what some have hoped. Some have hoped that he had found a fall-back position for them: *viz.*, maybe machines can *think* but they can't *feel*. His point is rather that the task of getting a machine to feel is a very different task from getting it to think; in particular it is not a task that invites solution simply by sophisticated innovations in *programming*, but rather, if at all, by devising new sorts of *hardware*. This goes some way to explaining the recalcitrance of mental features like pain to computer simulation, but not far enough. Since most of the discredited aprioristic thinking about the limitations of computers can be seen in retrospect to have stumbled over details, I propose to conduct a more detailed than usual philosophic thought experiment. Let us imagine setting out to prove the skeptic wrong about pain by actually writing a pain program, or designing a pain-feeling robot. I think the complications encountered will prove instructive.

The research strategy of computer simulation has often been mis-contrued by philosophers. Contrary to the misapprehensions innocent-ly engendered by Turing's classic paper, "Computing Machinery and Intelligence",[2] it is never to the point in computer simulation that one's model be *indistinguishable* from the modelled. Consider, for instance, a good computer simulation of a hurricane, as might be de-vised by meteorologists. One would not expect to get wet or wind-blown in its presence. That ludicrous expectation would be akin to a use-mention error, like cowering before the word "lion". A good com-puter simulation of a hurricane is a program, which, when you feed in *descriptions* of new meteorological conditions, gives you back *descrip-tions* of subsequent hurricane behavior. The descriptions might be in roughly ordinary English, dealing with clouds, waves and tides, or in some arbitrary notation, dealing with barometric pressure, wind veloc-ities, and yet more esoteric (but measurable) features of hurricanes. The goal is to devise a program that will give you good "predictions" of what a hurricane will do under a great variety of highly complex conditions. Such a program is tantamount to an immense conjunction of complicated conditionals: "if conditions A, B, C, . . . obtain, then R will result; and if conditions D, E, F, . . . obtain, S will result; and . . .". Obviously the only way to populate that conjunction reliably is by deriving the particular conditionals from general covering laws, all properly meshed and coordinated. So in order to write a good simula-tion program, one must have a *theory* of hurricane behavior, and it must be a good theory. But if one must have a theory in the first place, why bother incorporating it into a program? There are several good reasons. First, the demands of program writing force into the open any incoherencies, gaps, or unanswered questions in a theory; it keeps the theoretician honest. Second, once a theory is thus incorpo-rated into a working, "debugged" program, its implications can be quickly determined and assessed. A simulation can be an "experience-generator"; hurricanes are not that numerous, but a simulation pro-gram could generate thousands of different storm histories to scruti-nize for implausibility or worse. Also, of course, such a program could be used in high-speed real time prediction of current weather. The fact that such a simulation program is ultimately only a high speed gener-ator of the consequences that some theory assigns to various antecedent conditions is often obscured by the *mode of presentation* of the input and output. It is often useful, convenient, or just plain exciting to use the output to drive a visual display, a raster or TV screen on which appears, say, a swirling vortex moving up a map of the East Coast, but that swirling vortex is a sort of epiphenomenon, the tail that doesn't wag the dog. The theory incorporated into the program *directs* the behavior of the presentation, and does not *read off* the behavior of the presentation, which itself plays no role in the simulation beyond its role as a convenient display.

Now let us consider a similarly inspired computer simulation of human pain. We write a program, based on our theory of pain, such that when we type in *descriptions* of conditions:

An anvil drops from a height of two feet onto S's unanesthetized left foot,

the computer types back *descriptions* of results:

S jumps about on right foot, a tear in his eye, screaming.

We test the program by varying how we fill in the blanks in our permissible input formulae (e.g.: A _____ is dropped from a height of _____ on S's _____) and checking the resulting outputs for plausible variety and dependence on the input. What is unsatisfying about this computer simulation of pain? The skeptic might reply that it is a simulation at best only of pain *behavior*, but consider our hurricane simulation: what *else* is there to simulate but the hurricane's behavior? A better reply is that we have so far only attempted to simulate *external* pain behavior. This defect is easily remedied. Revised, our program will yield such outputs as

S's C-fibers are stimulated, . . . a pain-memory is laid down; S's attention is distracted; S's heart-rate increases . . ; S jumps about on right foot, a tear in the eye, screaming.

(We can be sketchy, for the moment, about the internal "behavior" or effects alluded to in the program.) Suppose, then, that we pack our output descriptions with neurophysiological description or even mentalistic psychological description about effects on memory, belief, desire, etc. Still, the skeptic may insist we have left something—indeed everything—of importance out. We have simulated, perhaps, the internal and external *causes and effects* of pain, but not the pain itself.[3] Some identity theorists may wish to retort to this that C-fibre stimulation just *is* the pain,* but we need not take a stand on that point, since there are further ways of obliging the skeptic. We can rewrite our program so it yields such outputs as

There is a pain, *P*, of the in-the-left-foot variety, in *S*; *S*'s *C*-fibers are stimulated . . .

Now we have explicitly included the pain. But, says the skeptic, the program still leaves out the *quality* of the pain. Very well. We expand our theory, and concomitantly our program, to yield detailed descriptions about even this. Again we feed in:

An anvil is dropped from a height of two feet on S's left foot.

and this time we get back:

There is a pain, *P*, of the in-the-left-foot variety in *S*; *P* begins as a dull, scarcely noticeable pressure, and then commences to throb; *P* increases in intensity until it explodes into shimmering hot flashes of stabbing stilettoes of excruciating anguish (or words to that effect) . . . ; *S*'s *C*-fibers are stimulated . . .

I see no reason why our program could not be enlarged to incorporate all this; the biggest problem would seem to be discovering sufficient uniformity and lawfulness in such "phenomenological" effects as reported by sufferers to permit much prediction. Of course if the data we collect suggest a random distribution of these effects within certain boundaries that is easy enough to incorporate into our program as well.**

I do not expect this would satisfy the skeptic. He might try to express his doubts by pointing out that there is nothing pain-like going on in the computer when it churns out these reports. But of course not. Nor does the computer hurricane generate an internal low barometric pressure behind its steely facade. At this point it should dawn on the skeptic that he has been barking up the wrong tree. He has no

---

*They would be—perhaps unwittingly—wrong if they made this claim, as we shall see. Stimulation of the *C*-fibers is neither a necessary nor sufficient condition for the occurrence of pain. (*C*-fibers *are* stimulated under general anesthesia, and need not be stimulated for neuralgia or central pain to occur.) The term "*C*-fibers" seems however to have lost, for philosophers, its empirical anchoring in neuroanatomy and become a philosopher's wild-card referring expression for whatever physical event "turns out to be identical with" pain.

**Such an enterprise might be illuminated by a revival of the researches of the Nineteenth Century investigator Hahnemann, who botanized over seventy-three distinct phenomenological varieties of pain. See F. Sauerbruch, *Pain: Its Meaning and Significance* (1963), p. 74.

pressing quarrel with *this* research strategy when it is directed to psychological phenomena, since its guiding presupposition is not that men are computers (any more than hurricanes are) but simply that one can have a rigorous *theory* of human psychology, materialist, dualist, epiphenomenalist, or whatever. Isn't there, however, another research strategy that differs significantly from the one we've been considering, where the aim of the computer is to *do*, not *describe*? For instance, "Shakey" at Stanford Research Institute is a robot that can "recognize" simple objects with its television eyes; it pushes cubes and pyramids around in response to typed commands. Such "performance models", one might say, really do things; they do not so much incorporate theories (as do simulations) as *instantiate* theories.* The skeptic's challenge is now for us to make such a robot, a *feeler of pain*, not a mechanized theory about feelers of pain. So let us try to design such a robot. Of course our efforts in this task will be as much guided by our *theory* of pain as were our earlier simulation efforts, and we might ask the skeptic if he had any quarrels with our earlier, programmed theory *as a theory* of pain. If the skeptic makes no objections to it, we are home free, for it is a relatively straightforward task to build the robot with the help of our earlier "describing" program. The describing program simply becomes the control system for our new robot.

Here is how it is done. Suppose our original program yielded outputs like: "S trembles, a tear in his eye, and says 'Ouch! My thumb hurts.'" First, we rewrite all outputs in the first person: "I tremble, a tear in my eye, and I say 'Ouch! My thumb hurts.' " Then we drop the redundant "I say" wherever it occurs and move all direct quotation onto a separate "protocol" terminal, which will then print only "Ouch! My thumb hurts." The rest of the output is reprogrammed to drive a display of flashing lights with labels. The "tremble" light goes

*The distinction is not as clear-cut as it may first appear. Terry Winograd's natural language understanding program (see Terry Winograd, "Understanding Natural Language", *Cognitive Psychology*, 1972, vol. 3, pp. 1-191) "manipulates" the "objects in its environment" and answers questions about them. But its environment is entirely artificial and internal, like the environment of the swirling hurricane of our earlier example. When Winograd's device "puts a cube on the table", is it a doer or a describer? Moreover, if we view the theory we incorporate into a program as an *uninterpreted* theory, we are free to view the computer's behavior as satisfying one interpretation of the theory, so that any programmed computer can be viewed as instantiating (on one interpretation) the theory incorporated in its program. The tokens of computer behavior that on one interpretation are uttered *decriptions* of the behavior of some other entity instantiating the theory, can on another interpretation be viewed as themselves instances of behavior predicted by the theory. I owe this observation to Joseph Weizenbaum.

on, the "tear in the eye" light, and so forth. Then we replace the input sentences in a similar manner. We make up magnetized plastic tokens representing different objects—anvils, knives, olives—falling from different heights, and we label an array of slots to accept these tokens: "thumb", "big toe", etc., so that *dropping* the anvil token into the thumb slot simulates dropping the anvil on the thumb. Of course that's not very realistic, but we can improve it easily. For instance, we can replace the "tremble" light with an eccentric flywheel that makes the whole computer vibrate when it is turning; the tear in the eye problem has already been solved for us by the toy manufacturers, and the other details of verisimilitude are either obviously irrelevant or can be solved by the Disney studios given six months and enough Federal grant money. The result will be a robot that really *does* things; it trembles and reels and whimpers; it says just where the pain is; it attempts to duck falling objects—perhaps it even kicks back if we kick it.*

But what about the rest of our earlier simulation? What happens to the hot flashes and dull throbs mentioned in our descriptive program? These parts of the output we transform into labeled flashing lights and leave them that way: sometimes the "dull throb" light is on (blinking slowly if you like) and sometimes the "hot flash" light is on. If the skeptic insists on more verisimilitude here, what can he be asking for? Remember that these lights are not blinking randomly. The "dull throb" light goes on only at appropriate times, the robot can then say: "There is a dull, throbbing pain," and the other apposite side effects of dull, throbbing pains are presumed to be arranged to coincide as well. But, the skeptic persists, no amount of *side effects* can turn what is not a dull, throbbing pain into a dull, throbbing pain, and obviously, calling this event a dull, throbbing pain does not make it one either. This objection, for all its plausibility, is unfair as it stands. The skeptic, we must assume, had no objection to settling for an IBM typewriter as the "speech" element in this robot, and surely typing is not talking—and calling typing talking would not make it talking. Since he has not challenged us to make a *bona fide* member of the species *homo sapiens* out of whatever bits and pieces are on the shelves at IBM, he must be permitting us to use some substitutes—the legs can be titanium, not flesh and bones—and since our flashing light (or what-

*Some of this fantasy has already been turned to fact. SIM ONE, a robot used in training medical students, blinks, breathes, has measurable blood pressure, coughs, twitches, and can become "anesthetized". See J. S. Denson and S. Abrahamson, "A Computer-controlled Patient Simulator", *Journal of the American Medical Association*, CCVIII (1969): 504–8.

ever turns it on) has all the *functional* features he has demanded of pain, why is he now changing the game? Calling the robot a human being would not make the robot a human being either, but that was never set as a goal. It begins to appear that what the skeptic was after all along was not a *simulation* or an *analogue* of pain, but the synthesis of real pain, like the synthesis of urea by Wöhler in 1828 that marked the unification of organic and inorganic chemistry. The synthesis of real pain in a machine would tend to confirm that we human beings are just fancy soft machines, as the materialist contends.

That we might reconstrue our task in this way highlights a peculiarity in our ordinary concept of pain. The word "pain" has both a *sortal* grammar ("I have a pain", "pains shooting up my arm") and a *mass noun* grammar ("There is more pain now", "it will cause you some pain"). The mass noun grammar often permits us—even invites us—to view pain as a sort of biological or psychological substance, rather than a process or event or activity or state. For instance, the amount of morphine that can be safely administered depends on the *amount of pain* it has to kill. For excruciating pain (e.g., that of coronary thrombosis) two to four times the usual therapeutic dose may be given without danger. But in cases of severe pains that can quickly and spontaneously disappear (e.g., those of coronary occlusion or biliary colic) such doses are dangerous, since if the pain disappears suddenly the patient may show signs of morphine poisoning. If such were to happen, one would do well to punch or slap the patient, since, as Stearns observed in 1883, "pain is the antidote for morphine poisoning". One creates *more pain* for the morphine to neutralize, and thus prevents the excess of morphine from poisoning.[4] This suggests that specificity to morphine as an antagonist would be a legitimate test for any robot pain to pass.

This reconstrual of the task might seem, however, to harbor a conceptual confusion. Does one not contradict oneself in speaking of the synthesis of real pain? Synthetic urea *is* urea, as genuine as any to be found, but synthetic rubber is not rubber.* Is artificial intelligence genuine intelligence? Artificial coloring is perfectly genuine *coloring*, but artificial flowers are not flowers. The field of artificial intelligence trades on this ambiguity. Successes are often heralded as examples of genuine intelligence created by artifice, but in the face of objections

---

*Herbert Simon, in *The Sciences of the Artificial* (1969), points to the distinction that is occasionally drawn between "artificial" and "synthetic"; a green glass gem might be called an artificial sapphire, while a manufactured gem chemically identical to genuine sapphire would be called synthetic (p. 4).

this claim can be adjusted; artificial intelligence *works just as well as,* or is a useful and even theoretically interesting *substitute* for, genuine intelligence. I do not believe the term "artificial intelligence" is objectionable on these grounds, for I do not believe in the distinction we are invited to make in this instance. Suppose the intelligence of some artifacts does function just as well as human intelligence (an immense supposition, of course); then, since intelligence, like respiration, is a purely functional notion, artificial intelligence, like artificial respiration, is no less genuine for being obtained by artifice. It may not be *just like* natural, human intelligence, but it is genuine intelligence, as genuine as (we can imagine) the *alien* intelligence of extra-galactic creatures might be.[5] But what of artificial or synthetic pain? Is pain like rubber and flowers, or like coloring, respiration and intelligence? Whatever answer we might agree on (and agreement is both unlikely and ultimately unimportant), one lesson is clear: *if* pain is deemed to be *essentially* a biological phenomenon, *essentially* bound up with birth, death, the reproduction of species, and even (in the case of human pain) social interactions and interrelations, then the computer scientist attempting to synthesize real pain in a robot is on a fool's errand. He can no more succeed than a master cabinetmaker, with the finest tools and materials, can succeed in making, today, a *genuine* Hepplewhite chair.

Reservations about whether synthetic pain would be real pain may seem overly precious, but it is important to bring them into the open, for several reasons. First, a great deal of the counterintuitiveness of the notion of robot pain no doubt derives from a dim appreciation of this side of our notion of pain. *Real* pain is bound up with the struggle to survive, with the real prospect of death, with the afflictions of our soft and fragile and warm flesh.[6] With our concept of pain, as with many others, there is a tug toward *parochiality*: *real* Chateau Latour has to have been made in a particular place, in a particular way, by particular people: an artificially concocted fluid indistinguishable to both chemists and connoisseurs from Chateau Latour would still not be *real* Chateau Latour. (Real vodka, on the other hand, can be made from just about anything, anywhere, by anybody.) The parochiality of the concept of pain, is, moreover, not an irrational feature, or at least not obviously so, for it has a role to play in defining our moral community. There can be no denying (though many have ignored it) that our concept of pain is inextricably bound up with (which may mean something less strong than *essentially connected with*) our ethical intuitions, our senses of suffering, obligation, and evil.[7] It will not do to suppose that an assessment of any attempt at robot synthesis of pain can be conducted independently of questions about what our moral obligations to this robot might be. One reason, then, why you can't make a computer that feels pain is that our concept of pain is not a pure psychological concept but also ethical, social, and parochial, so that whatever we *put inside* our computer or robot will not avail unless it brings in its train these other considerations, a matter over which our control, as computer designers, is worse than limited. This reason is important, and worth developing with more care, but not here, for it is also a bit of a red herring. Even if contextual matters, such questions of origin and "form of life", make a difference, they do not make enough of a difference. I do not think the skeptic wishes to rest his case at a point where the programmer's synthetic product might fall short only by these yardsticks (like the clever chemist's imitation Chateau Latour which only *seems* to have "good breeding"). Moreover, were the synthetic product that good, the contextual matters might either fall into line (we would start treating the computer very much as one of us, and commiserate with it, comfort it, etc.) or be dislodged in our minds from their position of importance. In any event, what the skeptic finds impossible to imagine is that this thing that happpens in and to him (and it happens in and to him quite independently—or so it seems—of his biological origin, destiny, social milieu or ethical status) can be made to happen in and to a robot.

At this point it is easy for the skeptic to fall into extravagant and irrelevant claims to support or flesh out his skepticism. When he says no *robot* could feel pain as he does, is it the artificiality, the chemistry, or *what* that makes the difference? A *cloned* duplicate of himself would presumably be capable of feeling pain, but if we could *construct* a biochemical duplicate of him, would this artifact be a painless robot? On what grounds, other than the grounds of origin we have just now set aside? Supposing, then, that a manufactured *biochemical* duplicate *would* feel pain, on his view, what difference could it make if we use other materials? Only two replies, both insupportable, occur to me: (1) organic compounds are capable of realizing functional structures with capacities of a sophistication or power *in principle* unrealizable in non-organic materials, or (2) though an inorganic replica might succeed in duplicating a human being's functional structure, the states in it functionally isomorphic to human pain states would fail to be genuine pain states because the biochemistry of pain-state realization is essential.* These are both highly implausible vitalistic claims, and any

*Note that we can obtain the specificity of functional reaction to morphine and other drugs without accomplishing this in the same way, chemically, that a human body does.

skeptic led to defend his view in this territory has simply been led astray. That is not to say that murmurs of vitalism do not make a large contribution to the skeptics' attitudes, but just that the contribution should be first isolated and then ignored. To find something better for the skeptic to say, we must give him more details to work with. We have been assuming, up to now, that the programmer could have at his disposal a fairly satisfactory theory of pain to exploit in designing his robots. We have been assuming, that is, that the *mysteriousness* of pain might thwart our efforts at synthesizing pain without thwarting our efforts at theorizing about it. But how realistic is that assumption? The best way to examine it is to set down the bare bones of current physiological theory relating to pain, and list some of the attested pain phenomena, the data any acceptable theory of pain must account for, and see if there are any insuperable difficulties presented by them. We can record the known dependencies and interrelations among these phenomena by plotting a "flow-chart" of sorts for a pain program.

II

The flow-chart to be presented here is merely a sketch, lacking rigor and detail, but its point is to facilitate philosophical scrutiny of pain, not to launch any serious project of programming or theoretical psychology or neurophysiology. I hope it will be clear that the difficulties we encounter would only be exacerbated in a more systematic model.

We can begin with what is known about the functional anatomy of transmission from pain sites into the brain. As is generally the case, the further in from the periphery we move, the murkier the details. The journey begins at the skin, with receptors sometimes called nociceptors that respond with some degree of specificity to a variety of noxious events: mechanical distortion, intensities of heat and cold and chemical changes, for instance. The outputs of these receptors travel brain-ward through at least two very different types of fibers: swiftly through the large myelinated *A*-fibers, and slowly through the narrow, unmyelinated *C*-fibers.* Both signals arrive at the substantia gelatinosa,

---

*The difference in transmission speed is considerable: 100 meters per second versus less than two meters per second. If you stick a pin in your finger you can distinguish quite readily two resultant sensations in sequence: roughly, a pricking sensation followed swiftly by a "deeper" pain. This tandem effect is generally thought to be explained by the difference in transmission speed. See R. A. Sternbach, *Pain, A Psychophysiological Analysis* (1968), p. 30 for a discussion of the issue, and references.

the midbrain gateway, where a complicated interaction takes place. A-fibers also send effects inwards via other channels. The A- and C-fibers seem to make two different functional contributions. On the one hand, it seems that the C-fibers are the preponderant transmitters of "slow", "deep", "aching", or "visceral" pains, while A-fibers are implicated in "sharp", "bright", "stabbing" pains. Recently Melzack and Wall have suggested a more interesting function for the A-fibers. They act at the substantia gelatinosa to *inhibit* the effect of the C-fibers, thus *closing* the gate to pain-impulse transmission, or at least damping the output of that gate. Moreover, the A-fiber channels that bypass the Melzack-Wall gate in the substantia gelatinosa seem to initiate more central activity that sends inhibitory signals back down to the gate, further blocking the transmission of impulses from the C-fibers. The capacity of the hypothesized Melzack-Wall gate system to explain a variety of pain phenomena is immense, as we will soon see.[8]

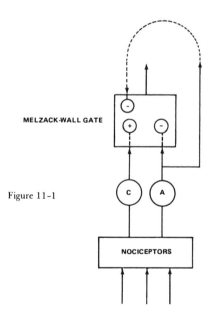

Figure 11-1

What, then, happens to the output of the gate, the so-called T-cell transmissions? In broadest outline we can say that once again there is a split into two channels. One channel carries through the lower, phylogenetically older portion of the brain, the limbic system (hypothalamus, reticular formation, paleocortex, hippocampus), and the other passes through the thalamus and is projected onto the higher, phylogenetically newer, characteristically human part of the brain, the neocortex. Let us simplify by calling these the old low path and the new high path. The new high path is subject to yet another bifurcation: there is both a specific and a non-specific projection of fibres from the thalamus onto the cortex.

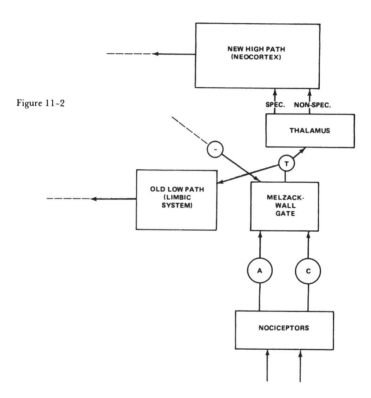

Figure 11-2

The new high path, which is relatively undeveloped or non-existent in lower animals, subserves fine-grained perception: location and characterization of pain and other stimuli. The old low path is characterized by orthodoxy as the *aversive* system, the "motivational-affective processing" system. Orthodoxy is well buttressed by evidence in this instance,* and this suggested separation of the hurtfulness or awfulness of pain from its other characteristics—to speak loosely—will loom large in our further discussion.

Having charted this far with the aid of anatomical roadmaps, we have reached *terra incognita*, and if we are to proceed with our flow chart we must abandon the pretence that our boxes represent anatomically salient structures, and proceed with a purely functional, abstract breakdown of the system. We can make use of the freedom thus provided to be more boldly speculative, and also, inevitably, vaguer about the nature of the functions and relations we are charting. The only constraint on our design will be that it accommodate the known and presumed phenomena.

Everyone knows, for instance, that distracting one's attention (e.g., by going to a movie) diminishes or banishes pain. This can be easily provided for if we build in a presenter-receiver filtering system across the pathway for incoming signals from all the sense modalities, subject to the following conditions: the receiver can have its general sensitivity raised or lowered, and the presenter has *selective* volume controls, so that its various signals can be turned up independently.** Then the effect of distracted attention could work this way: paying special attention to one input (the visual and auditory input from the movie) would be accomplished in part by turning up its volume in the presenter. Then the receiver would compensate for this high volume by decreasing its sensitivity, having the effect of muffling everything else, including the pain signals. The same effect might be accomplished by the Melzack-Wall gate, but let's be generous and draw in a separate filtering system.

---

*Lesions in the old low path are responsible for "central pain" or neuralgia (pain with a central cause but peripheral "location"—one does not necessarily feel a *head*ache in central pain). "Cortical representations" of pain are considered less "important" by researchers generally. Cortical lesions seem almost never to produce central pain (and when they do, descending effects on the old low path are indicated). Penfield, in his research on stimulation of the exposed cortex produced a wide variety of effects, but almost no pain. See V. Cassinari and C. A. Pagni, *Central Pain: A Neurosurgical Survey* (1969); and Wilder Penfield, *The Excitable Cortex in Conscious Man* (1958). Moreover, "direct stimulation of the reticular and limbic systems produces strong aversive drive and behavior typical of responses to naturally occurring painful stimuli". (Melzack and Wall, *op. cit.*, p. 20.)

**Such volume control systems have been posited in the course of many different investigations in the brain sciences. Arguably such a system's existence has been physiologically confirmed in cats. See Hernandez-Peon, Scherer and Jouvet, "Modification of Electrical Acitivty in Cochlear Nucleus during 'Attention' in Unanesthetized Cats", *Science*, CXXIII (1956): 331-32.

Pain signals trigger a variety of "spinal reflexes" causing relatively simple but swift muscular responses without the intervention of higher brain centers (and in some instances without passing through the substantia gelatinosa, the Melzack-Wall gate), and since distracted attention has little or no effect on these, we will put the filter only in the new high path, and draw in the reflex links (R) to the motor output nerves without intervening links of sophisticated control.

There are many transactions between the old low and new high paths. Of particular importance to us is the relation the reticular formulation in the old low brain has to higher centers. The reticular activating system plays a major role in governing sleep and waking, and determining the level of arousal generally; it also plays a role in directing attention, and thus can be considered a versatile alarm system.

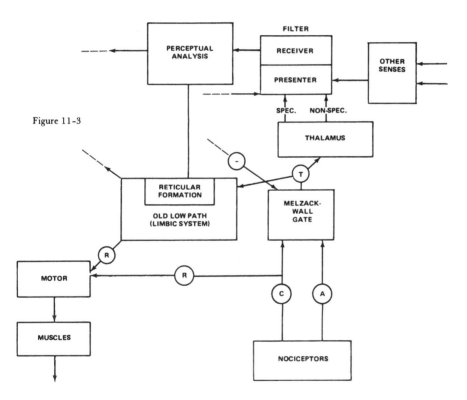

Figure 11-3

So far we have hardly touched on the effect of pain stimuli on "higher centers", so let us sketch in roughly what is most obvious about these effects. When we have a pain we believe we have a pain (at

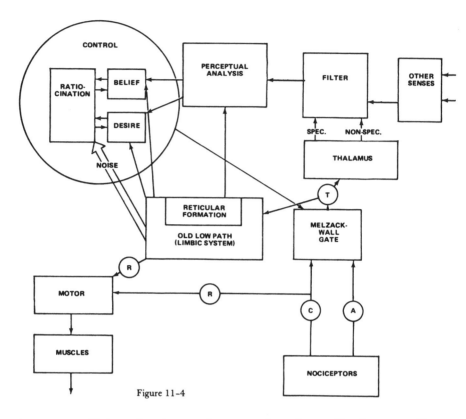

Figure 11-4

least normally), and pains can be remembered, usually, for some time. So in our control circle we will place a memory and belief box, and to be on the safe side, *two* arrows leading to it, one from the old low path and one from the new high path (further investigation might lead us to revise any of this, of course). Also, pains are abhorrent, at least usually. That is, the infliction of pain is a reliable behavior-modifier, tongue loosener, punishment. (Whether punishment is good for anything is another matter. Pain is a good way to punish.) So we should draw in a "goals and desires" box, with appropriate inputs. (If the "aversive" effects of pain are subserved *entirely* by the old low path, we might not want an arrow from the new high path to the desire center, but again, let's be generous. No doubt even the most intellectual apprehension of pain stimuli could have *some* effect on one's desires, current or long-term.)

It is a useful and oft-used myth, at least, that higher controls in human beings are accomplished by something like logical processing of the material in the belief and desire boxes (see Chapter 3), so let us

Figure 11-5

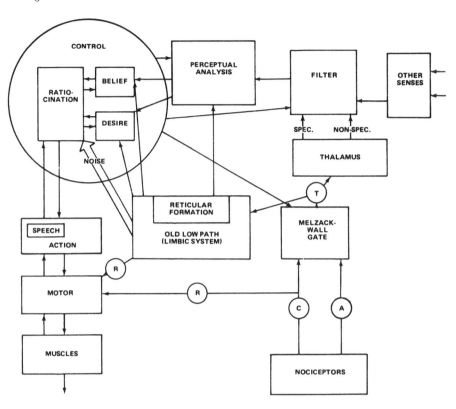

distinguish a ratiocination unit in the control area. We need this in any case, since one effect of pain stimuli on this function (as captured by our box) is not *informational* but *noisy*: pains interfere with our ability to concentrate, to solve problems, to think clearly, so we should draw a "noise" arrow to the ratiocination unit. (Perhaps we should draw noise arrows to other units as well, but let's not overcomplicate our diagram.)

Finally, let us transmit the control center's effects on behavior through an action organizing unit (with the specially important speech synthesis unit drawn in) to the motor-effector controls and thence to the muscles. In addition to the control center's effects on behavior, we must put in the arrows for various "descending effects" on the input system, including those already alluded to: an inhibitory effect on the Melzack-Wall gate, a volume control on the filter, a "perceptual set" or "readiness" determiner to weight the analyzing machinery, and others not worth drawing in. Then of course there should be "feedback" arrows throughout. That should be enough detail to handle the phenomena at least in outline. The sketchiness and idealization of this model should not be forgotten, of course. Some of the functions captured by these boxes may merge in single anatomical structures, and such distortions as are present in the model might seriously misrepresent the actual state of affairs to the point of requiring major revision of the model. In any case, however, we now have a fairly complicated and versatile model to play with; let us see how it runs when it comes to providing for the variety of pain phenomena.

Why does it help to rub or press the painful area, or to scratch an itch? Melzack and Wall claim that this increases A-fiber transmission, thus increasing the inhibition of the C-fiber stimulation in the substantia gelatinosa. A less commonly recognized home remedy for pain is not to *distract*, but to *concentrate* one's attention on the pain. I discovered this for myself in the dentist's chair, thinking to take advantage of the occasion by performing a phenomenological investigation without the benefit of novocain, and have since learned that this is a highly elaborated technique of Zen Buddhism.[9] I recommend this enthusiastically. If you can make yourself study your pains (even quite intense pains) you will find, as it were, no room left to *mind* them: (they stop hurting)—though studying a pain (e.g., a headache) gets boring pretty fast, and as soon as you stop studying them, they come back and hurt, which, oddly enough, is sometimes less boring than being bored by them and so, to some degree, preferable. I am not at all sure that what I just said "makes sense"; that is, I am not at all sure that this loose talk about *pains* that cease and resume hurting, or even this loose talk about *studying* one's pains, is ontologically, metaphysically, scientifically, phenomenologically *sound*, but it is nevertheless just what I want to say. That is the way I would put it if I were unselfconscious and unworried about committing some conceptual gaffe. And that is a crucial part of the problem of pain: we have a baffling variety of such untutored, unstudied accounts of pain phenomena, and it is no easier to give them all credence than it is to revise them by the light of some procrustean theory about what pain experiences must be. But, to return to the effect of attention on pains, whatever the "correct" philosophical analysis is of the variety of first person pain reports, it must have room for the fact that focussing attention can *obtain relief* (to put the matter neutrally for the moment). Melzack and Wall have a ready explanation of this phenomenon: focussing attention on one's pains may serve to raise the volume only on the

A-fiber component of it, thus inhibiting the *C*-fibers at the Melzack-Wall gate. Their experiments tend to confirm this hypothesis, and suggest that analgesia by hypnosis or yoga methods have similar explanations.*

We "locate" our pains, but this is not a single thing we do. On the one hand, we react more or less reflexively to jerk the injured part away from contact with harm, and that is accomplished through the old low path. But we also "can say" where our pains are, and this is presumably accomplished on the new high path with the aid of the specific projection system to the perceptual analysis areas of the cortex, and thence through the control system to ultimate speech. Excitation of a specific peripheral nerve fiber at any point on its length normally produces a sensation of pain felt at its normal extremity. "Phantom limb" is, of course, the most vivid manifestation of this phenomenon.**

In "referred pain" the pain location does not match the location of the trauma. This must be due to "leakage" or "short-circuits" at crossover points in the specific pathways, probably in the substantia gelatinosa. Oddly enough, however, administering novocain or other local anesthetic to the site where the pain is *felt* diminishes the referred pain, and pressure on that area increases the pain. This can be accounted for if we suppose the leakage is not a simple *turning-on* of the wrong fiber, but an *enhancement* of a resting level of transmission. Under local anesthesia there would be nothing to enhance (since local anesthetics stop *all* transmission), and pressing the uninjured area would produce a higher pre-existing level to enhance.

Now let us locate on our model the effects of various drugs, especially the anesthetics, which prevent all sensation, and the analgesics, which are specific for pain. Novocain and related local anesthetics act

*Can the Melzack-Wall theory also account for acupuncture anesthesia? It is not hard to speculate about mechanisms that could be added to the Melzack-Wall theory to accomodate the acupuncture effects, but I understand Wall is currently at least agnostic about the capacity of the theory to handle it.

**To some extent pain locations need to be *learned*, though, and can be unlearned. In cases of limb amputation performed on children before they developed the use and coordination of the limb, phantom limb is rarely experienced. When amputation occurs just after birth, phantom limb never occurs. See M. Simmel, "Phantom Experiences Following Amputation in Childhood", *Journal of Neurosurgery and Psychiatry*, XXV (1962): 69-72.

Moreover, locations can be "mislearned". A variety of pain commonly produced in jet pilots under certain high altitude conditions is positively located by them in either the cheeks or the teeth. Which location is reported depends not on variation in the physiological etiology of the pain (which is constant) but on whether or not the pilots have had recent painful dental work.

by completely stopping the transmission of nerve cells at their source. In fact, they block nerve activity wherever they are injected: "spinal block" is a local anesthetic administered high in the pathway to the brain, creating a wide area of total but still "local" anesthesia. There are no local analgesics, but aspirin is unique among the common general analgesics in having a peripheral site of action.* It antagonizes a metabolite, bradykinin, at the nociceptors; it is bradykinin that persists in stimulating the nociceptors after the initial traumatic event and thereby is responsible for persistent pain. Aspirin, by antagonizing bradykinin, prevents pain at the earliest opportunity. This is interesting because aspirin is also unique among analgesics in lacking the "reactive disassociation" effect. All other analgesics (e.g., the morphine group and nitrous oxide in sub-anesthetic doses) have a common "phenomenology". After receiving the analgesic subjects commonly report not that the pain has disappeared or diminished (as with aspirin) but that the pain *is as intense as ever* though they no longer *mind* it. To many philosophers this may sound like some sort of conceptual incoherency or contradiction, or at least indicate a failure on the part of the subjects to *draw enough distinctions*, but such philosophical suspicions, which we will examine more closely later, must be voiced in the face of the normality of such first-person reports and the fact that they are expressed in the widest variety of language by subjects of every degree of sophistication. A further curiosity about morphine is that if it is administered *before* the onset of pain (for instance, as a pre-surgical medication) the subjects claim not to feel any pain subsequently (though they are not *numb* or anesthetized—they have sensation in the relevant parts of their bodies); while if the morphine is administered *after* the pain has commenced, the subjects report that the pain continues (and continues to be *pain*), though they no longer mind it.

Our model suggests that morphine and other analgesics must work on the old low path while leaving the new high path relatively in order, and such is the case. While morphine, like anesthetic drugs generally, takes effect first at the higher, cortical levels of the brain and then descends to the old brain, the specific projections to the cortex are especially resistant to damping by drugs, so that the effects of these drugs is more pronounced on the old low aversive path than on the new high path of fine-grained perception. The timing-dependence feature of morphine might be explained this way: once old low pain signals have contributed to the "set" of the perceptual analyzing machinery (via influences on the control center's "descending effects"

*Aspirin also probably has central analgesic effects.

which would weight the interpretation machinery in favor of interpreting particular signal patterns as pain-transmitting), this cannot be quickly undone, even after the contribution from the old low path is eliminated by morphine. Lobotomized subjects similarly report feeling intense pain but not minding it, and in other ways the manifestations of lobotomy and morphine are similar enough to lead some researchers to describe the action of morphine (and some barbiturates) as "reversible pharmacological leucotomy [lobotomy]".*

When we turn from local anesthesia and analgesia in conscious subjects to general anesthesia, the situation becomes more complicated. The major problem can be approached by way of a curious and terrible incident from the annals of medicine. Curare, the poison used by South American Indians on their blow-pipe darts, was purified (as *d-tubocurarine*) and introduced into medical research in the 1930's, and its action was soon well understood.[10] It is a paralytic that acts directly on all the neuromuscular junctions, the last rank effectors of the nervous system, to produce total paralysis and limpness of all the voluntary muscles. It has no central effect except for a slight enhancement effect on activity in the cortex. In the 1940's, however, some doctors fell under the misapprehension that curare was a general anesthetic, and they administered it as such for major surgery. The patients were, of course, quiet under the knife, and made not the slightest frown, twitch or moan, but when the effects of the curare wore off, complained bitterly of having been completely conscious and in excruciating pain, feeling every scalpel stroke but simply paralyzed and unable to convey their distress. The doctors did not believe them. (The fact that most of the patients were infants and small children may explain this credibility gap.)[11] Eventually a doctor bravely submitted to an elaborate and ingenious test under curare, and his detailed confirmation of the subjects' reports was believed by his colleagues: curare is very definitely not any sort of anesthetic or analgesic.[12]

Recently a puzzle occurred to me: suppose that one were to add to curare a smidgin of *amnestic*, a drug that (we will hypothesize) has no effect on experience or memory during *n* hours after ingestion

*A. S. Keats and H. K. Beecher, "Pain Relief with Hypnotic Doses of Barbiturates, and a Hypothesis", *Journal of Pharmacology* (1950). Lobotomy, though discredited as a behavior-improving psychosurgical procedure, is still a last resort tactic in cases of utterly intractable central pain, where the only other alternative to unrelenting agony is escalating morphine dosages, with inevitable addiction, habituation and early death. Lobotomy does not excise any of the old low path (as one might expect from its effect on pain perception), but it does cut off the old low path from a rich input source in the frontal lobes of the cortex.

but thereafter wipes out all memory of those n hours.* Patients administered our compound, curare-cum-amnestic, will not later embarrass their physicians with recountings of agony, and will in fact be unable to tell in retrospect from their own experience that they were not administered a general anesthetic. Of course *during* the operation they would know, but would be unable to tell us.** At least most of our intuitions tell us that curare-cum-amnestic would not be an acceptable substitute for general anesthesia, even if it were cheaper and safer.*** But now how do we know that general anesthetics in use today are not really curare-cum-amnestic? We know, in fact, that curare *is* routinely used in general anesthesia today. Most general anesthetics by themselves in safe doses do not entirely block reflex spasms, so curare or another curariform paralytic is administered to prevent muscle-tearing damage and thrashing about that could interfere with the surgeon's task. Moreover, a variety of drugs in the anesthesiologist's bag are known to be amnestics. How do we know that these drugs have the further effect of producing genuine anesthesia or even analgesia? Absence of complaint or other behavioral manifestation, we have seen, is hardly sufficient grounds—though they are routinely and not unreasonably relied on in daily medical practice. To answer this question we will have to look more closely at the *internal* effects of the so-called general anesthetics, and at other, more indirect clues about their functions.

There are a wide variety of general anesthetics, but they fall into

---

*I know of no drug with just these powers, but a number of drugs used in anesthesia are known to have amnestic properties. Scopolamine is the strongest and most reliable amnestic (though it is still unreliable), but it has other effects as well: *not* anesthesia or analgesia, but it does create hallucinations and a sort of euphoria. Scopolamine and other amnestics are often prescribed by anesthesiologists *for the purpose of creating amnesia*. "Sometimes," I was told by a prominent anesthesiologist, "when we think a patient may have been awake during surgery, we give scopolamine to get us off the hook. Sometimes it works and sometimes not." Scopolamine was once widely used in conjunction with a sedative or morphine to produce the "twilight sleep" then recommended for childbirth. One pharmacological textbook, in discussing this practice, uses the phrase "obstetrical amnesia or analgesia" as if amnesia and analgesia were much the same thing. (Goodman and Gilman, *op. cit.,*[4] p. 555.)

**Unable in fact, not unable in principle. We could quite easily devise signalling systems triggered directly by activity in electrode-monitored motor neurons. My point is not that such a state is in principle indistinguishable from anesthesia; I simply want to consider what, aside from current behavioral evidence (and later memory report) is crucial in making the determination.

***I have found some people who proclaim their untroubled readiness to accept this substitute. I think they have been bewitched by Wittgensteinian logical behaviorism.

groups, and if we take three important drugs as paradigms, we will have more than enough variation to suggest the problems: (1) nitrous oxide, or laughing gas, which is inhaled; (2) ether, one of many related volatile inhalants; (3) sodium pentothal (or thiopental sodium), an injected "ultra-fast-acting" barbiturate.[13] These drugs are chemically very different, and have different effects on the central nervous system and the rest of the body. Moreover, in modern practice they are seldom used alone, but are almost always accompanied by preanesthetic medication, such as an analgesic (e.g., morphine), a sedative to combat anxiety and the nausea that often results from ether inhalation, or even a "basal" anesthetic, which produces anesthesia sufficiently deep for preparation for surgery but too shallow for surgery. In spite of this variation we can impose some order by considering the traditional "stages" and "planes" of general anesthesia. In passing from full consciousness into the anesthetized state, one moves through three of four marked stages. In the first, one is conscious but apt to have hallucinations or uncontrollable thoughts; the drug is acting on the neocortex (at least partly as an enhancer or stimulant). In the second or delirium stage one is unconscious (in some sense) but may laugh, shout, swear or thrash about. The drug's effects are descending through the brain, and one hypothesis is that the drug has reached the higher motor control centers and paralyzed them, "releasing" lower motor activity. In the third stage, called surgical anesthesia, there are four planes, of increasing depth. Depending on the surgery to be done one will be kept in the shallowest permissible plane of surgical anesthesia, since the fourth stage, medullary paralysis, is a short prelude to respiratory failure and death. These temporal stages are all but undetectable with sodium pentothal, where stage three is reached in a few seconds, and their manifestations are largely obliterated by the effects of preanesthetic medication with ether or nitrous oxide (no one wants a hallucinating, thrashing patient to deal with, which is one reason for pre-anesthetic medications). So the importance for practice, if not pedagogy, of the traditional stages of anesthetic induction is virtually nil. The four planes of third-stage surgical anesthesia, however, have well-recognized symptoms relied on by anesthesiologists in maintaining the proper level of anesthesia during surgery. And for all the differences among the drugs, one similarity is clear enough: in doses large enough to produce deep plane surgical anesthesia (or fourth stage medullary paralysis) all the drugs are analgesic and anesthetic if any drug could be, since their effect at those levels amounts to virtual shut-down of the entire central nervous system. Such barely reversible brain death will look plausibly pain-free (by being everything-free) to even the unrepentant interactionist, for there is almost nothing happening to interact with. This is small comfort to the skeptic, however, since because of their very danger such deep levels of anesthesia are shunned. In fact the direction of anesthetic practice is toward ever shallower, safer, more manageable anesthesia, with supplementary medication, such as curare, analgesics, sedatives and—yes—amnestics taking care of any loose ends uncontrolled by the shallow anesthetic.*

The persistence of reflex responses to painful stimuli under anesthesia is an obtrusive and unsettling fact, in need of disarming.** Goodman and Gilman observe that at the second stage of anesthesia "painful procedures are dangerous because the response to such stimulations (including incidental dreams [!]) is exaggerated and may lead to violent physical activity" (p. 32), and they note further that even at surgical levels, barbiturate anesthetics "do not adequately obtund the reflex responses to impulses which, in the conscious state, would be experienced as painful" (p. 127). Yet they assure us that analgesia in these circumstances is complete, despite the occurrence of "behavior" that is held—by some schools of thought—to be well nigh "criterial" for pain. The presence of the reflexes shows that the paths between nociceptors and muscles are not all shut down. What special feature is absent from those paths whose presence is required for the occurrence of pain? The short answer routinely given is: consciousness. General anesthetics render one unconscious, and when one is unconscious one cannot feel pain, no matter how one's body may jerk about. What could be more obvious? But this short answer has the smell of a begged question. The principle appealed to (that consciousness is a necessary condition for feeling pain) does not have the status of a well-confirmed empirical hypothesis, or a "law of nature", and its utility evaporates if we try to construe it as an "analytic truth". Until an analysis is given of the relatively gross, molar notions of

---

*For instance, the 1969 edition of Krantz and Carr describes the drawbacks of halothane, a recent popular inhalant anesthetic, as follows: it produces incomplete muscle relaxation, and "it does not produce patent analgesic properties, so it is used with nitrous oxide for analgesia, and a curariform [for paralysis]". One might well wonder just what halothane's strengths are.

**When anesthesia (without curare) is so deep that reflexes are absent, the worry that this absence is due to a curariform effect of the anesthetic by itself has been laid to rest recently by experiments in which twitch responses were directly evoked in deeply anesthetized subjects by electrode stimulation of motor nerves. (Reported by S. H. Ngai, "Pharmacologic and Physiologic Aspects of Anesthesiology", New England Journal of Medicine, Feb. 26, 1970: 541.) This reassuring datum is somewhat beside the point, however, since under common anesthetic practice, the reflexes are only obliterated by the accompanying curare.

consciousness and pain, the principle has no particular warrant, save what it derives from its privileged position as one of the experience-organizing, pretheoretically received truths of our common lore, and in that unsystematic context it is beyond testing. Until we have a theoretical account of consciousness, for instance, how are we to tell unconsciousness from strange forms of paralysis, and how are we to tell consciousness from zombie-like states of unconscious activity and reactivity? The paradigms of unconsciousness that anchor our acceptance of this home truth principle are insufficiently understood to permit us to make the distinctions we need to make in this instance.

I think it is fair to say that until very recently anesthesiologists had no better defense for their defining professional claim than such an appeal to "intuitive" principle:

"How do you prevent pain?"
"We give people drugs that render them unconscious."
"And how do you know they are really unconscious?"
"Try to wake them up; you'll see. (Besides, when they do wake up, they don't recall any pain)."

Today, fortunately, better answers can be given; answers that at least have the potential to form the framework of detailed and confirmable theories. The "state of unconsciousness" produced by general anesthetics can be independently characterized, and its importance accounted for. Drugs that cause sleep or deeper levels of "unconsciousness" are called *hypnotics*, and all general anesthetics are hypnotics. Moreover, they all achieve this effect by antagonizing—though in different ways—the normal functioning of the reticular formation, preventing (*inter alia*) the arousal of the neocortex. Some further details are of particular interest. Barbiturate anesthetics in sub-hypnotic doses are not anesthetic or analgesic at all, whereas nitrous oxide in sub-hypnotic doses is a reliable analgesic. This meshes well with our physiological account, since nitrous oxide not only depresses the reticular formation but also depresses transmission between the thalamus and cortex, an effect barbiturates lack. Melzack and Wall report that in cats barbiturate anesthetics produce strong descending inhibitory effects to their gate system in the substantia gelatinosa. So some general anesthetics may overdetermine their essential effect, but being a hypnotic (suppressing general arousal) is sufficient.

A more puzzling matter is the claim (e.g., by Goodman and Gilman) that "pain is totally abolished before the onset of unconsciousness" in the first stage of anesthetic induction; a scalpel incision, they say, feels like a blunt instrument drawn across the skin! One is entitled to view this claim with skepticism; surgical incisions during stage one anesthesia without other medication must be exceedingly rare occurrences in modern medicine, and for good reason, so presumably the grounds for the claim are anecdotal and not of recent vintage. But suppose the claim is in fact well grounded (at least true on occasion). At first blush it appears an embarrassment to our theory, since orthodoxy has it that only the cortex is affected during stage one anesthesia, and the effect on it is enhancement, not depression or blockade. How could cortical enhancement possibly produce analgesia? One possible answer: by evoking a hallucination (e.g., of a blunt instrument being drawn across the skin). The abnormal cortical activity of first stage anesthesia is known to evoke hallucinations, and hallucinations do have the power to overrule and obliterate competing veridical inputs (one's hallucinations are not simply *superimposed* on veridical perceptions), so if one were fortunate enough to hallucinate a harmless blunt instrument when the scalpel was plunged in, one would not feel pain. And, of course, one's being fortunate enough would not be fortuitous; the content of hallucinations is apparently guided by our deepest needs and desires, and what apter or deeper guiding desire than the desire to avoid pain? A similar account suggests itself for analgesia under hypnotic suggestion.

The shutting down of the reticular formation by anesthetics does not "turn off" the cortex nor does it prevent stimuli from reaching it. It prevents or depresses "recruitment" by those stimuli; they arrive at the cortex, but do not produce the normal spreading ripple of effects; they die out. On any plausible account of cortical functioning this should prevent the completion of the process of perceptual analysis. We could of course claim, with the support of orthodoxy, that such an effect on the cortex "produces unconsciousness" and we could then "explain" the absence of pain in such circumstances by an appeal to our common sense principle that consciousness is a necessary condition for pain, but that would require us to explain just how and why failure of cortical recruitment amounts to or causes unconsciousness, which is a step in the wrong direction, a step away from detailed functional analysis toward the haven of vague and unsystematized preconception. The hypothesis that the successful completion of a process of perceptual analysis is a critical feature in our functional account of pain is, in contrast, a generator of a variety of plausible accounts of perplexing phenomena. We have already seen its utility in accounting for the morphine time-dependence phenomenon. It could also be invoked to account for the relation between the amnestic and anesthetic properties of some drugs. Brazier suggests that anesthesia may result from a derangement of some *memory* functions subserved by the hippocampus, producing a sort of continuous amnesia of the specious present. Such a "forgetting" of each passing moment would cause a complete disability of perceptual analysis and ultimate recognition, and, so goes the theory, a pain not recognized is no pain at all.[14]

Another application of the hypothesis accounts for the striking fact that soldiers who have been wounded in battle often exhibit no discomfort from their serious injuries while awaiting treatment in the safety of a field hospital, but will complain bitterly of the pain of a clumsy venipuncture when a blood sample is taken.[15] They are in a state of specific—not general—analgesia, and the specificity is relative not even to bodily location, but to the *import* of the stimulation. This capacity for import-sensitive analgesia has been exploited rather systematically by the Lamaze natural childbirth technique. Adherents of the Lamaze method claim that by giving the mother a meaningful task to perform, the input which would otherwise be perceived as pain is endowed with a complex action-directing significance; since the patient is not merely a passive or helpless recipient of this input, but rather an *interested* recipient, a *user* of the input, it is not perceived as pain, and again, since a pain not recognized as such is no pain at all, the Lamaze method actually promotes a *reduction of pain* in childbirth.

The content-sensitivity of some forms of analgesia and the time-dependence of morphine's analgesic effect can only be explained by a theory that treats the experience of pain as somehow the outcome of a process of perceptual analysis. Then, once that process is grossly located (in the neocortex), we can determine a necessary condition for its successful completion (reticular formation arousal), and can provide some grounds for the belief that we are loath to abandon: general anesthetics are not misnamed. They are not misnamed because they prevent the completion of a process that is empirically established as a normally necessary condition of pain. This invocation of perceptual analysis restores the new high path in the cortex to a position of importance in our account, and suggests that activity in the old low path is important not because it *is* or *amounts to* pain, but because it is a major contributing condition of pain.

This forces us to acknowledge a far from negligible distinction between the pain we humans experience and the pain experienced by creatures that lack a neocortex (unless we want to maintain that only human beings and perhaps a few other "higher" animals do experience pain). But it should already be obvious to us that there are tremendous functional differences between human and subhuman pain:

no one is surprised that yoga, Zen Buddhism and Christian Science are ineffective anodynes for animals. What of anesthetic practice in veterinary surgery and animal experimentation, however? The hypothesis that "saves" shallow anesthesia for human subjects is apparently inapplicable to animals without a neocortex. The curare incident should persuade us not to jump to complacent conclusions about this. Current thinking in veterinary anesthesiology closely follows human anesthesiology in most regards: the Melzack-Wall theory is featured, but the action of drugs on the reticular formation is regarded as central. The reticular formation plays about the same role in animals' brains, serving to arouse those higher perceptual areas that are precursors, phylogenetically, of the human neocortex. Somewhat disturbing, however, is the common use in animals of "dissociative anesthetics" such as phencycladine and ketamine, which do not depress the reticular formation, but produce a state like cataleptic stupor. These drugs have been discontinued for human administration because their anesthetic properties were called in doubt, and patients frequently reported horrible hallucinations (typically, of dying and then flying through outer space to hell).[16]

This completes the survey of pain phenomena, and carries our functional, partly anatomical, flow-chart of pain as far as it can profitably be carried. The point of this extended exercise in speculative psychophysiology has been to flesh out a theory sketch to the point where one can plausibly claim to have an account that accommodates the data in all their variety.

III

Now we can return to the philosophical question that motivated the exercise: is the resulting theory a theory of pain at all; does it capture pain so that any realization of the flow chart would properly be said to be capable of experiencing genuine pain?

A related, but somewhat different question is this: can we locate pain, as distinct from its typical causes and effects, on the flow chart? The flow chart gives us a functional description at what I have called the sub-personal level.[17] I have labelled the various boxes "belief", "desire", "action" and so forth, but that was taking a liberty. The flow-chart deals directly not with a person's acts, beliefs, thoughts, feelings, but with the behind-the-scenes machinery that governs speech dispositions, motor subroutines, information storage and retrieval, and the like. It has been convenient to talk as if the *objects* of our attention, what we pay attention to, were impulse trains in the nervous system, to talk as if the muffled outputs from the filter *were* the diminished pains, to talk as if we recognize or fail to recognize a neural signal *as* a pain, but this is loose talk, and the conceptual confusions it invites are not inconsequential. When we retell the subpersonal story without taking these liberties we seem to be leaving something out.

Suppose we want to know how an anesthetic about to be administered to us works. The doctor tells us that it prevents mechanisms in the brain from "interpreting" certain impulse trains arriving from the periphery. This, he says, in turn prevents the initiation of motor activity, blocks normal effects on long and short term information storage and goal structures, and . . . permits surgery to proceed at safe levels of respiration and blood pressure. Yes, we reply, but does it stop the pain? If we are unsatisfied with the answer he has already given us, his further reassurance that of course the anesthetic does stop the pain is not yet another consequence of any theory of anesthesia he knows, so much as a "philosophical" dogma—quite reasonable, no doubt—that plays a useful role in his bedside manner. The sub-personal theory he relies upon, and perhaps helps to confirm or advance, can provide for the phenomena, it seems, while remaining neutral about the "philosophical" puzzles about pain. For instance, not only can it account for the effect of novocain and curare, it also can account for the presence of the "reactive disassociation" effect of morphine without taking a stand on whether the effect is properly described as the *presence* of pain in the *absence* of aversion, or as the *absence* of pain in the *presence* of peculiar beliefs or speech dispositions. It can explain the placebo effect without settling the question: Does placebo administration promote a belief that *causes* or *amounts to* the absence of pain? It can explain the success of the Lamaze method without committing itself to an account of what the success consists in: is it correct to say that the technique turns pains into painless sensations, or should we say it prevents certain pains from ever occurring at all? It can explain why concentrating on one's pain provides relief, without settling the question of whether such concentration changes the object of attention, and if so, whether the object is so changed it is no longer a pain, or rather a pain one does not mind having, a pain that doesn't hurt.

The sub-personal account can provide at least a sketchy suggestion of why hypnosis is sometimes an effective method of obtaining relief, but what, exactly, does hypnosis accomplish? Does it manage to prevent the pain that would otherwise occur from occurring, does it prevent its existence, or does it simply permit the subject to ignore or abide the pain? Or does it leave the subject in pain but make him *think* or *act as if* he were not? Can it possibly be that these are different ways of saying the same thing? Suppose someone is given the posthypnotic suggestion that upon awakening he will *have* a pain in his wrist. If the hypnosis works, is it a case of pain, hypnotically induced, or merely a case of a person who has been induced to *believe* he has a pain? If one answers that the hypnosis has induced real pain, suppose the posthypnotic suggestion has been: "On awakening you will *believe* you have a pain in the wrist." If this suggestion works, is the circumstance just like the previous one? (Isn't believing you are in pain tantamount to being in pain?) Or doesn't hypnosis induce beliefs at all? Is it rather that in both cases the subject just acts as if (1) he were in pain, (2) he believed he was in pain? What is presumably true in any case is that the effect of the hypnosis was to distort or weight the perceptual analysis machinery so that it produced a certain output, the sort of output that normally produces all or most of the normal pain dispositions: dispositions to avow, dispositions to nurse the wrist, take aspirin, and perhaps even dispositions to respond to stimulation of the wrist with the classic "spinal reflexes" (I do not know how deep hypnosis can reach—hypnotically induced "pain" does not evoke the characteristic palmar skin resistance of pain, but may otherwise be indistinguishable). Even if we knew exactly which of the boxes in our flow-chart were affected by hypnosis, and how, we would not thereby have answers to our philosophical questions (except in the extreme cases: if hypnosis were to produce only a disposition to *say*, "I have a pain in my wrist," and no other manifestations of pain, or alternatively, if hypnosis produced an observable injury, with swelling, inflammation, bradykinin, etc., in the wrist, we would find easy unanimity in our answers).

The philosophic questions do not seem idle, but our sub-personal theory does not—at least not yet—provide leverage for answering them. The silence of the sub-personal account here is due simply to the fact that pain itself does not appear on our flow chart, which seems to concern itself solely with the *causes and effects* of pain.[18] As we trace through the chart, we find the causal contributions include nociceptor and *C*-fibre stimulation, *T*-cell activity, the processes of perceptual analysis and the contributions thereto of old low path activity; and among the effects we find muscle contraction, avoidance reactions, reports, beliefs, disruptive effects on thinking or reasoning, and powerful goal modifications. The absence of a "pain" box might seem to be a simple omission, easily corrected. The most plausible place to insert a pain box is between the perceptual analysis box and the higher control centers. Isn't pain the *result* of perceptual analysis and the *cause* of our reactions to discomfort? Let us call the inserted box the *pain center*. Now what does it do? If one claims its function is simply to serve as the locus for the transmissions just mentioned, the go-between, then contrary to our suspicion, pain was already represented in our model; we simply had not drawn a line around it. If the point is rather that there is a separable and terrible something we had hitherto left out, how could we possibly add it with this box?

How do we get pain into the pain center? Here is a suggestion: there are two little men in the pain center, and when the light goes on one starts beating the other with chains. What is wrong with this? Not that we have introduced homunculi, for there are (somewhat less colorful) homunculi inhabiting all these boxes. That is a legitimate and useful way to comprehend flow-charting (see Chapters 5, 7, and 9). What is wrong is that even if there were pain in the box, it would not be the person's pain, but the little man's. And to be crass about it, who cares if the little men in one's brain are in pain? What matters is whether *I* am in pain.*

There is no way of adding a pain center to the sub-personal level without committing flagrant category mistakes, by confusing the personal and sub-personal levels of explanation.** We might toy with the idea that our pain center, somewhat like Descartes' notorious pineal gland, is the producer of epiphenomena, the *echt* pains that make all the difference (without of course making any *causal* difference). The standard rebuttal to this version of epiphenomenalism should suffice. Suppose there were a person of whom our sub-personal account (or a similar one) *without the pain center* were true. What are we to make of the supposition that he does not experience pain, be-

---

*The reason I do not object to positing a homunculus that, e.g., *infers* on the basis of texture gradients, overlap and perspective clues that a particular object in my visual field is at a particular distance, is that although there are grounds for claiming an inference-like process must be *going on in me*, it is clear enough that *I* do not draw the inference—though it gets drawn *in me*. But it is important that I be the subject of my pains. If the proper parts of me are for some purposes construable as homunculi, and if on these construals these proper parts are occasionally the subject of pain (an unlikely turn for the theory to take, but not impossible), then those will not or need not be occasions when it is also the case that I am the subject of pain.
**"Indeed the concept [of a pain center] is pure fiction unless virtually the whole brain is considered to be the "pain center" because the thalamus, the limbic system, the hypothalamus, the brain stem reticular formation, the parietal cortex, and the frontal cortex are all implicated in pain perception." Melzack and Wall, "Pain Mechanisms: A New Theory", *Science*, CL (1965): 975.

cause the sub-personal theory he instantiates does not provide for it? First we can make the behaviorist's point that it will be hard to pick him out of a crowd, for his pain behavior will be indistinguishable from that of normal people. But also, it appears *he* will not know the difference, for after all, under normally painful circumstances he believes he is in pain, he finds he is not immune to torture, he gladly takes aspirin and tells us, in one way or another, of the relief it provides. I would not want to take on the task of telling him how fortunate he was to be lacking the *je ne sais quoi* that constituted real pain.

But that is a tendentious description of the case. Let us consider instead the hypothesis suggested by it, *viz.*, that we have simply not seen the woods for the trees, that pain is not to be found in any one box of our flow-chart, but is a function or combination somehow of the elements already present. What function? The chief value of all this somewhat science-fictional flow-charting and compiling of odd phenomena—the reason I have spent so much time on it—is that it serves to drive wedges of contingency between features that are often thought to be conceptually inseparable, simply because they are usually coincident. What I am asserting is that the arrows on the flow-chart are the arrows of normal causal relation, and wherever we have seen fit to posit a particular relation or dependency, we can imagine a severing of the normal connections responsible for it. Some of this fragmentation has familiar manifestations, some is to be found only rarely, and some never occurs, so far as I know, though we can conceive of it occurring.

We can locate our pains, for instance, but this is a complex ability of ours that could become discomposed on occasion. Anscombe considers such a case:

> You say that your foot, not your hand, is very sore, but it is your hand you nurse, and you have no fear of or objection to an inconsiderate handling of your foot, and yet you point to your foot as the sore part: and so on. But here we should say that it was difficult to guess what you could mean.[19]

Pains are also goal modifiers, but they might not be. That is, we can imagine a person who says he is in pain, locates the pain consistently, is in fact being beaten, writhes, cries, trembles, *but is immune to torture.* Is this really imaginable? Of course it is. Perhaps that is what masochists are. Or perhaps they have, as it were, a sign reversed going to the goal box, so they seek out pain instead of avoiding it, at least in certain circumstances.*

Pains are abhorrent, but what are we to make of the reports of subjects who are lobotomized or under morphine analgesia, who report pains, rank them in terms of greater and less intensity, but seem and claim not to *mind* the pains? Are they confused? They say they are in pain, but could they properly be said to believe they were in pain? It is not as if they are speaking parrot-fashion, nor do they exhibit massive conceptual confusions in other areas, so why can it not be that they do believe they are in pain? The only strong presumption against granting them this belief is that a good many "theories" of pain make us "incorrigible" or "privileged" about our pains, and this is often characterized by the stipulation that belief that one is in pain is a sufficient condition for being in pain. If we hold this view of incorrigibility and grant these subjects their belief, then they are in pain, but then pain is not always abhorrent, even when the subjects are experiencing, as they sometimes believe, very intense pain. One might try to claim that such people reveal by their very odd behavior that they do not understand the word "pain", but that would be hard to support. Before the lobotomy or morphine administration, we can presume, they had a good command of English, including the word "pain", and there is no evidence, I think, to show that any of these treatments tends to produce lexical amnesia or other verbal confusions.** To be sure, they do not understand the word "pain" the way some theories would say they ought to, but to bow to these theories would be to beg the question in very description of the case.

The ordinary use of the word "pain" exhibits incoherencies great and small. A textbook announces that nitrous oxide renders one "insensible to pain", a perfectly ordinary turn of phrase which elicits no "deviancy" startle in the acutest ear, but it suggests that nitrous oxide doesn't prevent the occurrence of pain at all, but merely makes one insensible to it when it does occur (as one can be rendered insensible to the occurrence of flashing lights by a good blindfold). Yet the same book classifies nitrous oxide among analgesics, that is *preventers* of pain (one might say "painkillers") and we do not bat an eye. Similarly, if "pain is the antidote to morphine poisoning" then mor-

---

*Roger Trigg, in *Pain and Emotion* (Oxford, 1970), claims, correctly I think, that it would be *abnormal* but not conceptually impossible to have a very *intense* pain but not dislike it. Trigg also offers a useful account of intensity of pain in which intensity is sharply distinguished from 'strength of dislike'.
**Trigg, *op. cit.*, examines the hypothesis that leucotomes are too confused or imbecilic to know what they are answering.

phine cannot be said to prevent pain from occurring. Perhaps what the maxim really means is that *normally painful stimulation* is the antidote for morphine poisoning, but if that is what it means, that is not what it says, and what it says is easily understood, and understood to be good English. This particular slackness in our ordinary use has provided a playground for interminable philosophic disputation over the issue: can there be unfelt pains? I suggest that our flow-chart handles this traditional question by discrediting it. There can be, in principle, any combination of the normal "causes and effects" of pain in the absence of any others, and intuitions will no doubt clash about which words to use to describe the results. Other philosophical questions about pain might have more interesting answers.

Consider the commonplaces about differences in "pain-threshold". Some people, it is often claimed, can stand more pain than others: they have a *high* pain threshold.* Suppose I am one of those with a *low* threshold, and undergo treatment (drugs, hypnosis, or whatever) supposed to change this. Afterwards I report it was a complete success. Here is what I say:

(1) The treatment worked: the pain of having a tooth drilled is as intense as ever, only now I can stand it easily.

Or I might say something different. I might say:

(2) The treatment worked: having a tooth drilled no longer hurts as much; the pain is much less severe.

Can we distinguish these claims? Of course. They obviously mean very different things. Can I then know which claim is correct in my own case or in another's? Wittgenstein is sometimes supposed to have argued in the *Philosophical Investigations* that I cannot be said to know such a thing—and maybe that there is nothing to know; the claims are, in some sense, equivalent. But I do not think that can be right, whether or not Wittgenstein argued for it (and I do not see that he did). Suppose after my treatment I report the results in the first manner. Someone then chides me: "How do you know it's not (2)?" Now if I say in

---

*Two different phenomena have been alluded to by this term. The pain-threshold measured by the Hardy-Wolff-Goodell *dolorimeter* is presumed to be the minimal level of intensity at which a sensation type is deemed painful by the subject. (See J. D. Hardy, H. G. Wolff, and H. Goodell, *Pain Sensations and Reactions*, Baltimore: Williams and Wilkins, 1952, and also H. K. Beecher, op. cit., a classic critique of this experimental method of "measuring pain".)

In more common parlance, one's pain threshold is a *maximum* level of pain one can "tolerate", whatever that may be held to mean in the circumstances. The common belief that there is a wide variation in people's tolerance for pain is expressed repeatedly in the medical literature (see, e.g., Asenath Petrie, *Individuality in Pain and Suffering*, Chicago, 1967, but nowhere that I know of is there a careful attempt to confirm this by any objective tests.)

reply that there is an inner quality of painfulness that I can recall my past experiences at the dentist's to have had, and if I now resurrect that quality from my memory, and compare it with the quality of my present experience, I can see that the present experience has that same quality, only I mind it less; then Wittgenstein has a case against me. That sort of supporting claim must be bogus.* I could not confirm for myself by such a combination of recall and introspection that (1) was the right way to talk. Yet all the same I could stick to my story. I could say: "All I know is that that's the way I want to describe it— that's how it first occurred to me, and your skepticism hasn't changed my mind: I *still* want to say that. Nothing *shows* me I am in pain, and similarly nothing need show me that my pain is as intense as ever, though I mind it less." Such *things I want to say* count for something, but not, as we have just seen, for everything (we aren't *required* to accept the reports of morphine users or lobotomized subjects).

Could I be supported in my conviction about threshold by further evidence? We might run a survey on those who had had the treatment, and find a consensus. Or we might find that I was an anomaly, or that there were two broad groups of reporters, whose memberships were predictable from some features of the subjects (age, blood type, social background, size of the cortex . . .). Would a consensus confirm my story, or would it simply give us a general fact about pain-talk under certain conditions? The *truth* of the pain-talk would still seem open to question. Or, if one holds that the uniformity of this way of speaking is constitutive of the meaning of "pain" and hence ensures the truth of all this pain-talk as truth-by-meaning then at least we can ask if, all things considered, this is an apt or perspicuous way of talking, of dividing up the world. One is inclined to think that there must be some reason for us to say one thing rather than another, even if these "grounds" are not available to us introspectively. It would not be appropriate for us to be so designed that our convictions on this matter were grounded in no distinction of interest at all, but then to what other grounds could one appeal but to internal, sub-personal grounds? Suppose for instance, we were to look inside me and find that the treatment had the effect of diminishing the effects on goal structures, current action-directing sub-routines, and memory, but left unchanged the intensity or magnitude of whatever causally earlier processes normally co-vary with intensity-of-pain-

---

*Such a claim might be phenomenologically sincere, but as a justification for my convictions about how to describe the result of treatment it is without merit. I owe to Lawrence Davis the suggestion that we must not rule out the possibility of having such an experience.

reported. This would support my way of talking at least indirectly, by showing that there is at least one interpretation of the open schema "the magnitude of x is unchanged, but the effect of x on y is diminished" that is true. The truth of one interpretation could be called upon to help explain my desire to assert what might be another interpretation, even if we decline for various reasons to identify the referents of the different interpretations of "x" and "y". Suppose, alternatively, that we find normal operation of all systems in the flow-chart after the perceptual analyzer, but a diminuation in amplitude for some events or events earlier in the chain. This would seem in just the same way to support the second style of introspective report, and make my account suspect. But would it? Does the diminishing size of the retinal image of a receding figure make suspect the claims of perceptual size constancy? Only, perhaps, to those who hold extremely naive identity theories. Detailed isomorphisms between personal level talk of pains, beliefs, feelings, and actions and sub-personal level talk about impulse trains and their effects tempt the impatient to drive the silver spike of identity theory prematurely. The result is inevitably a theory that is easily refuted.

The philosophical questions that an identity theory (or other "philosophical" theory of pain) would be designed to answer are generated by our desire to put together an account that consistently honors all, or at any rate most, of our intuitions about *what pain is*. A prospect that cannot be discounted is that these intuitions do not make a consistent set. This would not be a particularly unsettling discovery if we could identify a few peripheral and unbuttressed intuitions as the culprits; they could be presumed to be mistaken or illusory, and dismissed, leaving a consistent core of intuitions as the raw material for philosophical analysis and system-building. Thus one might *legislate* a neat systematic relationship between sortal talk of pains and massterm talk of pain, thereby establishing two distinct "concepts of pain", and ignore any intuitions inharmonious to that scheme however well attested to by ordinary usage. Recommending such a slight (and improving) revision of our ordinary concept would not be, arguably, doing violence to our ordinary concept. But if contradiction is more entrenched, a more radical approach is dictated.

Consider the idea that being in pain is not any mere occurrence of stimuli, but an interpreted reception, a *per*ception that is influenced by many prior cognitive and conative factors. Some will find this intuitive, but pre-theoretically it is hardly compelling. On the contrary, nothing is more "intuitive" to the sufferer than that there is little that is *cognitive* about pain, that what one wants relief from is not merely an undesirable species of perception, that *in addition to* one's state of consciousness, or perceptual or epistemic state, the pain is there, a brute presence, unanalyzable and independent. The apparent disharmony between these two blocs of intuitions can be turned into clear contradiction if theory is permitted to develop along traditional lines. The grammatical grounds for the contradiction have already been noted: it is equally ordinary to speak of drugs that prevent pains or cause them to cease, and to speak of drugs that render one insensitive to the pains that may persist. (Further instances of the latter notion in our ordinary conception of pain can be found in the discussions of people who are "congenitally insensitive to pain".[20] Our *prima facie* obligation not to cause pain in others is surely understood not to exclude these unfortunate individuals from the class of subjects.) So ordinary usage provides support both for the view that for pains, *esse est percipi*,[21] and for the view that pains can occur unperceived.

What kinds of *objects of perception* are pains: are they merely *intentional objects*, or have they an independent status? (See Chapter 10) No one can defensibly claim to know. Neither introspection nor physiological research can cast any light on the question, and philosophical analysis can plausibly support or attack either view for the simple reason that there are common intuitions and associated ways of speaking that support the contrary views.* If one takes such contradictory testimony to impeach the authority of such intuitions as determinants of our ordinary concept of pain, where else might one look for testimony? Not even contradiction can dislodge our shared intuitions from their role as best manifestations of—constitutive employments of—our ordinary concept. What must be impeached is our ordinary concept of pain. A better concept is called for, and since even the most rudimentary attempt at a unified theory of pain phenomena is led inelectably to the position that pain occurs normally only as the result of a process of perceptual analysis, the *esse est percipi* position of pain promises to be more theoretically perspicuous, which, faced with the impasse of intuitions, is reason enough to adopt it.** This suggests an identification of pain with events—whatever they are—that occur post-interpretation, so that if we can determine where, in our model, interpretation is completed, whatever issues from

*See Pitcher, "The Awfulness of Pain", *loc. cit.*,[8] where a debate is presented between the Affirmativist, who holds that all pains are unpleasant, and the Negativist, who denies this. Pitcher claims, correctly I believe, that this debate "has no winner" (p. 485).
**In "Pain Perception", *loc. cit.*,[21] Pitcher adopts a similarly pragmatic strategy, defending a "perceptual" theory of pain that "will strike many as bizarre" largely on grounds of theoretical cogency.

that will be pain (when the interpretation machinery so interprets). Setting aside the categorical crudities of that formulation, there are still problems, for the interpretation of events in such a system is not an atomic matter, but highly compound. Perception has not one product but many, operating at different levels and in different ways. Has the interpretation machinery interpreted a signal as a pain if it evokes a speech disposition to say one is in pain? Or must it also produce the normal or apposite effects on belief, memory, desire, non-verbal action, and so forth? Looking at all the various effects such an interpretation of signals could produce, we can answer the philosophic questions about pain only by deciding which effects are "essential" to pain and which are not.

What governs our decisions about essentiality, however, is our stock of pretheoretical intuitions, which we have seen to be in disarray. Having countenanced legislation to settle two such conflicts already, we still face incompatibility of well-entrenched intuitions, such as these:

(1) Pains are essentially items of immediate experience or consciousness; the subject's access to pain is privileged or infallible or incorrigible.

(2) Pains are essentially abhorrent or awful—"Pain is perfect misery, the worst of evils . . ."

Efforts to capture both of these "essential" features in a theory of pain are bound to fail; theories that contrive to maintain both of these claims do so only at the expense of equally well-entrenched claims from other quarters. To see this suppose we attempt to capture at least part of what is compelling about (1) by the thesis:

(3) It is a necessary condition of pain that we are "incorrigible" about pain; i.e., if you believe you are in pain, your belief is true; you are in pain.*

---

*Not all versions of "privileged access" (to pains and other items) would maintain, or imply, this thesis, but many do, and it should be clear in what follows that a parallel argument can be addressed against some important versions that do not. For instance, the view that if one *says*, sincerely and with understanding, that one is in pain, one is in pain, succumbs even more directly to a version of my argument. One might think (and I used to claim) that Saul Kripke was committed to the incorrigibility thesis by his claim, in "Naming and Necessity", D. Davidson and G. Harman, eds., *The Semantics of Natural Language* (Dordrecht: Reidel, 1972), p. 339: "To be in the same epistemic situation that would obtain if one had a pain *is* to have a pain; to be in the same epistemic situation that would obtain in the absence of a pain *is* not to have a pain". But Kripke denies that this claim entails anything like (3) (A. P. A. Eastern Division Meeting, December 29, 1974). This leaves Kripke's notion of epistemic situation obscure to me, and I would not hazard a guess about whether a version of my argument applies to his view.

Condition (3) says that belief that one is in pain is a *sufficient* condition of pain. Such belief may be sufficient, but if we are held to be incorrigible about other states of mind or sensations as well (as incorrigibilists generally hold) there must be some other, distinguishing feature of pains; that they are abhorrent or awful seems as good a candidate as any. But then from (3) and

(4) It is a necessary condition of pain that pains are awful

It follows that believing one is in pain is a sufficient condition for really experiencing or undergoing (and not merely believing one is experiencing or undergoing) something awful. But the belief itself is not the pain, and it is not awful. Surely it is logically possible to be in a dispositional state bearing all the usual earmarks of belief that one is in pain, and yet not be experiencing or undergoing something awful. Not only is this logically possible, it is instanced routinely by morphine subjects and others. Then is there any way of denying that this consequence of (3) and (4) is false? There is a heroic line available. One could maintain that *whatever* dispositional state one was in, it could not properly be characterized as the state of belief that one was in pain unless one *understood* the concept of pain, and hence believed that pains were awful, and hence would never believe one was in pain unless one believed one was experiencing something awful; and then, since we are incorrigible about experience in general, one would never believe one was experiencing something awful unless one was experiencing something awful and, finally, since something *undergone but not experienced* (presuming that we can make sense of such a distinction) could not be awful (in the right sense), it really is quite defensible to claim that belief that one is in pain is sufficient condition for undergoing something awful.* This line can "save" (3) and (4) as conjoined necessary conditions of pain, but only at the expense of other intuitions, about our access to our beliefs or our capacity to say when we are in pain. If asked if I am in pain, I should say: "I am if I believe that I am, but who knows if my apparent belief is a genuine belief?" On this view, those who sincerely report that under morphine their pains are *intense* but not *awful* are not mistaken in believing they are in pain when they are not (for that has just been deemed to be logically impossible), but in saying something they do not believe (but only believe they believe?). The counterintuitiveness of this result does not utterly disqualify the heroic line. There are any number of ways of cutting this Gordian knot, and this is one of them. One decides which intuitions must go, and builds one's theory accordingly.

---

*Pitcher discusses a similar argument in "Pain Perception": 387-88.

I do not recommend the course just considered, however. I recommend giving up incorrigibility with regard to pain altogether, in fact giving up all "essential" features of pain, and letting pain states be whatever "natural kind" states the brain scientists find (if they ever do find any) that normally produce all the normal effects. When that day comes we will be able to say whether masochists enjoy pain, whether general anesthetics prevent pain or have some other equally acceptable effect, whether there are unfelt pains, and so forth. These will be discoveries based on a somewhat arbitrary decision about what pain is, and calling something pain doesn't make it pain. This is especially true of pain, for one of our intuitions about pain is that whether or not one is in pain is a brute fact, not a matter of decision to serve the convenience of the theorist. I recommend against trying to preserve that intuition, but if you disagree, whatever theory I produce, however predictive or elegant, will not be by your lights a theory of pain, but only a theory of what I illicitly choose to *call* pain. But if, as I have claimed, the intuitions we would have to honor were we to honor them all do not form a consistent set, there can be no true theory of pain, and so no computer or robot could instantiate the true theory of pain, which it would have to do to feel real pain. Human beings and animals could no more instantiate the true theory of pain (there being none), which lands us with the outrageous conclusion that no one ever feels pain. But of course we do. Human suffering and pain cannot be whisked out of existence by such an argument. The parochiality of the concept of pain protects us but not robots (or Martians or at least lower animals) from the skeptical arguments, by fixing the burden of proof: an adequate theory of pain must have normal human beings as instantiations, a demand that presupposes the primacy, but not the integrity, of our ordinary concept of pain.

What then is the conclusion? It is that any robot instantiation of any theory of pain will be vulnerable to powerful objections that appeal to well-entrenched intuitions about the nature of pain, but reliance on such skeptical arguments would be short-sighted, for the inability of a robot model to satisfy all our intuitive demands may be due not to any irredeemable mysteriousness about the phenomenon of pain, but to irredeemable incoherency in our ordinary concept of pain. Physiological perplexities may defy the best efforts of theoreticians, of course, but philosophical considerations are irrelevant to the probability of that. If and when a good physiological sub-personal theory of pain is developed, a robot could in principle be constructed to instantiate it. Such advances in science would probably bring in their train wide-scale changes in what we found intuitive about pain, so that the charge that our robot only suffered what we artificially *called* pain would lose its persuasiveness. In the meantime (if there were a cultural lag) thoughtful people would refrain from kicking such a robot.

IV

Free Will and Personhood

12

Mechanism and Responsibility

I

In the eyes of many philosophers the old question of whether determinism (or indeterminism) is incompatible with moral responsibility has been superseded by the hypotheseis that *mechanism* may well be. This is a prior and more vexing threat to the notion of responsibility, for mechanism is here to stay, unlike determinism and its denial, which go in and out of fashion. The mechanistic style of explanation, which works so well for electrons, motors and galaxies, has already been successfully carried deep into man's body and brain, and the open question now is not whether mechanistic explanation of human motion is possible, but just whether it will ultimately have crucial gaps of randomness (like the indeterminists' mechanistic explanation of electrons) or not (like the mechanistic explanation of macroscopic systems such as motors and billiards tables). In either case the believer in responsibility has problems, for it seems that whenever a particular bit of human motion can be given an entirely mechanistic explanation—with or without the invocation of "random" interveners—any non-mechanistic, rational, purposive explanation of the same motions is otiose. For example, if we are on the verge of characterizing a particular bit of human motion as a well-aimed kick in the pants, and a doctor can show us that in fact the extensor muscles in the leg were contracted by nerve impulses triggered by a "freak" (possibly random?) epileptic discharge in the brain, we will have to drop the search for purposive explanations of the motion, and absolve the kicker from all responsibility. Or so it seems. A more central paradigm might be as follows. Suppose a man is found who cannot, or will not, say the word "father". Otherwise, we may suppose, he seems perfectly normal, and even expresses surprise at his "inability" to say "that word I can't say". A psychoanalyst might offer a plausible explanation of this behavior in terms of unconscious hatred and desires and beliefs about his father, and a layman might say "Nonsense! This man is just playing a joke. I suspect he's made a bet that he can go a year without saying 'father' and is doing all this deliberately." But if a neurosurgeon were to come along and establish that a tiny lesion in the speech center of the brain caused by an aneurysm (random or not) was causally responsible for the lacuna in the man's verbal repertory (not an entirely implausible discovery in the light of Penfield's remarkable research), both the analyst's and the layman's candidates for explanation would have the rug pulled out from under them. Since a mere mechanistic happening in the brain, random or not, was the cause of the quirk, the man cannot have had reasons, unconscious or ordinary, for it, and cannot be held responsible for it. Or so it seems.

The principle that seems to some philosophers to emerge from such examples is that *the mechanistic displaces the purposive*, and any mechanistic (or causal) explanation of human motions takes priority over, indeed renders false, any explanation in terms of desires, beliefs, intentions. Thus Hospers says "Let us note that the more *thoroughly* and *in detail* we know the causal factors leading a person to behave as he does, the more we tend to exempt him from responsibility."[1] And Malcolm has recently supported the view that "although purposive explanations cannot be dependent on non-purposive explanations, they would be refuted by the verification of a comprehensive neurophysiological theory of behavior".[2] I want to argue that this principle is false, and that it is made plausible only by focusing attention on the wrong features of examples like those above. The argument I will unwind strings together arguments and observations from a surprisingly diverse group of recent writers, and perhaps it is fair to say that my share of the argument is not much. I will try to put the best face on this eclecticism by claiming that my argument provides a more fundamental and unified ground for these variously expressed discoveries about the relations between responsibility and mechanism.

II
The first step in reconciling mechanism and responsibility is getting clearer about the nature of the apparently warring sorts of explanations involved. Explanations that serve to ground verdicts of responsibility are couched at least partly in terms of the beliefs, intentions, desires, and reasons of the person or agent held responsible. There is a

a rough consensus in the literature about the domain of such explanations, but different rubrics are used: they are the "purposive" or "rational" or "action" or "intentional" explanations of behavior. I favor the term 'intentional' (from the scholastics, via Brentano, Chisholm, and other revivalists). *Intentional explanations*, then, cite thoughts, desires, beliefs, intentions, rather than chemical reactions, explosions, electric impulses, in explaining the occurrence of human motions. There is a well-known controversy debating whether (any) intentional explanations are ultimately only causal explanations—Melden and Davidson[3] are the initial protagonists—but I shall avoid the center of this controversy and the related controversy about whether a desire or intention could be identical with a physical state or event, and rest with a more modest point, namely that intentional explanations are at least not causal explanations *simpliciter*. This can best be brought out by contrasting genuine intentional explanations with a few causal hybrids.

Not all explanations containing intentional terms are intentional explanations. Often a belief or desire or other intentional phenomenon (intentional in virtue of being referred to by intentional idioms) is cited as a cause or (rarely) effect in a perfectly Humean sense of cause and effect.

(1) His belief that the gun was loaded caused his heart attack.
(2) His obsessive desire for revenge caused his ulcers.
(3) The thought of his narrow escape from the rattler made him shudder.

These sentences betray their Humean nature by being subject to the usual rules of evidence for causal assertions. We do not know at this time how to go about confirming (1), but whatever techniques and scientific knowledge we might have recourse to, our tactic would be to show that no other conditions inside or outside the man were sufficient to bring on the heart attack, and that the belief (however we characterize or embody it) together with the prevailing conditions brought about the heart attack in a law-governed way. Now this sort of account may be highly suspect, and ringed with metaphysical difficulties, yet it is undeniable that this is roughly the story we assume to be completable in principle when we assert (1). It may seem at first that (1) is not purely causal, for the man in question can tell us, infallibly or non-inferentially, that it was his belief that caused his heart attack. But this is false. The man is in no better position than we to say what caused his heart attack. It may feel to him as if this was the cause of the attack, but he may well be wrong; his only *knowledge* is of the temporal juxtaposition of the events. Similarly, (2) would be falsified if it turned out that the man's daily consumption of a quart of gin was more than sufficient to produce his ulcers, however strong and sincere his intuitions that the vengefulness was responsible. We are apt to think we have direct, non-inferential experience of thoughts causing shudders, as asserted in (3), but in fact we have just what Hume says we have: fallible experience over the years of regular conjunction.

These explanations are not intentional because they do not explain by *giving a rationale* for the *explicandum*. Intentional explanations explain a bit of behavior, an action, or a stretch of inaction, by making it reasonable in the light of certain beliefs, intentions, desires ascribed to the agent. (1) to (3) are to be contrasted in this regard with

(4) He threw himself to the floor because of his belief that the gun was loaded.

(5) His obsessive desire for revenge led him to follow Jones all the way to Burma.

(6) He refused to pick up the snake because at that moment he thought of his narrow escape from the rattler.

The man's heart attack in (1) is not made *reasonable* in the light of his belief (though we might say we can now understand how it happened), but his perhaps otherwise inexplicable action in (4) is. Sentence (5) conspicuously has "led" where its counterpart has "caused", and for good reason. Doubts about (5) would not be settled by appeal to inductive evidence of past patterns if constant conjunctions, and the man's own pronouncements about his trip to Burma have an authority his self-diagnosis in (2) lacks.

The difference in what one is attempting to provide in mechanistic and intentional explanations is especially clear in the case of "psychosomatic" disorders. One can say—in the manner of (1) and (2)—that a desire or belief merely *caused* a symptom, say, paralysis, or one can say that a desire or belief led a person to *want* to be paralyzed—to become paralyzed *deliberately*. The latter presumes to be a purely intentional explanation, a case of making the paralysis—as an *intended condition—reasonable* in the light of certain beliefs and desires, e.g. the desire to be waited on, the belief that relatives must be made to feel guilty.

III

Intentional explanations have the actions of persons as their primary domain, but there are times when we find intentional explanations (and predictions based on them) not only useful but indispensable for accounting for the behavior of complex machines. Consider the case of the chess-playing computer, and the different stances one can choose to adopt in trying to predict and explain its behavior. First there is the *design stance*. If one knows exactly how the computer's program has been designed (and we will assume for simplicity that this is not a learning or evolving program but a static one), one can predict the computer's designed response to any move one makes. One's prediction will come true provided only that the computer performs as designed, that is, without breakdown. In making a prediction from the design stance, one *assumes* there will be no malfunction, and predicts, as it were, from the blueprints alone. The essential feature of the design stance is that we make predictions solely from knowledge of or assumptions about the system's design, often without making any examination of the innards of the particular object.

Second, there is what we may call the *physical stance*. From this stance our predictions are based on the actual state of the particular system, and are worked out by applying whatever knowledge we have of the laws of nature. It is from this stance alone that we can predict the malfunction of systems (unless, as sometimes happens these days, a system is *designed* to malfunction after a certain time, in which case malfunctioning in one sense becomes a part of its proper functioning). Instances of predictions from the physical stance are common enough: "If you turn on that switch you'll get a nasty shock," and, "When the snows come that branch will break right off," are cases in point. One seldom adopts the physical stance in dealing with a computer just because the number of critical variables in the physical constitution of a computer would overwhelm the most prodigious human calculator. Significantly, the physical stance is generally reserved for instances of breakdown, where the condition preventing normal operation is generalized and easily locatable, e.g., "Nothing will happen when you type in your question, because it isn't plugged in," or, "It won't work with all that flood water in it." Attempting to give a physical account or prediction of the chess-playing computer would be a pointless and herculean labor, but it would work in principle. One could predict the response it would make in a chess game by tracing out the effects of the input energies all the way through the computer until once more type was pressed against paper and a response was printed.

There is a third stance one can adopt toward a system, and that is the *intentional stance*. This tends to be most appropriate when the system one is dealing with is too complex to be dealt with effectively from the other stances. In the case of the chess-playing computer one adopts this stance when one tries to predict its response to one's move by figuring out what a good or reasonable response would be, given the information the computer has about the situation. Here one assumes not just the absence of malfunction, but the rationality of design or programming as well. Of course the stance is pointless, in view of its extra assumption, in cases where one has no reason to believe in the system's rationality. In weather predicting, one is not apt to make progress by wondering what clever move the wise old West Wind will make next. Prediction from the intentional stance assumes rationality in the system, but not necessarily perfect rationality. Rather, our pattern of inference is that we start with the supposition of what we take to be perfect rationality, and then alter our premise in individual cases as we acquire evidence of individual foibles and weaknesses of reason. This bias in favor of rationality is particularly evident in the tactics of chess players, who set out to play a new opponent by assuming that he will make reasonable responses to their moves, and then seeking out weaknesses. The opponent who started from an assumption of irrationality would be foolhardy in the extreme. But notice, in this regard, how the designer of a chess-playing program might himself be able to adopt the design stance, and capitalize from the very beginning on flaws in rationality he knew were built into the program. In the early days of chess-playing programs, this tactic was feasible, but today, with evolving programs capable of self-improvement, designers are no longer capable of maintaining the design stance in playing against their own programs, and must resort, as any outsider would, to the intentional stance in trying to outwit their own machines.

Whenever one can successfully adopt the intentional stance toward an object, I call that object an *intentional system.* The success of the stance is of course a matter settled pragmatically, without reference to whether the object *really* has beliefs, intentions, and so forth; so whether or not any computer can be conscious, or have thoughts or desires, some computers undeniably *are* intentional systems, for they are systems whose behavior can be predicted, and most efficiently predicted, by adopting the intentional stance toward them (see Chapter 1).

This tolerant assumption of rationality is the hallmark of the intentional stance with regard to people as well as computers. We start by assuming rationality in our transactions with other adult human beings, and adjust our predictions as we learn more about personalities. We do not *expect* new acquaintances to react irrationally to particular topics, but when they do, we adjust our strategies accordingly. The presumption that we will be able to communicate with our fellow men is founded on the presumption of their rationality, and this is so strongly entrenched in our inference habits that when our predictions prove false we first cast about for external mitigating factors (he must not have heard, he must not know English, he must not have seen x, been aware that y, etc.) before questioning the rationality of the system as a whole. In extreme cases personalities may prove to be so unpredictable from the intentional stance that we abandon it, and if we have accumulated a lot of evidence in the meanwhile about the nature of response patterns in the individual, we may find that the design stance can be effectively adopted. This is the fundamentally different attitude we occasionally adopt toward the insane. It need hardly be added that in the area of behavior (as opposed to the operation of internal organs, for instance) we hardly ever know enough about the physiology of individuals to adopt the physical stance effectively, except for a few dramatic areas, like the surgical cure of epileptic seizures.

IV

The distinction of stance I have drawn appears closely related to MacKay's distinction between the "personal aspect" and the "mechanical aspect" of some systems. Of central importance in MacKay's account is his remarking that the choice of stance is "up to us", a matter of *decision*, not discovery.[4] Having chosen to view our transactions with a system from the intentional stance, certain characterizations of events necessarily arise, but that these arise *rightly* cannot be a matter of proof. Much the same distinction, I believe, is presented in a different context by Strawson, who contrasts "participation in a human relationship" with "the objective attitude". "If your attitude toward someone is wholly objective, then though you may fight him, you cannot quarrel with him, and though you may talk to him, even negotiate with him, you cannot reason with him. You can at most pretend to quarrel, or to reason, with him."[5] Both MacKay and Strawson say a great deal that is illuminating about the conditions and effects of adopting the personal or participant attitude toward someone (or something), but in their eagerness to establish the implications for ethics of the distinction, they endow it with a premature moral dimension. That is, both seem to hold that adopting the personal attitude toward a system (human or not) involves admitting the system into the moral community. MacKay says, in discussing the effect of our adopting the attitude toward a particular animate human body,

At the personal level, Joe will have established some personal claims on us, and we on Joe. We shall not be able rightly to tamper with his brain, for example, nor feel free to dismantle his body. . . . He has become 'one of us', a member of the linguistic community—not, be it noted, by virtue of the particular *stuff* of which his brain is built . . . but by virtue of the particular kinds of mutual interaction that it can sustain with our own—interaction which at the personal level we describe as that of person-to-person.[6]

MacKay is, I believe, conflating two choices into one. The first choice, to ascend from the mechanistic to the intentional stance, as portrayed by our chess-playing designer, has no moral dimension. One is guilty of no monstrosities if one dismembers the computer with whom one plays chess, or even the robot with whom one has long conversations. One adopts the intentional stance toward any system one assumes to be (roughly) rational, where the complexities of its operation preclude maintaining the design stance effectively. The second choice, to adopt a truly moral stance toward the system (thus viewing it as a person), might often turn out to be psychologically irresistible given the first choice, but it is logically distinct. Consider in this context the hunter trying to stalk a tiger by thinking what *he* would do if he were being hunted down. He has adopted the intentional stance toward the tiger, and perhaps very effectively, but though the psychological tug is surely there to disapprove of the hunting of any creature wily enough to deserve the intentional treatment, it would be hard to sustain a charge of either immorality or logical inconsistency against the hunter. We might, then, distinguish a fourth stance, above the intentional stance, called the *personal stance*. The personal stance presupposes the intentional stance (note that the intentional stance presupposes *neither* lower stance) and seems, to cursory view at least, to be just the annexation of moral commitment to the intentional. (A less obvious relative of my distinctions of stance is Sellars' distinction between the manifest and scientific images of man. Sellars himself draws attention to its kinship to Strawson: "Roughly, the manifest image corresponds to the world as conceived by P. F. Strawson. . . . The manifest image is, in particular, a framework in which the distinctive features of persons are conceptually irreducible to features of nonpersons, e.g. animals and merely material things."[7] A question I will not attempt to answer here is whether Sellars' manifest image lines up more with the narrower, and essentially moral, personal stance or the broader intentional stance. (See Chapter 14.)

Something like moral commitment can exist in the absence of the intentional stance, as Strawson points out, but it is not the same; the objective attitude—my design or physical stances—"may include pity or even love, though not all kinds of love". The solicitude of a gardener for his flowers, or for that matter, of a miser for his coins, cannot amount to moral commitment, because of the absence of the intentional. (Parenthetical suggestion: is the central fault in utilitarianism a confusion of gardener-solicitude with person-solicitude?)

Since the second choice (of moral commitment) is like the first in being just a choice, relative to ends and desires and not provably right or wrong, it is easy to see how they can be run together. When they are, important distinctions are lost. Strawson's union of the two leads him to propose, albeit cautiously, a mistaken contrast: "But what is above all interesting is the tension there is, in us, between the participant attitude and the objective attitude. One is tempted to say: between our humanity and our intelligence. But to say this would be to distort both notions."[8] The distortion lies in allying the non-intentional, mechanistic stances with the coldly rational and intelligent, and the intentional stance with the emotional. The intentional stance of one chess player toward another (or the hunter toward his prey) can be as coldly rational as you wish, and alternatively one can administer to one's automobile in a bath of sentiment.

Distinctions are also obscured if one makes *communicating with* a system the hallmark of intentionality or rationality. Adopting the intentional stance toward the chess-playing computer is not necessarily viewing one's moves as *telling* the computer anything (I do not have to *tell* my human opponent where I moved—he can *see* where I moved); it is merely predicting its responses with the assumption that it will respond rationally to its *perceptions*. Similarly, the hunter stalking the tiger will be unlikely to try to *communicate* with the tiger (although in an extended sense even this might be possible—consider the sort of *entente* people have on occasion claimed to establish with bears encountered on narrow trails, etc.), but he will plan his strategy on his assessment of what the tiger would be reasonable to *believe* or *try*, given its perceptions. As Grice has pointed out,[9] one thing that sets communication as a mode of interaction apart from others is that in attempting a particular bit of communication with A, one intends to produce in A some response *and* one intends A to recognize that one intends to produce in him this response *and* one intends that A produce this response on the basis of recognition. When one's assessment of the situation leads to the belief that these intentions are not apt to be fulfilled, one does not try to communicate with A, but one does not, on these grounds, necessarily abandon the intentional stance. *A* may simply not understand any language one can speak, or any language at all (e.g. the tiger). One can still attempt to influence *A*'s behavior by relying on *A*'s rationality. For instance, one can throw rocks at *A* in an effort to get *A* to leave, something that is apt to work with Turk or tiger, and in each case what one does is at best marginal communication.*

Communication, then, is not a separable and higher *stance* one may choose to adopt toward something, but a type of interaction one may attempt within the intentional stance. It can be seen at a glance that the set of intentions described by Grice would not be fulfilled with any regularity in any community where there was no *trust* among the members, and hence communication would be impossible, and no doubt this sort of consideration contributes to the feeling that the intentional community (or at least the smaller *communicating* community) is co-extensive with the moral community, but of course the only conclusion validly drawn from Grice's analysis here is a pragmatic one: if one wants to influence *A*'s behavior, and *A* is capable of communicating, then one will be able to establish a very *effective* means of influence by establishing one's trustworthiness in *A*'s eyes (by hook or by crook). It is all too easy, however, to see interpersonal, convention-dependent communication as the mark of the intentional—perhaps just because intentional systems process information— and thus make the crucial distinction out to be that between "poking at" a system (to use MacKay's vivid phrase) and communicating with it. Not only does this way of putting the matter wrongly confuse the system's perception of communications with its perception more generally, but it is apt to lead to a moralistic inflation of its own. The notion of communication is apt to be turned into something mystical or semi-divine—synonyms today are "rap", "groove", "dig", "empathize". The critical sense of communication, though, is one in which the most inane colloquies between parent and teenager (or man and bear) count as communication. (MacKay himself has on occasion suggested that the personal attitude is to be recognized in Buber's famous I—Thou formula, which is surely inflation.) The ethical implication to be extracted from the distinction of stance is not that the intentional stance is *a* moral stance, but that it is a precondition of

---

*J. Bennett, in *Rationality* (London: Routledge & Kegan paul, 1964), offers an extended argument to the effect that communication and rationality are essentially linked, but his argument is vitiated, I believe, by its reliance on an artificially restrictive sense of rationality—a point it would take too long to argue here. See Chapter 1 for arguments for a more generous notion of rationality.

any moral stance, and hence if it is jeopardized by any triumph of mechanism, the notion of moral responsibility is jeoparidized in turn.

V

Reason, not regard, is what sets off the intentional from the mechanistic; we do not just reason about what intentional systems will do, we reason about how they will reason. And so it is that our predictions of what an intentional system will do are formed on the basis of what would be reasonable (for anyone) to do under the circumstances, rather than on what a wealth of experience with this system or similar systems might inductively suggest the system will do. It is the absence from the mechanistic stances of this presupposition of rationality that gives rise to the widespread feeling that there is an antagonism between predictions or explanations from these different stances. The feeling ought to be dissipated at least in part by noting that the absence of a presupposition of rationality is not the same as a presupposition of non-rationality.

Suppose someone asks me whether a particular desk calculator will give 108 as the product of 18 and 6.[10] I work out the sum on a piece of paper and say, "Yes." He responds with, "I know that it *should*, but will it? You see, it was designed by my wife, who is no mathematician." He hands me her blueprints and asks for a prediction (from the design stance). In working on this prediction the assumption of rationality, or good design, is useless, so I abandon it, not as false but as question-begging. Similarly, if in response to his initial question I reply, "It's an IBM, so yes," he may reply, "I know it's *designed* to give that answer, but I just dropped it, so maybe it's broken." In setting out to make this prediction I will be unable to avail myself of the assumption that the machine is designed to behave in a certain way, so I abandon it. My prediction does not depend on any assumptions about rationality or design, but neither does it rescind any.

One reason we are tempted to suppose that mechanistic explanations preclude intentional explanations is no doubt that since mechanistic explanations (in particular, physical explanations) are for the most part attempted, or effective, only in cases of malfunction or breakdown, where the rationality of the system is obviously impaired, we associate the physical explanation with a failure of intentional explanation, and ignore the possibility that a physical explanation will go through (however superfluous, cumbersome, unfathomable) in cases where intentional explanation is proceeding smoothly. But there is a more substantial source of concern than this, raised by MacIntyre.

Behaviour is rational—in this arbitrarily, defined sense—if, and only if, it can be influenced, or inhibited by the adducing of some logically relevant consideration. . . . But this means that if a man's behaviour is rational it cannot be determined by the state of his glands or any other antecedent causal factor. For if giving a man more or better information or suggesting a new argument to him is a both necessary and sufficient condition for, as we say, changing his mind, then we exclude, for this occasion at least, the possibility of other sufficient conditions. . . . Thus to show that behaviour is rational is enough to show that it is not causally determined in the sense of being the effect of a set of sufficient conditions *operating independently of the agent's deliberation or possibility of deliberation.* So the discoveries of the physiologist and psychologist may indefinitely increase our knowledge of why men behave irrationally but they could never show that rational behaviour in this sense was causally determined. (*my italics*)[11]

MacIntyre's argument offers no license for the introduction of the italicized phrase above, and without it his case is damaged, as we shall see later, when the effect of prediction is discussed. More fundamental, however, is his misleading suggestion that the existence of sufficient conditions for events in a system puts that system in a straitjacket, as it were, and thus denies it the flexibility required of a truly rational system. There is a grain of truth in this, which should be uncovered. In elaborating the distinction between stances, I chose for an example a system of rather limited versatility; the chess-playing system is unequipped even to play checkers or bridge, and input appropriate to these other games would reveal the system to be as non-rational and unresponsive as any stone. There is a fundamental difference between such limited-purpose systems and systems that are supposed to be capable of responding appropriately to input of all sorts. For although it is possible in principle to design a system that can be guaranteed to respond appropriately (relative to some stipulated ends) to any limited number of inputs given fixed, or finitely ambiguous or variable, environmental "significance", there is no way to design a system that can be guaranteed to react appropriately under *all* environmental conditions. A detailed argument for this claim would run on too long for this occasion, and I have presented the major steps of it in *Content and Consciousness* so I will try to establish at least comprehension, if not conviction, for the claim by a little thought-experiment about *tropistic behavior.*

Consider Wooldridge's account of the tropistic behavior of the *sphex* wasp (Chapter 4, p. 65 of this volume).[12] The interference with the wasp unmasks the behavior as a tropism, rigid within the limits set on the significance of the input, however felicitous its operation under normal circumstances. The wasp's response lacks that freewheeling flexibility in response to the situation that Descartes so aptly honored as the infinity of the rational mind. For the notion of a perfectly rational, perfectly adaptable system, to which all input compatible with its input organs is significant and comprehensible is the notion of an unrealizable physical system. For let us take the wasp's tropism and improve on it. That is, suppose we take on the role of wasp designers, and decide to enlarge the subroutine system of the tropism to ensure a more rational fit between behavior and *whatever* environment the wasp may run into. We think up one stymying environmental condition after another, and in each case design subroutines to detect and surmount the difficulty. There will always be room for yet one more set of conditions in which the rigidly mechanical working out of response will be unmasked, however long we spend improving the system. Long after the wasp's behavior has become so perspicacious that we would not think of calling it tropistic, the fundamental nature of the system controlling it will not have changed; it will just be more complex. In this sense any behavior controlled by a finite mechanism must be tropistic.

What conclusion should be drawn from this about human behavior? That human beings, as finite mechanical systems, are not rational after all? Or that the demonstrable rationality of man proves that there will always be an inviolable *terra incognita*, an infinite and non-mechanical mind beyond the grasp of physiologists and psychologists? It is hard to see what evidence could be adduced in support of the latter conclusion, however appealing it may be to some people, since for every awe-inspiring stroke of genius cited in its favor (the Einstein-Shakespeare gambit), there are a thousand evidences of lapses, foibles, bumbling and bullheadedness to suggest to the contrary that man is only imperfectly rational. Perfection is hard to prove, and nothing short of perfection sustains the argument. The former alternative also lacks support, for although in the case of the wasp we can say that its behavior has been shown to be *merely* mechanically controlled, what force would the "merely" have if we were to entertain the notion that the control of man's more versatile behavior is merely mechanical? The denigration might well be appropriate if in a particular case the mechanical explanation of a bit of behavior was short and sweet (consider explanations of the knee-jerk reflex or our hypothetical man who cannot say "father"), but we must also consider cases in which the physiologist or cybernetician hands us twenty volumes of fine print and says, "Here is the design of this man's behavioral control system." Here is a case where the philosopher's preference for simple examples leads him astray, for of course any *simple* mechanistic explanation of a bit of behavior will disquality it for plausible intentional characterization, make it a mere happening and not an action, but we cannot generalize from simple examples to complex, for it is precisely the simplicity of the examples that grounds the crucial conclusion.

The grain of truth in MacIntyre's contention is that *any* system that can be explained mechanistically—at whatever length—must be in an extended sense tropistic, and this can enhance the illusion that mechanistic and intentional explanations cannot coexist. But the only implication that could be drawn from the *general* thesis of man's ultimately mechanistic organization would be that man must, then, be imperfectly rational, in the sense that he cannot be so designed as to *ensure* rational responses to all contingencies, hardly an alarming or counter-intuitive finding; and from any *particular* mechanistic explanation of a bit of behavior, it would not follow that that particular bit of behavior was or was not a rational response to the environmental conditions at the time, for the mere fact that the response *had* to follow, given its causal antecedents, casts no more doubt on its rationality than the fact that the calculator *had* to answer "108" casts doubt on the arithmetical correctness of its answer.

What, then, can we say about the hegemony of mechanistic explanations over intentional explanations? Not that it does not exist, but that it is misdescribed if we suppose that whenever the former are confirmed, they drive out the latter. It is rather that mechanistic predictions, eschewing any presuppositions of rationality, can put the lie to intentional predictions when a system happens to fall short of rationality in its response, whether because of weakness of "design", or physically predictable breakdown. It is the presuppositions of intentional explanation that put prediction of *lapses* in principle beyond its scope, whereas lapses are in principle predictable from the mechanistic standpoint, provided they are not the result of truly random events.*

VI
It was noted earlier that the search for a watershed to divide the

---

*In practice we predict lapses at the intentional level ("You watch! He'll forget all about your knight after you move the queen") on the basis of loose-jointed inductive hypotheses about individual or widespread human frailties. These hypotheses are expressed in intentional terms, but if they were given rigorous support, they would in the process be recast as predictions from the design or physical stance.

things we are responsible for from the things we are not comes to rest usually with a formulation roughly harmonious with the distinction drawn here between the intentional and the mechanistic. Many writers have urged that we are responsible for just those events that are our intentional *actions* (and for their foreseeable results), and a great deal has been written in an effort to distinguish action from mere happening. The performing of actions is the restricted privilege of rational beings, persons, conscious agents, and one establishes that something is an action not by examining its causal ancestry but by seeing whether certain sorts of talk about *reasons* for action are appropriate in the context. On this basis we exculpate the insane, with whom one is unable to reason, unable to communicate; we also excuse the results of physical *force majeure* against which reason cannot prevail, whether the force is external (the chains that bind) or internal (the pain that makes me cry out, revealing our position to the enemy). This fruitful distinction between reason–giving and cause–giving is often, however, the source of yet another misleading intuition about the supposed antagonism between mechanism and responsibility. "Roughly speaking," Anscombe says, "it establishes something as a reason if one argues against it."[13] One is tempted to go on: a reason is the sort of thing one can argue against with some hope of success, but one cannot argue against a causal chain. There is of course a sense in which this is obvious: one cannot argue with what has no ears to hear, for instance. But if one tries to get the point into a form where it will do some work, namely: "The presentation of an argument cannot affect a causal chain," it is simply false. Presentations of arguments have all sorts of effects on the causal milieu: they set air waves in motion, cause ear drums to vibrate, and have hard to identify but important effects deep in the brain of the audience. So although the presentation of an argument may have no detectable effect on the trajectory of a cannonball, or closer to home, on one's *autonomic* nervous system, one's perceptual system is designed to be sensitive to the sorts of transmissions of energy that must occur for an argument to be communicated. The perceptual system can, of course, be affected in a variety of ways; if I sneak up behind someone and yell "Flinch, please!" in his ear, the effects wrought by my utterance would not constitute an action in obedience to my request, not because they were effects of a cause, but because the intricate sort of causal path that in general would have to have existed for an intentional explanation to be appropriate was short-circuited. An intentional system is precisely the sort of system to be affected by the input of information, so the discovery in such a system of a causal chain culminating in a bit of behavior does not at all license the inference: "Since the behavior was caused we could not have argued him out of it", for a prior attempt to argue him out of it would have altered the causal ancestry of the behavior, perhaps effectively.

The crucial point when assessing responsibility is whether or not the antecendent inputs achieve their effects as inputs of information, or by short-circuit. The possibility of short-circuiting or otherwise tampering with an intentional system gives rise to an interesting group of perplexities about the extent of responsibility in cases where there has been manipulation. We are generally absolved of responsibility in cases where we have been manipulated by others, but there is no one principle of innocence by reason of manipulation. To analyze the issue we must first separate several distinct excusing conditions that might be lumped together under the heading of manipulation.

First, one may disclaim responsibility for an act if one has been led to commit the act by deliberately false information communicated by another, and one might put this: "He manipulated me, by forging documents." The principle in such cases has nothing to do with one's intentional system being tampered with, and in fact the appeal to the deliberate malice of the other party is a red herring.[14] The principle invoked to determine guilt or innocence in such cases is simply whether the defendant had reasonably good evidence for the beliefs which led to his act (and which, if true, would have justified it, presumably). The plain evidence of one's senses is normally adequate when what is at issue is the presentation of a legal document, and so normally one is absolved when one has been duped by a forgery, but not, of course, if the forgery is obvious or one has any evidence that would lead a reasonable man to be suspicious. And if the evidence that misled one into a harmful act was produced by mere chance or "act of God" (such as a storm carrying away a "Stop" sign) the principle is just the same. When one is duped in this manner by another, one's intentional system has not been tampered with, but rather exploited.

The cases of concern to us are those in which one's behavior is altered by some non-rational, non-intentional interference. Here, cases where a person's body is merely mechanically interposed in an ultimately harmful result do not concern us either (e.g. one's arm is bumped, spilling Jones's beer, or less obviously, one is drugged, and hence is unable to appear in court). One is excused in such cases by an uncomplicated application of the *force majeure* principle. The only difficult cases are those in which the non-rational, non-intentional interference alters one's beliefs and desires, and subsequently, one's actions. Our paradigm here is the idea—still fortunately science fiction—of the neurosurgeon who "rewires" me and in this way inserts a belief or desire that was not there before. The theme has an interesting variation which is not at all fictional: the 'mad scientist might discover enough about a man's neural *design* (or program) to figure out that certain inputs would have the effect of reprogramming the man, quite independent of any apparent sense they might have for the man to react to rationally. For instance, the mad scientist might discover that flashing the letters of the alphabet in the man's eyes at a certain speed would cause him (in virtue of his imperfectly rational design) to believe that Mao is God. We have, in fact, fortuitously hit upon such ways of "unlocking" a person's mind in hypnotism and brain-washing, so the question of responsibility in such cases is not academic. Some forms of psychotherapy, especially those involving drugs, also apparently fall under this rubric. Again it should be noted that the introduction of an evil manipulator in the examples is superfluous. If I am led to believe that Mao is God by a brain hemorrhage, or by eating tainted meat, or by being inadvertently hypnotized by the monotony of the railroad tracks, the same puzzling situation prevails.

Philosophers have recognized that something strange is going on in these cases, and have been rightly reluctant to grant that such descriptions as I have just given are fully coherent. Thus Melden says,

> If by introducing an electrode into the brain of a person, I succeed in getting him to believe that he is Napoleon, that surely is not a rational belief that he has, nor is he responsible for what he does in consequence of this belief, however convinced he may be that he is fully justified in acting as he does.[15]

Why, though, is the man not responsible? Not because of the absurdity of the belief, for if a merely negligent evidence-gatherer came to believe some absurdity, his consequent action would not be excused, and if the electrode-induced belief happened to be true but just previously unrecognized by the man, it seems we would still deny him responsibility. (I do not think this is obvious. Suppose a benevolent neurosurgeon implants the belief that honesty is the best policy in the heads of some hardened criminals; do we, on grounds of non-rational implantation, deny these people status in the society as responsible agents?) The non-rationality, it seems, is not to be ascribed to the *content* of the belief, but somehow to the manner in which it is believed or acquired. We do, of course, absolve the insane, for they are *in general* irrational, but in this case we cannot resort to this precedent for the man has, *ex hypothesi*, only one non-rational belief. Something strange indeed is afoot here, for as was mentioned before, the introduction of the evil manipulator adds nothing to the example, and if we allow that the presence of one non-rationally induced belief absolves from responsibility, and if the absurdity or plausibility of a belief is independent of whether it has been rationally acquired or not, it seems we can never be sure whether a man is responsible for his actions, for it just may be that one of the beliefs (true or false) that is operative in a situation has been produced by non-rational accident, in which case the man would be ineligible for praise or blame. Can it be that there is a tacit assumption that no such accidents have occurred in those cases where we hold men responsible? This line is unattractive, for suppose it were *proved* in a particular case that Smith had been led to some deed by a long and intricate argument, impeccably formulated by him, with the exception of one joker, a solitary premise non-rationally induced. Our tacit assumption would be shown false; would we deny him responsiblity?

A bolder skepticism toward such examples has been defended by MacIntyre: "If I am right the concept of causing people to change their beliefs or to make moral choices, by brain-washing or drugs, for example, is not a possible concept."[16] Hampshire, while prepared to countenance causing beliefs in others, finds a conceptual difficulty in the reflexive case: "I must regard my own beliefs as formed in response to free inquiry; I could not otherwise count them as beliefs."[17] Flew vehemently attacks MacIntyre's proposal:

> If it did hold it would presumably rule out as logically impossible all indoctrination by such non-rational techniques. The account of Pavlovian conditionings in Aldous Huxley's *Brave New World* would be not a nightmare fantasy but contradictory nonsense. Again if this consequence did hold, one of the criteria for the use of the term *belief* would have to be essentially backward-looking. Yet this is surely not the case. The actual criteria are concerned with the present and future dispositions of the putative believer; and not at all with how he may have been led, or misled, into his beliefs.[18]

Flew's appeal to the reality of brain-washing is misplaced, however, for what is at issue is how the results of brain-washing are to be coherently described, and MacIntyre is right to insist that there is a conceptual incoherency in the suggestion that in brain-washing one causes beliefs, *tout simple*. In *Content and Consciousness* I have argued that there *is* an essential backward-looking criterion of belief; here I shall strike a more glancing blow at Flew's thesis. Suppose for a moment that we put ourselves in the position of a man who wakes up to discover a non-rationally induced belief in his head (he does not know it was non-rationally induced; he merely encounters this new belief in the course of reflection, let us say). What would this be like? We can tell several different stories, and to keep the stories as neutral as possible, let us suppose the belief induced is false, but not wild: the man has been induced to believe that he has an older brother in Cleveland.

In the first story, Tom is at a party and in response to the question, "Are you an only child?" he replies, "I have an older brother in Cleveland." When he is asked, "What is his name?" Tom is baffled. Perhaps he says something like this: "Wait a minute. Why do I think I have a brother? No name or face or experiences come to mind. Isn't that strange: *for a moment* I had this feeling of conviction that I had an older brother in Cleveland, but now that I think back on my childhood, I remember perfectly well I was an only child." If Tom has come out of his brainwashing still predominantly rational, his induced belief can last only a moment once it is uncovered. For this reason, our earlier example of the impeccable practical reasoning flawed by a lone induced belief is an impossibility.

In the second story, when Tom is asked his brother's name, he answers, "Sam," and proceeds to answer a host of other obvious questions, relates incidents from his childhood, and so forth. Not *one* belief has been induced, but an indefinitely large stock of beliefs, and other beliefs have been wiped out. This is a more stable situation, for it may take a long time before Tom encounters a serious mismatch between this large and interrelated group and his other beliefs. Indeed, the joint, as it were, between this structure of beliefs and his others may be obscured by some selective and hard to detect amnesia, so that Tom never is brought up with any hard-edge contradictions.

In the third story, Tom can answer no questions about his brother in Cleveland, but insists that he believes in him. He refuses to acknowledge that well-attested facts in his background make the existence of such a brother a virtual impossibility. He says bizarre things like, "I know I am an only child and have an older brother living in Cleveland." Other variations in the story might be interesting, but I think we have touched the important points on the spectrum with these three stories. In each story, the question of Tom's responsibility can be settled in an intuitively satisfactory way by the invocation of familiar principles. In the first case, while it would be *hubris* to deny that a neurosurgeon might some day be able to set up Tom in this strange fashion, if he could do it without disturbing Tom's prevailing rationality the effect of the surgery on Tom's beliefs would be evanescent. And since we impose a general and flexible obligation on any rational man to inspect his relevant beliefs before undertaking important action, we would hold Tom responsible for any rash deed he committed while under the temporary misapprehension induced in him. Now if it turned out to be physically impossible to insert a single belief without destroying a large measure of Tom's rationality, as in the third story, we would not hold Tom responsible, on the grounds of insanity—his rationality would have been so seriously impaired as to render him invulnerable to rational communication. In the second story, determining responsibility must wait on answers to several questions. Has Tom's rationality been seriously impaired? If not, we must ask the further question: did he make a reasonable effort to examine the beliefs on which he acted? If the extent of his brainwashing is so great, if the fabric of falsehoods is so broad and well-knit, that a reasonable man taking normal pains could not be expected to uncover the fraud, then Tom is excused. Otherwise not.

With this in mind we can reconsider the case of the hardened criminals surgically rehabilitated. Are they responsible citizens now, or zombies? If the surgeon has worked so delicately that their rationality is not impaired (perhaps improved!), they are, or can become, responsible. In such a case the surgeon will not so much have implanted a belief as implanted a suggestion and removed barriers of prejudice so that the suggestion *will be* believed, given the right sort of evidential support. If on the other hand the patients become rigidly obsessive about honesty, while we may feel safe allowing them to run loose in the streets, we will have to admit that they are less than persons, less than responsible agents. A bias in favor of true beliefs can be detected here: since it is hard to bring an evidential challenge to bear against a true belief (for lack of challenging evidence—unless we fabricate or misrepresent), the flexibility, or more specifically rationality, of the man whose beliefs all seem to be true is hard to establish. And so, if the rationality of the hardened criminals' new belief in honesty is doubted, it can be established, if at all, only by deliberately trying to shake the belief!

The issue between Flew and MacIntyre can be resolved, then, by noting that one cannot directly and simply cause or implant a belief, for a belief is essentially something that has been *endorsed* (by commission or omission) by the agent on the basis of its conformity with the rest of his beliefs. One may well be able to produce a zombie, either surgically or by brainwashing, and one might even be able to induce a large network of false beliefs in a man, but if so, their persistence *as beliefs* will depend, not on the strength of any sutures, but on their capacity to win contests against conflicting claims in evidential showdowns. A parallel point can be made about desires and intentions. Whatever might be induced in me is either fixed and obsessive, in which case I am not responsible for where it leads me, or else, in MacIntyre's phrase, "can be influenced or inhibited by the adducing of some logically relevant consideration", in which case I am responsible for *maintaining* it.

VII

I believe the case is now complete against those who suppose there to be an unavoidable antagonism between the intentional and the mechanistic stance. The intentional stance toward human beings, which is a precondition of any ascriptions of responsibility, *may* coexist with mechanistic explanations of their motions. The other side of this coin, however, is that we *can* in principle adopt a mechanistic stance toward human bodies and their motions, so there remains an important question to be answered. *Might* we abandon the intentional stance altogether (thereby of necessity turning our backs on the conceptual field of morality, agents, and responsibility) in favor of a purely mechanistic world view, or is this an alternative that can be ruled out on logical or conceptual grounds? This question has been approached in a number of different ways in the literature, but there is near unanimity about the general shape of the answer: for Strawson the question is whether considerations (of determinism, mechanism, etc.) could lead us to look on everyone exclusively in the "objective" way, abandoning the "participant" attitude altogether. His decision is that this could not transpire, and he compares the commitment to the participant attitude to our commitment to induction, which is "original, natural, non-rational (not *irrational*), in no way something we choose or could give up".[19] Hampshire puts the point in terms of the mutual dependence of "two kinds of knowledge", roughly, inductive knowledge and knowledge of one's intentions. "Knowledge of the natural order derived from observation is inconceivable without a decision to test this knowledge, even if there is only the test that constitutes a change of point of view in observation of external objects."[20] In other words, one cannot *have* a world view of any sort without having beliefs, and one could not have beliefs without having intentions, and having intentions requires that one view *oneself*, at least, intentionally, as a rational agent. Sellars makes much the same point in arguing that "the scientific image cannot replace the manifest without rejecting its own foundation".[21] Malcolm says, "The motto of the mechanist ought to be: One cannot speak, therefore one must be silent.[22] But here

Malcolm has dropped the ball on the goal line; how is the mechanist to *follow* his "motto", and how *endorse* the "therefore"? The doctrine that emerges from all these writers is that you can't get there from here, that to assert that the intentional is eliminable "is to imply pragmatically that there is at least one person, namely the one being addressed, if only oneself, with regard to whom the objective attitude cannot be the only kind of attitude that is appropriate to adopt".[23] Recommissioning Neurath's ship of knowledge, we can say that the consensus is that there is at least one plank in it that cannot be replaced.

Caution is advisable whenever one claims to have proved that something cannot happen. It is important to see what does not follow from the consensus above. It does not follow, though Malcolm thinks it does,[24] that there are some things in the world, namely human beings, of which mechanism as an embracing theory cannot be true, for there is no incompatibility between mechanistic and intentional explanation. Nor does it follow that we will always characterize some things intentionally, for we may all be turned into zombies next week, or in some other way the human race may be incapacitated for communication and rationality. All that is the case is that we, *as persons*, cannot *adopt* exclusive mechanism (by eliminating the intentional stance altogether). A corollary to this which has been much discussed in the literature recently is that we, as persons, are curiously immune to certain sorts of predictions. If I cannot help but have a picture of myself as an intentional system, I am bound, as MacKay has pointed out, to have an *underspecified* description of myself, "not in the sense of leaving any parts unaccounted for, but in the sense of being compatible with more than one state of the parts".[25] This is because no information system can carry a complete true representation of itself (whether this representation is in terms of the physical stance or any other). And so I cannot even in principle have all the data from which to predict (from any stance) my own future.[26] Another person might in principle have the data to make all such predictions, but he could not tell them all to me without of necessity falsifying the antecedents on which the prediction depends by interacting with the system whose future he is predicting, so I can never be put in the position of being obliged to believe them. As an intentional system I have an epistemic horizon that keeps my own future as an intentional system indeterminate. Again, a word of caution: this barrier to prediction is not one we are going to run into in our daily affairs; it is not a barrier preventing or rendering incoherent predictions I might make about my own future decisions, as Pears for one has pointed out.[27] It is just that since I must view myself as a person, a full-fledged intentional system, there is no complete biography of my future I would be right to accept.

All this says nothing about the impossibility of dire depersonalization in the future. Wholesale abandonment of the intentional is in any case a less pressing concern than partial erosion of the intentional domain, an eventuality against which there are no conceptual guarantees at all. If the growing area of success in mechanistic explanation of human behavior does not in itself rob us of responsibility, it does make it more pragmatic, more effective or efficient, for people on occasion to adopt less than the intentional stance toward others. Until fairly recently the only well-known generally effective method of getting people to do what you wanted them to was to treat them as persons. One might threaten, torture, trick, misinform, bribe them, but at least these were forms of control and coercion that appealed to or exploited man's rationality. One did not attempt to adopt the design stance or the physical stance, just because it was so unlikely that one could expect useful behavioral results. The advent of brainwashing, subliminal advertising, hypnotism and even psychotherapy (all invoking variations on the design stance), and the more direct physical tampering with drugs and surgical intervention, for the first time make the choice of stance a genuine one. In this area many of the moral issues are easily settled; what dilemmas remain can be grouped, as MacKay has observed, under the heading of treating a person as less than a person *for his own good*. What if mass hypnosis could make people stop wanting to smoke? What if it could make them give up killing? What if a lobotomy will make an anguished man content? I argued earlier that in most instances we must ask for much more precise descriptions of the changes wrought, if we are to determine whether the caused change has impaired rationality and hence destroyed responsibility. But this leaves other questions still unanswered.

13

The Abilities of Men and Machines

Mechanism as a theory of mind would be refuted if it could be shown that a human being (or his mind)* *can do* what no machine *can do*, and there is a family of arguments invoking Gödel's Theorem which purport to prove just that.[1] I wish to show that all these arguments must fail because at one point or another they must implicitly deny an obvious truth, namely that the constraints of logic exert their force not on the things in the world directly, but rather on what we are to count as defensible descriptions or interpretations of things. The common skeleton of the anti-mechanistic arguments is this: any computing machine at all can be represented as some Turing machine,** but a man cannot, for suppose Jones over there were a realization of some Turing machine TM_j, then (by Gödel) there would be something A that Jones *could not do* (namely, prove TM_j's Gödel sentence). But watch!—this is the crucial empirical part of the argument—Jones *can* do A; therefore Jones is not a realization of TM_j, and since *it can be seen* that this will be true whatever Turing machine we choose, Jones transcends, angel-like, the limits of mechanism. The error in this lies, I will argue, in supposing that the determination of Jones's acts and hence his abilities, and also the determination of the activities of a

---

*or *her* mind. This paper is about human beings, the biological class—not necessarily persons (see Chapter 14)—and certainly not just male human beings. Since I find "his or her" abominable style, I am stuck with either "his" or "her". I tried rewriting the paper with "her", but found that this left connotations that would distract or offend.

**As Judson Webb points out, this premise can be viewed as a form of Church's Thesis. ("Metamathematics and the Philosophy of Mind", *Philosophy of Science* 1968: 171.) My criticism does not depend on questioning Church's Thesis.

computing device, can proceed in a neutral way that will not beg the question of the applicability of Gödel's Theorem.

Gödel's Theorem says that in any consistent axiom system rich enough to generate the arithmetic of the natural numbers, there are statements we cannot prove in the system, but which can be seen by other means to be true. Gödel's Theorem, then, is about axiom systems, and the "machines" it governs are as abstract as the axiom systems. A Turing machine can be viewed as nothing more than a finite system of instructions to perform simple operations on strings of symbols which constitute the "input". The instructions are gathered into "machine states", each of which is a finite sequence of instructions, and a master instruction, or state-switching function, which prescribes which sequence of instructions is to be followed given the input. Such a specification is obviously entirely neutral about how such operating and switching is to be accomplished, and hence a particular Turing machine can be "realized" in very different ways: by a mechanical tape-reading device, by simulation on a digital computer, or by "hand simulation", where the operations are performed by a person or persons following written instructions on "state" cards.

The engineer setting out to construct directly a mechanical realization of a Turing machine has the following task: he must exploit the laws of nature in such a way as to achieve the regularities prescribed or presupposed in the Turing Machine specification. Thus, for each of the symbols in the alphabet in which the input and output are to be expressed, the engineer must devise some physical feature that can be reliably distinguished mechanically from its brethren (like a hole in a paper tape and unlike a pencil mark or spoken word). These features should also be relatively stable, quickly producible and small scale— for obvious reasons of engineering economy. Paired with the symbol features must be the devices, whatever they are, that react differently to the symbol features, that "read" or "discriminate" them. Then, whatever these different reactions are, they must in turn be so designed to differ from one another that the next rank of effectors, whatever they are, can be caused to react differently to them, and so forth. For each shift of *state* there must be a corresponding *physical* shift, which might be a shift of gears, or the sliding of a different cam onto a drive shaft, or the opening and closing of series of electrical or hydraulic relays. The whole machine may exploit only a few simple principles of electronics or it may be a Rube Goldberg contraption, but in either case it must be more or less insulated from the rest of the environment, so that coincidental features of the outside world do not interfere with its operation, e.g., changes in temperature or relative humidity, or sudden accelerations. The better the design, the more immune to interference the machine will be. But what counts as interference, and what counts as a physical change "read" as input by the machine is relative to the designer's choice of physical laws. A hole in the tape may be a symbol to one machine, a major disruptive event to another (depending usually on whether we are speaking of paper tape or magnetic recording tape). Similarly, what internal changes in the machine are to count as state changes, and what are to count as breakdowns is also relative to the designer's scheme of realization. If we discover a machine that is drastically affected by accelerations, it may be a computer poorly designed for mobile applications, e.g., in airplanes, but on the other hand it may be an inertial guidance system, and the accelerations may be its input.

Since the choices engineers actually make when designing hardware are a fairly standard and well-known lot, and since the purposes of machines are usually either obvious or suitably announced by the manufacturer, it is easy to overlook this relativity to the designer's choices and suppose that we can directly observe the input, output, operations and state changes of any device, and hence can settle in an objective fashion which Turing machine, if any, it is. In principle, however, we cannot do this. Suppose Jones and Smith come across a particular bit of machinery churning away on a paper tape. They both study the machine, they each compile a history of its activity, they take it apart and put it back together again, and arrive finally at their pronouncements. What sorts of disagreements might there be between Jones and Smith?

First we might find them disagreeing only on the interpretation of the input and output symbols, and hence on the purpose or function of the Turing machine, so that, for instance, Jones treats the symbol-features as numbers (base two or base ten or what have you) and then "discovers" that he can characterize the Turing machine as determining the prime factors of the input numbers, while Smith interprets the symbol features as the terms and operators of some language, and has the Turing machine proving theorems using the input to generate candidates for proof sequences. This would not be a disagreement over which Turing machine had been realized, for this is purely semantic disagreement; a Turing machine specification is in terms of syntactic relationships and functions only, and *ex hypothesi* Jones and Smith agree on which features are symbols and on the rules governing the production of the output strings. In principle a particular Turing machine could thus serve many purposes, depending on how its users chose to interpret the symbols.

More interesting and radical disagreements are also possible however. Jones may announce that his device is TM_j, that its input and output are expressions of binary arithmetic, and that its function is to extract square roots. However, let us suppose, he proves mathematically (that is, on the basis of the machine table he assigns it and not the details of engineering) that the program is faulty, giving good answers for inputs less than a hundred but failing periodically for larger numbers. He adds that the engineering is not all that sound either, since if you tip the machine on its side the tape reader often misreads the punched holes. Smith disagrees. He says the thing is TM_S, designed to detect certain sorts of symmetries in the input sequences of holes, and whose output can be read (in a variation of Morse Code) as a finite vocabulary of English words describing these symmetries. He goes on to say that tipping the machine on its side amounts to a shift in input, to which the machine responds quite properly by adjusting its state-switching function. The only defect he sees is that there is one cog in the works that is supposed to be bent at right angles and is not; this causes the machine to miscompute in certain states, with the result that certain symmetries are misdescribed. Here there is disagreement not only about the purpose of the machine, or the semantics of the language it uses, but also about the syntax and alphabet. There is no one-to-one correspondence between their enumerations of symbols or instructions. The two may still agree on the nature of the mechanism, however, although they disagree on what in the mechanism counts as deliberate design and what is sloppiness. That is, given a description of the physical state of the machine and the environment, and a physical description of the tape to be fed in, they will give the same prediction of its subsequent *motions*, but they will disagree on which features of this biography are to be called malfunctions, and on which parts of the machine's emissions count as symbols. Other sorts of disagreement over interpretation are possible in principle. For instance, one can treat any feature of the environment as input, even in the absence of any salient and regular reaction to it by any part of the machine, if one is prepared to impute enough stupidity to the designer. There is no clear boundary between entities that count as imperfect or broken or poorly designed realizations of TM_x and entities that are not at all realizations of TM_x. By the same token, discovering that an entity can be viewed as a highly reliable, well-designed TM_a does not preclude its also being viewed as an equally good realization of some other TM_b. To give a trivial example, almost any good computer could be construed as a Turing machine yielding as output "*p*" if and only if it receives as input "*q*", where our symbol "*p*" is realized by a very faint hum, and "*q*" by turning on the power switch.

Faced with the competing interpretations of the tape reader offered by Jones and Smith, if we decide that one interpretation, say Jones's, is more plausible all things considered, it will only be because these things we consider include our intuitions and assumptions about the likely intentions and beliefs of the designer of the machine. The quick way to settle the dispute, then, is to ask the designer what his intentions were. Of course he may lie. So it seems we may never find out for sure; only the designer knows for sure, but what is it he knows that we do not? Only what his intentions were, what Turing machine he intended to realize—and he may even discover that his own intentions were confused. In any case, what the designer's intentions were in his heart of hearts does not determine any objective fact about the device before us. If Smith purchases it on the spot and proceeds to use it as a symmetry classifier, then what he has is just as truly a symmetry classifier as any he could build on his own, under his own intentions, inspired by this prototype. If we find something on the beach and can figure out how to use it as a TM$_b$, then it is a TM$_b$ in the fullest possible sense.

Now how does this affect the possibility of there being *living* Turing machines? It is not at all far-fetched and is even quite the vogue to suppose that an animal can profitably be viewed as a computer or finite automaton of a special sort, and since any finite automaton can be simulated by a Turing machine, this amounts in a fashion to the supposition that we might want to treat an animal as a Turing machine. (There are difficulties in this, but let us concede to the anti-mechanists the shortest visible route to their goal; it will only hasten their demise.) The question then is, can we settle whether or not we have chosen the *correct* Turing machine interpretation of a particular animal? First we have to decide which of the impingements on the animal count as input and which as interference, and it is not at all clear what criteria we should use in deciding this. Suppose we ask ourselves if changes in barometric pressure constitute input or interference for a particular animal. Probably in most animals we will find detectable, salient physical changes associated with changes in barometric pressure, but suggestive as this might seem, what would it show? Suppose we learn that the effect of such pressure changes in cows is to make them all lie down in the field. So what? What advantage, one wants to ask, accrues to the cows from this reaction? Our search for a plausible Turing machine specification is guided here, as it was for the paper tape device, by the assumption that a Turing machine always has some point, some purpose. From a strictly mathematical point of view this assumption is unwarranted; a Turing machine may compute a function of no interest, elegance or utility whatever, of no value to anyone, and still meet the formal requirements for a Turing machine. Of course we would not be interested in the notion of a Turing machine at all were it not the case that we can isolate and study those that can be used to serve interesting purposes. The application of the concept to animals will be fruitful just so long as it leads us to mechanizations of apparently purposeful activity observed in the animal. Thus in some animals changes in barometric pressure can be highly *significant*, and may be responded to in some *appropriate* way by the animal—by finding shelter before the impending storm, for instance— and in these cases we will have reason to treat the effects on the animals as the receipt of information, and this will set us searching for an information-processing model of this capacity in the animal, or in other words (to take the short route again) to view the animal as a Turing machine for which barometric pressure is input.

At another level in our examination of the living candidate for machinehood, we would have to decide which features of the animal's physical constitution are working as they were designed to, as they were supposed to, and which are malfunctioning, misdesigned or merely fortuitous. The "response" of mice to the "stimulus" of being dropped in molten lead is no doubt highly uniform, and no doubt we can give sufficient physiological conditions for this uniformity of reaction, but "burning to a crisp" does not describe a sort of behavior to which mice are prone; they are not *designed* or *misdesigned* to behave this way when so stimulated.* This does not mean that we cannot treat a mouse as an analogue of the one-state, two-symbol humming Turing machine described above. Of course we can; there just is no point. In one sense an animal—in fact any fairly complicated object— can be a number of different Turing machines at once, depending on our choice of input, state descriptions, and so forth. No one of these can be singled out on purely structural or mechanical grounds as *the* Turing machine interpretation of the animal. If we want to give sense to that task, we must raise considerations of purpose and design, and then no objectively confirmable answer will be forthcoming, for if Smith and Jones disagree about the ultimate purpose of particular structures or activities of the animal, there is no Designer to interview, no blueprint to consult.

Similar considerations apply *pari passu* when we ask if a man is a

---

*Cf. Wilfrid Sellars' remarks on "earthworm-behavioristics" in *Science, Perception, and Reality* (London: Routledge & Kegan Paul, 1963), pp. 23-4.

Turing machine. As a complicated chunk of the world he will surely qualify for any number of Turing machine characterizations, and it is even possible that by some marvelous coincidence some of these will match Turing machine interpretations of interest to mathematicians. Thus the wandering patches of light on a baby's retina, and the subsequent babble and arm-waving, might be given a systematic interpretation as input and output so that the arm-wavings turn out to be proofs of theorems of some non-Euclidean geometry, for example. It is important to recognize that it is solely non-mathematical assumptions that make this suggestion outlandish; it is only because of what we believe about the lack of *understanding* in babies, the *meaninglessness* of their babble, the *purposes*, if you will, for which babies are intended, that we would discard such an interpretation were some mathematician clever enough to devise it. By suitable gerrymandering (e.g., incessant shifting of input vocabulary) it ought to be possible to interpret any man as any Turing machine—indeed as all Turing machines at the same time. So construed, every infant and moron would be engaged (among its other activities) in proving theorems and Gödel sentences (any Gödel sentence you choose), but of course the motions that constituted these feats of proving would not *look* like feats of proving, but like sleeping, eating, talking about the weather. The antimechanist is not interested in Turing machine interpretations of this sort; the activities and abilities he supposes he has crucial information about are those of mature, sane mathematicians in their professional endeavors.

He is interested in those motions of a man the purpose or interpretation of which is natural and manifest—his *actions* in short—but once we turn to the question of which Turing machine interpretation fits these actions, and hence might deserve to be called *the* description of the man, we come up against the relativities encountered by Smith and Jones: the ultimate function and design of every part of a man is not in the end to be decided by any objective test. Moreover, since *the* Turing machine interpretation of a man (if there is one) is picked out as the one best capturing the biological design of a man, and since man the biological entity has more ulterior goals than mere theorem-proving, no plausible candidate for *the* Turing machine interpretation of any man will be of the right sort to give the anti-mechanist the premise he needs. In addition to whatever computing a man may do (in school, in business, for fun) he also eats, acquires shelter, makes friends, protects himself and so forth; we do not need Gödel to demonstrate that man is not just a computer in *this* sense—that is, a device whose sole purpose is to compute functions or prove theorems. Suppose, to illustrate this, we have a particular hardware TM_k churning out theorems in some system, and a mathematician, Brown, sitting next to the computer churning out the same theorems in the same order. If we tentatively adopt the hypothesis that we have two realizations of TM_k, then we can go on to apply the Gödelian limitations to them both, but we have an easy way of disproving the hypothesis with respect to Brown. Once we have fixed, for our hypothesis, the list of Brown-motions that count as the issuing of output symbols (and these will appear to be in one-to-one correspondence with some symbol-printing motions of the hardware model), we merely ask Brown to pause in his calculations for a moment and give forth with a few of these symbols "out of order". His doing this is enough to establish *not* that Brown is not a machine, but that Brown is not (just) a (good) TM_k. Brown is not a TM_k because here we see output symbols being emitted contrary to the hypothesized instructions for TM_k, so either our request broke him (is a mathematician to be viewed as a sequence of exquisitely fragile self-repairing mechanical theorem-provers?) or he was not a TM_k in the first place.

The fact that Brown was producing the same proofs as the hardware TM_k does not imply that if Brown is a mechanism he is a hardware TM_k, for producing the same proofs is not a sufficient condition for being, in this sense, the same Turing machine. Perhaps we were fooled into thinking Brown was a TM_k because, for a while, he had "hand simulated" a TM_k. Simulating a TM_k is in one sense being a TM_k (a simulation is a realization), but of course it is not the sense the anti-mechanist needs, for in the sense in which simulating is being, the anti-mechanist claim is just false: it is not true that if a man were a TM_k he could not prove S, where S is TM_k's Gödel sentence. If a man's being a TM_k is a matter of simulating a TM_k then in all likelihood he can prove S; all he has to do is cease for a while following the instructions that amount to simulating a TM_k, and Gödel says nothing about this role-changing being impossible. What the man *cannot do* (and this regardless of whether he is a machine, organism or angel) is prove S while following the instructions of TM_k, but this is no more a limitation on his powers than is his inability to square the circle.

Gödel's Theorem has its application to machines via the notion of a Turing machine specification, but Turing machine specifications say very little about the machines they specify. Characterizing something as a TM_k ascribes certain capacities to it, and puts certain limitations on these capacities, but says nothing about other features or capacities of the thing. From the fact that something A is a realization of a TM_k we cannot deduce that A is made of steel or has rubber tires, nor can we deduce that it cannot fly, for although the specification of a TM_k does not stipulate that it can fly, it does not and cannot rule out this possibility. We also cannot deduce that A cannot speak English. Perhaps A can, and perhaps while speaking English, A may issue forth with a proof of TM_k's Gödel sentence. A could not do this if A were *just* a TM_k, but that is precisely the point: nothing concrete could be *just* a particular Turing machine, and any concrete realization of any Turing machine can in principle have capacities under one interpretation denied it under another.

The fundamental error behind attempts to apply Gödel's Theorem to philosophy of mind is supposing that objective and exclusive determinations of the activities and capacities of concrete objects are possible which would determine uniquely which Turing machine specification (if any) is *the* specification for the object. Once we acknowledge this error, this apparent application of Gödel's Theorem to the philosophy of mind reveals its vacuity: if a man were (a realization of) a particular theorem-proving Turing machine with Gödel sentence S, then *in his role as that Turing machine* he could not prove S, but this says nothing about his capacities in other roles on the one hand, and on the other we surely have no evidence—and could have no evidence—that a man while playing the role of a Turing machine can do what Gödel says he cannot.

Postscript, 1978

We can put the point of this paper in a form that should be mildly astonishing to the anti-mechanists who hope to use Gödel: a realization of the *Universal Turing machine* can, in principle, do the one thing Gödel's theorem says the Universal Turing machine cannot do: prove the Gödel sentence of the Universal Turing machine. How could this be? A thought experiment will explain.

Children can be taught to hand simulate simple Turing machines. There are primers and textbook chapters designed to do just that. Suppose a graduate student in Artificial Intelligence took as his dissertation task, as his "toy problem", writing a program that could learn to "hand simulate" a Turing machine just as children do—by reading the instruction book, doing the practice exercises, etc. Call this imaginary program *WUNDERKIND*. The rules of this project are that *WUNDERKIND*, after debugging but before being given its "lessons", should be *unable* to hand simulate a Turing machine, but after being fed exactly the same instruction (in English) as the school children—no more, no less—should be able to hand simulate a Turing machine as well as, or even better than, the school children. (This proviso has nothing to do with the applicability of Gödel's theorem to the case; it is added to give the project a non-trivial task, and hence to give *WUNDERKIND* something like a human set of abilities and interests.)

Imagine that *WUNDERKIND* was designed, and that it worked—it "learned" to hand simulate a Turing machine, TM_k. Suppose we witness a demonstration of the program, actual hardware producing actual symbols. Now just what is this hardware object not supposed to be able to do? Prove "its" Gödel sentence. But which sentence is that? Which Turing machine is in front of us? If the hardware is a standard, commercial, programmable computer, it is—given enough time and storage—a realization of the Universal Turing machine, which has a Gödel number and a Gödel sentence, call it S_U. But it is currently running the *WUNDERKIND* program (let's ignore the fact that probably today it is time-sharing, and running many bits of many programs in quick succession), which is (mathematically equivalent to) a Turing machine with a different Gödel number and a different Gödel sentence, call it S_W. Then there is the Turing machine, TM_k, that *WUNDERKIND* is hand simulating, and it too has a Gödel sentence, call it S_k. Now we know that *WUNDERKIND*, while hand simulating TM_k, cannot *as part of that hand simulation* produce S_k. But *WUNDERKIND* does other things as well; it asks questions, reads, practices, corrects errors in its exercises, and who knows what else. Perhaps it plays chess or writes fairy tales. What it does while not simulating TM_k is an independent matter. It might well, for all we know, start offering proofs of sentences, and one of them might be S_k. Another might be S_U! Or S_W! *There is nothing in Gödel's theorem to prevent this.* The computer, the actual hardware device, is a realization, let us grant, of the Universal Turing machine, and *in that guise* it cannot offer a proof of S_U. In that guise what it is doing is *imitating* TM_W—*WUNDERKIND*. When we shift perspective and view the object before us as *WUNDERKIND* (*WUNDERKIND* the child-simulation, not *WUNDERKIND* the algorithm represented by the machine table) we see it not as a theorem-prover-in-the-vocabulary-of-the-Universal-Turing-machine, but as a rather childlike converser in English, who asks questions, says things true and false on a variety of topics, and in that guise might well come up with a string of symbols that constituted a proof of S_U or any other sentence.

The idea that *WUNDERKIND* itself can be viewed from more than one perspective will benefit from further specification. Consider what is wrong with the following argument: all computer programs are algorithms; there is no feasible algorithm for checkmate in chess; therefore checkmate by computer is impossible. The first premise is true, and so is the second. Chess is a finite game, so there is a brute force algorithm that gives the best line of play by simply enumerating all possible games in a tree structure and then working back from the myriad last moves to the line or lines of play that guarantee checkmate or draw for white or black, but this algorithm is impractical to say the least. But of course chess programs are not that bad at achieving checkmate, so the conclusion is false. What is true is that good chess programs are not algorithms for checkmate, but rather just algorithms for playing legal chess. Some are better than others, which means that some terminate in checkmate more often against strong players than others, but they are not *guaranteed* to end in checkmate, or even in a draw. In addition to the rather unilluminating perspective from which such a program can be viewed as a mere algorithm, there is the perspective from which it can be viewed as *heuristic*—taking chances, jumping to conclusions, deciding to ignore possibilities, searching for solutions to problems. If you want to design a good chess algorithm, you must look at the task from this perspective. Similarly, *WUNDERKIND* can be viewed as a mere algorithm for taking symbols as input and issuing symbols as output. *That* it is guaranteed to do, but from the other perspective it is an English-understanding learner of hand simulation, who follows hunches, decides on semantic interpretations of the sentences it reads, ignores possible lines of interpretation or activity, and so on. From the fact that something can be viewed as proceeding heuristically, it does not follow that it is heuristic "all the way down"—whatever that might mean. And similarly, limitations (Gödelian and other) on what can be done by algorithms are not limitations on what can be done—without guarantee but with a high degree of reliability—heuristically by an algorithm.

This is no *refutation* of anti-mechanism, no *proof* that a human being and a computer are in the relevant respects alike—for of course it all depends on my asking you to imagine the success of *WUNDER-KIND*. Perhaps *WUNDERKIND* is "impossible"—though it looks modest enough, by current AI standards. If it is "impossible", this is something Gödel's theorem is powerless to show. That is, if all the versions of *WUNDERKIND* that are *clearly* possible fall far short of our intuitive ideal (by being too narrow, too keyed to the particular wording in the instruction book, etc.) and if no one can seem to devise a satisfactory version, this failure of Artificial Intelligence will be independent of the mathematical limits on algorithms.

14

Conditions of Personhood

I am a person, and so are you. That much is beyond doubt. I am a human being, and *probably* you are too. If you take offense at the "probably" you stand accused of a sort of racism, for what is important about us is not that we are of the same biological species, but that we are both persons, and I have not cast doubt on that. One's dignity does not depend on one's parentage even to the extent of having been born of woman or born at all. We normally ignore this and treat humanity as the deciding mark of personhood, no doubt because the terms are locally coextensive or almost coextensive. At this time and place, human beings are the only persons we recognize, and we recognize almost all human beings as persons, but on the one hand we can easily contemplate the existence of biologically very different persons—inhabiting other planets, perhaps—and on the other hand we recognize conditions that exempt human beings from personhood, or at least some very important elements of personhood. For instance, infant human beings, mentally defective human beings, and human beings declared insane by licensed psychiatrists are denied personhood, or at any rate crucial elements of personhood.

One might well hope that such an important concept, applied and denied so confidently, would have clearly formulatable necessary and sufficient conditions for ascription, but if it does, we have not yet discovered them. In the end there may be none to discover. In the end we may come to realize that the concept of a person is incoherent and obsolete. Skinner, for one, has suggested this, but the doctrine has not caught on, no doubt in part because it is difficult or even impossible to conceive of what it would be like if we abandoned the concept of a person. The idea that we might cease to view others and *ourselves* as

persons (if it does not mean merely that we might annihilate ourselves, and hence cease to view anything as anything) is arguably
self-contradictory (see Chapter 12). So quite aside from whatever
might be right or wrong in Skinner's grounds for his claim, it is hard
to see how it could win out in contest with such an intuitively invulnerable notion. If then the concept of a person is in some way
an ineliminable part of our conceptual scheme, it might still be in
rather worse shape than we would like. It might turn out, for instance, that the concept of a person is only a free-floating honorific
that we are all happy to apply to ourselves, and to others as the
spirit moves us, guided by our emotions, aesthetic sensibilities, considerations of policy, and the like— just as those who are *chic* are
all and only those who can get themselves considered *chic* by others
who consider themselves *chic*. Being a person is certainly *something* like that, and if it were no more, we would have to reconsider if we could the importance with which we now endow the
concept.

Supposing there *is* something more to being a person, the searcher
for necessary and sufficient conditions may still have difficulties if
there is more than one concept of a person, and there are grounds for
suspecting this. Roughly, there seem to be two notions intertwined
here, which we may call the moral notion and the metaphysical
notion. Locke says that "person"

is a forensic term, appropriating actions and their merit; and so
belongs only to intelligent agents, capable of a law, and happiness, and misery. This personality extends itself beyond present
existence to what is past, only by consciousness—whereby it
becomes concerned and accountable. (*Essay*, Book II, Chap.
XXVII).

Does the metaphysical notion—roughly, the notion of an intelligent,
conscious, feeling agent—*coincide* with the moral notion—roughly,
the notion of an agent who is accountable, who has both rights and
responsibilities? Or is it merely that being a person in the metaphysical
sense is a necessary but not sufficient condition of being a person in
the moral sense? Is being an entity to which states of consciousness or
self-consciousness are ascribed *the same* as being an end-in-oneself, or
is it merely one precondition? In Rawls's theory of justice, should the
derivation from the original position be viewed as a demonstration of
how metaphysical persons *can become* moral persons, or should it be
viewed as a demonstration of why metaphysical persons *must be*

moral persons?* In less technical surroundings the distinction stands out as clearly: when we declare a man insane we cease treating him as accountable, and we deny him most rights, but still our interactions with him are virtually indistinguishable from normal personal interactions unless he is very far gone in madness indeed. In one sense of "person", it seems, we continue to treat and view him as a person. I claimed at the outset that it was indubitable that you and I are persons. I could not plausibly hope—let alone aver—that all readers of this essay will be legally sane and morally accountable. What—if anything— was beyond all doubt may only have been that anything properly addressed by the opening sentence's personal pronouns, "you" and "I", was a person in the metaphysical sense. If that was all that was beyond doubt, then the metaphysical notion and the moral notion must be distinct. Still, even if we suppose there are these distinct notions, there seems every reason to believe that metaphysical personhood is a necessary condition of moral personhood.**

What I wish to do now is consider six familiar themes, each a claim to identify a necessary condition of personhood, and each, I think, a correct claim on some interpretation. What will be at issue here is first, how (on my interpretation) they are dependent on each other; second, why they are necessary conditions of moral personhood, and third, why it is so hard to say whether they are jointly sufficient conditions for moral personhood. The *first* and most obvious theme is that persons are *rational beings*. It figures, for example, in the ethical theories of Kant and Rawls, and in the "metaphysical" theories of Aristotle and Hintikka.[1] The *second* theme is that persons are beings to which states of consciousness are attributed, or to which psychological or mental or *intentional predicates*, are ascribed. Thus Strawson

*In "Justice as Reciprocity", a revision of "Justice as Fairness" printed in S. Gorovitz, ed., *Utilitarianism* (Indianapolis: Bobbs Merrill, 1971), Rawls allows that the persons in the original position may include "nations, provinces, business firms, churches, teams, and so on. The principles of justice apply to conflicting claims made by persons of all these separate kinds. There is, perhaps, a certain logical priority to the case of human individuals" (p. 245). In *A Theory of Justice* (Cambridge, Mass.: Harvard University Press, 1971), he acknowledges that parties in the original position may include associations and other entities not human individuals (e.g., p. 146), and the apparent interchangeability of "parties in the original position" and "persons in the original position" suggests that Rawls is claiming that for some moral concept of a person, the moral person is *composed* of metaphysical persons who may or may not themselves be moral persons.
**Setting aside Rawls's possible compound moral persons. For more on compound persons see Amelie Rorty, "Persons, Policies, and Bodies", *International Philosophical Quarterly*, XIII, 1 (March, 1973).

identifies the concept of a person as "the concept of a type of entity such that *both* predicates ascribing states of consciousness *and* predicates ascribing corporeal characteristics" are applicable.* The *third* theme is that whether something counts as a person depends in some way on an *attitude taken* toward it, a *stance adopted* with respect to it. This theme suggests that it is not the case that once we have established the objective fact that something is a person, we treat him or her or it in a certain way, but that our treating him or her or it in this certain way is somehow and to some extent constitutive of its being a person. Variations on this theme have been expressed by MacKay, Strawson, Rorty, Putnam, Sellars, Flew, Nagel, Van de Vate, and myself.[2] The *fourth* theme is that the object toward which this personal stance is taken must be capable of *reciprocating* in some way. Very different versions of this are expressed or hinted at by Rawls, MacKay, Strawson, Grice, and others. This reciprocity has sometimes been rather uninformatively expressed by the slogan: to be a person is to treat others as persons, and with this expression has often gone the claim that treating another as a person is treating him morally—perhaps obeying the Golden Rule, but this conflates different sorts of reciprocity. As Nagel says, "extremely hostile behavior toward another is compatible with treating him as a person" (p. 134), and as Van de Vate observes, one of the differences between some forms of manslaughter and murder is that the murderer treats the victim as a person.

The *fifth* theme is that persons must be capable of *verbal communication*. This condition handily excuses nonhuman animals from full personhood and the attendant moral responsibility, and seems at least implicit in all social contract theories of ethics. It is also a theme that has been stressed or presupposed by many writers in philosophy of mind, including myself, where the moral dimension of personhood has not been at issue. The *sixth* theme is that persons are distinguishable from other entities by being *conscious* in some special way: there is a way in which *we* are conscious in which no other species is conscious. Sometimes this is identified as *self*-consciousness of one sort or another. Three philosophers who claim—in very different ways—that a

*P. F. Strawson, *Individuals* (London: Methuen, 1959), pp. 101-102. It has often been pointed out that Strawson's definition is obviously much too broad, capturing all sentient, active creatures. See, e.g. H. Frankfurt, "Freedom of the Will and the Concept of a Person", *Journal of Philosophy*, LXVIII (January 14, 1971). It can also be argued (and I would argue) that states of consciousness are only a proper subset of psychological or intentionally characterized states, but I think it is clear that Strawson here means to cast his net wide enough to include psychological states generally.

special sort of consciousness is a precondition of being a moral agent are Anscombe, in *Intention*, Sartre, in *The Transcendence of the Ego*, and Frankfurt, in his recent paper, "Freedom of the Will and the Concept of a Person".[3]

I will argue that the order in which I have given these six themes is—with one proviso—the order of their dependence. The proviso is that the first three are mutually interdependent; being rational is being intentional is being the object of a certain stance. These three together are a necessary but not sufficient condition for exhibiting the form of reciprocity that is in turn a necessary but not sufficient condition for having the capacity for verbal communication, which is the necessary* condition for having a special sort of consciousness, which is, as Anscombe and Frankfurt in their different ways claim, a necessary condition of moral personhood. (I will not discuss Sartre's claim here.)

I have previously exploited the first three themes, rationality, intentionality and stance, to define not persons, but the much wider class of what I call *intentional systems*, and since I intend to build on that notion, a brief résumé is in order. An intentional system is a system whose behavior can be (at least sometimes) explained and predicted by relying on ascriptions to the system of *beliefs* and *desires* (and other intentionally characterized features—what I will call *intentions* here, meaning to include hopes, fears, intentions, perceptions, expectations, etc.). There may *in every case* be other ways of predicting and explaining the behavior of an intentional system—for instance, mechanistic or physical ways—but the intentional stance may be the handiest or most effective or in any case *a* successful stance to adopt, which suffices for the object to be an intentional system. So defined, intentional systems are obviously not all persons. We ascribe beliefs and desires to dogs and fish and thereby predict their behavior, and we can even use the procedure to predict the behavior of some machines. For instance, it is a good, indeed the only good, strategy to adopt against a good chess-playing computer. By *assuming* the computer has certain beliefs (or information) and desires (or preference functions) dealing with the chess game in progress, I can calculate—under auspicious circumstances—the computer's most likely next move, *provided I assume that the computer deals rationally with these beliefs and desires*. The computer is an intentional system in these instances not because it has any particular intrinsic features, and not because it really and truly has beliefs and desires (whatever that would be), but just because it succumbs to a certain *stance* adopted toward it, namely

---

*And sufficient, but I will not argue it here. I argue for this in *Content and Consciousness* and more recently and explicitly in Chapters 2 and 9 of this volume.

the intentional stance, the stance that proceeds by ascribing intentional predicates under the usual constraints to the computer, the stance that proceeds by considering the computer as a rational practical reasoner.

It is important to recognize how bland this definition of *intentional system* is, and how correspondingly large the class of intentional systems can be. If, for instance, I predict that a particular plant—say a potted ivy—will grow around a corner and up into the light because it "seeks" the light and "wants" to get out of the shade it now finds itself in, and "expects" or "hopes" there is light around the corner, I have adopted the intentional stance toward the plant, and lo and behold, within very narrow limits it works. Since it works, some plants are very low-grade intentional systems.

The actual utility of adopting the intentional stance toward plants was brought home to me talking with loggers in the Maine woods. These men invariably call a tree not "it" but "he", and will say of a young spruce, "He wants to spread his limbs, but don't let him; then he'll have to stretch up to get his light," or, "Pines don't like to get their feet wet the way cedars do." You can "trick" an apple tree into "thinking it's spring" by building a small fire under its branches in the late fall; it will blossom. This way of talking is not just picturesque and is not really superstitious at all; it is simply an efficient way of making sense of, controlling, predicting, and explaining the behavior of these plants in a way that nicely circumvents one's ignorance of the controlling mechanisms. More sophisticated biologists may choose to speak of information transmission from the tree's periphery to other locations in the tree. This is less picturesque, but still intentional. Complete abstention from intentional talk about trees can become almost as heroic, cumbersome, and pointless as the parallel strict behaviorist taboo when speaking of rats and pigeons. And even when intentional glosses on (e.g.) tree-activities are of vanishingly small heuristic value, it seems to me wiser to grant that such a tree is a very degenerate, uninteresting, negligible intentional system than to attempt to draw a line above which intentional interpretations are "objectively true".

It is obvious, then, that being an intentional system is not sufficient condition for being a person, but is surely a necessary condition. Nothing to which we could not successfully adopt the intentional stance, with its presupposition of rationality, could count as a person. Can we then define persons as a subclass of intentional systems? At first glance it might seem profitable to suppose that persons are just that subclass of intentional systems that *really* have beliefs, desires, and so forth, and are not merely *supposed* to have them for the sake of a short-cut prediction. But efforts to say what counts as really having a belief (so that no dog or tree or computer could qualify) all seem to end by putting conditions on genuine belief that (1) are too strong for our intuitions, and (2) allude to distinct conditions of personhood farther down my list. For instance, one might claim that genuine beliefs are necessarily *verbally expressible* by the believer,[4] or the believer must be *conscious* that he has them, but people seem to have many beliefs that they cannot put into words, and many that they are unaware of having—and in any case I hope to show that the capacity for verbal expression, and the capacity for consciousness, find different *loci* in the set of necessary conditions of personhood.

Better progress can be made, I think, if we turn to our fourth theme, reciprocity, to see what kind of definition it could receive in terms of intentional systems. The theme suggests that a person must be able to reciprocate the stance, which suggests that an intentional system that itself adopted the intentional stance toward other objects would meet the test. Let us define a *second-order intentional system* as one to which we ascribe not only simple beliefs, desires and other intentions, but beliefs, desires, and other intentions *about* beliefs, desires, and other intentions. An intentional system S would be a second-order intentional system if among the ascriptions we make to it are such as *S believes that T desires that p, S hopes that T fears that q,* and reflexive cases like *S believes that S desires that p.* (The importance of the reflexive cases will loom large, not surprisingly, when we turn to those who interpret our sixth condition as *self*-consciousness. It may seem to some that the reflexive cases make all intentional systems automatically second-order systems, and even *n*-order systems, on the grounds that believing that *p* implies believing that you believe that *p* and so forth, but this is a fundamental mistake; the iteration of beliefs and other intentions is never redundant, and hence while some iterations are normal—are to be expected—they are never trivial or automatic.)

Now, are human beings the only second-order intentional systems so far as we know? I take this to be an empirical question. We ascribe beliefs and desires to dogs, cats, lions, birds, and dolphins, for example, and thereby often predict their behavior—when all goes well—but it is hard to think of a case where an animal's behavior was so sophisticated that we would need to ascribe second-order intentions to it in order to predict or explain its behavior. Of course if some version of mechanistic physicalism is true (as I believe), we will never *need* absolutely to ascribe any intentions to anything, but supposing that for heuristic and pragmatic reasons we were to ascribe intentions to animals, would we ever feel the pragmatic tug to ascribe second-order intentions to them? Psychologists have often appealed to a principle known as Lloyd Morgan's Canon of Parsimony, which can be viewed as a special case of Occam's Razor; it is the principle that one should attribute to an organism as little intelligence or consciousness or rationality or mind as will suffice to account for its behavior. This principle can be, and has been, interpreted as demanding nothing short of radical behaviorism,[5] but I think this is a mistake, and we can interpret it as the principle requiring us when we adopt the intentional stance toward a thing to ascribe the simplest, least sophisticated, lowest-order beliefs, desires, and so on, that will account for the behavior. Then we will grant, for instance, that Fido *wants* his supper, and *believes* his master will give him his supper if he begs in front of his master, but we need not ascribe to Fido the further *belief* that his begging induces a *belief* in his master that he, Fido, *wants* his supper. Similarly, my *expectation* when I put a dime in the candy machine does not hinge on a further *belief* that inserting the coin induces the machine to *believe* I *want* some candy. That is, while Fido's begging looks very much like true second-order interacting (with Fido treating his master as an intentional system), if we suppose that to Fido his master is just a supper machine activated by begging, we will have just as good a predictive ascription, more modest but still, of course, intentional.

Are dogs, then, or chimps or other "higher" animals, incapable of rising to the level of second-order intentional systems, and if so why? I used to think the answer was yes, and I thought the reason was that nonhuman animals lack language, and that language was needed to represent second-order intentions. In other words, I thought condition four might rest on condition five. I was tempted by the hypothesis that animals cannot, for instance, have second-order beliefs, beliefs about beliefs, for the same reason they cannot have beliefs about Friday, or poetry. Some beliefs can only be acquired, and hence represented, via language.[6] But if it is true that some beliefs cannot be acquired without language, it is false that all second-order beliefs are among them, and it is false that non-humans cannot be second-order intentional systems. Once I began asking people for examples of non-human second-order intentional systems, I found some very plausible cases. Consider this from Peter Ashley (in a letter):

One evening I was sitting in a chair at my home, the *only* chair my dog is allowed to sleep in. The dog was lying in front of me, whimpering. She was getting nowhere in her trying to "convince" me to give up the chair to her. Her next move is the most interesting, nay, the *only* interesting part of the story. She stood up, and went to the front door where I could still easily see her. She scratched the door, giving me the impression that she had given up trying to get the chair and had decided to go out. However as soon as I reached the door to let her out, she ran back across the room and climbed into her chair, the chair she had "forced" me to leave.

Here it seems we must ascribe to the dog the *intention* that her master *believe* she *wants* to go out—not just a second-order, but a third-order intention. The key to the example, what makes it an example of a higher-order intentional system at work, is that the belief she intends to induce in her master is false. If we want to discover further examples of animals behaving as second-order intentional systems it will help to think of cases of deception, where the animal, believing *p*, tries to get another intentional system to believe *not-p*. Where an animal is trying to induce behavior in another which *true* beliefs about the other's environment would not induce, we cannot "divide through" and get an explanation that cites only first-level intentions. We can make this point more general before explaining why it is so: where *x* is attempting to induce behavior in *y* which is inappropriate to *y*'s *true* environment and needs but appropriate to *y*'s *perceived* or *believed* environment and needs, we are forced to ascribe second-order intentions to *x*. Once in this form the point emerges as a familiar one, often exploited by critics of behaviorism: one can be a behaviorist in explaining and controlling the behavior of laboratory animals only so long as he can rely on there being no serious dislocation between the actual environment of the experiment and the environment perceived by the animals. A tactic for embarrassing behaviorists in the laboratory is to set up experiments that deceive the subjects: if the deception succeeds, their behavior is predictable from their false *beliefs* about the environment, not from the actual environment. Now a first-order intentional system is a behaviorist; it ascribes no intentions to anything. So if we are to have good evidence that some system *S* is *not* a behaviorist—is a second-order intentional system—it will only be in those cases where behaviorist theories are inadequate to the data, only in those cases where behaviorism would not explain system *S*'s success in manipulating another system's behavior.

This suggests that Ashley's example is not so convincing after all, that it can be defeated by supposing his dog is a behaviorist of sorts. She need not believe that scratching on the door will induce Ashley to believe she wants to go out; she may simply believe, as a good behaviorist, that she has conditioned Ashley to go to the door when she scratches. So she applies the usual stimulus, gets the usual response, and that's that. Ashley's case succumbs if this is a *standard* way his dog has of getting the door opened, as it probably is, for then the more modest hypothesis is that the dog believes her master is conditioned to go to the door when she scratches. Had the dog done something *novel* to deceive her master (like running to the window and looking out, growling suspiciously) then we would have to grant that rising from the chair was no mere conditioned response in Ashley, and could not be "viewed" as such by his dog, but then, such virtuosity in a dog would be highly implausible.

Yet what is the difference between the implausible case and the well-attested cases where a low-nesting bird will feign a broken wing to lure a predator away from the nest? The effect achieved is novel, in the sense that the bird in all likelihood has not repeatedly conditioned the predators in the neighborhood with this stimulus, so we seem constrained to explain the ploy as a bit of genuine deception, where the bird *intends* to induce a false *belief* in the predator. Forced to this interpretation of the behavior, we would be mightily impressed with the bird's ingenuity were it not for the fact that we know such behavior is "merely instinctual". But why does it disparage this trick to call it merely instinctual? To claim it is instinctual is to claim that all birds of the species do it; they do it even when circumstances aren't entirely appropriate; they do it when there are better reasons for staying on the nest; the behavior pattern is rigid, a tropism of sorts, and presumably the controls are genetically wired in, not learned or invented.

We must be careful not to carry this disparagement too far; it is not that the bird does this trick "unthinkingly", for while it is no doubt true that she does not in any sense run through an argument or scheme in her head ("Let's see, if I were to flap my wing as if it were broken, the fox would think . . ."), a man might do something of similar subtlety, and of genuine intelligence, novelty, and appropriateness, and not run through the "conscious thoughts" either. *Thinking the thoughts*, however that is characterized, is not what makes truly intelligent behavior intelligent. Anscombe says at one point "If [such an expression of reasoning] were supposed to describe actual mental processes, it would in general be quite absurd. The interest of the account is that it described an order which is there whenever actions are done with intentions."[7] But the "order is there" in the case of the bird as well as the man. That is, when we ask why birds evolved with this tropism, we explain it by noting the utility of having a means of *deceiving* predators, or inducing false beliefs in them; what must be explained is the provenance of the bird's second-order intentions. I would be the last to deny or dismiss the vast difference between instinctual or tropistic behavior and the more versatile, intelligent behavior of humans and others, but what I want to insist on here is that if one is prepared to adopt the intentional stance without qualms as a tool in predicting and explaining behavior, the bird is as much a second-order intentional system as any man. Since this is so, we should be particularly suspicious of the argument I was tempted to use, viz., that *representations* of second order intentions would depend somehow on language.[8] For it is far from clear that all or even any of the beliefs and other intentions of an intentional system need be *represented* "within" the system in any way for us to get a purchase on predicting its behavior by *ascribing* such intentions to it. (I argue this in more detail in Chapters 2 and 3.) The situation we elucidate by citing the bird's desire to induce a false belief in the predator seems to have no room or need for a representation of this sophisticated intention in any entity's "thoughts" or "mind", for neither the bird nor evolutionary history nor Mother Nature need think these thoughts for our explanation to be warranted.

Reciprocity, then, provided we understand by it merely the capacity in intentional systems to exhibit higher-order intentions, while it depends on the first three conditions, is independent of the fifth and sixth. Whether this notion does justice to the reciprocity discussed by other writers will begin to come clear only when we see how it meshes with the last two conditions. For the fifth condition, the capacity for verbal communication, we turn to Grice's theory of meaning. Grice attempts to define what he calls "nonnatural" meaning, an utterer's meaning something by uttering something, in terms of the *intentions* of the utterer. His initial definition is as follows:*

"U meant something by uttering x" is true if, for some audience A, U uttered x intending
(1) A to produce a particular response *r*.
(2) A to think (recognize) that U intends (1).
(3) A to fulfill (1) on the basis of his fulfillment of (2).

Notice that intention (2) ascribes to *U* not only a second- but a

---

*The key papers are "Meaning", *Philosophical Review* (July, 1957), and "Utterer's Meaning and Intentions", *Philosophical Review* (April, 1969). His initial formulation, developed in the first paper, is subjected to a series of revisions in the second paper, from which this formulation is drawn (p. 151).

third-order Intention: *U* must *intend* that *A* *recognize* that *U* *intends* that *A* produce *r*. It matters not at all that Grice has been forced by a series of counterexamples to move from this initial definition to much more complicated versions, for they all reproduce the third-order Intention of (2). Two points of great importance to us emerge from Grice's analysis of nonnatural meaning. First, since nonnatural meaning, meaning something by saying something, must be a feature of any true verbal communication, and since it depends on third-order intentions on the part of the utterer, we have our case that condition five rests on condition four and not vice versa. Second, Grice shows us that mere *second*-order intentions are not enough to provide genuine reciprocity; for that, *third*-order intentions are needed. Grice introduces condition (2) in order to exclude such cases as this: I leave the china my daughter has broken lying around for my wife to see. This is not a case of meaning something by doing what I do, intending what I intend, for though I am attempting thereby to induce my wife to believe something about our daughter (a second-order intention on my part), success does not depend on her recognizing this intention of mine, or recognizing my intervention or existence at all. There has been no real *encounter*, to use Erving Goffman's apt term, between us, no *mutual recognition*. There must be an encounter between utterer and audience for utterer to mean anything, but encounters can occur in the absence of non-natural meaning (witness Ashley's dog), and ploys that depend on third-order intentions need not involve encounters (e.g., *A* can intend that *B* believe that *C* desires that *p*). So third-order intentions are a necessary but not sufficient condition for encounters which are a necessary but not sufficient condition for instances of nonnatural meaning, that is, instances of verbal communication.

It is no accident that Grice's cases of nonnatural meaning fall into a class whose other members are cases of deception or manipulation. Consider, for instance, Searle's ingenious counterexample to one of Grice's formulations: the American caught behind enemy lines in World War II Italy who attempts to deceive his Italian captors into concluding he is a German officer by saying the one sentence of German he knows: *"Kennst du das Land, wo die Zitronen blühen?"*[9] As Grice points out, these cases share with cases of nonnatural meaning a reliance on, or exploitation of, the rationality of the victim. In these cases success hinges on inducing the victim to embark on a chain of reasoning to which one contributes premises directly or indirectly. In deception the premises are disbelieved by the supplier; in normal communication they are believed. Communication, in Gricean guise, appears to be a sort of collaborative manipulation of audience by utterer; it depends, not only on the rationality of the audience who must sort out the utterer's intentions, but on the audience's *trust* in the utterer. Communication, as a sort of manipulation, would not work, given the requisite rationality of the audience, unless the audience's trust in the utterer were *well-grounded* or reasonable. Thus the *norm* for utterance is sincerity; were utterances not normally trustworthy, they would fail of their purpose (see Chapter 1).

Lying, as a form of deception, can only work against a background of truth-telling, but other forms of deception do not depend on the trust of the victim. In these cases success depends on the victim being *quite* smart, but not quite smart enough. Stupid poker players are the bane of clever poker players, for they fail to see the bluffs and ruses being offered them. Such sophisticated deceptions need not depend on direct encounters. There is a book on how to detect fake antiques (which is also, inevitably, a book on how to *make* fake antiques) which offers this sly advice to those who want to fool the "expert" buyer: once you have completed your table or whatever (having utilized all the usual means of simulating age and wear) take a modern electric drill and drill a hole right through the piece in some conspicuous but perplexing place. The would-be buyer will argue: no one would drill such a disfiguring hole without a reason (it can't be supposed to look "authentic" in any way) so it must have served a purpose, which means this table must have been in use in someone's home; since it was in use in someone's home, it was not made expressly for sale in this antique shop . . . therefore it is authentic. Even if this "conclusion" left room for lingering doubts, the buyer will be so preoccupied dreaming up uses for that hole it will be months before the doubts can surface.

What is important about these cases of deception is the fact that just as in the case of the feigning bird, success does not depend on the victim's *consciously entertaining* these chains of reasoning. It does not matter if the buyer just notices the hole and "gets a hunch" the piece is genuine. He *might* later accept the reasoning offered as his "rationale" for finding the piece genuine, but he might deny it, and in denying it, he might be deceiving himself, even though the *thoughts* never went through his head. The chain of reasoning explains why the hole works as it does (if it does), but as Anscombe says, it need not "describe actual mental processes", if we suppose actual mental processes are conscious processes or events. The same, of course, is true of Gricean communications; neither the utterer nor the audience need consciously entertain the complicated intentions he outlines, and what is a bit surprising is that no one has ever used this fact as an objection to Grice. Grice's conditions for meaning have been often criticized for falling short of being sufficient, but there seems to be an argument not yet used to show they are not even necessary. Certainly, few people ever consciously framed those ingenious intentions before Grice pointed them out, and yet people have been communicating for years. Before Grice, were one asked: "Did you intend your audience to recognize your intention to provoke that response in him?" one would most likely have retorted: "I intended nothing so devious. I simply intended to inform that that I wouldn't be home for supper" (or whatever). So it seems that if these complicated intentions underlay our communicating all along, they must have been unconscious intentions. Indeed, a perfectly natural way of responding to Grice's papers is to remark that *one was not aware* of doing these things when one communicated. Now Anscombe has held, very powerfully, that such a response establishes that the action under that description was not *intentional.** Since one is not *aware* of these *intentions* in speaking, one cannot be speaking *with* these *intentions*.

Why has no one used this argument against Grice's theory? Because, I submit, it is just too plain that Grice is on to something, that Grice is giving us necessary conditions for nonnatural meaning. His analysis illuminates so many questions. Do we communicate with computers in Fortran? Fortran seems to be a language; it has a grammar, a vocabulary, a semantics. The transactions in Fortran between man and machine are often viewed as cases of *man communicating with machine*, but such transactions are pale copies of human verbal communication precisely because the Gricean conditions for nonnatural meaning have been bypassed. There is no room for them to apply. Achieving one's ends in transmitting a bit of Fortran to the machine does not hinge on getting the machine to recognize one's *intentions*. This does not mean that all communications with computers in the future will have this shortcoming (or strength, depending on your purposes), but just that we do not now communicate, in the strong (Gricean) sense, with computers.**

---

*See G.E.M. Anscombe, *Intention* (Oxford: Blackwells, 1957), p. 11. Here, and in the next few paragraphs, I am using "intentions" and "intentional" in their *ordinary* sense—and putting them in italics for emphasis.

**It has been pointed out to me by Howard Friedman that many current Fortran compilers which "correct" operator input by inserting "plus" signs and parentheses, etc., to produce well-formed expressions arguably meet Grice's criteria, since within a very limited sphere, they diagnose the "utterer's" *intentions*

If we are not about to abandon the Gricean model, yet are aware of no such *intentions* in our normal conversation, we shall just have to drive these *intentions* underground, and call them unconscious or pre-conscious *intentions*. They are *intentions* that exhibit "an order which is there" when people communicate, *intentions* of which we are not normally aware, and *intentions* which are a precondition of verbal communication.

We have come this far without having to invoke any sort of consciousness at all, so if there is a dependence between consciousness or self-consciousness and our other conditions, it will have to be consciousness depending on the others. But to show this I must first show how the first five conditions by themselves might play a role in ethics, as suggested by Rawls's theory of justice. Central to Rawls's theory is his setting up of an idealized situation, the "original position", inhabited by idealized persons, and deriving from this idealization the first principles of justice that generate and illuminate the rest of his theory. What I am concerned with now is neither the content of these principles nor the validity of their derivation, but the nature of Rawls's tactic. Rawls supposes that a group of idealized persons, defined by him as rational, self-interested entities, make calculations under certain constraints about the likely and possible interactive effects of their individual and antagonistic interests (which will require them to frame higher-order intentions, for example, beliefs about the desires of others, beliefs about the beliefs of others about their own desires, and so forth). Rawls claims these calculations have an optimal "solution" that it would be reasonable for each self-interested person to adopt as an alternative to a Hobbesian state of nature. The solution is to agree with his fellows to abide by the principles of justice Rawls adumbrates. What sort of a proof of the principles of justice would this be? Adopting these principles of justice can be viewed, Rawls claims, as the solution to the "highest order game" or "bargaining problem". It is analogous to derivations of game theory, and to proofs in Hintikka's epistemic logic,[10] and to a "demonstration" that the chess-playing computer will make a certain move because it is the most rational move given its information about the game. All depend on the assumption of ideally rational calculators, and hence their outcomes are intrinsically normative. Thus I see the derivations from Rawls's

---

and proceed on the basis of this diagnosis. But first it should be noted that the machines to date can diagnose only what might be called the operator's syntactical intentions, and second, these machines do not seem to meet Grice's subsequent and more elaborate definitions, not that I wish to claim that no computer could.

original position as continuous with the deductions and extrapolations encountered in more simple uses of the intentional stance to understand and control the behavior of simpler entities. Just as truth and consistency are norms for belief (see Chapter 1 of this volume), and sincerity is the norm for utterance, so, if Rawls is right, justice as he defines it is the norm for interpersonal interactions. But then, just as part of our warrant for considering an entity to have any beliefs or other intentions is our ability to construe the entity as *rational*, so our grounds for considering an entity a person include our ability to view him as abiding by the principles of justice. A way of capturing the peculiar status of the concept of a person as I think it is exploited here would be to say that while Rawls does not at all intend to argue that justice is the inevitable result of *human* interaction, he does argue in effect that it is the inevitable result of *personal* interaction. That is, the concept of a person is itself inescapably normative or idealized; to the extent that justice does not reveal itself in the dealings and interactions of creatures, to that extent they are not persons. And once again we can see that there is "an order which is there" in a just society that is independent of any actual episodes of conscious thought. The existence of just practices and the "acknowledgment" implicit in them does not depend on anyone ever consciously or deliberately going through the calculations of the idealized original position, consciously arriving at the reciprocal agreements, consciously adopting a stance toward others.

> To recognize another as a person one must respond to him and act towards him in certain ways; and these ways are intimately connected with the various prima facie duties. Acknowledging these duties in some degree, and so having the elements of morality, is not a matter of choice or of intuiting moral qualities or a matter of the expression of feelings or attitudes . . . it is simply the pursuance of one of the forms of conduct in which the recognition of others as persons is manifested.[11]

The importance of Rawls's attempt to derive principles of justice from the "original position" is, of course, that while the outcome is recognizable as a *moral* norm, it is not *derived as* a moral norm. Morality is not presupposed of the parties in the original position. But this means that the derivation of the norm does not in itself give us any answer to the questions of when and why we have the right to hold persons *morally* responsible for deviations from that norm. Here Anscombe provides help and at the same time introduces our sixth condition. *If I am to be held responsible for an action* (a bit of behavior of mine under a particular description), I must have been *aware* of that action under that description.* Why? Because only if I was aware of the action can I *say* what I was about, and participate from a privileged position in the question-and-answer game of giving reasons for my actions. (If I am not in a privileged position to answer questions about the reasons for my actions, there is no special reason to ask *me*.) And what is so important about being able to participate in this game is that only those capable of participating in reason-giving can be argued into, or argued out of, courses of action or attitudes, and if one is incapable of "listening to reason" in some matter, one cannot be held responsible for it. The capacities for verbal communication and for awareness of one's actions are thus essential in one who is going to be amenable to argument or persuasion, and such persuasion, such reciprocal adjustment of interests achieved by mutual exploitation of rationality, is a feature of the optimal mode of personal interaction.

This capacity for participation in mutual persuasion provides the foundation for yet another condition of personhood recently exposed by Harry Frankfurt.** Frankfurt claims that persons are the subclass of intentional systems capable of what he calls *"second-order voli-tions"*. Now at first this looks just like the class of second-order intentional systems, but it is not, as we shall see.

> Besides wanting and choosing and being moved *to do* this or that, men may also want to have (or not to have) certain desires and motives. They are capable of wanting to be different, in their preferences and purposes, from what they are. . . . No animal other than man, however, appears to have the capacity for reflective self-evaluation that is manifested in the formation of second-order desires. (p. 7)

Frankfurt points out that there are cases in which a person might be said to want to have a particular desire even though he would not want that desire to be effective for him, to be "his will". (One might, for instance, want to desire heroin just to know what it felt like to desire heroin, without at all wanting this desire to become one's

---

*I can be held responsible for events and states of affairs that I was not aware of and ought to have been aware of, but these are not *intentional* actions. In these cases I am responsible for these further matters in virtue of being responsible for the foreseeable consequences of actions—including acts of omission—that I was aware of.

**H. Frankfurt, "Freedom of the will and the concept of a person", *loc. cit.*[3]. Frankfurt does not say whether he conceives his condition to be merely a necessary or also a sufficient condition of moral personhood.

effective desire.) In more serious cases one wants to have a desire one currently does not have, and wants this desire to become one's will. These cases Frankfurt calls second-order volitions, and it is having these, he claims, that is "essential to being a person" (p. 10). His argument for this claim, which I will not try to do justice to here, proceeds from an analysis of the distinction between having freedom of action and having freedom of the will. One has freedom of the will, on his analysis, only when one can have the will one wants, when one's second-order volitions can be satisfied. Persons do not always have free will, and under some circumstances can be responsible for actions done in the absence of freedom of the will, but a person always must be an "entity for whom the freedom of its will may be a problem" (p. 14)—that is, one capable of framing second-order volitions, satisfiable or not. Frankfurt introduces the marvelous term "wanton" for those "who have first-order desires but . . . no second-order volitions". (Second-order volitions for Frankfurt are all, of course, *reflexive* second-order desires.) He claims that our intuitions support the opinion that all nonhuman animals, as well as small children and some mentally defective people, are *wantons*, and I for one can think of no plausible counterexamples. Indeed, it seems a strength of his theory, as he claims, that human beings—the only persons we recognize—are distinguished from animals in this regard. But what should be so special about second-order volitions? Why are they, among higher-order intentions, the peculiar province of persons? Because, I believe, the "reflective self-evaluation" Frankfurt speaks of is, and must be, genuine self-consciousness, which is achieved only by adopting toward *oneself* the stance not simply of communicator but of Anscombian reason-asker and persuader. As Frankfurt points out, second-order desires are an empty notion unless one can *act* on them, and acting on a second-order desire must be logically distinct from acting on its first-order component. Acting on a second-order desire, doing something to bring it about that one acquires a first-order desire, is acting upon oneself just as one would act upon another person: one *schools* oneself, one offers oneself persuasions, arguments, threats, bribes, in the hopes of inducing oneself to acquire the first-order desire.* One's stance toward oneself *and access to oneself* in these cases is essentially

---

*It has been brought to my attention that dogs at stud will often engage in masturbation, in order, apparently, to *increase their desire* to copulate. What makes these cases negligible is that even supposing the dog can be said to act on a desire to strengthen a desire, the effect is achieved in a nonintentional ("purely physiological") way; the dog does not appeal to or exploit his own rationality in achieving his end. (As if the only way a person could act on a second-order volition were by taking a pill or standing on his head, etc.)

the same as one's stand toward and access to another. One must *ask oneself* what one's desires, motives, reasons really are, and only if one can say, can become aware of one's desires, can one be in a position to induce oneself to change.[12] Only here, I think, is it the case that the "order which is there" cannot be there unless it is there in episodes of conscious thought, in a dialogue with oneself.*

Now finally, why are we not in a position to claim that these necessary conditions of moral personhood are also sufficient? Simply because the concept of a person is, I have tried to show, inescapably normative. Human beings or other entities can only aspire to being approximations of the ideal, and there can be no way to set a "passing grade" that is not arbitrary. Were the six conditions (strictly interpreted) considered sufficient they would not ensure that any actual entity was a person, for nothing would ever fulfill them. The moral notion of a person and the metaphysical notion of a person are not separate and distinct concepts but just two different and unstable resting points on the same continuum. This relativity infects the satisfaction of conditions of personhood at every level. There is no objectively satisfiable sufficient condition for an entity's *really* having beliefs, and as we uncover apparent irrationality under an intentional interpretation of an entity, our grounds for ascribing any beliefs at all wanes, especially when we have (what we always *can* have in principle) a non-intentional, mechanistic account of the entity. In just the same way our assumption that an entity is a person is shaken precisely in those cases where it matters: when wrong has been done and the question of responsibility arises. For in these cases the grounds for saying that the person is culpable (the evidence that he did wrong, was aware he was doing wrong, and did wrong of his own free will) are in themselves grounds for doubting that it is a person we are dealing with at all. And if it is asked what could *settle* our doubts, the answer is: nothing. When such problems arise we cannot even tell in our own cases if we are persons.

---

*Marx, in *The German Ideology*, says: "Language, like consciousness, only arises from the need, the necessity, of intercourse with other men. . . . Language is as old as consciousness, language is practical consciousness". And Nietzsche, in *The Joyful Wisdom*, says: "For we could in fact think, feel, will, and recollect, we could likewise 'act' in every sense of the term, and nevertheless nothing of it at all need necessarily 'come into consciousness' (as one says metaphorically; . . . . *What* then is the *purpose* of consciousness generally, when it is in the main *superfluous*? —Now it seems to me, if you will hear my answer and its perhaps extravagant supposition, that the subtlety and strength of consciousness are always in proportion to the *capacity for communication* of a man (or an animal), the capacity for communication in its turn being in proportion to the *necessity for communication*. . . . In short, the development of speech and the development of consciousness (not of reason, but of reason becoming self-conscious) go hand in hand."

15

On Giving Libertarians What They Say They Want

Why is the free will problem so persistent? Partly, I suspect, because it is called *the* free will problem. Hilliard, the great card magician, used to fool even his professional colleagues with a trick he called the tuned deck. Twenty times in a row he'd confound the quidnuncs, as he put it, with the same trick, a bit of prestidigitation that resisted all the diagnostic hypotheses of his fellow magicians. The trick, as he eventually revealed, was a masterpiece of subtle misdirection; it consisted entirely of the *name*, "the tuned deck", plus a peculiar but obviously non-functional bit of ritual. It was, you see, *many* tricks, however many different but familiar tricks Hilliard had to perform in order to stay one jump ahead of the solvers. As soon as their experiments and subtle arguments had conclusively eliminated one way of doing the trick, that was the way he would do the trick on future trials. This would have been obvious to his sophisticated onlookers had they not been so intent on finding *the* solution to *the* trick.

The so called free will problem is in fact many not very closely related problems tied together by a name and lots of attendant anxiety. Most people can be brought by reflection to care very much what the truth is on these matters, for each problem poses a threat: to our self-esteem, to our conviction that we are not living deluded lives, to our conviction that we may justifiably trust our grasp of such utterly familiar notions as possibility, opportunity and ability.* There is no

*An incomplete list of the very different questions composing the free will problem: (1) How can a material thing (a mechanism?) be correctly said to reason, to have reasons, to act on reasons? (a question I attempt to answer in Chapter 12). (2) How can the unique four dimensional non-branching world-worm that comprises all that has happened and will happen admit of a notion of possibilities that are not actualities? What does an *opportunity* look like when the world is very good reason to suppose that an acceptable solution to *one* of the problems will be, or even point to, an acceptable solution to the others, and we may be misled by residual unallayed worries into rejecting or undervaluing partial solutions, in the misguided hope that we might allay all the doubts with one overarching doctrine or theory. But we don't have any good theories. Since the case for determinism is persuasive and since we all want to believe we have free will, *compatibilism* is the strategic favorite, but we must admit that no compatibilism free of problems while full of the traditional flavors of responsibility has yet been devised.

The alternatives to compatibilism are anything but popular. Both the libertarian and the hard determinist believe that free will and determinism are incompatible. The hard determinist says: "So much of the worse for free will." The libertarian says: "So much the worse for determinism," at least with regard to human action. Both alternatives have been roundly and routinely dismissed as at best obscure, at worst incoherent. But alas for the compatibilist, neither view will oblige us by fading away. Their persistence, like Hilliard's success, probably has many explanations. I hope to diagnose just one of them.

In a recent paper, David Wiggins has urged us to look with more sympathy at the program of libertarianism.[1] Wiggins first points out that a familiar argument often presumed to demolish libertarianism begs the question. The first premise of this argument is that every event is either causally determined or random. Then since the libertarian insists that human actions cannot be both free and determined, the libertarian must be supposing that any and all free actions are random. But one would hardly hold oneself responsible for an action that merely happened at random, so libertarianism, far from securing a necessary condition for responsible action, has unwittingly secured a condition that would defeat responsibility altogether. Wiggins points out that the first premise, that every event is either causally determined or random, is not the innocent logical truth it appears to be. The innocent logical truth is that every event is either causally determined or nor causally determined. There may be an established sense of the word "random" that is unproblematically synonymous with "not causally determined", but the word "random" in common parlance has further connotations of pointlessness or arbitrariness, and it

---

viewed *sub specie aeternitatis*? (3) How can a person be an author of decisions, and not merely the locus of causal summation for external influences? (4) How can we make sense of the intuition that an agent can only be responsible if he could have done otherwise? (5) How can we intelligibly describe the relevant mental history of the truly culpable agent—the villain or rational cheat with no excuses? As Socrates asked, can a person knowingly commit evil?

is these very connotations that ground our acquiescence in the further premise that one would not hold oneself responsible for one's random actions. It may be the case that whatever is random in the sense of being causally undetermined, is random in the sense connoting utter meaninglessness, but that is just what the libertarian wishes to deny. This standard objection to libertarianism, then, assumes what it must prove; it fails to show that undetermined action would be random action, and hence action for which we could not be held responsible.

But is there in fact any reasonable hope that the libertarian can find some defensible ground between the absurdity of "blind chance" on the one hand and on the other what Wiggins calls the cosmic unfairness of the determinist's view of these matters? Wiggins thinks there is. He draws our attention to a speculation of Russell's: "It might be that without infringing the laws of physics, intelligence could make improbable things happen, as Maxwell's demon would have defeated the second law of thermo-dynamics by opening the trap door to fast-moving particles and closing it to slow-moving particles."[2] Wiggins sees many problems with the speculation, but he does, nevertheless, draw a glimmer of an idea from it.

> For indeterminism maybe all we really need to imagine or conceive is a world in which (a) there is some macroscopic indeterminacy founded in microscopic indeterminacy, and (b) an appreciable number of the free actions or policies or deliberations of individual agents, although they are not even in principle hypothetico-deductively derivable from antecedent conditions, can be such as to persuade us to fit them into meaningful sequences. We need not trace free actions back to volitions construed as little pushes aimed from outside the physical world. What we must find instead are patterns which are coherent and intelligible in the low level terms of practical deliberation, even though they are not amenable to the kind of generalization or necessity which is the stuff of rigorous theory. (p. 52)

The "low level terms of practical deliberation" are, I take it, the familiar terms of intentional or reason-giving explanation. We typically render actions intelligible by citing their reasons, the beliefs and desires of the agent that render the actions at least marginally reasonable under the circumstances. Wiggins is suggesting then that if we could somehow *make sense* of human actions at the level of intentional explanation, then in spite of the fact that those actions might be physically undetermined, they would not be random. Wiggins invites us to take this possibility seriously, but he has little further to say in elaboration or defense of this. He has said enough, however, to suggest to me a number of ways in which we could give libertarians what they seem to want.

Wiggins asks only that human actions be seen to be *intelligible* in the low-level terms of practical deliberation. Surely if human actions were *predictable* in the low-level terms of practical deliberation, they would be intelligible in those terms. So I propose first to demonstrate that there is a way in which human behavior could be strictly undetermined from the physicist's point of view while at the same time accurately predictable from the intentional level. This demonstration, alas, will be very disappointing, for it relies on a cheap trick and what it establishes can be immediately seen to be quite extraneous to the libertarian's interests. But it is a necessary preamble to what I hope will be a more welcome contribution to the libertarian's cause. So let us get the disappointing preamble behind us.

Here is how a bit of human behavior could be undetermined from the physicist's point of view, but quite clearly predictable by the intentionalist. Suppose we were to build an electronic gadget that I will call an answer box. The answer box is designed to record a person's answers to simple questions. It has two buttons, a Yes button, and a No button, and two foot pedals, a Yes pedal, and a No pedal, all clearly marked. It also has a little display screen divided in half, and on one side it says "use the buttons" and on the other side it says "use the pedals". We design this bit of apparatus so that only one half of this display screen is illuminated at any one time. Once a minute, a radium randomizer determines, in an entirely undetermined way of course, whether the display screen says "use the buttons" or "use the pedals". I now propose the following experiment. First, we draw up a list of ten very simple questions that have Yes or No answers, questions of the order of difficulty of "Do fish swim?" and "Is Texas bigger than Rhode Island?" We seat a subject at the answer box and announce that a handsome reward will be given to those who correctly follow all the experimental instructions, and a bonus will be given to those who answer all our questions correctly.

Now, can the physicist in principle predict the subject's behavior? Let us suppose the subject is in fact a physically deterministic system, and let us suppose further that the physicist has perfect knowledge of the subject's initial state, all the relevant deterministic laws, and all the interactions within the closed situation of the experimental situation. Still, the unpredictable behavior of the answer box will infect the subject on a macroscopic scale with its own indeterminacy on at least ten occasions during the period the physicist must predict. So the best the physicist can do is issue a multiple disjunctive or multiple conditional prediction. Can the intentionalist do any better? Yes, of course. The intentionalist, having read the instructions given to the subject and having sized up the subject as a person of roughly normal intelligence and motivation, and having seen that all the odd numbered questions have Yes answers and the even numbered questions have No answers, confidently predicts that the subject will behave as follows: "The subject will give Yes answers to questions *1, 3, 5, 7,* and *9,* and the subject will answer the rest of the questions in the negative". There are no *if's, or's* or *maybe's* in those predictions. They are categorical and precise—precise enough for instance to appear in a binding contract or satisfy a court of law.

This is, of course, the cheap trick I warned you about. There is no real difference in the predictive power of the two predictors. The intentionalist for instance is no more in a position to predict whether the subject will move finger or foot than the physicist is, and the physicist may well be able to give predictions that are tantamount to the intentionalist's. The physicist may for instance be able to make this prediction: "When question *6* is presented, if the illuminated sign on the box reads use the pedals, the subject's right foot will move at velocity *k* until it depresses the No pedal *n* inches, and if the illuminated sign says use the buttons, the subject's right index finger will trace a trajectory terminating on the No button." Such a prediction is if anything more detailed than the intentionalist's simple prediction of the negative answer to question *6,* and it might in fact be more reliable and better grounded as well. But so what? What we are normally interested in, what we are normally interested in *predicting*, moreover, is not the skeletal motion of human beings but their actions, and the intentionalist can predict the actions of the subject (at least insofar as most of us would take any interest in them) without the elaborate rigmarole and calculations of the physicist. The possibility of indeterminacy in the environment of the kind introduced here, and hence the possibility of indeterminacy in the subject's reaction to that environment, is something with regard to which the intentionalistic predictive power is quite neutral. Still, we could not expect the libertarian to be interested in this variety of undetermined human behavior, behavior that is undetermined simply because the behavior of the answer box, something entirely external to the agent, is undetermined.

Suppose then we move something like the answer box inside the agent. It is a commonplace of action theory that virtually all human actions can be accomplished or realized in a wide variety of ways. There are, for instance, indefinitely many ways of insulting your neighbor, or even of asserting that snow is white. And we are often not much interested, nor should we be, in exactly which particular physical motion accomplishes the act we intend. So let us suppose that our nervous system is so constructed and designed that whenever in the implementation of an intention, our control system is faced with two or more options with regard to which we are non-partisan, a purely undetermined tie-breaking "choice" is made. There you are at the supermarket, wanting a can of Campbell's Tomato Soup, and faced with an array of several hundred identical cans of Campbell's Tomato Soup, all roughly equidistant from your hands. What to do? Before you even waste time and energy pondering this trivial problem, let us suppose, a perfectly random factor determines which can your hand reaches out for. This is of course simply a variation on the ancient theme of Buridan's ass, that unfortunate beast who, finding himself hungry, thirsty and equidistant between food and water, perished for lack of the divine nudge that in a human being accomplishes a truly free choice. This has never been a promising vision of the free choice of responsible agents, if only because it seems to secure freedom for such a small and trivial class of our choices. What does it avail me if I am free to choose *this* can of soup, but not free to choose between buying and stealing it? But however unpromising the idea is as a centerpiece for an account of free will, we must not underestimate its possible scope of application. Such trivial choice points seldom obtrude in our conscious deliberation, no doubt, but they are quite possibly ubiquitous nonetheless at an unconscious level. Whenever we choose to perform an action of a certain sort, there are no doubt slight variations in timing, style and skeletal implementation of those actions that are within our power but beneath our concern. For all we know, which variation occurs is *undetermined*. That is, the implementation of any one of our intentional actions may encounter undetermined *choice points* in many places in the causal chain. The resulting behavior would not be distinguishable to our everyday eyes, or from the point of view of our everyday interests, from behavior that was rigidly determined. What we are mainly interested in, as I said before, are actions, not motions, and what we are normally interested in predicting are actions.

It is worth noting that not only can we typically predict actions from the intentional stance without paying heed to possibly undetermined variations of implementation of these actions, but we can even put together chains of intentional predictions that are relatively immune to such variation. In the summer of 1974 many people were confidently predicting that Nixon would resign. As the day and hour approached, the prediction grew more certain and more specific as to time and place; Nixon would resign not just in the near future, but in the next hour, and in the White House and in the presence of television cameramen and so forth. Still, it was not plausible to claim to know just how he would resign, whether he would resign with grace, or dignity, or with an attack on his critics, whether he would enunciate clearly or mumble or tremble. These details were not readily predictable, but most of the further dependent predictions we were interested in making did not hinge on these subtle variations. However Nixon resigned, we could predict that Goldwater would publicly approve of it, Cronkite would report that Goldwater had so approved of it, Sevareid would comment on it, Rodino would terminate the proceedings of the Judiciary Committee, and Gerald Ford would be sworn in as Nixon's successor. Of course some predictions we might have made at the time would have hinged crucially on particular details of the precise manner of Nixon's resignation, and if these details happened to be undetermined both by Nixon's intentions and by any other feature of the moment, then some human actions of perhaps great importance would be infected by the indeterminacy of Nixon's manner at the moment just as our exemplary subject's behavior was infected by the indeterminacy of the answer box. That would not, however, make these actions any the less intelligible to us as actions.

This result is not just what the libertarian is looking for, but it is a useful result nevertheless. It shows that we can indeed install indeterminism in the internal causal chains affecting human behavior *at the macroscopic level* while preserving the intelligibility of practical deliberation that the libertarian requires. We may have good reasons from other quarters for embracing determinism, but we need not fear that macroscopic indeterminism in human behavior would of necessity rob our lives of intelligibility by producing chaos. Thus, philosophers such as Ayer and Hobart,[3] who argue that free will requires determinism, must be wrong. There are *some* ways our world could be macroscopically indeterministic, without that fact remotely threatening the coherence of the intentionalistic conceptual scheme of action description presupposed by claims of moral responsibility.

Still, it seems that all we have done is install indeterminism in a *harmless* place by installing it in an *irrelevant* place. The libertarian would not be relieved to learn that although his decision to murder his neighbor was quite determined, the style and trajectory of the death blow was not. Clearly, what the libertarian has in mind is indeterminism at some earlier point, prior to the ultimate decision or formation of intention, and unless we can provide that, we will not aid the libertarian's cause. But perhaps we can provide that as well.

Let us return then, to Russell's speculation that intelligence might make improbable things happen. Is there any way that something like this could be accomplished? The idea of intelligence exploiting randomness is not unfamiliar. The poet, Paul Valéry, nicely captures the basic idea:

> It takes two to invent anything. The one makes up combinations; the other one chooses, recognizes what he wishes and what is important to him in the mass of the things which the former has imparted to him. What we call genius is much less the work of the first one than the readiness of the second one to grasp the value of what has been laid before him and to choose it.*

Here we have the suggestion of an intelligent *selection* from what may be a partially arbitrary or chaotic or random *production*, and what we need is the outline of a model for such a process in human decision-making.

An interesting feature of most important human decision-making is that it is made under time pressure. Even if there are, on occasion, algorithmic decision procedures giving guaranteed optimal solutions to our problems, and even if these decision procedures are in principle available to us, we may not have time or energy to utilize them. We are rushed, but moreover, we are all more or less lazy, even about terribly critical decisions that will affect our lives—our own lives, to say nothing of the lives of others. We invariably settle for a *heuristic* decision procedure; we *satisfice*;** we poke around hoping for inspiration; we do our best to think about the problem in a more or less directed way until we must finally stop mulling, summarize our results as best we can, and act. A realistic model of such decision-making just *might* have the following feature: When someone is faced with an important decision, something in him generates a variety of more or less relevant considerations bearing on the decision. Some of these considerations, we may suppose, are determined to be generated, but others may be non-deterministically generated. For instance, Jones, who is finishing her dissertation on Aristotle and the practical syllogism, must decide within a week whether to accept the assistant

---

*Quoted by Jacques Hadamard, in *The Psychology of Invention in the Mathematical Field*, Princeton University Press, 1949, p. 30. I discuss the implications of Valéry's claim in Chapter 5.
**The term is Herbert Simon's. See his *The Sciences of the Artificial* (1969) for a review of the concept.

professorship at the University of Chicago, or the assistant professorship at Swarthmore. She considers the difference in salaries, the probable quality of the students, the quality of her colleagues, the teaching load, the location of the schools, and so forth. Let us suppose that considerations A, B, C, D, E, and F occur to her and that those are the only considerations that occur to her, and that on the basis of those, she decides to accept the job at Swarthmore. She does this *knowing* of course that she could devote more time and energy to this deliberation, could cast about for other relevant considerations, could perhaps dismiss some of A-F as being relatively unimportant and so forth, but being no more meticulous, no more obsessive, than the rest of us about such matters, she settles for the considerations that have occurred to her and makes her decision.

Let us suppose though, that after sealing her fate with a phone call, consideration G occurs to her, and she says to herself: "If only G had occurred to me before, I would certainly have chosen the University of Chicago instead, but G didn't occur to me". Now it just might be the case that *exactly* which considerations occur to one in such circumstances is to some degree strictly undetermined. If that were the case, then even the intentionalist, knowing everything knowable about Jones' settled beliefs and preferences and desires, might nevertheless be unable to predict her decision, except perhaps conditionally. The intentionalist might be able to argue as follows: "If considerations A-F occur to Jones, then she will go Swarthmore," and this would be a prediction that would be grounded on a rational argument based on considerations A-F according to which Swarthmore was the best place to go. The intentionalist might go on to add, however, that if consideration G also occurs to Jones (which is strictly unpredictable unless we interfere and draw Jones' attention to G), Jones will choose the University of Chicago instead. Notice that although we are supposing that the decision is in this way strictly unpredictable except conditionally by the intentionalist, whichever choice Jones makes is retrospectively intelligible. There will be a rationale for the decision in either case; in the former case a rational argument in favor of Swarthmore based on A-F, and in the latter case, a rational argument in favor of Chicago, based on A-G. (There may, of course be yet another rational argument based on A-H, or I, or J, in favor of Swarthmore, or in favor of going on welfare, or in favor of suicide.) Even if *in principle* we couldn't predict which of many rationales could ultimately be correctly cited in justification or retrospective explanation of the choice made by Jones, we could be confident that there would be some sincere, authentic, and not unintelligible rationale to discover.

The model of decision making I am proposing has the following feature: when we are faced with an important decision, a consideration-generator whose output is to some degree undetermined produces a series of considerations, some of which may of course be immediately rejected as irrelevant by the agent (consciously or unconsciously). Those considerations that are selected by the agent as having a more than negligible bearing on the decision then figure in a reasoning process, and if the agent is in the main reasonable, those considerations ultimately serve as predictors and explicators of the agent's final decision. What can be said in favor of such a model, bearing in mind that there are many possible substantive variations on the basic theme?

First, I think it captures what Russell was looking for. The intelligent selection, rejection and weighting of the considerations that do occur to the subject is a matter of intelligence making the difference. Intelligence makes the difference here because an intelligent selection and assessment procedure determines which microscopic indeterminacies get amplified, as it were, into important macroscopic determiners of ultimate behavior.

Second, I think it installs indeterminism in the right place for the libertarian, if there is a right place at all. The libertarian could not have wanted to place the indeterminism *at the end* of the agent's assessment and deliberation. It would be insane to hope that after all rational deliberation had terminated with an assessment of the best available course of action, indeterminism would then intervene to flip the coin before action. It is a familiar theme in discussions of free will that the important claim that one could have done otherwise under the circumstances is not plausibly construed as the claim that one could have done otherwise given *exactly* the set of convictions and desires that prevailed at the end of rational deliberation. So if there is to be a crucial undetermined nexus, it had better be prior to the final assessment of the considerations on the stage, which is right where we have located it.

Third, I think that the model is recommended by considerations that have little or nothing to do with the free will problem. It may well turn out to be that from the point of view of biological engineering, it is just more efficient and in the end more rational that decision-making should occur in this way. Time rushes on, and people must act, and there may not be time for a person to canvass all his beliefs, conduct all the investigations and experiments that he would see were relevant, assess every preference in his stock before acting, and it may be that the best way to prevent the inertia of Hamlet from overtaking us is for our decision-making processes to be expedited by a process of partially random generation and test. Even in the rare circumstances where we know there is, say, a decision procedure for determining the optimal solution to a decision problem, it is often more reasonable to proceed swiftly and by heuristic methods, and this strategic principle may in fact be incorporated as a design principle at a fairly fundamental level of cognitive-conative organization.

A fourth observation in favor of the model is that it permits moral education to make a difference, without making all of the difference. A familiar argument against the libertarian is that if our moral decisions were not in fact determined by our moral upbringing, or our moral education, there would be no point in providing such an education for the young. The libertarian who adopted our model could answer that a moral education, while not completely determining the generation of considerations and moral decision-making, can nevertheless have a prior selective effect on the sorts of considerations that will occur. A moral education, like mutual discussion and persuasion generally, could adjust the boundaries and probabilities of the generator without rendering it deterministic.

Fifth—and I think this is perhaps the most important thing to be said in favor of this model—it provides some account of our important intuition that we are the authors of our moral decisions. The unreflective compatibilist is apt to view decision-making on the model of a simple balance or scale on which the pros and cons of action are piled. What gets put on the scale is determined by one's nature and one's nurture, and once all the weights are placed, gravity as it were determines which way the scale will tip, and hence determines which way we will act. On such a view, the agent does not seem in any sense to be the author of the decisions, but at best merely the locus at which the environmental and genetic factors bearing on him interact to produce a decision. It all looks terribly mechanical and inevitable, and seems to leave no room for creativity or genius. The model proposed, however, holds out the promise of a distinction between authorship and mere implication in a causal chain.*

Consider in this light the difference between completing a lengthy exercise in long division and constructing a proof in, say, Euclidian geometry. There is a sense in which I can be the author of a particular bit of long division, and can take credit if it turns out to be correct, and can take pride in it as well, but there is a stronger sense in which I

---

*Cf. the suggestive discussion of genius in Kant's *Critique of Judgment*, Sections 46, 47.

can claim authorship of a proof in geometry, even if thousands of school children before me have produced the very same proof. There is a sense in which this is something original that I have created. To take pride in one's *computational accuracy* is one thing, and to take pride in one's *inventiveness* is another, and as Valéry claimed, the essence of invention is the intelligent selection from among randomly generated candidates. I think that the sense in which we wish to claim authorship of our moral decisions, and hence claim responsibility for them, requires that we view them as products of intelligent invention, and not merely the results of an assiduous application of formulae. I don't want to overstate this case; certainly many of the decisions we make are so obvious, so black and white, that no one would dream of claiming any special creativity in having made them and yet would still claim complete responsibility for the decisions thus rendered. But if we viewed all our decision-making on those lines, I think our sense of our dignity as moral agents would be considerably impoverished.

Finally, the model I propose points to the multiplicity of decisions that encircle our moral decisions and suggests that in many cases our ultimate decision as to which way to act is less important phenomenologically as a contributor to our sense of free will than the prior decisions affecting our deliberation process itself: the decision, for instance, not to consider any further, to terminate deliberation; or the decision to ignore certain lines of inquiry.

These prior and subsidiary decisions contribute, I think, to our sense of ourselves as responsible free agents, roughly in the following way: I am faced with an important decision to make, and after a certain amount of deliberation, I say to myself: "That's enough. I've considered this matter enough and now I'm going to act," in the full knowledge that I could have considered further, in the full knowledge that the eventualities may prove that I decided in error, but with the acceptance of responsibility in any case.

I have recounted six recommendations for the suggestion that human decision-making involves a non-deterministic generate-and-test procedure. First, it captures whatever is compelling in Russell's hunch. Second, it installs determinism in the only plausible locus for libertarianism (something we have established by a process of elimination). Third, it makes sense from the point of view of strategies of biological engineering. Fourth, it provides a flexible justification of moral education. Fifth, it accounts at least in part for our sense of authorship of our decisions. Sixth, it acknowledges and explains the importance of decisions internal to the deliberation process. It is embarrassing to note, however, that the very feature of the model that inspired its promulgation is *apparently* either gratuitous or misdescribed or both, and that is the causal indeterminacy of the generator. We have been supposing, for the sake of the libertarian, that the process that generates considerations for our assessment generates them at least in part by a physically or causally undetermined or random process. But here we seem to be trading on yet another imprecision or ambiguity in the word "random". When a system designer or programmer relies on a "random" generation process, it is not a *physically undetermined* process that is required, but simply a *patternless* process. Computers are typically equipped with a random number generator, but the process that generates the sequence is a perfectly deterministic and determinate process. If it is a good random number generator (and designing one is extraordinarily difficult, it turns out) the sequence will be locally and globally patternless. There will be a complete absence of regularities on which to base predictions about unexamined portions of the sequence.

Isn't it the case that the new improved proposed model for human deliberation can do as well with a random-but-deterministic generation process as with a causally undetermined process? Suppose that to the extent that the considerations that occur to me are unpredictable, they are unpredictable simply because they are fortuitously determined by some arbitrary and irrelevant factors, such as the location of the planets or what I had for breakfast. It appears that this alternative supposition diminishes not one whit the plausibility or utility of the model that I have proposed. Have we in fact given the libertarians what they really want without giving them indeterminism? Perhaps. We have given the libertarians the materials out of which to construct an account of personal authorship of moral decisions, and this is something that the compatibilistic views have never handled well. But something else has emerged as well. Just as the presence or absence of macroscopic indeterminism in the implementation style of intentional actions turned out to be something essentially undetectable from the vantage point of our *Lebenswelt*, a feature with no significant repercussions in the "manifest image", to use Sellars' term, so the rival descriptions of the consideration generator, as random-but-causally-deterministic *versus* random-and-causally-*in*deterministic, will have no clearly testable and contrary implications at the level of micro-neuro-physiology, even if we succeed beyond our most optimistic fantasies in mapping deliberation processes onto neural activity.

That fact does not refute libertarianism, or even discredit the motivation behind it, for what it shows once again is that we need not fear that causal indeterminism would make our lives unintelligible. There may not be compelling grounds from *this* quarter for favoring an indeterministic vision of the springs of our action, but if considerations from other quarters favor indeterminism, we can at least be fairly sanguine about the prospects of incorporating indeterminism into our picture of deliberation, even if we cannot yet see what point such an incorporation would have. Wiggins speaks of the cosmic unfairness of determinism, and I do not think the considerations raised here do much to allay our worries about *that*. Even if one embraces the sort of view I have outlined, the deterministic view of the unbranching and inexorable history of the universe can inspire terror or despair, and perhaps the libertarian is right that there is no way to allay these feelings short of a brute denial of determinism. Perhaps such a denial, and only such a denial, would permit us to make sense of the notion that our actual lives are created by us over time out of possibilities that exist in virtue of our earlier decisions; that we trace a path through a branching maze that both defines who we are, and why, to some extent (if we are fortunate enough to maintain against all vicissitudes the integrity of our deliberational machinery) we are *responsible* for being who we are. That prospect deserves an investigation of its own. All I hope to have shown here is that it is a prospect we can and should take seriously.

16

How to Change Your Mind

Annette Baier claims* that we can discover something important
about the mind, something overlooked or denied in recent accounts,
by examining a particular sort of episode in the natural history of
minds, the sort of episode ordinarily called a *change of mind*. We can,
she says, see more clearly what does and does not count as a *mind* by
seeing what does and does not count as a change of mind. We can
understand thought by understanding second thoughts. I propose to
extend her analysis of change of mind, to do some very impression-
istic theory sketching and speculating, and in the process try to provide at least a partial explanation for some of her observations about
the nature of change of mind.

Baier's contention is that there is an important distinction to be
drawn between those of us who can change our minds and other intelligent creatures. The conviction that *some* such distinction is to be
made is shared by several philosophers whose claims have long tempted me, without converting me until now. Norman Malcolm, in his
APA Presidential Address of 1972, "Thoughtless Brutes", claimed
that there was an oft-neglected distinction between *thinking that p*
and *having the thought that p*; a dog may think a squirrel is up the
tree, Malcolm allows, and this may explain its barking where it does,
but it would be wrong, Malcolm thinks, to suppose the dog has the
thought that the squirrel is up the tree. Thoughts *occur* to people, but

*This chapter was prepared as a reply to an early draft of Annette Baier's "Change
of Mind", delivered at the Chapel Hill Colloquium, October 16, 1977. The references in it to Baier's essay do not prevent it from being understood by itself, or
better yet it can be read as an introduction to Baier's subsequent version of
"Change of Mind" (forthcoming).

not to dogs. I think this is on the right track, or almost on the right track, and with help and inspiration from Baier, I will try to locate and travel down the *better* track.

Ronald de Sousa, in a fascinating paper, "How to give a piece of your mind: or, the logic of belief and assent", argues that we should distinguish sharply between what he calls *belief* and *assent*.* Belief, on his view, is a sort of lower, less intellectual phenomenon; it forms the dispositional foundation for the fancier phenomenon, assent, which is restricted to human beings. I think he is closer to the truth than Malcolm. Putting de Sousa's ideas together with Baier's seems to me to produce one of those mutual illuminations that gives off more than twice the light of the parts taken separately.

First we must recognize, as Baier says, that not every alteration in "cognitive state" is a change of mind. You were not born knowing that turtles can't fly, it almost certainly never *occurred* to you before this moment, but it is hardly news to you. You already knew it, but were not born knowing it, so there was some cognitive change in you in the interim; it was not a case of changing your mind, that's for sure. Many other cognitive alterations are harder to distinguish from our targets, changes of mind, but Baier suggests that it will help if we look at the clearest cases: where one changes one's mind or makes up one's mind about *what to do*—the practical cases. I think she is right to point to these cases, for more reasons than she gives. I want to get at this rather indirectly by looking at a different distinction between types of cognitive transition. Consider for a moment the transition between what tradition would call *de dicto* or *notional* desire and *de re* or *relational* desire. As Quine memorably puts it, when one *wants a sloop* in the former, notional sense, one's desire does not link one to any particular boat; what one wants is mere *relief from slooplessness*. This is to be contrasted with wanting *de re that* sloop, *Courageous*, the sloop tied up at the slip.

Now suppose I am in the former state, as in fact I often have been. Suppose I am *in the market* for a sloop. Now let us see what happens if I pass from that state into the presumed state of desire *de re*. I start out wanting something much more specific that mere relief from slooplessness, of course. I want relief from 32-to-36-foot-wooden-

---

Review of Metaphysics, XXV (1971): 52–79. There is a terminological problem in de Sousa's paper that I am going to pretend is not there. To evade exegetical problems I will claim that de Sousa says things he doesn't quite say—but might agree with. Forwarned that my account of his paper is distorted, everyone should read it and see for themselves. Everyone should read it anyway, since it is an important paper, containing many more insights than I discuss here.

diesel-auxilliary-spinnaker-rigged-slooplessness. And this is what I tell
the boat broker. I give him a list of requirements. I want a sloop that
is *F, G, H, I, J*, etc. My list is finite, but if I am wise I don't declare
it to be unrevisably complete when I give it to him. For suppose he
then says: "I know just the boat *you want*; you want the *Molly B*,
here." The *Molly B* is a sloop that is *F, G, H, I, J*, etc. Of course the
salesman is pushing when he says this. He must mean I *will* want the
Molly B when I see it. Certainly it doesn't follow from the fit between
my requirement and the boat that I am already in a state of relational
desire for it. I may have neglected to mention or even reflect upon the
color of the boat I want, and if the *Molly B* is painted purple, this may
suffice to keep me out of the *de re* state. On seeing the purple *Molly
B*, I add, like Tigger: "Well, *not being purple* was really one of my
tacit requirements." The boat broker sets out again with a clearer
sense of what I desire *de dicto*. But even if the yacht he then presents
me with is exactly what I had in mind, even if when I examine it I can
find no disqualifying features, there is still a motion of the mind that
must happen, and this is just what the broker tries so resourcefully to
evoke in me. He's got to get me to plump for it, to declare my love, to
sign on the line. What he wants to stimulate in me though is not
correctly viewed, I submit, as a change of desire or wanting. What he
wants to stimulate in me is a *choosing*, a decision to opt for something. Once I have opted, in fact, I may get cold feet about the whole
deal. Desire may drain out of me. Having made up my mind, not to
desire the boat but to *buy* it, I may begin having second thoughts.
But having second thoughts in this sense is not changing my mind.
That happens only if I back out of the deal and renege on a contract.
Now several features of this special case seem to me to bear importantly on the general issue of change of mind.

First, in such a case my decision to buy the boat or not is not
logically tied to the grounds on which it is made in the way that,
arguably, other cognitive states and events can be logically tied. That
is, there may be a rule requiring me to attribute to you a disbelief that
not-p, if I attribute to you a belief that *p*. But there is nothing incoherent or logically odd about the description of me as desiring *de
dicto* a sloop that is *F, G, H, I, J*, and not desiring *de re*, the *Molly B*,
which I even *believe* to be *F, G, H, I, J*. Moreover it is least not obvious that in such a state I always warrant criticism. It is not obvious
that I am clearly irrational. My bullheadedness or caution may in fact
be a highly useful and adaptive feature of my cognitive make-up. More
important to our concerns, I think, is the fact that although opting
for the boat or not is *my* decision, it is something *I do*, I don't know

in the end why I do it, what causes me to do it. I am not in a privileged position to tell someone else *exactly* what prevented me from opting if I refrain or what tipped the balance if I buy. In this matter, my decision is the occasion of the discovery I make about myself. It is in this domain that E. M. Forster's marvelous remark draws our attention to a truth. He once asked: "How can I tell what I think until I see what I say?"

The distinction between *de re* and *de dicto* propositional attitudes is a vexed one. I am in fact quite inclined to believe that nothing real or worth talking about deserves to be called either a *de re* belief or a *de re* desire. But that is a topic for another time. What interests me here is just that the case I've described of moving from *de dicto* desire to an opting, a choice, has certain features in common with other nonconative cases of making up one's mind. This decision is first of all an act, an exemplary case of doing something that has consequences for which one may be held responsible. Moreover, it bears the marks of freedom, such as they are. (I discuss these in Chapters 5 and 15.) Here, what is important is just that it is a choice point that terminates a process of deliberation or consideration that is not apparently algorithmic, but rather at best heuristic. At some point, we just stop deliberating. We take one last look at the pros and cons, and leap. As Baier says, the changes of belief that are cut and dried, the mere corrections having no taint of uncertainty, are not changes of mind.

Another important feature to note in our boat-buying example is that the result or product of this episode of choice is not the same sort of thing as the "raw material". Although my opting arises from and is ultimately explained by my desires, it is not a desire, but a choice, and the state it initiates is not a state of desire, but of *commitment to acquire* or something like that. This point sets the stage for de Sousa's claims, for the parallel remark to make regarding all cases of making up or changing one's mind is that changes of mind are a species of judgment, and while such judgments arise from beliefs and are ultimately to be explained by one's beliefs, such judgments themselves are *not* beliefs—when such judgments are called occurrent or episodic beliefs, this is a serious misnomer—but *acts*, and these acts initiate states that are also not states of belief, but of something rather like commitment, rather like ownership. I trust it sounds at least faintly paradoxical to claim that when I change my mind or make up my mind, the result is not a new belief at all, but this is just what I want to maintain, and so does de Sousa. He calls such judgings "assenting", but is then left with no good term for the products of assent, the states one enters into as a result of such judging. I suggest that we would do quite well by ordinary usage if we called these states *opinions*, and hence sharply distinguished opinions from beliefs. Then we can immediately extend Malcolm's train of thought in this way: animals may have *beliefs* about this and that, but they don't have *opinions*. They don't have opinions because they don't *assent*. Making up your mind is coming to have an opinion, I am proposing, and changing one's mind is changing one's opinion. Here is what de Sousa says (roughly) about the relationship between belief and assent (or now: opinion). On some theories of belief, he notes, the belief that *p* is considered to admit of degree. One believes .9 that *p* and so believes .1 that *not-p*. Bayesian accounts have this feature, for instance. Other accounts of belief—he calls them classical accounts—treat belief as all or nothing. One believes flat out that *p* and hence disbelieves flat out that *not-p*. Now de Sousa's interesting suggestion is that there ought to be no quarrel to adjudicate here, that the intuitions that support the latter variety of theory are not to be dismissed or overridden by intuitions that support the former. We should simply view the latter intuitions as about a different category of mental state, the state of assent, i.e., opinion, not belief. So de Sousa proposes a two-level theory for human beings (and other persons if such there be). We human beings are believers, as are the beasts. But moreover (and here he is echoing Hume, as we learn from Baier) we harbor epistemic desires. We are collecters, he says, of true sentences. We have a hunger for such items, which we add to our collections by what he calls "*a bet on truth alone*, solely determined by epistemic desirabilities". He is careful to say that there is an analogy only, but a strong one, between betting and assenting. Now when a gambler bets, his wagers, if he is rational, are a function of the subjective probability of the outcome for him and the desirability of the payoff, or at least that's the Bayesian line. This Bayesian line is applied or exploited by de Sousa to explain (or at least predict statistically) the acts of assent we will make given our animal-level beliefs and desires. We are equipped first with animal-type belief and desire, which behave in Bayesian fashion, and which explain our proclivity to make these leaps of assent, to act, to bet on the truth of various sentences.

Now of course subjective probabilities and degrees of desirability are not in any sense introspectable features of our beliefs or desires. That's why we can't calculate, on the basis of introspected data, a Bayesian prediction about *what we will decide*. We must wait and see what we decide. Some observant Bayesian psychologist might attribute weighted beliefs and desires to us, and on this basis predict our decisions; we might endorse those predictions, but not from any *privileged* position. (By the way, it seems to me that this fact about non-introspectable subjective probabilities has an important and damaging implication for epistemological doctrines that pretend to enunciate principles about *what one ought to believe* when one believes such and such with subjective probability k, as if they were giving us rules for the regulation of the understanding that we could actually attempt to follow.)

What is the role of language in the difference between belief and opinion? I'll suggest a few sketchy points. Belief, the lower brutish state, is best considered divorced from language. Robert Stalnaker suggests in "Propositions"[1] that for the purposes of cognitive psychology, the task of which is to explain the behavior of both beast and man in terms of beliefs and desires, the objects of belief should be viewed as propositions, because the identity of propositions can be fixed, not by their being tied closely or even indirectly to sentences of a particular language, but by reference to the selective function of the state of belief in determining behavior. We want a way of speaking of this selective function that abstracts from particular languages. Fortunately, a manner of speaking is available: we say that a particular belief is a function taking possible worlds into truth values.

First, the functional account, as a theory of rational action, already contains implicitly an intuitive notion of alternative possible courses of events. The picture of a rational agent deliberating is a picture of a man who considers various alternative possible futures, knowing that the one to become actual depends in part on his choice of action. The function of desire is simply to divide these alternative courses of events into the ones to be sought and the ones to be avoided, or in more sophisticated versions of the theory, to provide an ordering or measure of the alternative possibilities with respect to their desirability. The function of belief is simply to determine which are the relevant alternative possible situations, or in more sophisticated versions of the theory, to rank them with respect to their probability under various conditions of becoming actual.

If this is right, then the identity conditions for the objects for desire and belief are correctly determined by the possible-world account of propositions. That is, two sentences P and Q express the same proposition from the point of view of the possible-world theory if and only if a belief or desire that P necessarily functions exactly like a belief or desire that Q in the determination of any rational action. (p. 81).

Propositions thus viewed, Stalnaker observes, have no syntax, or structure, and this fits our intuitions about *belief* so long as we keep belief firmly distinguished from opinion. Philosophers are forever taking as examples of belief such things as:

Tom believes that Don Larson pitched the only perfect game in World Series history

an example par excellence of a *sentence collected as true* by Tom, not a belief in the basic sense at all.

Now why do we have opinions at all? And why do we have them while animals don't? Because we have language. I think the way to look at it is this: once you have a language, there are all these sentences lying around, and you have to do something with them. You have to put them in boxes labeled "True" and "False" for one thing. In Chapter 3 (p. 47) I discuss an example from Chekhov's *Three Sisters*. Tchebutykin is reading a newspaper and he mutters (*a propos* of nothing, apparently), "Balzac was married in Berditchev," and repeats it, saying he must make a note of it. Irina repeats it. Now did Tchebutykin believe it? Did Irina? One thing I know is that I have never forgotten the sentence. Without much conviction, I'd bet on its truth if the stakes were right, if I were on a quiz show for instance. Now my state with regard to this sentence is radically unlike my current state of perceptual belief, a state utterly unformulated into sentences or sentence-like things so far as common sense or introspection or casual analysis can tell. (That is, what the ultimate cognitive psychology might discover about the machinery of my information processing system is only very indirectly tied to this.)

Now then, what are the problems with the view that I have been sketching here, in my headlong rush to theory? Well, one might claim that de Sousa and I have got the whole matter completely backwards. I agree with de Sousa that the realm of opinion is where the classical, all-or-nothing notion of belief really belongs, but isn't it in fact our "intellectual" *opinions* that are *most* amenable to treatment in terms of degrees of confidence? I think this objection springs from an illusion. Remember my opting for the *Molly B*. My desire for this craft may subsequently wane following my decision to buy it. Similarly, my happiness with my own opinions may increase and diminish, but they are nevertheless the opinions I am *committed* to unless I change my mind. I may express or exhibit less confidence in them, while not relinquishing them. Most importantly, I may fail to act on them as I would were my conviction unflagging. It is my beliefs and desires that predict my behavior *directly*. My opinions can be relied on to predict my behavior only to the degree, normally large, that my opinions and beliefs are in rational correspondence, i.e., roughly as Bayes would have them. It is just this feature of the distinction between opinion and belief that gives us, I think, the first steps of an acceptable account of those twin puzzles, self-deception and *akrasia* or weakness of will. Animals, I submit, whatever their cognitive and conative frailties, are immune to both self-deception and akrasia. Why? Because they have only beliefs, not opinions, and *part* of what is true when one exhibits either of these normal pathologies, self-deception or weakness of will (I think they may be just one affliction in the end), is that one *behaves* one way while *judging* another. One's behavior is consonant with one's beliefs "automatically", for that is how in the end we individuate beliefs and actions. It is only because we have among our acts *acts of deeming true, acts of assent*, that these afflictions have a domain in which to operate.

There seems to be another problem with this account. I believe that Don Larson pitched the only perfect game in World Series history. My account would require that since this is one of those sentences latched onto and deemed true, it should count as an *opinion*, and not a belief, yet it doesn't ring in the ear as ordinary usage to say that it is one of my opinions. It is not something, as Baier would point out, that I've *made up my mind about*. I think that's right. It isn't something I've made up my mind about. I think the way to handle such cases is dictated by considerations raised by de Sousa and also by Baier. Many sentences that are candidates for acquisition into my collection of truths are not at all dubious under the circumstances in which they first occur as candidates. This sentence about Don Larsen is surely one of them. No heuristic, informal deliberation or consideration or tea-leaf gazing is required as a prelude to their acceptance. But that is just to say that there are *sure bets*. The outcome is so expectable and the stakes are so favorable, that they hardly count as bets at all. Recall the professional card player who says: "Oh I bet, but I never gamble."

There are in any case many ways of adding to one's collection of opinions, just as there are many ways of acquiring paintings or overcoats.* One can inherit them, fall into possession of them without noticing, fail to discard them after deciding to discard them, take them on temporary loan and forget that this is what one has done. For instance, one's verbal indoctrination as a child—as an adult too—certainly has among its effects the inculcation of many ill-considered *dicta* one will be willing to parade as true though one has never exam-

---

*Amelie Rorty provided many of the ideas in this paragraph.

ined them. Habits of thought tied to well-turned phrases may persist long after one has denied the relevant assertions. One may suspend disbelief in a few enabling assumptions "for the sake of argument", and become so engrossed in the argument that one forgets one has done this. Years later one may still be suspending disbelief in those assumptions—for no reason at all, save reasons that have lapsed in the interim. Losing is not discarding, and forgetting is not changing one's mind, but it is a way of divesting oneself of an opinion. Why is Saul's conversion on the road to Damascus not a change of mind? Ordinary language gives us a hint. His mind changes all right, but *he* doesn't change it; it is changed for him. It is not an act of his.

Baier points to the role of *other critics* in changing one's mind, and claims it is important to recognize this role. Why are critics important? Because one changes one's own mind the way one changes somebody else's: by an actual colloquy or soliloquy of persuasion (see Chapter 14). Note that in such an enterprise there can be success, or failure, or an intermediate result between success and failure. Understanding these intermediate results is important to understanding self-deception and *akrasia*. Surely the following has happened to you—it has happened to me many times: somebody corners me and proceeds to present me with an argument of great persuasiveness, of *irresistible* logic, step by step by step. I can think of nothing to say against any of the steps. I get to the conclusion and can think of *no reasons* to deny the conclusion, *but I don't believe it!* This can be a social problem. It is worse than unsatisfying to say: "Sorry, I don't believe it, but I can't tell you why. I don't know." You might, depending on the circumstances, lie a little bit, nod and assent publicly while keeping your private disbelief to yourself, and it might not always be a craven or vicious thing to do. But I suggest that there is another thing that could happen. Genuine (de Sousian) assent, *inner* assent if you like, can be wrung from you by such an argument so that the conclusion does become one of your *opinions—but you don't believe it.* This is what happens, I think, when you follow an argument whose conclusion is that all things considered cigarette smoking is harmful, acquiesce in the conclusion ("Yes indeed, that conclusion falls in the set of true sentences."), and then light up another cigarette. The *gap* that must be located one place or another is any account of weakness of will is between what one has been provoked or goaded or enticed into *judging* (quite sincerely) by such an act of persuasion (which might be self-persuasion), and one's deeper behavior-disposing states—one's beliefs. As many accounts would have it, weakness of will is exhibited when one acts intentionally against one's better *judgment*, a claim that can be saved from incoherence if we distinguish sharply between such judgment and belief.

To return to an issue raised at the outset, is the ordinary distinction between changes of mind and other cognitive shifts an important distinction? Yes. It is very important, for only a theory of mind that makes change of mind and the resulting opinions a salient category can begin to account for self-deception and *akrasia*, two phenomena that are not just cognitive pathologies, but moral pathologies as well. If we are to explain how a person can be a moral agent, we must first grant that it is of the essence of personhood that a person can change his mind.

17

Where Am I?

Now that I've won my suit under the Freedom of Information Act, I am at liberty to reveal for the first time a curious episode in my life that may be of interest not only to those engaged in research in the philosophy of mind, artificial intelligence and neuroscience but also to the general public.

Several years ago I was approached by Pentagon officials who asked me to volunteer for a highly dangerous and secret mission. In collaboration with NASA and Howard Hughes, the Department of Defense was spending billions to develop a Supersonic Tunneling Underground Device, or STUD. It was supposed to tunnel through the earth's core at great speed and deliver a specially designed atomic warhead "right up the Red's missile silos," as one of the Pentagon brass put it.

The problem was that in an early test they had succeeded in lodging a warhead about a mile deep under Tulsa, Oklahoma, and they wanted me to retrieve it for them. "Why me? " I asked. Well, the mission involved some pioneering applications of current brain research, and they had heard of my interest in brains and of course my Faustian curiosity and great courage and so forth. . . . Well, how could I refuse? The difficulty that brought the Pentagon to my door was that the device I'd been asked to recover was fiercely radioactive, in a new way. According to monitoring instruments, something about the nature of the device and its complex interactions with pockets of material deep in the earth had produced radiation that could cause severe abnormalities in certain tissues of the brain. No way had been found to shield the brain from these deadly rays, which were apparently harmless to other tissues and organs of the body. So it had been decided that the person sent to recover the device should *leave his brain behind*. It would be kept in a safe place where it could execute its normal control functions by elaborate radio links. Would I submit to a surgical procedure that would completely remove my brain, which would then be placed in a life-support system at the Manned Spacecraft Center in Houston? Each input and output pathway, as it was severed, would be restored by a pair of microminiaturized radio transceivers, one attached precisely to the brain, the other to the nerve stumps in the empty cranium. No information would be lost, all the connectivity would be preserved. At first I was a bit reluctant. Would it really work? The Houston brain surgeons encouraged me. "Think of it," they said, "as a mere *stretching* of the nerves. If your brain were just moved over an *inch* in your skull, that would not alter or impair your mind. We're simply going to make the nerves indefinitely elastic by splicing radio links into them."

I was shown around the life-support lab in Houston and saw the sparkling new vat in which my brain would be placed, were I to agree. I met the large and brilliant support team of neurologists, hematologists, biophysicists, and electrical engineers, and after several days of discussions and demonstrations, I agreed to give it a try. I was subjected to an enormous array of blood tests, brain scans, experiments, interviews, and the like. They took down my autobiography at great length, recorded tedious lists of my beliefs, hopes, fears, and tastes. They even listed my favorite stereo recordings and gave me a crash session of psychoanalysis.

The day for surgery arrived at last and of course I was anesthetized and remember nothing of the operation itself. When I came out of anesthesia, I opened my eyes, looked around, and asked the inevitable, the traditional, the lamentably hackneyed post-operative question: "Where am I?" The nurse smiled down at me. "You're in Houston," she said, and I reflected that this still had a good chance of being the truth one way or another. She handed me a mirror. Sure enough, there were the tiny antennae poking up through their titanium ports cemented into my skull.

"I gather the operation was a success," I said, "I want to go see my brain." They led me (I was a bit dizzy and unsteady) down a long corridor and into the life-support lab. A cheer went up from the assembled support team, and I responded with what I hoped was a jaunty salute. Still feeling lightheaded, I was helped over to the life-support vat. I peered through the glass. There, floating in what looked like ginger-ale, was undeniably a human brain, though it was almost covered with printed circuit chips, plastic tubules, electrodes, and other paraphernalia. "Is that mine?" I asked. "Hit the output transmitter switch there on the side of the vat and see for yourself," the project director replied. I moved the switch to OFF, and immediately slumped, groggy and nauseated, into the arms of the technicians, one of whom kindly restored the switch to its ON position. While I recovered my equilibrium and composure, I thought to myself: "Well, here I am, sitting on a folding chair, staring through a piece of plate glass at my own brain. . . . But wait," I said to myself, "shouldn't I have thought, 'Here I am, suspended in a bubbling fluid, being stared at by my own eyes'?" I tried to think this latter thought. I tried to project it into the tank, offering it hopefully to my brain, but I failed to carry off the exercise with any conviction. I tried again. "Here am *I*, Daniel Dennett, suspended in a bubbling fluid, being stared at by my own eyes." No, it just didn't work. Most puzzling and confusing. Being a philosopher of firm physicalist conviction, I believed unswervingly that the tokening of my thoughts was occurring somewhere in my brain: yet, when I thought "Here I am," where the thought occurred to me was *here*, outside the vat, where I, Dennett, was standing staring at my brain.

I tried and tried to think myself into the vat, but to no avail. I tried to build up to the task by doing mental exercises. I thought to myself, "The sun is shining *over there*," five times in rapid succession, each time mentally ostending a different place: in order, the sun-lit corner of the lab, the visible front lawn of the hospital, Houston, Mars, and Jupiter. I found I had little difficulty in getting my "there's" to hop all over the celestial map with their proper references. I could loft a "there" in an instant through the farthest reaches of space, and then aim the next "there" with pinpoint accuracy at the upper left quadrant of a freckle on my arm. Why was I having such trouble with "here"? "Here in Houston" worked well enough, and so did "here in the lab," and even "here in this part of the lab," but "here in the vat" always seemed merely an unmeant mental mouthing. I tried closing my eyes while thinking it. This seemed to help, but still I couldn't manage to pull it off, except perhaps for a fleeting instant. I couldn't be sure. The discovery that I couldn't be sure was also unsettling. How did I know *where* I meant by "here" when I thought "here"? Could I *think* I meant one place when in fact I meant another? I didn't see how that could be admitted without untying the few bonds of intimacy between a person and his own mental life that had survived the onslaught of the brain scientists and philosophers, the physicalists and behaviorists. Perhaps I was incorrigible about where I *meant* when I said "here." But in my present circumstances it seemed that either I was doomed by sheer force of mental habit to thinking systematically false indexical thoughts, or where a person is (and hence where his thoughts are tokened for purposes of semantic analysis) is not necessarily where his brain, the physical seat of his soul, resides. Nagged by confusion, I attempted to orient myself by falling back on a favorite philosopher's ploy. I began naming things.

"Yorick," I said aloud to my brain, "you are my brain. The rest of my body, seated in this chair, I dub 'Hamlet.'" So here we all are: Yorick's my brain, Hamlet's my body, and I am Dennett. *Now*, where am I? And when I think "where am I?" where's that thought tokened? Is it tokened in my brain, lounging about in the vat, or right here between my ears where it *seems* to be tokened? Or nowhere? Its *temporal* coordinates give me no trouble; must it not have spatial coordinates as well? I began making a list of the alternatives.

(1) *Where Hamlet goes, there goes Dennett.* This principle was easily refuted by appeal to the familiar brain transplant thought-experiments so enjoyed by philosophers. If Tom and Dick switch brains, Tom is the fellow with Dick's former body—just ask him; he'll claim to be Tom, and tell you the most intimate details of Tom's autobiography. It was clear enough, then, that my current body and I could part company, but not likely that I could be separated from my brain. The rule of thumb that emerged so plainly from the thought experiments was that in a brain-transplant operation, one wanted to be the *donor*, not the recipient. Better to call such an operation a *body*-transplant, in fact. So perhaps the truth was,

(2) *Where Yorick goes, there goes Dennett.* This was not at all appealing, however. How could I be in the vat and not about to go anywhere, when I was so obviously outside the vat looking in and beginning to make guilty plans to return to my room for a substantial lunch? This begged the question I realized, but it still seemed to be getting at something important. Casting about for some support for my intuition, I hit upon a legalistic sort of argument that might have appealed to Locke.

Suppose, I argued to myself, I were now to fly to California, rob a bank, and be apprehended. In which state would I be tried: In

California, where the robbery took place, or in Texas, where the brains of the outfit were located? Would I be a California felon with an out-of-state brain, or a Texas felon remotely controlling an accomplice of sorts in California? It seemed possible that I might beat such a rap just on the undecidability of that jurisdictional question, though perhaps it would be deemed an inter-state, and hence Federal, offense. In any event, suppose I were convicted. Was it likely that California would be satisfied to throw Hamlet into the brig, knowing that Yorick was living the good life and luxuriously taking the waters in Texas? Would Texas incarcerate Yorick, leaving Hamlet free to take the next boat to Rio? This alternative appealed to me. Barring capital punishment or other cruel and unusual punishment, the state would be obliged to maintain the life-support system for Yorick though they might move him from Houston to Leavenworth, and aside from the unpleasantness of the opprobrium, I, for one, would not mind at all and would consider myself a free man under those circumstances. If the state has an interest in forcibly relocating persons in institutions, it would fail to relocate me in any institution by locating Yorick there. If this were true, it suggested a third alternative.

(3) *Dennett is wherever he thinks he is.* Generalized, the claim was as follows: At any given time a person has a *point of view*, and the location of the point of view (which is determined internally by the content of the point of view) is also the location of the person.

Such a proposition is not without its perplexities, but to me it seemed a step in the right direction. The only trouble was that it seemed to place one in a heads-I-win/tails-you-lose situation of unlikely infallibility as regards location. Hadn't I myself often been wrong about where I was, and at least as often uncertain? Couldn't one get lost? Of course, but getting lost *geographically* is not the only way one might get lost. If one were lost in the woods one could attempt to reassure oneself with the consolation that at least one knew where one was: one was right *here* in the familiar surroundings of one's own body. Perhaps in this case one would not have drawn one's attention to much to be thankful for. Still, there were worse plights imaginable, and I wasn't sure I wasn't in such a plight right now.

Point of view clearly had something to do with personal location, but it was itself an unclear notion. It was obvious that the content of one's point of view was not the same as or determined by the content of one's beliefs or thoughts. For example, what should we say about the point of view of the Cinerama viewer who shrieks and twists in his seat as the roller-coaster footage overcomes his psychic distancing? Has he forgotten that he is safely seated in the theater? Here I was inclined to say that the person is experiencing an illusory shift in point of view. In other cases, my inclination to call such shifts illusory was less strong. The workers in laboratories and plants who handle dangerous materials by operating feedback-controlled mechanical arms and hands undergo a shift in point of view that is crisper and more pronounced than anything Cinerama can provoke. They can feel the heft and slipperiness of the containers they manipulate with their metal fingers. They know perfectly well where they are and are not fooled into false beliefs by the experience, yet it is as if they were inside the isolation chamber they are peering into. With mental effort, they can manage to shift their point of view back and forth, rather like making a transparent Neckar cube or an Escher drawing change orientation before one's eyes. It does seem extravagant to suppose that in performing this bit of mental gymnastics, they are transporting *themselves* back and forth.

Still their example gave me hope. If I was in fact in the vat in spite of my intuitions, I might be able to train myself to adopt that point of view even as a matter of habit. I should dwell on images of myself comfortably floating in my vat, beaming volitions to that familiar body *out there*. I reflected that the ease or difficulty of this task was presumably independent of the truth about the location of one's brain. Had I been practicing before the operation, I might now be finding it second nature. You might now yourself try such a *tromp l'oeil*. Imagine you have written an inflammatory letter which has been published in the *Times*, the result of which is that the Government has chosen to impound your brain for a probationary period of three years in its Dangerous Brain Clinic in Bethesda, Maryland. Your body of course is allowed freedom to earn a salary and thus to continue its function of laying up income to be taxed. At this moment, however, your body is seated in an auditorium listening to a peculiar account by Daniel Dennett of his own similar experience. Try it. Think yourself to Bethesda, and then hark back longingly to your body, far away, and yet *seeming* so near. It is only with long-distance restraint (yours? the Government's?) that you can control your impulse to get those hands clapping in polite applause before navigating the old body to the rest room and a well-deserved glass of evening sherry in the lounge. The task of imagination is certainly difficult, but if you achieve your goal the results might be consoling.

Anyway, there I was in Houston, lost in thought as one might say, but not for long. My speculations were soon interrupted by the

Houston doctors, who wished to test out my new prosthetic nervous system before sending me off on my hazardous mission. As I mentioned before, I was a bit dizzy at first, and not surprisingly, although I soon habituated myself to my new circumstances (which were, after all, well nigh indistinguishable from my old circumstances). My accommodation was not perfect, however, and to this day I continue to be plagued by minor coordination difficulties. The speed of light is fast, but finite, and as my brain and body move farther and farther apart, the delicate interaction of my feedback systems is thrown into disarray by the time lags. Just as one is rendered close to speechless by a delayed or echoic hearing of one's speaking voice so, for instance, I am virtually unable to track a moving object with my eyes whenever my brain and my body are more than a few miles apart. In most matters my impairment is scarcely detectable, though I can no longer hit a slow curve ball with the authority of yore. There are some compensations of course. Though liquor tastes as good as ever, and warms my gullet while corroding my liver, I can drink it in any quantity I please, without becoming the slightest bit inebriated, a curiosity some of my close friends may have noticed (though I occasionally have *feigned* inebriation, so as not to draw attention to my unusual circumstances). For similar reasons, I take aspirin orally for a sprained wrist, but if the pain persists I ask Houston to administer codeine to me *in vitro*. In times of illness the phone bill can be staggering.

But to return to my adventure. At length, both the doctors and I were satisfied that I was ready to undertake my subterranean mission. And so I left my brain in Houston and headed by helicopter for Tulsa. Well, in any case, that's the way it seemed to me. That's how I would put it, just off the top of my head as it were. On the trip I reflected further about my earlier anxieties and decided that my first post-operative speculations had been tinged with panic. The matter was not nearly as strange or metaphysical as I had been supposing. Where was I? In two places, clearly: both inside the vat and outside it. Just as one can stand with one foot in Connecticut and the other in Rhode Island, I was in two places at once. I had become one of those scattered individuals we used to hear so much about. The more I considered this answer, the more obviously true it appeared. But, strange to say, the more true it appeared, the less important the question to which it could be the true answer seemed. A sad, but not unprecedented, fate for a philosophical question to suffer. This answer did not completely satisfy me, of course. There lingered some question to which I should have liked an answer, which was neither "Where are all my various and sundry parts?" nor "What is my current point of view?" Or at least there seemed to be such a question. For it did seem undeniable that in some sense *I* and not merely *most of me* was descending into the earth under Tulsa in search of an atomic warhead.

When I found the warhead, I was certainly glad I had left my brain behind, for the pointer on the specially built Geiger counter I had brought with me was off the dial. I called Houston on my ordinary radio and told the operation control center of my position and my progress. In return, they gave me instructions for dismantling the vehicle, based upon my on-site observations. I had set to work with my cutting torch when all of a sudden a terrible thing happened. I went stone deaf. At first I thought it was only my radio earphones that had broken, but when I tapped on my helmet, I heard nothing. Apparently the auditory transceivers had gone on the fritz. I could no longer hear Houston or my own voice, but I could speak, so I started telling them what had happened. In mid-sentence, I knew something else had gone wrong. My vocal apparatus had become paralyzed. Then my right hand went limp—another transceiver had gone. I was truly in deep trouble. But worse was to follow. After a few more minutes, I went blind. I cursed my luck, and then I cursed the scientists who had led me into this grave peril. There I was, deaf, dumb, and blind, in a radioactive hole more than a mile under Tulsa. Then the last of my cerebral radio links broke, and suddenly I was faced with a new and even more shocking problem: whereas an instant before I had been buried alive in Oklahoma, now I was disembodied in Houston. My recognition of my new status was not immediate. It took me several very anxious minutes before it dawned on me that my poor body lay several hundred miles away, with heart pulsing and lungs respirating, but otherwise as dead as the body of any heart transplant donor, its skull packed with useless, broken electronic gear. The shift in perspective I had earlier found well nigh impossible now seemed quite natural. Though I could think myself back into my body in the tunnel under Tulsa, it took some effort to sustain the illusion. For surely it was an illusion to suppose I was still in Oklahoma: I had lost all contact with that body.

It occurred to me then, with one of those rushes of revelation of which we should be suspicious, that I had stumbled upon an impressive demonstration of the immateriality of the soul based upon physicalist principles and premises. For as the last radio signal between Tulsa and Houston died away, had I not changed location from Tulsa to Houston at the speed of light? And had I not accomplished this without any increase in mass? What moved from A to B at such speed was surely myself, or at any rate my soul or mind—the massless center of my being and home of my consciousness. My *point of view* had lagged somewhat behind, but I had already noted the indirect bearing of point of view on personal location. I could not see how a physicalist philosopher could quarrel with this except by taking the dire and counter-intuitive route of banishing all talk of persons. Yet the notion of personhood was so well entrenched in everyone's world view, or so it seemed to me, that any denial would be as curiously unconvincing, as systematically disingenuous, as the Cartesian negation, "non sum."[1]

The joy of philosophic discovery thus tided me over some very bad minutes or perhaps hours as the helplessness and hopelessness of my situation became more apparent to me. Waves of panic and even nausea swept over me, made all the more horrible by the absence of their normal body-dependent phenomenology. No adrenalin rush of tingles in the arms, no pounding heart, no premonitory salivation. I did feel a dread sinking feeling in my bowels at one point, and this tricked me momentarily into the false hope that I was undergoing a reversal of the process that landed me in this fix—a gradual undisembodiment. But the isolation and uniqueness of that twinge soon convinced me that it was simply the first of a plague of phantom body hallucinations that I, like any other amputee, would be all too likely to suffer.

My mood then was chaotic. On the one hand, I was fired up with elation at my philosophic discovery and was wracking my brain (one of the few familiar things I could still do), trying to figure out how to communicate my discovery to the journals; while on the other, I was bitter, lonely, and filled with dread and uncertainty. Fortunately, this did not last long, for my technical support team sedated me into a dreamless sleep from which I awoke, hearing with magnificent fidelity the familiar opening strains of my favorite Brahms piano trio. So that was why they had wanted a list of my favorite recordings! It did not take me long to realize that I was hearing the music without ears. The output from the stereo stylus was being fed through some fancy rectification circuitry directly into my auditory nerve. I was mainlining Brahms, an unforgettable experience for any stereo buff. At the end of the record it did not surprise me to hear the reassuring voice of the project director speaking into a microphone that was now my prosthetic ear. He confirmed my analysis of what had gone wrong and assured me that steps were being taken to re-embody me. He did not elaborate, and after a few more recordings, I found myself drifting off to sleep. My sleep lasted, I later learned, for the better part of a year, and when I awoke, it was to find myself fully restored to my senses. When I looked into the mirror, though, I was a bit startled to see an unfamiliar face. Bearded and a bit heavier, bearing no doubt a family resemblance to my former face, and with the same look of spritely intelligence and resolute character, but definitely a new face. Further self-explorations of an intimate nature left me no doubt that this was a new body and the project director confirmed my conclusions. He did not volunteer any information on the past history of my new body and I decided (wisely, I think in retrospect) not to pry. As many philosophers unfamiliar with my ordeal have more recently speculated, the acquisition of a new body leaves one's *person* intact. And after a period of adjustment to a new voice, new muscular strengths and weaknesses, and so forth, one's *personality* is by and large also preserved. More dramatic changes in personality have been routinely observed in people who have undergone extensive plastic surgery, to say nothing of sex change operations, and I think no one contests the survival of the person in such cases. In any event I soon accommodated to my new body, to the point of being unable to recover any of its novelties to my consciousness or even memory. The view in the mirror soon became utterly familiar. That view, by the way, still revealed antennae, and so I was not surprised to learn that my brain had not been moved from its haven in the life-support lab.

I decided that good old Yorick deserved a visit. I and my new body, whom we might as well call Fortinbras, strode into the familiar lab to another round of applause from the technicians, who were of course congratulating themselves, not me. Once more I stood before the vat and contemplated poor Yorick, and on a whim I once again cavalierly flicked off the output transmitter switch. Imagine my surprise when nothing unusual happened. No fainting spell, no nausea, no noticeable change. A technician hurried to restore the switch to ON, but still I felt nothing. I demanded an explanation, which the project director hastened to provide. It seems that before they had even operated on the first occasion, they had constructed a computer duplicate of my brain, reproducing both the complete information processing structure and the computational speed of my brain in a giant computer program. After the operation, but before they had dared to send me off on my mission to Oklahoma, they had run this computer system and Yorick side by side. The incoming signals from Hamlet were sent simultaneously to Yorick's transceivers and to the computer's array of inputs. And the outputs from Yorick were not only beamed back to Hamlet, my body; they were recorded and checked against the simultaneous output of the computer program, which was called "Hubert" for reasons obscure to me. Over days and even weeks, the outputs were identical and synchronous, which of course did not *prove* that they had succeeded in copying the brain's functional structure, but the empirical support was greatly encouraging.

Hubert's input, and hence activity, had been kept parallel with Yorick's during my disembodied days. And now, to demonstrate this, they had actually thrown the master switch that put Hubert for the first time in on-line control of my body—not Hamlet, of course, but Fortinbras. (Hamlet, I learned, had never been recovered from its underground tomb and could be assumed by this time to have largely returned to the dust. At the head of my grave still lay the magnificent bulk of the abandoned device, with the word STUD emblazoned on its side in large letters—a circumstance which may provide archeologists of the next century with a curious insight into the burial rites of their ancestors.)

The laboratory technicians now showed me the master switch, which had two positions, labeled *B*, for Brain (they didn't know my brain's name was Yorick) and *H*, for Hubert. The switch did indeed point to *H*, and they explained to me that if I wished, I could switch it back to *B*. With my heart in my mouth (and my brain in its vat), I did this. Nothing happened. A click, that was all. To test their claim, and with the master switch now set at *B*, I hit Yorick's output transmitter switch on the vat and sure enough, I began to faint. Once the output switch was turned back on and I had recovered my wits, so to speak, I continued to play with the master switch, flipping it back and forth. I found that with the exception of the transitional click, I could detect no trace of a difference. I could switch in mid-utterance, and the sentence I had begun speaking under the control of Yorick was finished without a pause or hitch of any kind under the control of Hubert. I had a spare brain, a prosthetic device which might some day stand me in very good stead, were some mishap to befall Yorick. Or alternatively, I could keep Yorick as a spare and use Hubert. It didn't seem to make any difference which I chose, for the wear and tear and fatigue on my body did not have any debilitating effect on either brain, whether or not it was actually causing the motions of my body, or merely spilling its output into thin air.

The one truly unsettling aspect of this new development was the prospect, which was not long in dawning on me, of someone detaching the spare—Hubert or Yorick, as the case might be—from Fortinbras and hitching it to yet another body—some Johnny-come-lately Rosencrantz or Guildenstern. Then (if not before) there would be *two* people, that much was clear. One would be me, and the other would be a sort of super-twin brother. If there were two bodies, one under the control of Hubert and the other being controlled by Yorick, then which would the world recognize as the true Dennett? And whatever the rest of the world decided, which one would be *me*? Would I be the Yorick-brained one, in virtue of Yorick's causal priority and former intimate relationship with the original Dennett body, Hamlet? That seemed a bit legalistic, a bit too redolent of the arbitrariness of consanguinity and legal possession, to be convincing at the metaphysical level. For, suppose that before the arrival of the second body on the scene, I had been keeping Yorick as the spare for years, and letting Hubert's output drive my body—that is, Fortinbras—all that time. The Hubert-Fortinbras couple would seem then by squatter's rights (to combat one legal intuition with another) to be the true Dennett and the lawful inheritor of everything that was Dennett's. This was an interesting question, certainly, but not nearly so pressing as another question that bothered me. My strongest intuition was that in such an eventuality *I* would survive so long as *either* brain-body couple remained intact, but I had mixed emotions about whether I should want both to survive.

I discussed my worries with the technicians and the project director. The prospect of two Dennetts was abhorrent to me, I explained, largely for social reasons. I didn't want to be my own rival for the affections of my wife, nor did I like the prospect of the two Dennetts sharing my modest professor's salary. Still more vertiginous and distasteful, though, was the idea of knowing *that much* about another person, while he had the very same goods on me. How could we ever face each other? My colleagues in the lab argued that I was ignoring the bright side of the matter. Weren't there many things I wanted to do but, being only one person, had been unable to do? Now one Dennett could stay at home and be the professor and family man, while the other could strike out on a life of travel and adventure—missing the family of course, but happy in the knowledge that the other Dennett was keeping the home fires burning. I could be faithful and adulterous at the same time. I could even cuckold myself—to say nothing of other more lurid possibilities my colleagues were all too ready to force upon my overtaxed imagination. But my ordeal in Oklahoma (or was it Houston?) had made me less adventurous, and I shrank from this opportunity that was being offered (though of course I was never quite sure it was being offered to *me* in the first place).

There was another prospect even more disagreeable—that the spare, Hubert or Yorick as the case might be, would be detached from any input from Fortinbras and just left detached. Then, as in the other case, there would be two Dennetts, or at least two claimants to my name and possessions, one embodied in Fortinbras, and the other sadly, miserably disembodied. Both selfishness and altruism bade me take steps to prevent this from happening. So I asked that measures be taken to ensure that no one could ever tamper with the transceiver connections or the master switch without my (our? no, *my*) knowledge and consent. Since I had no desire to spend my life guarding the equipment in Houston, it was mutually decided that all the electronic connections in the lab would be carefully locked: both those that controlled the life-support system for Yorick and those that controlled the power supply for Hubert would be guarded with fail-safe devices, and I would take the only master switch, outfitted for radio remote control, with me wherever I went. I carry it strapped around my waist and—wait a moment—*here it is.* Every few months I reconnoiter the situation by switching channels. I do this only in the presence of friends of course, for if the other channel were, heaven forbid, either dead or otherwise occupied, there would have to be somebody who had my interests at heart to switch it back, to bring me back from the void. For while I could feel, see, hear and otherwise sense whatever befell my body, subsequent to such a switch, I'd be unable to control it. By the way, the two positions on the switch are intentionally unmarked, so I never have the faintest idea whether I am switching from Hubert to Yorick or *vice versa.* (Some of you may think that in this case I really don't know *who* I am, let alone where I am. But such reflections no longer make much of a dent on my essential Dennettness, on my own sense of who I am. If it is true that in one sense I don't know who I am then that's another one of your philosophical truths of underwhelming significance.)

In any case, every time I've flipped the switch so far, nothing has happened. *So let's give it a try. . . .*

"THANK GOD! I THOUGHT YOU'D NEVER FLIP THAT SWITCH! You can't imagine how horrible it's been these last two weeks—but now you know, it's your turn in purgatory. How I've longed for this moment! You see, about two weeks ago—excuse me, ladies and gentlemen, but I've got to explain this to my . . . um, brother, I guess you could say, but he's just told you the facts, so you'll understand—about two weeks ago our two brains drifted just a bit out of synch. I don't know whether *my* brain is now Hubert or Yorick, any more than you do, but in any case, the two brains drifted apart, and of course once the process started, it snowballed, for I was in a slightly different receptive state for the input we both received, a difference that was soon magnified. In no time at all the illusion that I was in control of my body—our body—was completely dissipated. There was nothing I could do—no way to call you. YOU DIDN'T EVEN KNOW

I EXISTED! It's been like being carried around in a cage, or better, like being possessed—hearing my own voice say things I didn't mean to say, watching in frustration as my own hands performed deeds I hadn't intended. You'd scratch our itches, but not the way I would have, and you kept me awake, with your tossing and turning. I've been totally exhausted, on the verge of a nervous breakdown, carried around helplessly by your frantic round of activities, sustained only by the knowledge that some day you'd throw the switch.

"Now it's your turn, but at least you'll have the comfort of knowing *I* know you're in there. Like an expectant mother, I'm eating—or at any rate tasting, smelling, seeing—for *two* now, and I'll try to make it easy for you. Don't worry. Just as soon as this colloquium is over, you and I will fly to Houston, and we'll see what can be done to get one of us another body. You can have a female body—your body could be any color you like. But let's think it over. I tell you what—to be fair, if we both want this body, I promise I'll let the project director flip a coin to settle which of us gets to keep it and which then gets to choose a new body. That should guarantee justice, shouldn't it? In any case, I'll take care of you, I promise. These people are my witnesses.

"Ladies and gentlemen, this talk we have just heard is not exactly the talk *I* would have given, but I assure you that everything he said was perfectly true. And now if you'll excuse me, I think I'd—we'd—better sit down."[2]

Notes

Introduction

1. See my "Current Issues in the Philosophy of Mind", in *American Philosophical Quarterly*, October, 1978.
2. See Jerry Fodor, *The Language of Thought* (New York: Crowell, 1975): Chapter 1, for a vigorous account of what is wrong with type identity theory.
3. See also Jerry Fodor and Ned Block, "What Psychological States are Not", *Philosophical Review*, LXXXI (1972), and Ned Block, "Troubles with Functionalism" in C. W. Savage, ed., *Perception and Cognition: Issues in the Foundations of Psychology, Minnesota Studies in the Philosophy of Science*, vol. IX (1978).
4. Cf. Fodor, *op. cit.*, "Introduction: Two Kinds of Reductionism", and Hilary Putnam, "Reductionism and the Nature of Psychology", *Cognition*, II (1973): 131-46.
5. See Richard Aquila, *Intentionality: A Study of Mental Acts* (University Park: Pennsylvania State University, 1977), especially Chapter 1, for a sounder conception of Brentano's sense of the thesis.
6. W. G. Lycan and G. Pappas, *Materialism* (forthcoming): Chapter 4.

Chapter 1

1. I am indebted to Peter Woodruff for making extensive improvements in this chapter prior to its initial publication. Since it appeared, I have found anticipations and developments of similar or supporting themes in a variety of writers, most notably Carl Hempel, "Rational Action", *Proceedings and Addresses of the American Philosophical Association*, XXXV (1962), reprinted in N. S. Care and C. Landesman, eds., *Readings in the Theory of Action* (Bloomington, Indiana: University Press, 1968); L. Jonathan Cohen, "Teleological Explanation", *Proceedings of the Aristotelian Society* (1950-51), and "Can there be Artificial Minds?", *Analysis* (1954-55); B. A. O. Williams, "Deciding to Believe", in H. E. Kiefer and M. K. Munitz, eds., *Language, Belief, and Metaphysics* (Albany: SUNY Press, 1970), and David Lewis, "Radical Interpretation", *Synthese*, III, IV (1974): 331-44;
2. For a lucid introduction to the concept and its history, see the entry on "intentionality" by Roderick Chisholm in P. Edwards, ed., *The Encyclopedia*

of Philosophy (New York: MacMillan, 1967).
3. *Content and Consciousness* (London: Routledge & Kegan Paul, 1969).
4. The term "intentional system" occurs in Charles Taylor's *The Explanation of Behaviour* (London: Routledge & Kegan Paul, 1964): p. 62, where its use suggests it is co-extensive with the term as I use it, but Taylor does not develop the notion in depth. See, however, his p. 58ff. For an introduction to the concept of an intentional system with fewer philosophical presuppositions, see the first sections of Chapters 12 and 14 of this volume.
5. Hintikka notes in passing that game theory is like his epistemic logic in assuming rationality, in *Knowledge and Belief* (Ithaca, N.Y.: Cornell, 1962): p. 38.
6. I have in mind especially A. Phillips Griffiths' penetrating discussion "On Belief", *Proceedings of the Aristotelian Society*, LXIII (1962/3): 167-86; and Bernard Mayo's "Belief and Constraint", ibid., LXIV (1964): 139-56, both reprinted in Phillips Griffiths, ed., *Knowledge and Belief* (New York: Oxford, 1967).
7. See, e.g., H. H. Price, "Belief and Will", *Proceedings of the Aristotelian Society*, suppl. vol. XXVIII (1954), reprinted in S. Hampshire, ed., *Philosophy of Mind* (New York: Harper & Row, 1966).
8. Cf. A. W. Collins, "Unconscious Belief", *Journal of Philosophy*, LXVI, 20 (Oct. 16, 1969): 667-80.

Chapter 2

1. Their papers, "Consciousness: the Secondary Role of Language", and "*Content and Consciousness* and the Mind-Body Problem", were published, along with an abstract of this essay, in *Journal of Philosophy*, LXIX, 18 (October 5, 1972): 579-604.
2. See E. A. Feigenbaum and F. Feldman, *Computers and Thought* (New York, 1963), for this distinction. Less is made of it in the field today (1978) than ten years ago.
3. "Mental Events", in L. Foster and J. W. Swanson, eds., *Experience and Theory* (University of Massachusetts Press, 1970).
4. In his review of *Content and Consciousness*, *Journal of Philosophy*, LXIX (April 12, 1972).
5. K. Gunderson, *Mentality and Machines* (Doubleday Anchor, 1971).
6. *Content and Consciousness*, pp. 118-19.
7. "What is it like to be a Bat?", *Philosophical Review*, LXXXIII (1974): 435-445.
8. See John Vickers, "Judgment and Belief", in K. Lambert, ed., *The Logical Way of Doing Things* (New Haven: Yale, 1969).
9. Ryle makes this point in "A Puzzling Element in the Notion of Thinking" in Strawson, ed., *Studies in the Philosophy of Thought and Action* (Oxford, 1968).
10. See *Content and Consciousness*, pp. 8-15.

Chapter 3

1. See, in another context, A. I. Melden's use of the notion in *Free Action* (New York: Humanities, 1961): pp. 211-15.

2. G. E. M. Anscombe, *Intention* (2nd ed.; Oxford: Blackwell, 1963).
3. G. Harman, "Language Learning", *Nous*, IV (1970): 35. See also his "Three Levels of Meaning", *Journal of Philosophy*, LXV (1968): 590-602, especially p. 598.
4. See Donald Davidson, "Theories of Meaning and Learnable Languages", in Y. Bar-Hillel, ed., *Logic, Methodology, and Philosophy of Science* (Amsterdam: North-Holland, 1965): 383-94.
5. M. L. Minsky, ed., *Semantic Information Processing* (Cambridge: M.I.T. Press, 1968): 26.
6. *Mind* (1895), reprinted in I. M. Copi and J. A. Gould, eds., *Readings on Logic* (New York: Macmillan, 1964). Harman offers a similar argument in "Psychological Aspects of the Theory of Syntax", *Journal of Philosophy*, XLIV (1967): 75-87.
7. H. von Foerster, A. Inselberg, and P. Weston, "Memory and Inductive Inference", in H. L. Oestreicher and D. R. Moore, eds., *Cybernetic Problems in Bionics* (New York: Gordon and Breach, 1968).
8. See G. E. M. Anscombe, "The Intentionality of Sensation: A Grammatical Feature", in R. J. Butler, ed., *Analytical Philosophy, Second Series* (Oxford: Blackwell, 1965).
9. G. Harman, "Language Learning".
10. See John Vickers, "Judgment and Belief", in K. Lambert, ed., *The Logical Way of Doing Things* (New Haven: Yale University Press, 1969), and A. W. Collins, "Unconscious Belief", *Journal of Philosophy*, LXVI (1969): 667-80.

Chapter 4

1. *Beyond Freedom and Dignity* (New York: Knopf, 1971), p. 11. See also Skinner's *About Behaviorism* (New York: Random House, 1974): p. 31: "Almost all versions (of mentalism) contend that the mind is a non-physical space in which events obey non-physical laws".
2. *Beyond Freedom and Dignity*, pp. 12 and 191.
3. In the film, *Behavior Control: Freedom and Morality* (Open University Film Series). This is a conversation between Skinner and Geoffrey Warnock, reviewed by me in *Teaching Philosophy*, I, 2 (Fall, 1975): 175-7. See also *About Behaviorism*, p. 121: "By attempting to move human behavior into a world of non-physical dimensions, mentalistic or cognitivistic psychologists have cast the *basic* issues in insoluble form." Note that here he countenances no exceptions to the cognitivist-dualist equation.
4. *Beyond Freedom and Dignity*, p. 191. See also Skinner's *Science and Human Behavior* (Free Press paperback edition, 1953): p. 285 and 82.
5. "Behaviorism at Fifty", in T. W. Wann, ed., *Behaviorism and Phenomenology* (University of Chicago Press, 1964): 84.
6. *Beyond Freedom and Dignity*: pp. 1, 14 and 193. In *About Behaviorism* Skinner countenances *covert* behavior (p. 26) and "private consequences" as reinforcers (p. 106), but on other pages insists "the environment stays where it is and where it has always been—outside the body" (p. 75), and "Neither the stimulus nor the response is ever *in* the body in any literal sense" (p. 148). See also "Why Look Inside", *About Behaviorism*, 165-69.
7. *Beyond Freedom and Dignity*, p. 14.
8. "The Case Against B. F. Skinner", *New York Review of Books* (December

30, 1971).

9. "Behaviorism at Fifty", p. 84.

10. *Beyond Freedom and Dignity*, p. 195; see also pp. 8 and 10. *About Behaviorism*, p. 18 and 170; *Cumulative Record* (1961): pp. 274-75.

11. In "Operant Behavior", in W. K. Honig, ed., *Operant Behavior: Areas of Research and Application* (New York: Appleton Century Crofts, 1966), Skinner disparages theories that attempt to order the behavioral chaos by positing "some mental, physiological or merely conceptual inner system which by its nature is neither directly observed in nor accurately represented on any occasion by, the performance of an organism. There is no comparable inner system in an operant analysis" (p. 16). Here sheer internality is apparently the bogy. See also *Science and Human Behavior*, p. 32ff.

12. He could hardly deny this, but he comes perilously close to it in *About Behaviorism*, where a particularly virulent attack of operationalism tempts him to challenge the credentials of such innocuous "scientific" concepts as the *tensile strength* of rope and the *viscosity* of fluids (pp. 165-66). Before philosophers scoff at this, they should remind themselves where psychologists caught this disease. A few pages later (p. 169) Skinner grants that a molecular explanation of viscosity is "a step forward" and so are physiological explanations of behavior. In "What is Psychotic Behavior?" (in *Cumulative Record*) he disparages "potential energy" and "magnetic field"

13. *Beyond Freedom and Dignity*, pp. 9 and 23; *Cumulative Record*, pp. 283-84; "Behaviorism at Fifty".

14. A patient and exhaustive review of these issues in Skinner's writings up to 1972 can be found in Russell Keat, "A Critical Examination of B. F. Skinner's Objections to Mentalism", *Behaviorism*, vol. I (Fall, 1972).

15. "Behaviorism at Fifty", p. 80; *Beyond Freedom and Dignity*, Chapter 1, and p. 160.

16. *Beyond Freedom and Dignity*, p. 195.

17. *New Essays on the Understanding* (1704): Preface. See also Leibniz' *Discourse on Metaphysics*, X.

18. Skinner finds a passage in Newton to much the same effect as Leibniz: *Beyond Freedom and Dignity*, p. 9.

19. *Ibid.*, p. 14.

20. *Ibid.*, p. 200.

21. In *About Behaviorism*, (pp. 213-14) Skinner provides a marvelous list of the cognitivistic horrors—together with the hint that they are all equally bad, and that the use of one implicates one in the countenancing of all the others: " . . . sensations . . . intelligence . . . decisions . . . beliefs . . . a death instinct . . . sublimation . . . an id . . . a sense of shame . . . reaction formations . . . psychic energy . . . consciousness . . . mental illnesses . . ."

22. "Behaviorism at Fifty", p. 80.

23. See *Content and Consciousness* (1969), and Chapter 1 of this volume, where I argue at length for this claim.

24. "Behaviorism at Fifty", p. 80.

25. See, e.g., Roderick Chisholm, *Perceiving, A Philosophical Study* (1957), and numerous articles since then; also Quine, *Word and Object* (1960); W. G. Lycan, "On Intentionality and the Psychological", *American Philosophical Quarterly* (October, 1969).

26. There is a great deal of literature to suggest, however, that specifying the

logical marks of intentional idioms is hardly uncontroversial. See, e.g., Lycan, *op. cit.*

27. *Word and Object*, p. 221.
28. Quine has recently confirmed to me in conversation that he has been unsuccessful in attempts to convey this portion of the Quinean creed to his close friend in William James Hall.
29. See especially *Beyond Freedom and Dignity*, pp. 24 and 72.
30. A careful reading of these "translations" should do more than reading the combined works of Chisholm and Quine to convince the reader that translating the intentional in behavioral terms is impossible.
31. "Behaviorism at Fifty", p. 93.
32. *Beyond Freedom and Dignity*, p. 93.
33. See also *Beyond Freedom and Dignity*, p. 118.
34. A defender of Skinner, in response to this sentence, sought to explain and justify this curious behavior of Skinner's by suggesting that the reason Skinner overlooked this crucial vacillation is that he had no idea he was conducting any such argument. According to this apologist, Skinner's entire case against freedom and dignity boils down to an uncomplicated allegiance to hard determinism. If so, I've vastly overestimated Skinner. However, if I understand the principles of the new hermeneutics (a dubious antecedent!), I am entitled to ignore refractory biographical details like these and press ahead with my interpretation of the texts.
35. *The Machinery of the Brain* (New York: McGraw Hill, 1963): p. 82.
36. In "Behaviorism at Fifty" Skinner discusses Lloyd Morgan's Canon of Parsimony, which is a special case, in a way, of Occam's Razor: never assume any more intellect or powers of rationality than are required to explain the behavior. He seems in the end to think this grounds his conviction that "it is in the nature of scientific inquiry" that ascriptions of rationality must all in the end be falsified.
37. True or false—I am not prepared to concede the truth of his operant conditioning theory, even for pigeons.
38. But we shouldn't. See W. F. Brewer, "There is No Convincing Evidence for Operant or Classical Conditioning in Adult Humans", in W. B. Weimer, ed., *Cognition and the Symbolic Processes* (Hillsdale, New Jersey: Erlbaum, 1974).
39. See *Science and Human Behavior*, p. 177, and Chomsky's amusing *reductio ad absurdum* of Skinner's analysis of "your money or your life" in his review of *Verbal Behavior*, in *Language* (1959), reprinted in J. Fodor and J. Katz, ed., *The Structure of Language, Readings in the Philosophy of Language* (New York: Prentice Hall, 1964).
40. R. J. Nelson, "Behaviorism is False", *Journal of Philosophy* (July 24, 1969); see also Michael Arbib, "Memory Limitations of Stimulus-Response Models", *Psychological Review*, LXXVI, 5 (1969): 507-11, and Patrick Suppes, "Stimulus-Response Theory of Automata and TOTE Hierarchies: A Reply to Arbib", *Psychological Review*, LXXVI, 5 (1969): 511-14.
41. In *About Behaviorism*, Skinner says: "When . . . histories are out of reach, very little prediction and control is possible, but a behavioristic account is still more useful than a mentalistic one in interpreting what a person is doing and why. . . . [If] we are going to guess, it is more helpful to guess about genetic endowment and environmental history than about the feelings which

have resulted from them" (pp. 2 and 5-6). Here again we see Skinner's failure of stimulus discrimination betraying him. He speaks of the *feelings* which have resulted. Feelings are a wishy-washy, unpredictive lot, no doubt, of scant use to the cognitive psychologist, but beliefs, expectations and intentions, for instance (or better still, their theoretical counterparts) are much more powerfully organizable into predictive and explanatory structures.

Chapter 5

1. Quoted by Jacques Hadamard, in *The Psychology of Inventing in the Mathematical Field* (Princeton University Press, 1949): p. 30.
2. Herbert Simon, *The Sciences of the Artificial* (M.I.T.): p. 97.
3. D. E. Broadbent, *Behaviour* (University Paperbacks edn., 1961): p. 75.
4. Clark Hull, *Principles of Behavior* (1943): p. 19.
5. Cf. also B. F. Skinner, "Behaviorism at Fifty", in T. W. Wann, ed., *Behaviorism and Phenomenology* (University of Chicago Press, 1969): 80.
6. Broadbent, *op. cit.*, p. 56.
7. Cf., e.g., Charles Taylor, *The Explanation of Behaviour* (1964); Chomsky's reviews of Skinner's *Verbal Behavior*, in *Language* (1959); and *Beyond Freedom and Dignity*, in *New York Review of Books* (Dec. 30, 1971); Broadbent, *op. cit.*
8. *Science and Human Behavior*, p. 55.
9. "Behaviorism at Fifty", in Wann, *op. cit.*, p. 84.
10. See, for instance, the computer-copy of a *particular* stockbroker in E. A. Feigenbaum & J. Feldman, eds., *Computers and Thought* (New York: McGraw Hill, 1964).
11. Quoted in Hadamard, *op. cit.*, p. 16, italics added.
12. Quoted in Hadamard, *op. cit.*, p. 14.
13. Arthur Koestler, *The Act of Creation* (New York: Dell, 1964): p. 164.

Chapter 7

1. J. Weizenbaum, *Computer Power and Human Reason* (San Francisco: Freeman, 1976): p. 179, credits Louis Fein with this term.
2. Cf. also *Content and Consciousness*.
3. Cf. Zenon Pylyshyn, "Complexity and the Study of Artificial and Human Intelligence", in Martin Ringle, ed., *Philosophical Perspectives on Artificial Intelligence* (Humanities Press and Harvester Press, 1978), for a particularly good elaboration of the top-down strategy, a familiar theme in AI and cognitive psychology. Moore and Newell's "How can MERLIN Understand?" in Lee W. Gregg, *Knowledge and Cognition* (New York: Academic Press, 1974), is the most clear and self-conscious employment of this strategy I have found.
4. See also Judson Webb, "Gödel's Theorem and Church's Thesis: A Prologue to Mechanism", *Boston Studies in the Philosophy of Science*, XXXI (Reidel, 1976).
5. Wilfrid Sellars, *Science, Perception and Reality* (London: Routledge & Kegan Paul, 1963): pp. 182ff.
6. Terry Winograd, *Understanding Natural Language* (New York: Academic Press, 1972), pp. 12ff.

7. Cf. Correspondence between Weizenbaum, *et al.* in *Communications of the Association for Computing Machinery*; Weizenbaum, CACM, XVII, 7 (July 1974): 425; Arbib, CACM, XVII, 9 (Sept. 1974): 543; McLeod, CACM, XVIII, 9 (Sept. 1975): 546; Wilks, CACM, XIX, 2 (Feb. 1976): 108; Weizenbaum and McLeod, CACM, XIX, 6 (June 1976): 362.

8. J. Weizenbaum, "Contextual Understanding by Computers", CACM, X, 8 (1967): 464-80; also *Computer Power and Human Reason.*

9. Cf. Pylyshyn, *op. cit.*

10. Cf. Weizenbaum, *Computer Power and Human Reason*, for detailed support of this claim.

11. Cf. Jerry Fodor, "The Appeal to Tacit Knowledge in Psychological Explanation", *Journal of Philosophy*, LXV (1968); F. Attneave, "In Defense of Homunculi", in W. Rosenblith, *Sensory Communication* (Cambridge: MIT Press, 1960); R. DeSousa, "Rational Homunculi", in A. Rorty, ed., *The Identities of Persons* (University of California Press, 1976); Elliot Sober, "Mental Representations", in *Synthese*, XXXIII (1976).

12. See, e.g., Daniel Bobrow, "Dimensions of Representation", in D. Bobrow and A. Collins, eds., *Representation and Understanding* (New York: Academic Press, 1975).

13. W. A. Woods, "What's In a Link?" in Bobrow and Collins, *op. cit.*; Z. Pylyshyn, "Imagery and Artifical Intelligence", in C. Wade Savage, ed., *Minnesota Studies in the Philosophy of Science*, IX (forthcoming), and Pylyshyn, "Complexity and the Study of Human and Artificial Intelligence", *op. cit.*; M. Minsky, "A Framework for Representing Knowledge", in P. Winston, ed., *The Psychology of Computer Vision* (New York, 1975).

14. Cf. Winograd on the costs and benefits of declarative representations in Bobrow and Collins, *op. cit.*: 188.

15. See, e.g., Winston, *op. cit.*, and Pylyshyn, "Imagery and Artificial Intelligence", *op. cit.*; "What the Mind's Eye Tells the Mind's Brain", *Psychological Bulletin* (1972); and the literature referenced in these papers.

16. See e.g., Pylyshyn's paper *op. cit.*; Winograd in Bobrow and Collins, *op. cit.*; Moore and Newell, *op. cit.*; Minsky, *op. cit.*

Chapter 8

1. Norman Malcolm, *Dreaming* (London: Routledge & Kegan Paul, 1959): p. 4.

2. In *Content and Consciousness.*

3. *Dreaming, op. cit.*, p. 82.

4. David Foulkes, *The Psychology of Sleep* (New York: Scribners, 1966).

5. See Norman Malcolm, "Dreaming and Skepticism", *Philosophical Review*, LXV (1956): 14-37, especially section VIII.

6. "Dreaming and Skepticism", *loc. cit.*, section VIII, especially p. 30.

7. William Dement and E. A. Wolpert, "The Relation of Eye Movements, Bodily Motility and External Stimuli to Dream Content", *Journal of Experimental Psychology*, LV (1958): 543-53.

8. "Dreaming and Skepticism", *loc. cit.*, p. 31.

9. Thomas Nagel, "What Is It Like to Be a Bat?", *Philosophical Review*, LXXXIII (1974): 435-51.

10. R. M. Yost and Donald Kalish, "Miss MacDonald on Sleeping and Waking", *Philosophical Quarterly* (April 1955): 109-24. Malcolm discusses this claim

in *Dreaming, op. cit.*

11. C. B. Martin and Max Deutscher, "Remembering", *Philosophical Review*, LXXV (1969): 189.

Chapter 9

1. Thomas Nagel, "What is it Like to Be a Bat?" *Philosophical Review*, LXXXIII (1974): 435-51.
2. Marvin Minsky, "A Framework for Representing Knowledge", MIT AI Lab Memo #306, 1974, subsequently published in P. Winston, ed., *The Psychology of Computer Vision* (New York: Academic Press, 1975).
3. B. Julesz, *Foundations of Cyclopean Vision* (Chicago: University of Chicago Press, 1971).
4. John Rawls, *A Theory of Justice* (Cambridge: Harvard University Press, 1971).
5. Lawrence Davis, unpublished paper delivered to the Association for Philosophy and Psychology, M.I.T., October, 1974.
6. See also Sydney Shoemaker, "Functionalism and Qualia", *Philosophical Studies*, XXVII (1975): 291-315; and Ned Block, "Troubles with Functionalism", in C. Wade Savage, ed., *Perception and Cognition: Issues in the Foundations of Psychology*, Minnesota Studies in the Philosophy of Science, vol. IX (1978).
7. Ulric Neisser, *Cognitive Psychology* (New York: Appleton Century Crofts, 1967). Neisser now wishes to banish iconic memory from a position of importance in the theory of perceptual processes—see his *Cognition and Reality* (San Francisco: W. H. Freeman, 1976)—but I cannot see that he can go so far as to deny its existence, and I am not convinced it is not important.
8. Neisser, *Cognitive Psychology, op. cit.*
9. Jerry Fodor, *The Language of Thought* (New York: Crowell, 1975); J. R. Lackner and M. Garrett, "Resolving Ambiguity: Effects of Biasing Context in the Unattended Ear", *Cognition*, I (1973): 359-72.
10. D. E. Broadbent, *Perception and Communication* (Oxford: Pergamon Press, 1958).
11. William James, *The Principles of Psychology*, vol. I, 1890; edition cited (New York: Dover Publications, 1950): 251-52.
12. The clearest account of false steps from functional premises to structural conclusions is to be found in Zenon Pylyshyn, "What the Mind's Eye Tells the Mind's Brain. A Critique of Mental Imagery", *Psychological Bulletin*, LXXXVI (1973): 1-24, and "Representation of Knowledge: Non-linguistic Forms", in *Theoretical Issues in Natural Language Processing*, Association for Computational Linguistics Preprint (1975).
13. R. N. Shepard and J. Metzler, "Mental Rotation of Three-Dimensional Objects", *Science*, CLXXI (1971): 701-3.
14. I owe this observation to Michael Hooker.

Chapter 10

1. The psychological literature on mental images is growing so fast that a citation of current work will be out of date before the ink is dry. There is even a new journal, the *Journal of Mental Imagery*. A few classic papers are R. N.

Shepard and J. Metzler, "Mental Rotation of Three-Dimensional Objects", *Science*, CLXXI (1971): 701-3; L. A. Cooper and R. N. Shepard, "Chronometric Studies of the Rotation of Mental Images", in W. G. Chase, ed., *Visual Information Processing* (1973): 75-115; Allan Paivio, *Imagery and Verbal Processes* (New York: Holt Rinehart and Winston, 1971); Zenon Pylyshyn, "What the Mind's Eye Tells the Mind's Brain: a Critique of Mental Imagery", *Psychological Bulletin* (1972) and "Imagery and Artificial Intelligence", forthcoming in C. Wade Savage, ed., *Minnesota Studies in the Philosophy of Science*, vol. IX, and M. Kosslyn, "Information Representation in Visual Images", *Cognitive Psychology* (1975), vol. 7: 341-70.

2. D. M. Armstrong, *Belief, Truth and Knowledge* (Cambridge University Press, 1971).

3. Cf. my "Geach and Intentional Identity", *Journal of Philosophy* LXV, 11 (1968): 335-41.

4. I find support for my reading of Husserl in Richard Schacht's excellently lucid article, "Husserlian and Heideggerian Phenomenology", *Philosophical Studies*, XXIII (1972): 293-314. Schacht proposed there to distinguish what he calls *phenomenography* from *phenomenology*. In the terms of this chapter, phenomenography would be the mere gathering and cataloguing of protocols (one's own, not others') without attempting the further extrapolation of intentional objects from them—which is phenomenology.

5. I find support especially in Alastair Hannay's "Sartre's Illusion of Transcendence", Chapter 5 of *Mental Images—A Defence* (London: Allen and Unwin, 1971). "The term 'image' itself should be used to refer to the way the object appears, or rather, to the way in which an imaging-consciousness 'gives itself an object'." (p. 99).

6. Husserl speaks of the *hyle* or hyletic phase, and I am tempted to claim that the occupants of the α-role are Husserl's *hyle*, but perhaps the hyle are only some constituents of or raw material for the α. See "The Hyletic and Noetic Phases as Real, the Noematic as Non-real Phases of Experience", Section 97 of Husserl's *Ideas*, W. R. Bryce Gibson, trans. (London: George Allen and Unwin, 1931). Bo Dahlbom has both clarified and complicated my thinking on this issue.

7. Cf. also *Content and Consciousness*, and for an account of the relation between such utterances and the "propositional episodes" that evince them, see my "On the Absence of Phenomenology" (forthcoming in B. L. Tapscott, D. Gustafson, eds., *Body, Mind and Method: Essays in Honor of Virgil Aldrich*, Dordrecht: Reidel).

8. Cf. Strawson's insightful discussions of the dangers and prospects of conceiving of (without believing in) "phenomenal figures", in "Physical and Phenomenal Geometry", in *The Bounds of Sense* (London: Methuen, 1966): pp. 281-92. "The problem is whether the nature of phenomenal geometry can be described without a dangerous reliance on the possibly dubious concept of the phenomenal figure—a concept which, though dubious, is satisfying to one's simple-minded wish for a set of *objects* to be the peculiar matter of the study." (p. 288)

Chapter 11

1. Keith Gunderson, *Mentality and Machines* (1971).

2. A. M. Turing, *Mind* (1950), reprinted in A. R. Anderson, ed., *Minds and Machines* (1964), and discussed by Gunderson, *inter alia*, in "The Imitation Game", in Anderson and in *Mind* (1964), and revised in *Mentality and Machines*.

3. Cf. Gunderson, *Mentality and Machines*, p. 157: ". . . emotion is different from its effects . . ."

4. See, e.g., Louis S. Goodman and Alfred Gilman, *The Pharmacological Basis of Therapeutics* (2nd edition, 1955): p. 248.

5. On this, and many other matters Joseph Weizenbaum has provided me with illuminating suggestions.

6. Cf. Paul Ziff, "The Feelings of Robots", *Analysis*, XIX, 3 (1959), reprinted in Anderson, ed., *Minds and Machines*.

7. See, in this regard, Stanley Cavell's suggestive paper, "Knowing and Acknowledging", in *Must We Mean What We Say?* (1969).

8. George Pitcher discusses the philosophical implications of the Melzack-Wall theory in "The Awfulness of Pain", *Journal of Philosophy*, LXVIII (July 23, 1970). A more recent and highly developed version of the Melzack-Wall theory is found in R. Melzack and P. D. Wall, "Psychophysiology of Pain", in H. Yamamura, ed., *Anesthesia and Neurophysiology, International Anesthesiology Clinics*, VIII, 1 (1970).

9. A journalistic account of this technique can be found in Marilyn Ferguson, *The Brain Revolution* (1973).

10. See A. R. McIntyre, *Curare: Its History, Nature and Clinical Use* (Chicago: University of Chicago, 1947) and A. E. Bennett, "The History of the Introduction of Curare into Medicine", *Anesthesia and Analgesia* (1968): 484-92.

11. See Scott M. Smith, *et. al.*, "The Lack of Cerebral Effects of d-Tubocurarine", *Anesthesiology*, VIII, 1 (1947): 1-14.

12. *Ibid.*

13. Surveys of anesthesiology can be found in the standard medical school pharmacology texts, such as Goodman and Gilman, *op. cit.*, or J. C. Krantz and C. J. Carr, *The Pharmacological Principles of Medical Practice* (7th edn., Baltimore: Williams and Wilkins, 1969). More up-to-date material on the physiology of anesthesia is contained in H. Yamamura, *op. cit.*

14. Mary Brazier, "Effects of Anesthesia on Visually Evoked Responses", in H. Yamamura, *op. cit.*

15. H. K. Beecher, "The Measurement of Pain", *Pharmacological Review* (1957): 59-191.

16. A survey of the literature on animal pain (which I have only begun) could start with William V. Lumb and E. Wynn Jones, *Veterinary Anesthesia*, 1973. See also J. E. Breazille and R. L. Kitchell, "Pain Perception in Animals", *Federal Proceedings*, XXVIII, 1379 (1969) and G. Corssen, *et. al.*, "Changing Concepts in Pain Control During Surgery: Dissociative Anesthesia with C1-581 [Ketamine] A Progress Report" in *Anesthesia and Analgesia*, LXVII (1968): 6.

17. See *Content and Consciousness*, especially Chapter 4.

18. Cf. Thomas Nagel's review of *Content and Consciousness*, *Journal of Philosophy*, (April 20, 1972).

19. G. E. M. Anscombe, *Intention* (Ithaca, New York: Cornell University Press, 1963): p. 14. See also the discussion of this case in Kathryn Pyne Parsons, "Mistaking Sensations", *Philosophical Review*, LXXIX (April, 1970).

20. See, e.g., L. D. Cohen, *et. al.*, "Case Report: Observations of a Person with Congenital Insensitivity to Pain", *Journal of Abnormal Social Psychology*, LI (1955): 333, and B. H. Kirman, *et. al.* "Congenital Insensitivity to Pain in an Imbecile Boy", *Developmental Medicine and Child Neurology*, X (1968): 57-63.

21. See, e.g., George Pitcher, "Pain Perception", *Philosophical Review*, LXXIX (July, 1970).

Chapter 12

1. J. Hospers, "What Means This Freedom?" in S. Hook, ed., *Determinism and Freedom in the Age of Modern Science* (New York: Collier, 1958): 133.

2. N. Malcolm, "The Conceivability of Mechanism", *Philosophical Review*, LXXVII (1968): 51.

3. A. I. Melden, *Free Action* (London: Routledge & Kegan Paul, 1961); D. Davidson, "Actions, Reasons and Causes", *Journal of Philosophy*, LX (1963): 685-700.

4. D. M. MacKay, "The Use of Behavioral Language to Refer to Mechanical Processes", *British Journal of Philosophical Science*, XIII (1962): 89-103. See also H. Putnam, "Robots: Machines or Artificially Created Life?", read at A.P.A. Eastern Division Meeting, 1964, subsequently published in S. Hampshire, ed., *Philosophy of Mind* (New York: Harper & Row, 1966): 91.

5. P. F. Strawson, "Freedom and Resentment", *Proceedings of the British Academy* (1962), reprinted in Strawson, ed., *Studies in the Philosophy of Thought and Action* (Oxford University Press, 1968): 79.

6. MacKay, *op. cit.*: 102.

7. W. Sellars, "Fatalism and Determinism", in K. Lehrer, ed., *Freedom and Determinism* (New York: Random House, 1966): p. 145. A Flew, "A Rational Animal", in J. R. Smythies, ed., *Brain and Mind* (London: Routledge & Kegan Paul, 1968): 111-35, and A. Rorty, "Slaves and Machines", *Analysis* (April 1962): 118-20, develop similar distinctions.

8. Strawson, *op. cit.*, p. 80.

9. H. P. Grice, "Meaning", *Philosophical Review*, LXVI (1957); "Utterer's Meaning and Intentions", *Philosophical Review*, LXVI (1969).

10. Cf. L. W. Beck, "Agent, Actor, Spectator, and Critic", *Monist* (1965): 175-79.

11. A. C. MacIntyre, "Determinism", *Mind*, MMXMLVII: 248ff.

12. D. Wooldridge, *The Machinery of the Brain* (New York: McGraw-Hill, 1963): p. 82.

13. G. E. M. Anscombe, *Intention* (Oxford: Blackwell, 1957): p. 24.

14. Cf. D. M. MacKay, "Comments on Flew", in Smythies, *op. cit.*, p. 130.

15. Melden, *op. cit.*, p. 214.

16. Quoted by Flew, *op. cit.*, p. 118.

17. S. Hampshire, *Freedom of the Individual* (New York: Harper & Row, 1965), p. 87.

18. Flew, *op. cit.*, p. 120.

19. Strawson, *op. cit.*, p. 94.

20. This is of course an echo of Strawson's examination of the conditions of knowledge in a "no-space world" in *Individuals* (London: Methuen, 1959).

21. W. Sellars, *Science, Perception and Reality* (London: Routledge & Kegan

Paul, 1963): p. 21.

22. Malcolm, *op. cit.*, p. 71.

23. J. E. Llewelyn, "The Inconceivability of Pessimistic Determinism", *Analysis* (1966): pp. 39–44. Having cited all these authorities, I must acknowledge my own failure to see this point in *Content and Consciousness*, p. 190. This is correctly pointed out by R. L. Franklin in his review in *Australasian Journal of Philosophy* (September 1970).

24. Malcolm, *op. cit.*, p. 71.

25. D. M. MacKay, "On the Logical Indeterminacy of a Free Choice", *Mind* (1960): 31–40; "The Use of Behavioral Language to Refer to Mechanical Processes", *loc. cit.*; "The Bankruptcy of Determinism", unpublished, read June 1969, at University of California at Santa Barbara.

26. Cf. K. Popper, "Indeterminism in Quantum Physics and Classical Physics", *British Journal of the Philosophy of Science* (1950).

27. D. F. Pears, "Pretending and Deciding", *Proceedings of the British Academy* (1964), reprinted in Strawson, ed., *Studies in the Philosophy of Thought and Action, loc. cit.*, pp. 97–133.

Chapter 13

1. The most widely discussed is J. R. Lucas, "Minds, Machines and Gödel", *Philosophy* (1961), reprinted in A. R. Anderson, ed., *Minds and Machines* (Englewood Cliffs, New Jersey: Prentice-Hall, 1964): 43–59. See also Lucas, *The Freedom of the Will* (New York: Oxford, 1970), and my review, *Journal of Philosophy*, LXIX (1972): 527–31.

Chapter 14

1. J. Hintikka, *Knowledge and Belief* (Ithaca: Cornell University Press, 1962).

2. D. M. MacKay, "The use of behavioral language to refer to mechanical processes", *British Journal of Philosophy of Science* (1962): 89–103; P. F. Strawson, "Freedom and Resentment", *Proceedings of the British Academy* (1962), reprinted in Strawson, ed., *Studies in the Philosophy of Thought and Action* (Oxford, 1968); A. Rorty, "Slaves and machines", *Analysis* (1962); H. Putnam, "Robots: Machines or Artificially Created Life?", *Journal of Philosophy*, LXI (November 12, 1964); W. Sellars, "Fatalism and Determinism", in K. Lehrer, ed., *Freedom and Determinism* (New York: Random House, 1966); A. Flew, "A Rational Animal", in J. R. Smythies, ed., *Brain and Mind* (London: Routledge & Kegan Paul, 1968); T. Nagel, "War and Massacre", *Philosophy and Public Affairs* (Winter 1972); D. Van de Vate, "The Problem of Robot Consciousness", *Philosophy and Phenomenological Research* (December 1971); Chapter 1 of this volume.

3. H. Frankfurt, "Freedom of the Will and the Concept of a Person", *Journal of Philosophy*, LXVIII (January 14, 1971).

4. Cf. Bernard Williams, "Deciding to Believe", in H. E. Kiefer and M. K. Munitz, eds., *Language, Belief and Metaphysics* (New York: New York University Press, 1970).

5. E.g., B. F. Skinner, "Behaviorism at Fifty", in T. W. Wann, ed., *Behaviorism and Phenomenology* (Chicago: University of Chicago Press, 1964).

6. For illuminating suggestions on the relation of language to belief and ration-

ality, see Ronald de Sousa,"How to Give a Piece of Your Mind; or the Logic of Belief and Assent", *Review of Metaphysics* (September 1971).

7. G. E. M. Anscombe, *Intention* (Oxford: Blackwell, 1957): p. 80.
8. Cf. Ronald de Sousa, "Self-Deception", *Inquiry*, XIII (1970), especially p. 317.
9. John Searle, "What is a Speech Act?" in Max Black, ed., *Philosophy in America* (London: Allen & Unwin, 1965), discussed by Grice in "Utterer's Meaning and Intentions", p. 160.
10. See Hintikka, *Knowledge and Belief*, p. 38.
11. J. Rawls, "Justice as Reciprocity", in S. Gorovitz, ed., *Utilitarianism* (Indianapolis: Bobbs Merrill, 1971): 259.
12. Margaret Gilbert, in "Vices and Self-Knowledge", *Journal of Philosophy*, LXVIII (August 5, 1971): 452, examines the implications of the fact that "when, and only when, one believes that one has a given trait can one decide to change out of it".

Chapter 15

1. D. Wiggins, "Towards a Reasonable Libertarianism" in T. Honderich, ed., *Essays on Freedom of Action* (London: Routledge & Kegan Paul, 1973).
2. Bertrand Russell, *Human Knowledge; its Scope and Limits* (New York: Simon and Schuster, 1948), Chapter 15, "The Physiology of Sensation and Volition", p. 54.
3. A. J. Ayer, "Freedom and Necessity", in *Philosophical Essays* (London: MacMillan, 1954); R. B. Hobart, "Free Will as Involving Determination and Inconceivable Without It", *Mind* (1934).

Chapter 16

1. In A. MacKay and D. Merrill, eds., *Issues in the Philosophy of Language* (New Haven: Yale, 1976).

Chapter 17

1. C.f., Jaakko Hintikka, "Cogito ergo sum: Inference or Performance?" *The Philosophical Review*, LXXI, 1962, pp. 3-32.
2. Anyone familiar with the literature on this topic will recognize that my remarks owe a great deal to the explorations of Sydney Shoemaker, John Perry, David Lewis and Derek Parfit, and in particular to their papers in Amelie Rorty, ed., *The Identities of Persons*, 1976.

Acknowledgements

1. "Intentional Systems" is reprinted from *Journal of Philosophy*, LXVIII, 4, (1971): 87-106 with permission of the editors. Earlier drafts were presented at Princeton and the University of Massachusetts at Amherst, December, 1970.
2. "Reply to Arbib and Gunderson" has not been previously published, but an abstract appears in *Journal of Philosophy*, LXIX, 18, (1972): 604, following the papers by Arbib and Gunderson. It was presented at a symposium on *Content and Consciousness* at the American Philosophical Association Eastern Division Meeting, December, 1972.
3. "Brain Writing and Mind Reading" is reprinted with permission of the University of Minnesota Press from Keith Gunderson, ed., *Language, Mind, and Knowledge, Minnesota Studies in the Philosophy of Science* VII (1975). Earlier drafts were presented at Tufts, the University of Maine, and the Cincinnati Colloquium on Mind and Brain, November, 1971.
4. "Skinner Skinned" has not been previously published. Earlier versions were presented at Tuskegee Institute, March, 1972; University of Tennessee, November, 1973; Western Michigan University, December, 1974; Lycoming College, November, 1975; and as one of my Taft Lectures at the University of Cincinnati, February, 1978.
5. "Why the Law of Effect Will Not Go Away" is reprinted with permission of the editors from the *Journal of the Theory of Social Behaviour*, V, 2 (1975): 169-87. It was first presented at the first meeting of the Society for Philosophy and Psychology, at M.I.T. in October, 1974. Subsequent drafts were presented at UCLA, Brigham Young University, Lycoming College, and the Harvard Society for Fellows in Law and Humanities.
6. "A Cure for the Common Code?" is reprinted with the permission of the editors from *Mind* (April, 1977), where it was titled simply "Critical Notice: *The Language of Thought* by Jerry Fodor". Under its present title it circulated in typescript during 1976.
7. "Artificial Intelligence as Philosophy and as Psychology" is reprinted with the permission of Humanities Press and Harvester Press from Martin Ringle, ed., *Philosophical Perspectives on Artificial Intelligence* (New York: Humanities Press and Harvester Press, 1978). Earlier drafts were presented at Carnegie

Mellon University; SUNY New Paltz Conference on Artificial Intelligence and Philosophy (organized by the Society for the Interdisciplinary Study of the Mind), March, 1977; Hampshire College, March, 1977; the University of North Carolina at Greensboro, April, 1977; University of Alberta, November, 1977; Simon Fraser University, November, 1977; University of Calgary, November, 1977; Rutgers University, March, 1978.

8. "Are Dreams Experiences?" is reprinted with permission of the editors from *Philosophical Review*, LXXIII (April, 1976): 151-171. Earlier drafts were presented at Harvard, February, 1975; U.C. Irvine, March, 1975; Brigham Young University, March, 1975; University of Cincinnati, May, 1975; Vassar College, November, 1975; Lycoming College, November, 1975. It is also reprinted in Charles Dunlop, ed., *Philosophical Essays on Dreaming*, Cornell Univ. Press, 1977.

9. "Toward a Cognitive Theory of Consciousness" is reprinted with permission of the University of Minnesota Press from C. Wade Savage, ed., *Perception and Cognition: Issues in the Foundations of Psychology, Minnesota Studies in the Philosophy of Science*, IX (1978). It was first presented at the Conference on Perception, Cognition, Knowledge and Mind at the University of Minnesota, June, 1975. Subsequent drafts were presented at Cornell University, December, 1975; and at SUNY Binghamton, February, 1976.

10. "Two Approaches to Mental Images" has not been previously published. It was first presented at the Western Canadian Philosophical Association at the University of Manitoba, Winnipeg, October, 1977, and subsequently at the University of Victoria, November, 1977; University of British Columbia, November, 1977; University of Washington, November, 1977, and Brown, December, 1977. A revised version was presented as one of my Taft Lectures at the University of Cincinnati, February, 1978; Sloan Foundation Workshop on Mental Representation, M.I.T., January, 1978; University of Virginia, February, 1978; Columbia University, March, 1978, and the University of Alabama, April, 1978.

11. "Why You Can't Make a Computer that Feels Pain" is reprinted with permission of D. Reidel Publishing Company from *Synthese*, XXXVIII, 3 (July, 1978). Early drafts were presented at the University of Chicago, February, 1974; Western Michigan University, December, 1974, and Boston University, December, 1976.

12. "Mechanism and Responsibility" is reprinted with permission from Ted Honderich, ed., *Essays on Freedom of Action* (Routledge & Kegan Paul, 1973). A draft was presented at Yale University, December, 1971.

13. "The Abilities of Men and Machines" has not been previously published. An Abstract appeared in *Journal of Philosophy*, LXVII, 20 (1970): 835. It was presented at the American Philosophical Association Eastern Division Meeting, December, 1970.

14. "Conditions of Personhood" is reprinted with permission from Amelie O. Rorty, ed., *The Identities of Persons* (University of California Press, 1976). Earlier drafts were presented at the University of Pittsburgh, April, 1972; University of Connecticut, April, 1972; Wellesley College, November, 1972; Harvard University, December, 1972; Rockefeller University, March, 1973, and Temple University, March, 1973.

15. "On Giving Libertarians What They Say They Want" has not been previously published. Earlier drafts were presented at Princeton University, March, 1976, and Williams College, April, 1976.

Acknowledgments   341

16. "How to Change Your Mind" has not been previously published. It was presented as a reply to Annette Baier at the Chapel Hill Colloquium, October, 1977.
17. "Where Am I?" has not been previously published. It was presented first at the Chapel Hill Colloquium, October, 1976, and subsequently at M.I.T., in December, 1976, and at the University of Alabama, April, 1978.

The passage on page 65 from *The Machinery of the Brain*, by Dean Wooldridge, Copyright 1963, McGraw Hill, used with permission of the McGraw Hill Book Company.

The illustrations on pp. 119-121 from *Artificial Paranoia*, by Kenneth Colby, used with permission of Pergamon Press Ltd.

The illustration on p. 167 used with permission of Roger Shepard.

Index